Effective Implementation in Practice

INTEGRATING PUBLIC POLICY AND MANAGEMENT

Jodi Sandfort and
Stephanie Moulton

JB JOSSEY-BASS™
A Wiley Brand

Cover design by Wiley
Cover image: © iStock.com / rbv
Sandfort photo by Matt Sandfort.
Moulton photo by Henry Wilson.

Published by Jossey-Bass
A Wiley Brand
One Montgomery Street, Suite 1200, San Francisco, CA 94104-4594—www.josseybass.com

Jossey-Bass books and products are available through most bookstores. To contact Jossey-Bass directly call our Customer Care Department within the U.S. at 800-956-7739, outside the U.S. at 317-572-3986, or fax 317-572-4002.

Wiley publishes in a variety of print and electronic formats and by print-on-demand. Some material included with standard print versions of this book may not be included in e-books or in print-on-demand. If this book refers to media such as a CD or DVD that is not included in the version you purchased, you may download this material at http://booksupport.wiley.com. For more information about Wiley products, visit www.wiley.com.

Library of Congress Cataloging-in-Publication Data
Library of Congress Cataloging-in-Publication Data has been applied for and is on file with the Library of Congress.

ISBN 978-1-118-77548-6 (pbk.); ISBN 978-1-118-98615-8 (ebk.); ISBN 978-1-118-98616-5 (ebk.)

Printed in the United States of America
FIRST EDITION
PB Printing 10 9 8 7 6 5 4 3 2 1

Effective
Implementation in
Practice

Essential Texts for Public and Nonprofit Leadership and Management

Public Participation for 21st Century Democracy by Tina Nabatchi and Matt Leighninger

Managing and Measuring Performance in Public and Nonprofit Organizations, 2nd Edition by Theodore H. Poister

Public Budgeting in Context: Structure, Law, Reform, and Results by Katherine Willoughby

Applied Research Methods in Public and Nonprofit Organizations by Mitchell Brown and Kathleen Hale

Governing Cross-Sector Collaboration by John J. Forrer, James Edwin (Jed) Kee, and Eric Boyer

Visual Strategy: A Workbook for Strategy Mapping in Public and Nonprofit Organizations by John M. Bryson, Fran Ackermann, and Colin Eden

Social Entrepreneurship: An Evidence-Based Approach to Creating Social Value by Chao Guo and Wolfgang Bielefeld

Smart Communities: How Citizens and Local Leaders Can Use Strategic Thinking to Build a Brighter Future, 2nd Edition by Suzanne W. Morse

Leading Forward: Successful Public Leadership Amidst Complexity, Chaos, and Change by Tim A. Flanagan and John S. Lybarger

Creating Value in Nonprofit-Business Collaborations: New Thinking and Practice by James E. Austin and M. May Seitanidi

Understanding and Managing Public Organizations, 5th Edition by Hal G. Rainey

The Effective Public Manager: Achieving Success in Government Organizations, 5th Edition by Steven Cohen, William Eimicke, and Tanya Heikkila

Human Resources Management for Public and Nonprofit Organizations: A Strategic Approach, 4th Edition by Joan E. Pynes

The Practitioner's Guide to Governance as Leadership: Building High-Performing Nonprofit Boards by Cathy A. Trower

Meta-Analysis for Public Management and Policy by Evan Ringquist

Social Media in the Public Sector: Participation, Collaboration, and Transparency in the Networked World by Ines Mergel

Managing Nonprofit Organizations by Mary Tschirhart and Wolfgang Bielefeld

The Ethics Challenge in Public Service, 3rd Edition by Carol W. Lewis and Stuart C. Gilman

The Responsible Administrator, 6th Edition by Terry L. Cooper

The Handbook of Nonprofit Governance by BoardSource

Strategic Planning for Public and Nonprofit Organizations, 4th Edition by John M. Bryson

Hank Rosso's Achieving Excellence in Fundraising, 3rd Edition edited by Eugene R. Tempel, Timothy Seiler, and Eva Aldrich

The Jossey-Bass Handbook of Nonprofit Leadership and Management, 3rd Edition edited by David O. Renz, Robert D. Herman, and Associates

Handbook of Practical Program Evaluation, 3rd Edition edited by Joseph S. Wholey, Harry P. Hatry, and Kathryn E. Newcomer

Handbook of Human Resources Management in Government, 3rd Edition edited by Stephen E. Condrey

CONTENTS

Tables, Figures, and Boxes ix

The Authors xi

Preface xiii

PART ONE The Implementation Landscape 1

ONE Framing Implementation 5

Exploring Policy and Program Implementation 9

Defining Implementation Effectiveness 12

Unpacking Implementation Systems 16

Bringing the Analysis to Life 28

TWO Conventional Perspectives on Policy and Program Implementation 35

Political Processes and Authority 37

Governance and Management 43

Policy and Program Evaluation 52

Conclusion 64

THREE A New Perspective for Implementation: Strategic Action Fields 67

Introducing Strategic Action Fields 69

Core Programs 74

Unpacking Social Structures and Dynamics 82

Conclusion 96

PART TWO The Implementation System at Multiple Levels 99

FOUR Policy Fields 103

Policy Fields in Focus 107

Analyzing the Development of the Core Program 120

Applying Policy Field Analysis 131

Conclusion 136

FIVE Organizations 139

Organizations in Focus 141

Analyzing the Integration of the Core Program 148

Applying Organizational Analysis 155

Conclusion 162

SIX Front Lines 163

Front Lines in Focus 166

Analyzing the Application of the Core Program 174

Applying Frontline Analysis 181

Conclusion 188

PART THREE The Practice of Effective Implementation 191

SEVEN Exploring Implementation in Practice 195

Implementation Dynamics: The Hardest Hit Fund 196

Implementation Dynamics: The Quality Rating and Improvement System 211

Opportunities for Change 222

EIGHT Leading Learning in Implementation Systems   225

Investigating Technical Challenges   228
Engaging Others in Adaptive Challenges   246
Bringing It All Together   259

Appendix A Policy Field Audit   261
Appendix B Policy Field Visual Diagram   263
Appendix C Program Process Flow   265
Appendix D Organization Program Integration Audit   267
Appendix E Frontline Interactions Audit   271
Appendix F Target Experiences Analysis   275
Appendix G Implementation Dynamics and Outcomes Analysis   279
Appendix H Implementation Improvement Blueprint   283

Notes   287
Bibliography   339
Index   379

TABLES, FIGURES, AND BOXES

TABLES

Table 1.1	Indicators of Implementation Effectiveness	14
Table 1.2	Multiple Levels of the Implementation System	24
Table 1.3	Principles for Cultivating Effective Implementation Practice	25
Table 1.4	Comparison of Illustrative Cases	32
Table 2.1	Three Traditional Perspectives on Implementation	36
Table 3.1	Power and Culture in Strategic Action Fields	85
Table 4.1	Institutions Involved in Policy Fields	111
Table 4.2	Examples of Implementation Resources	123
Table 4.3	Selected Government Tools Important to Implementation	127
Table 6.1	Variation in Illustrative Frontline Occupations	167
Table 7.1	Indicators of Effectiveness in the HHF Program	202
Table 7.2	Indicators of Effectiveness in the QRS Program	213
Table 8.1	Tactics and Tools for Technical Change in Implementation Systems	231
Table 8.2	Indicators of Public Value Failure for Implementation	235
Table 8.3	Common Behavioral Biases	241
Table 8.4	Tactics and Tools for Adaptive Change in Implementation Systems	247
Table D.1	Organization Program Integration Audit (OPIA) Template	268
Table E.1	Frontline Interactions Audit Template	272
Table G.1	Indicators of Implementation Effectiveness	280

Table G.2   Mechanisms of Authority and Culture That Shape Social
             Structure and Influence Social Dynamics in Strategic
             Action Fields   281

FIGURES

Figure 3.1   Illustration of a Multilevel System with Common and
             Distinct Elements   72
Figure 4.1   Early Childhood Education Policy Field in Minnesota, 2012   134
Figure 5.1   Coordination Continuum for Implementation Activities
             within Organizations   152
Figure 5.2   QRS Program Process Flow   156
Figure 6.1   Engagement Continuum for Implementation Activities with
             Different Target Groups   176
Figure 8.1   Practices for Improving Implementation Effectiveness   227
Figure 8.2   Trade-offs when Initiating Project Management   253
Figure 8.3   Process of Group Development and Problem Solving   254

BOXES

Box 1.1   Overview of National Health Care Reform   5
Box 1.2   Introduction to the Hardest Hit Fund Program   29
Box 1.3   Introduction to the Quality Rating and Improvement Systems
             Program   30
Box 4.1   HHF Policy Field Actors   114
Box 4.2   QRS Policy Field Actors   118
Box 4.3   Ohio's HHF Program   129
Box 4.4   Minnesota's QRS Program   130
Box 6.1   Frontline Interactions in HHF   185
Box 7.1   HHF Program Objectives   200

THE AUTHORS

Photo by Matt Sandfort

Jodi Sandfort is an associate professor and area chair at the Hubert Humphrey School of Public Affairs, University of Minnesota. Her research and practice focus on improving the implementation of social policy, particularly that designed to support low-income children and their families. Her research is published in top journals, including the *Journal of Public Administration Research and Theory*, *Public Administration Review*, *Nonprofit and Voluntary Sector Quarterly*, *Journal of Policy Analysis and Management*, and *Social Service Review*. Her career has spanned academia and various positions in private philanthropy and nonprofit organizations at the state and national levels.

Photo by Henry Wilson

Stephanie Moulton is an associate professor at the John Glenn School of Public Affairs, The Ohio State University. Her research and practice focus on the implementation and evaluation of housing and consumer finance policies and programs. Her research is published in top journals such as the *Journal of Public Administration Research and Theory*, *Public Administration Review*, *Nonprofit and Voluntary Sector Quarterly*, *the Journal of Money, Credit and Banking*, the *Journal of Housing Economics*, and the *Journal of Consumer Affairs*. Prior to her academic career, Moulton worked in the nonprofit sector, designing and managing asset building, home ownership, and community development programs at the local and state levels.

We dedicate this book to our children: Hannah, Abby, Andrew, and Ethan

PREFACE

This book is fundamentally about change. Policy and program implementation requires changing systems and organizations, changing the hearts and minds of both people who work within them and those who are served by them. And there is a lot already written about change. In the early twenty-first century, we are fascinated by it. Popular social commentators' blogs and books help us make sense of the massive societal, environmental, and economic changes occurring around the world. Management gurus provide accounts of organizational change, models to describe it, and ideas for engaging those resistant to it. Self-help books and podcasts describe individual change in spirituality, family dynamics, exercise regimes, and nutrition, providing five-step, eight-step, twelve-step plans to structure our intention and enable personal transformation. All of these many resources help us make sense of these changes; they help us describe it, understand it, and shape it.

In writing this book, we begin with the presumption that amid all of these other resources, ideas, and guides, there is something unique to be learned regarding change in public policies and programs. What is unique, in part, is the ambition. When people in democracies need to address collective problems, they turn to formulating public policies or developing new programs and initiatives. They must accomplish things together they cannot accomplish alone or through purely private activities. They need safe roads, Internet access in remote regions, schools for their children. Yet many such initiatives are what scholars have called "wicked problems," or "grand challenges," difficult to solve because of their complexity. There are often conflicting interpretations of the problem: *what* should be done about it, *who* should do it, and *how* it shall be accomplished.

In the face of such complexity, one response is to attempt to centralize decision making and adopt tools such as written rules, structured protocols, or benchmarks in an attempt to reduce uncertainty. During the 1970s and 1980s, scholars at policy schools in the United States initially saw implementation in this way—as a mere management task that would be propelled through centralization or, at a minimum, professional standardization. It was something to turn to once policymaking was complete to achieve policy outcomes, understood as a distinct phase of the policy process, following agenda setting, policy formation, adoption, and preceding evaluation. Yet thirty years of research documents both the fallacy of trying to control implementation and the limitations of a "phases" model.

An alternative approach is to acknowledge that implementation is about making change in complex systems. It is about how policy ideas come to be embedded in operations and everyday actions. And while it unfolds in unexpected ways, there are lessons that can be learned and patterns that can be identified to improve how this process occurs. In this book, we aim to share these lessons and provide techniques for seeing these patterns. We integrate considerable research in public policy, economics, sociology, public administration, design, medicine, political science, social work, urban planning, education, and public health. We offer stories of challenges and successes. We describe tools that can be applied to your particular interests or professional projects to help improve implementation in those instances and enable you to be a more strategic actor and leader of productive change. We also provide more extensive analysis of cases we each know well: programs developed to respond to the US housing crisis and improve early childhood education. Through these various means, we provide a way to engage in making change in complex implementation systems in ways that improve desirable results.

Attending to policy and program implementation is rarely in anyone's job description, but often is everyone's responsibility. So we focus here on enabling people at various levels in systems to see their implementation roles and responsibilities more clearly. We also highlight the skills necessary to cultivate and seize change moments that present themselves to improve implementation results. In our efforts, though, we want to be clear: implementation is more akin to gardening than engineering or architecture.[1] While effective implementation practice benefits from knowing relevant scientific concepts, it also involves attending to the unpredictable environment and engaging in creative problem solving.

Like gardeners, many implementers have an unconscious preference for how to approach their work. One friend of ours started her garden by first testing the soil, assessing the composition and determining whether it was acidic, neutral, or alkaline. Once diagnosed, she systematically introduced additives to improve the soil conditions so she could grow a wider array of plants, testing it every few weeks for the first year. She turned similar attention to eliminating weeds, fertilizing lawns, and fighting pests. When we talk with her about gardening, there are always debates about biotechnology or the best heirloom variety of seeds. She loves consulting and comparing the vast array of scientific knowledge. She combs through it for insights or suggestions about what might be useful in responding to a particular challenge, such as her poorly drained bed in her corner yard or her tomatoes that don't ever seem to ripen.

Yet we know many other gardeners who jump right in and select whatever looks good at the local gardening store each spring. Some of them end up killing almost everything, but they keep repeating the same process each year because their springtime enthusiasm is uncontainable. One of our friends who took this approach is now almost a master gardener. Literally, he started by getting his hands dirty. His approach was intuitive: he plants new additions in his garden each spring and waits to see how well they grow, adding fertilizer, watering, yanking out pesky weeds, and cursing squirrels who always seem to be attacking his tulips and lilies. But as his interest grew, he began to consult gardening blogs and books, learning more about how specific fertilizers could enhance the blooms of his roses.

Obviously for both of our friends, the environment really determines what unfolds under their watchful eyes. The science-oriented gardener reads about microclimates and adjusts her planting given the light, wind, and moisture present in the corner between the house and the garage. But after two months without rain, the plants in that microclimate struggle to survive as much as any other. The forces of nature—sun, rain, and wind—determine whether one will spend most of his or her time in a given summer watering, weeding, or relaxing with a cool glass of lemonade surrounded by colorful beauty. All gardeners respond to the unpredictability of nature. They observe, take risks, and adapt their plans given what is unfolding around them.

In this book, we are trying to support implementers who resemble either of these types of gardeners. We identify and integrate relevant science because we know that both benefit from the insights that emerge from systematic study of policy and program change. Our close reading has uncovered helpful ways to talk about what happens in policy and program implementation across contexts. This allows for better communication about implementation processes and challenges, even when people work at different levels or different scales. We also share case illustrations because in some areas, there is not yet research to probe what occurs in practice.

Yet we want to be clear. Even when consulting these resources, implementation practice is not merely applying technical skills. Rather, improving implementation requires engaging the unpredictable—the people who shape the understanding and activities of the program at various levels, the resources of money and talent that are almost always constrained, and the political environment that is changeable. This environment is often quite influential in policy and program implementation. Elections happen, newly appointed officials are brought in to lead state agencies, foundations change their priorities, organizational boards develop pet programs, and professional accreditation boards alter their standards. Things rarely occur just as they were intended, but through engaging intellect and imagination, the complex and rewarding challenges of policy and program implementation can captivate you for many years to come.

We focus here on policy and program implementation that occurs in public bureaucracies, networks and collaboratives, and public-private partnerships. It happens in nonprofit service organizations, schools, banks, and local governments. In our treatment, we combine policy and program implementation because one's definition about whether something is a "policy" or a "program" depends more on one's reference point than on any inherent characteristic of the change. We also concentrate on change that spans the responsibilities of more than one organization and change undertaken to achieve public rather than private results. A vast array of policy and program implementation projects falls into this definition, from significant federal policy such as new national health care reform, to new local service models developed by food shelves. While there are many, many differences among these initiatives, they all involve the central concern of engaging others to bring about change that benefits people other than themselves.

Although it is very important to refine professional abilities to deliver on this noble calling, there are not many sources to turn to for relevant insights about implementation practice. While implementation activities happen every day, few people stop and are consciously aware of their roles in the larger process. The to-do tasks of work occupy our attention, this grant proposal or report to write, that meeting to plan or follow up, the client who needs to be responded to. Yet the way one shapes a grant proposal, facilitates an important meeting, or develops a systematic way to respond to a citizen's needs actually becomes the way policies and programs are implemented. It is important to help professionals understand their own responsibilities for improving policy and program implementation and what ultimately results.

OUR PERSPECTIVE

In spite of the significance of implementation practice, scholarly investigations of it have become balkanized and, in some cases, almost defunct. Yet our own professional practice, teaching, and research emphasize the critical need to build implementation skills among professionals. That is fundamentally what motivated us to write this book. We combed through the literature, but also filtered the lessons through our professional experiences.

Jodi has worked at different levels in implementation systems across a number of fields: documenting variation in state policies in early childhood education; working on the front lines of the HIV/AIDS service system as a case manager in Detroit; making annual investments of $20 million in state human services fields at a major regional foundation. She also studied implementation at the organizational and systems levels through her dissertation on welfare and welfare-to-work providers and subsequent studies on early childhood education, human service networks, and welfare programs. She consults with many private philanthropic organizations around developing strategies for public service system reform and develops leadership training programs for professionals in public agencies and nonprofits. Stephanie comes with a similarly relevant background: serving low-income households in a local nonprofit housing organization as a frontline staff member; leading a statewide network of nonprofit organizations, private banks, and state agencies for an asset-building program; and providing policy analysis and technical assistance to state and federal agencies. She has used this experience to craft an extensive research program on housing and economic stability, particularly focused on vulnerable populations, partnering closely with national and state public agencies, foundations, and nonprofits. The national press seeks her insights regularly about the realities of housing policies and program implementation, with her research highlighted in, for example, the *New York Times*, *Bloomberg*, CNBC, and *Forbes Magazine*. In this book, we capitalize on both sets of these experiences.

We drew on these diverse experiences and integrated them through a collaborative process that, for each of us, was unrivaled. Each idea and example, table and appendix reflects this partnership; all parts of the book were cowritten. While we hope this process improved the overall product, any intellectual oversights contained are, likewise, limitations we both must claim. This book was truly an equal effort. The order of authorship does not reflect the substance of our contributions.

Our experiences lead us to believe that while public systems may appear impenetrable, there are endless opportunities, large and small, for individuals to make implementation more effective. While a grant proposal might be motivated to bring more dollars into your organization, it might also provide an opportunity to build relationships with people from another organization who could offer a better service model for the effort. While a meeting might be scheduled to report progress on assigned tasks, it might also provide an opportunity to invite people into problem solving or shape their emerging understanding of an issue. While responding to a young mother's needs for child care might just be a way to move her application to the next frontline worker, it might also provide an opportunity to reinforce her tenacity at pursuing higher education or connect her with other parents with similar needs. By taking the time to better understand the full variety of implementation tasks, you will be poised to improve desired results.

As might be clear by now, we have not written a how-to book that provides a recipe that can be perfected by close adherence to set rules or know-how. Rather, we see this as an effort to integrate and translate research and experience, draw attention to the significance of implementation activities, and encourage readers to step more overtly into roles focused on cultivating effective implementation. Through this attention, we believe more potent results desired by the public will grow and thrive.

ACKNOWLEDGMENTS

We have both grown considerably in our collaboration on this project. Our different but complementary skills as policy and management practitioners and scholars were assets throughout, helping us bring insights from both the research literature and our experiences to this effort.

Many people supported us throughout this project, and we are humbled with gratitude for their belief in our work and the importance of this project. In particular, we thank Stephen Roll and Sook Jin Ong for their support in deeper investigation of the vast implementation studies literature that informs this book. Brint Milward welcomed us to the University of Arizona and provided invaluable space for our collaborative writing. And Mary Lou Middleton and Danielle

Harlow provided editing support. We also would like to thank two anonymous reviewers who helped us improve these ideas.

Our colleagues at our current and former institutions enabled us to develop and hone the understanding of policy and program implementation that we share here. In particular, Jodi's collaborations with Kathryn Quick, Melissa Middleton Stone, Sally Coleman Seldon, Jessica Sowa, Kate Conners, Leah Lundquist, Tuesday Ryan-Hart, and Gary De Cramer directly influenced her thinking about implementation theory and practice. Ongoing conversations with John Bryson, Barbara Crosby, Martha Feldman, Brint Milward, and Joe Soss also significantly influenced the contributions she made to this book. Finally, she is thankful for conversations with Kathryn Tout, Laurie Davis, and Barbara Yates, which informed the early childhood case recounted here. Stephanie's collaborations and ongoing discussions with Craig Boardman, Barry Bozeman, Michael Collins, Adam Eckerd, Rob Greenbaum, Jamie Levine-Daniel, Susan Miller, and Blair Russell directly influenced her approach to implementation as a melding pot of policy and management approaches and challenges. And she is indebted to her ongoing collaborations with the Ohio Housing Finance Agency, including Holly Holtzen, Cindy Flaherty, and Stephanie Casey-Pierce. The policy challenges presented in this book are our own views, not those of the Ohio Housing Finance Agency or its representatives.

Most important, we express sincere gratitude to our families, who were patient and compassionate supporters as we worked on this book, putting up with our late nights and time away from home for writing retreats together. In particular, our husbands, Steve Marchese and James Moulton, offered love and encouragement every step of the way.

PART ONE

The Implementation Landscape

Reformers are institutional gardeners more than architects and engineers. They reinterpret codes of behavior, impact causal and normative beliefs, foster civic and democratic identities and engagement, develop organized capabilities, and improve adaptability.[1]

The great thing about [gardening] is the way something new is always happening . . . Each year there are new varieties to discover in the annual crop of seed catalogs, new trends to dabble with and new planting schemes to explore. And apart from the dazzling variety of the plants themselves, there are the imponderables of pests, problems and weather that combine to make each season a new gardening adventure. But some things never change—the basic skills of sowing, planting, and cultivation.[2]

In part 1, we describe the landscape of our approach to policy and program implementation. While we integrate prior approaches to understanding implementation in public contexts, we devote attention to describing an alternative way to view implementation, suggesting criteria for assessing effectiveness, and explaining why things happen the way they do. Chapter 1 presents our definition of effective implementation and key elements in our approach. It is worth noting that this approach is purposefully pragmatic, grounded in academic thinking, but also drawing considerably from experience and reflection. And it is context dependent. Effective implementation cannot be reduced to a generic set of skills that can be applied universally across all settings. Policy-specific expertise is essential, and we introduce case examples that we follow throughout the book to elucidate the dynamics of implementation analysis in specific settings.

Chapter 2 situates our approach within the context of three other traditions of scholarship and practice: political processes and authority, governance and management, and policy and program evaluations. One of our motivations for writing this book is the cognitive dissonance we often feel when engaging scholarship in any one of these areas. On one hand, each directly speaks to the implementation system and its challenges. But on the other hand, each informs only one piece of the implementation puzzle—political and power dynamics, the governance system, or interventions targeting behavioral change. In our work as practitioners and now scholars, we navigate across these artificial boundaries, borrowing from each the relevant aspects for implementation. We think that this is an important contribution for future students and practitioners and therefore share these insights in chapter 2.

Finally, in chapter 3, we apply the concept of strategic action fields to the implementation system as a way to suggest a systematic way to explain what happens in implementation systems. By doing this, we emphasize that these systems are complex, not merely complicated. They cannot be neatly reduced to a set of factors or variables that predict success, but rather must be viewed as dynamic, living social systems. Each level in the implementation system is a strategic action field with a unique social structure and dynamics that shape the core program. The core program is what distinguishes implementation from other change initiatives—it involves establishing viable options, using a logic of change, and selecting a means for activity coordination. This is a new way of thinking about the implementation system. And like any other new idea, it may take some time to digest the concepts. We continue to weave the concepts presented in this chapter throughout the rest of the book. By its end, we believe this new way of thinking can become second nature and improve your own endeavors as implementation practitioners.

Framing Implementation

By April 2014, Sandra Martinez, manager at Connect with Health Colorado, could finally stop to breathe and reflect on the events of the previous year.[1] The federal Affordable Care Act (ACA) was a major change in public policy (see box 1.1), and her organization, a nonprofit formed by the legislature to implement the state's health care insurance marketplace, was at the center stage of Colorado's efforts to get the first wave of citizens enrolled. While in late 2013 public and national media attention reached fever pitch when operational challenges threatened the federal insurance website marketplace, Colorado was not caught in that controversy. Because it was one of the seventeen states that elected to operate its own insurance exchange, she and other leaders in the state's public, nonprofit, and private health organizations focused their attention on other important implementation activities. There had been some delays in the state-run enrollment process, largely because of the state's effort to sign up as many people as eligible into Medicaid to reduce citizens' expenses. Yet a sizable number had completed an application, some drawing on the support of navigators contracted to provide individual support in making insurance selections.

Box 1.1
Overview of National Health Care Reform

Lauded by some as the most significant social welfare law passed in the United States for half a century, the signing of the Patient Protection and Affordable Care Act by President Obama in March 2010 set into motion a complex series of events. Termed "Obamacare" by political adversaries, the law's goals focused

(continued)

---

on increasing the quality and affordability of health insurance, decreasing the number of uninsured Americans, and reducing health care costs. Implementation of some features began immediately, but political controversy and legal challenges created initial uncertainty for states as they considered how to craft their own health care policy in relation to federal action. When the Supreme Court ruled the act constitutional in June 2012, states began deciding which of the many options offered in the act they would pursue. For example, states had the option of expanding the Medicaid program to provide more affordable insurance for low-income people, creating health care marketplaces or exchanges to help individuals and small employers purchase private insurance, or making changes to existing state-based health programs. Other states chose to let the federal default options take effect.

Like other states, Colorado had established the Connect with Health exchange as a quasi-governmental agency, governed by a legislatively appointed board representing a range of stakeholders to oversee the program's direction and ensure public accountability. They had convened working groups to establish the plans and strategies of implementation focused on health care plans, disadvantaged communities, small businesses, and consumer services. Other groups in the state raised funds from private sources to investigate models for consumer support and public education. Martinez, along with some members from these work groups, participated in a number of national events and networks funded by private foundations that brought together state leaders to share the strategies being used to resolve implementation challenges. She found these efforts invaluable; they provided a neutral learning place and valuable information that helped improve decision making.

The need for health care reform in Colorado was high. Compared to other states, a large number of uninsured children and adults either had no health care or paid high out-of-pocket expenses.[2] In 2011, the governor had signed into law the state's policy authorizing Medicaid expansion[3] and the development of the insurance exchange. As in other states, eligibility for support was tied to income eligibility: the lowest-income citizens accessed health insurance through expansions in Medicaid, another group was eligible for tax credits to decrease out-of-pocket costs, and others could now access insurance through an unsubsidized marketplace benefiting from group-negotiated insurance terms. But in May 2013, following the lead of the Colorado Health Foundation, the governor also declared a goal of making the state the healthiest in the nation, raising the urgency and political salience of the issue in the state. Over the previous year, there had been an unprecedented number of public-private initiatives focused on the governor's goals of promoting prevention and wellness, improving service coordination, and making operational changes in payment and information technology. And while sometimes tensions had erupted between state leaders about the pace and consequence of the changes, the network between major organizations had held together.

The Colorado Department of Health Care Policy and Financing played an important role in the state as the agency that authorized many of the public programs. The department's managers, such as Maurice Brown, entered into the contracts with the ten insurance plans advertising on the Connect with Health Colorado website. Accountable to the federal Department of Health and Human Services, ACA activities were significantly influenced by the department's years of experience administering Medicaid, Medicare, and the Children's Health Insurance Program. The new policy also fit solidly into the organization's new articulated mission of improving health care access and outcomes for citizens while demonstrating sound stewardship of financial resources. Managers had developed six organizational goals, including strategies to improve services and align communication, technology, and staffing. The overarching intent was to transform the health care system from a traditional fee-for-service model into a regional outcomes-focused coordinated system of care. The ACA programs were included in this larger structure promoted by the department, although compared with his peers, Maurice was more extensively involved with external groups such as Connect with Health, the Colorado Health Foundation, and other implementation working groups because of the policy's visibility.

While the policy had an impact on many organizations that interacted with citizens—health insurance companies and co-ops, health providers that now processed bills for fewer uninsured people, mental health practices that now faced economic pressure to join larger groups to ease billing—the agencies providing outreach to disadvantaged groups were particularly important in the first few years because of the law's goal to enroll the uninsured. Informed by research conducted by a coalition of consumer advocates, the state contracted with public health and community-based agencies to provide exchange navigation, education, and support about the various insurance options. In original discussions, some exchange planners had believed it would operate like the travel website Travelocity, which allows easy comparison among various options. Yet the unveiling of Connect with Health Colorado revealed that enrolling in health care insurance is much more complex than booking an airline flight. At one time there were over sixty-five policies to choose among, and managers like Noah Manning soon discovered that enrollment assistance took considerably more time than what his organization had originally budgeted.

The face-to-face work fell to the cadre of navigators and health advocates who provided enrollment counseling. Yet at the front lines, the dynamics were complex. On the one hand, while navigators such as Cynthia Wang provided information for free to low-income citizens, other certified health advocates received commissions for their services. And consumers' needs were complex, often requiring individualized assistance. Cynthia had to remind some people to save documentation of expenses to qualify for tax credits at the end of the year. For others, after they had received their insurance cards, she coached them on how to find and use the health care, which many had been putting off for years. Outside of the metropolitan areas, this task was even more challenging because of the limited numbers of clinics and hospitals in many communities. As Cynthia sat with people, she heard each story in turn—the recently laid-off construction worker who couldn't afford the insurance fees, the elderly retail worker whose employer had joined the exchange but offered inadequate coverage for his needs, the disabled veteran who had a difficult time driving the long distances to get her regular checkups.

From each of their positions, Sandra, Maurice, Noah, and Cynthia face certain issues that must be resolved in the process of implementing the ACA. While resolving ideological debates among large institutions might seem quite different from responding to customers' confusion, these issues are interconnected. One level directly influences the implementation tasks and results at another; the Connect with Health Colorado working groups create the plans and online forms that the frontline navigators like Cynthia must fill out. The lessons Noah learned about work flow in outreach agencies are relevant to objectives articulated by the Department of Health Care Policy and Financing. The first policy implementation scholars described this reality as the "complexity of joint action" and, because of it, subtitled their book "why it is amazing that federal programs work at all."[4]

In this book focusing on policy and program implementation, we are more optimistic. We believe the more that people like Sandra, Maurice, Noah, and Cynthia recognize their interdependence and have ways for talking about and analyzing the complex implementation system they are part of, the more likely that policy and program implementation can help deliver desired results. However, this vision depends on implementers recognizing their essential roles in these systems. It requires professionals who will work hard to cultivate the analytical and social skills necessary to understand and intervene in complex systems. It requires courage to acknowledge ambiguity and still take action, particularly seizing opportunities to work across the multiple levels of the system.

In our understanding, implementation is a form of policy practice, distinct from yet influenced by policy debate. It is centrally important to democratic governance. And in its complexity, it can be both fascinating and challenging—solving one problem can reveal another layer needing to be addressed. In this book, we invite you to engage in the endeavor of studying implementation. Be curious about implementation dynamics, develop new conceptual language, and cultivate skills that will help you resolve the implementation quandaries you encounter. Throughout, keep in mind that while your actions are merely one part of the larger system's dynamics, sometimes small interventions can improve whole system operation. Opportunities present themselves, often in unexpected ways, to better align an implementation system toward improving public value results.

EXPLORING POLICY AND PROGRAM IMPLEMENTATION

Implementation issues appear in less-dramatic gestures than the passage of major health care reform. In fact, when any new program or idea for an initiative is shared, practical questions about implementation often follow right behind. How do we take these mandates and make them real in our state? How do we pull together the right people to respond to the large foundation's request for proposal? When a grant proposal is funded, how do we empower the program managers to develop procedures and training for staff? While we both recognize the urgency of these questions, we also believe that it is important to understand each question in its larger, systemic context. The first step in developing this ability is to internalize helpful lessons from social science that provide new ideas and consistent language for your analysis.

By definition, policy and program implementation is complex. The issues that make their way into the public arena are significant, the solutions illusive. Energy conservation, affordable and adequate housing, educational effectiveness—all are desirable goals that require changes in personal, market, and organizational behavior to attain. Very few policies or programs designed to achieve such goals are self-implementing. And yet the means, the *how* of developing these solutions, is often quite illusive. Merely acting from organizational or professional interests does little to create integrative solutions that foster collective action across boundaries to advance the common good.

This process is made more challenging because, as in Colorado's ACA example, much of policy and program implementation devolves from the central government. Around the world, traditional public bureaucracies directly provide fewer services than they used to, depending instead on private organizations under contracts, grants, or subsidies to deliver public services. The diversity of organizations and varied government tools in use raises the substantive importance of improving implementation, but it is not easy. Public sector managers, accustomed to focusing their attention on how best to navigate bureaucratic structures and legislative oversight, must acknowledge how much of policy implementation falls outside the direct control of publicly employed staff. They must cultivate skills of network management, such as facilitation and negotiation, to work effectively in implementation systems. Private business and nonprofit managers, accustomed to acting on narrow conceptions of their organizational bottom line or interests, must recognize the significance of their involvement in public service provision. They must recognize the legitimacy of public accountability and yield some autonomy to be part of larger solutions to public problems. Both must reorient themselves away from organizational interests toward attention to the policy or program target population, to understanding their behaviors, motivations, and concerns. Teachers, police officers, unemployment insurance clerks and doctors must recognize how their daily decisions—decisions to go beyond the formal requirements of their job in responding to students, citizens, and needy patients—often become the face of public policy.

It is common for public managers, private and nonprofit leaders, and direct service professionals to complain that target groups often do not follow policy or program requirements; they often fail to act in ways that designers intend. This disconnect between systems operation and target group behaviors is a fundamental challenge in most implementation projects. Yet seeking to understand the way such behavior is indeed logical by attending to the actual motivations and realities of these target groups is often essential for orienting what implementation improvements should address.

Compared to previous political science and public affairs scholarship, our notion of policy and program implementation grows more directly from sociology and organizational theories. As we discuss in chapter 2, many other scholars anchor implementation on policy intent or the characteristics of a particular legislative statute.[5] In this conception, policy implementation is focused on trying to bring the ideas of formal policy into reality. Policy implementation is viewed as the activities carried out by various institutions and implementers in pursuit of adherence to formal public policy and laws. As proponents of a government-centered, top-down approach to implementation, Dan Mazmanian and Paul Sabatier state, "Implementation is the carrying out of a basic policy decision, usually incorporated in a statute but which can also take the form of important executive orders or court decisions."[6] From this understanding, program implementation follows linearly from policy implementation. Implementers, county or regional governments or local service organizations, try to interpret and integrate policy directions into their ongoing operations through specific programs; they are a necessary component of policy implementation, operating at a smaller, more localized scale.

But this linear relationship does not hold. Many times national policy is created after the documented impact from programmatic innovation at state or local levels. Kindergarten, electrical smart grid, HIV/AIDS services, and countless other examples evolved in this way. These programmatic ideas can be described, evaluated, assessed by others, and adopted by other states before national legislation is forthcoming. As a result, we join other scholars in challenging how policy implementation is often described in textbooks, as a stage in the policy process that comes after policy adoption.[7]

Instead, we define effective implementation as deliberate, institutionally sanctioned change motivated by a policy or program oriented toward creating public value results on purpose. When implementation is successful, it becomes incorporated in everyday work and part of standard operating procedures. Effective implementation is deliberate because it involves conscious design, planning, and assessment of what occurs. Effective implementation also is institutionally sanctioned, backed by political authority and a pragmatic understanding of reasonable actions within the operational constraints of the setting. Yet effective implementation is focused on change, introducing new or modifying existing patterns of actions. But many times the process of change proceeds in unexpected ways. There are a number of important indicators of implementation effectiveness.

When successful, policy and program implementation creates public value by enabling collective impact beyond the narrow self-interest of any particular actor or institution.[8] When policy and program implementation is successful, what once was new and foreign becomes incorporated in everyday work, with the requisite resources necessary to sustain the change in behavior among program implementers. When successful, implementation also helps achieve changes in the target group as imagined by policymakers or program developers.

Rather than assuming a linear relationship between policy and program implementation, we understand implementation as a process of change occurring, sometimes simultaneously and in contrary directions, at different scales within a complex system.[9] It happens in a context where often there are already established ways of working. Said another way, it rarely happens on a clean slate. As a result, policy and program implementation requires continuous and intentional learning about changes focused on publicly desired results. And it raises significant questions: What is significant about a context that shapes change? How can changes yield publicly desired outcomes and minimize unintended consequences? How can others be engaged so that what was once new or threatening can be integrated into daily practices and operations? To help us begin to provide answers, we harvest insights from social science theory and research to ground us in concepts important to developing more skill in implementation practice. But there is also mystery in implementation, much like a gardener feels when watching spring flowers emerge from the ground. There is a social dimension to this type of policy practice that operates in unpredictable and sometimes awe-inspiring ways. To be effective, actors must cultivate subtle social skills that engage others in being part of the change.

DEFINING IMPLEMENTATION EFFECTIVENESS

To carry out programs successfully, it is essential for implementers to have a clear sense of the results desired to help shape implementation activities. But often it is difficult to narrow down the possible options. One can easily ask, "Desired results according to whom, and for what purpose?" However, just because desired results are often subjective it does not imply that anything goes. While this is not true for all implementation more generally (such as the implementation of a new technology in a private corporation), policy and program implementation systems normatively should ultimately create public value. It is what justifies the change that is being attempted—change that tries to counteract the tendency in large systems for inaction and drift.

But pursuing outcomes in line with public value requires explicit consideration of the public consensus regarding how a program ought to be carried out and the desired changes that should result.[10] Sometimes this public consensus is documented through democratic processes, in policy or legislative intent. As described in chapter 2, classic implementation scholars described effectiveness as whether the implementation achieved the policy intent. But many times, the formal policy intent is unclear or lacking altogether. When present, policy or program statements often identify large-scale desired results. For example, for the ACA, three results were articulated by national law: expanding health coverage to 25 million Americans by 2023, lowering costs and increasing benefits for consumers, and incentivizing quality and innovation in our health care system. While laudable, each is vast and difficult to use to anchor the numerous implementation decisions being carried out in the states and localities. It is well established that in public programs, definitions of effectiveness vary dramatically because of political differences, competing vantage points, and multiple goals.[11] Desired results often are left intentionally vague in formal policy statements not only to provide political cover, but also to allow localized interpretations and evaluations of effectiveness. In fact, many scholars note the irony that what is good for implementation—clear assignment of responsibilities, specification of change processes, and clear outcomes—is often very bad for politics.[12]

But public values explicitly extend beyond conventional notions of efficiency and effectiveness.[13] One can look to other sources beyond the formal policy to reflect public value consensus regarding a particular program, such as nonprofit membership associations within a certain policy area or accrediting bodies that define quality practices in a field.[14] In her research on mortgage lending, Stephanie has often found that institutions in the local community can be a stronger influence on public value outcomes than formal legislative policies.[15] And policy field and organizational actors can initiate processes of citizen engagement where members of the public are convened to provide feedback about desired activities and results.[16] Indeed, an important first-order task for implementation is to specify the desired outcomes given the formal policies and other assessments of public consensus in a particular policy area.

But what outcomes are important? As others have argued,[17] often people interested in public policy tend to ignore administrative and organizational processes and pay little attention to how the operations of programs significantly shape desired outcomes among target groups. In this frame, significant policy outcomes emerge from the alteration of individual, economic, or social factors—and the interventions designed to address these factors—rather than through interactions with the system delivering the policy. However, people interested in organizational management often focus their attention on improving the quality of work or attending to staff motivation, and identifying structures that facilitate coordination or manage the complexities of the agency's environment. To the extent that policy outcomes are considered, it is primarily about performance measurement and assessment of organizational outcomes. The risk, of course, is that management undertaken without awareness of desired changes in the target population may or may not achieve the ultimate policy and program outcomes.

As the title of this book suggests, we strongly believe that effective implementation requires integrating these policy and management mind-sets, leading us to realize that the multiple indicators for defining implementation effectiveness must be acknowledged. A multidimensional notion of effectiveness is also consistent with scholars' recognition that public policies and programs have multiple constituencies, often with their own assessment of what should result.[18] It is also consistent with the notion that the manner in which a service is delivered directly shapes how target groups engage with the intervention offered.[19] As illustrated in table 1.1, effective policy and program implementation entails changes in both system operations and the target population.

As suggested in our definition of implementation, we are concerned with two types of ultimate outcomes: integration of the change into system operations and

Table 1.1
Indicators of Implementation Effectiveness

	Process Quality Results	Ultimate Outcomes
Change in systems operations	Quality of program delivery	Integration of program processes into daily operations
Change in target groups	Target group satisfaction and engagement with the program	Desired change in the behaviors or conditions of the target group

desired change in the target group, in either target group behaviors or conditions. When systems change at the policy field, organization, or frontline levels, the new ideas and practices of the policy or program become integrated into standard operating procedures. They are institutionalized, no longer seen as new or "other" but as part of the way work is accomplished. This is one important outcome of implementation. However, a change in the conditions or behaviors of those targeted by the initiative is also essential; most often, the desire for this type of change motivated policymakers or program developers in the first place.

In addition to the ultimate change in the system or target population, we also suggest that quality is an integral result, including both the quality of the operational work environment and the quality of interactions with the target population. Sometimes these results are referred to in policy circles as a type of output, but we believe this underscores their significance in implementation practice. For public goods and services, quality is often difficult to measure. It is much easier to assess the quality of a consumer's hotel experience than to evaluate the quality of nursing home services provided to a patient with Alzheimer's disease. However, this is the very reason that quality is an important result for assessing the implementation of public services.[20] If our only goal for putting grandma in a nursing home is to increase her safety so she is less likely to fall, wander off, or otherwise hurt herself, then it doesn't matter if this is accomplished through sedatives or repeated interactions with nursing home staff. But most of us also care about the quality of engagement for grandma and hope that she is treated with dignity and respect. Hence, quality matters in implementation; it ensures that we attend as much to the means of public service delivery as the ends.

In policy and program implementation, we also care about not only the quality of the user experience (e.g., grandma in the nursing home), but also the quality of the work environment (e.g., the experiences of the nurse or social worker providing services). Normatively, this is linked to public service values.[21] Often public and nonprofit sector workers are paid less than private sector counterparts; yet it is believed the commitment to the public purpose brings intrinsic rather than extrinsic rewards because of their motivation toward the public good. Employee satisfaction and individual mastery also helps realize intrinsic rewards, and research suggests the quality of the work environment affects the extent to which change is successfully integrated within an organization.[22] Satisfied employees also improve the quality of citizens' experiences with the policy and program. Thus, the indicators of implementation effectiveness are not independent factors but rather steps that are significant in the ultimate goal of altering the conditions or behavior of groups targeted by the policy or program. We return to these ideas in chapter 8, where we discuss how such indicators of effectiveness provide an anchor to focus your own activities in improving implementation systems.

UNPACKING IMPLEMENTATION SYSTEMS

As we will see in chapter 2, implementation is a topic that has eluded simple explanations and modeling. In part, this is because of how much variation there is in the substantive concerns of public policy and programs. Implementing health care reform is quite different from implementing new requirements for smart appliances that use less electricity; implementing emergency food programs for the needy is quite different from implementing a national security mission. While the specific details of implementation vary widely, some elements are consistent across settings, which form the foundation of a more general understanding of the implementation process. We introduce these concepts here and probe them in more detail in chapters 2 and 3.

First, policy and program implementation occurs at different levels within a system. As with the illustration of Colorado's health care reform implementation, certain activities occur at the policy field level, where institutions craft and develop understandings and resources about the most effective way of carrying out policy and program objectives. At this level, many organizations are involved, such as government agencies, nonprofit associations, research groups, and foundations. Other types of implementation activities occur within the bounds of organizations. For policy and program implementation, two types of organizations are particularly significant: those, such as the Colorado Department of Health Care Policy and Financing, that authorize policies and programs through administration and those, such as Noah Manning's exchange navigation agency, that provide direct services. At this level, organizations operationalize the policy or program parameters into daily practice, often in relation to prior organizational experiences or competencies. The final level within the implementation system is the front lines, where the targets of the policy or program interact with the policy system or staff, such as Cynthia Wang. At this level, individual and collective identities are salient as staff and target groups negotiate their understandings and application of general program parameters to particular situations. These levels operate simultaneously within the same state context, within the same implementation system.

Sometimes, as is true in many other complex systems dynamics, they operate in competing directions.[23]

Second, to frame effective implementation practice, we have found it helpful to think of the settings found at these levels as *strategic action fields*. We find this helpful because while the specific details of people, programs, or power are unique to each context, strategic action field theory helps us recognize and analyze social processes that transcend particular contexts. Actors in a setting have shared knowledge about each other and a general understanding about their purpose, the relationships within it, and the spoken and unspoken rules.[24] Said more simply, people in the policy or program area share a common understanding about the task at hand, the relationships they have with each other, and the taken-for-granted assumptions of that setting. In the Colorado health reform illustration, while Sandra Martinez certainly had to address unique challenges and access different resources at the policy field level than Noah Manning or Cynthia Wang did within their organizations or working with clients, each operated within a strategic action field. Within each context, although the particulars differed, the social process of assembling resources and the authority to make change is consistent.

There are common dimensions of strategic action fields that can facilitate a more general understanding of processes across settings and levels in an implementation system. For one, all implementation settings are organized around a core set of program technologies that field members understand are being used. The central question in implementation is: How do we create desired change in the target population? We use the term *program technology* to refer to the means adopted to make such change. While often technology is understood as the hardware and software now shaping so many social interactions, technology has a broader definition within organizational sciences, referring to the full range of activities used to transform inputs into outputs or outcomes.[25] Inputs, often conceptualized as raw materials, can be people, other living things, material resources, objects, or symbols. Similarly, outputs can take many different forms. Technology is the full range of activities used to make a change. It is what we do to get the outcomes we want. At its most basic, policy and program implementation is concerned with accomplishing an effective program technology, of developing the means to accomplish desired ends. While there might be challenges about the validity of the means and debates about the ends, actors understand what is going on and what is at stake. Program technology processes are often represented through flowcharts, logic models, or process diagrams illustrating how activities are logically aligned into steps.

Second, within implementation contexts, there is always variation in power. In analyzing implementation contexts, we explore a critical question: How are resources and authority distributed and coordinated to induce actors to participate in the program? Various people and institutions have different abilities to make things happen. Both formal and informal authority structures shape each setting, and people working within it have a general understanding of the power distribution. There are formal manifestations of power, such as rules, contracts, and performance terms, and understanding how these forces directly shape implementation is one part of analysis of strategic action fields.

Third, there are informal influences that shape action, including shared understandings of what is possible and considered legitimate. Culture is the symbolic dimension of social action, the way a group makes sense of what is taking place. In analyzing implementation settings, we explore the question: How are meaning and commitment to the program cultivated? A strong culture creates shared understanding of what to do and how it should be done. It provides a collective interpretation of the problems to be solved, definitions of success and failure along the way, and the value assigned to what results. Getting people to work together toward a common goal is not just about formal inducements such as paychecks and contracts but also about shared commitment (or lack thereof) to the task at hand. By attending to culture in implementation systems, we are explicitly directing our attention to commitment as a powerful motivator. Thus, part of the work of effective implementation is cultivating commitment to the process.

Many strategic action fields exist within the implementation system for a particular policy or program.[26] Just as there are multiple fields within Colorado, there are distinct strategic action fields in other states. Neighboring Kansas and Nebraska decided not to develop their own state-based health care marketplace. As a result, the fall 2013 challenges with the federal HealthCare.gov online enrollment were a problem they needed to contend with; in addition, the choices their state leadership made by not claiming their state's expansion to the Medicaid programs changed implementation tasks. But beyond these large-scale decisions, other distinctions are significant for implementation. There are different health systems, large employers, and consumer groups involved in negotiation about the terms of implementation in each state. In Kansas, different service-providing organizations are integrating the new program with their existing operating procedures than in

Nebraska or Colorado. In each place, community-based navigators and citizens suddenly able to access health insurance for the first time interact with the structures developed at other levels of the implementation system.

So a third assumption of our approach is that while these strategic action fields might be related, they are still bounded as implementation contexts. Conventionally many policy implementation scholars assumed that formal policy parameters create the bounds around which implementation will take place. By contrast, our approach suggests that the strategic action fields operating at each level of the system create the boundaries around implementation—both constraining and enabling what is seen to be possible in the implementation process. Certainly formal policies and legislation are one component of strategic action fields. However, there are other constraints that emerge from other forces. Sometimes they are human factors, for example, in the mind-set of coworkers or organizational decision makers. Yet what is so interesting is that in other strategic action fields, a similar mind-set would not be significant enough to impede change. At other times, these constraints are material resources, such as limited facilities, finances, or information technology systems. But again, it often is not the objective amount of resources that is deterministic but rather the way it is understood and addressed within a particular context. As such, the meaning and significance of important factors in implementation—the understanding of them as constraints or opportunities—emerge from how the strategic action field is bounded.

Finally, our approach implies that to improve implementation practice, one must understand and seek to influence activities happening at different levels throughout the implementation system. In scholarly terminology, this is a problem referred to as collective action. Sociologist Carl May writes, "This problem of collective, coordinated and cooperative social action is the pivot upon which implementation . . . must turn."[27] Collective action—getting groups of individuals at different places in a system to apply themselves to a consistent direction of change—is at the heart of the matter. Implementation requires that actors engage each other in change processes so that ultimately, that which was old becomes established in daily routines. Perhaps it is applying a funding mechanism that creates different incentives for private organizations; creating a new program that better engages participants; or adopting a coaching program that reinforces an evidence-based mental health program. While the specific tactics and activities undertaken differ, the process of change requires collective action within and across the strategic action fields found in the whole implementation system.

As we will see in chapter 2, the existing research on policy and program implementation irrefutably documents its complexity. Yet our theoretically and empirically grounded approach helps professionals more effectively understand, navigate, and shape the process. To lay the foundation for a more in-depth exploration of the historical foundation of our approach and the dynamics within strategic action fields, it is useful to first investigate the various levels of scale found in implementation systems, introducing an awareness of implementation practice at these levels. We then conclude this chapter with an overview of two cases that we use throughout the rest of this book to bring the analysis to life.

Understanding Scale

We are not the first to suggest the importance of investigating implementation processes at multiple levels.[28] Such an approach, though, is particularly important in countries like the United States and in the European Union that have dense policy domains where multiple government, private business, and nonprofit agencies are already engaged in policy formation and public service provision. Rather than naively thinking that a new policy or program idea can be implemented as initially envisioned, our approach invites inquiry, learning about existing conditions within the implementation system, and considering the nature of the implementation challenges one might face. Certain implementation activities occur at the policy field level, and others unfold at the organization or frontline levels; certain types of challenges and possible solutions present themselves as well. Said another way, there are different levels in an implementation system that influence both the scope of problems and solutions, as well as the observed results. Strategic action fields operate at each level, and each requires the cultivation of particular strategic actions at different scales.

The notion of scale here is important. Think about gardening. It is clear that gardeners use different knowledge and tools to address problems, depending on their scale. When wanting to make significant alterations at her home, a gardener will hire a landscape architect to assess the naturally existing contours of the plot, recommend grading, and bring in bulldozers and backhoe loaders to create tiered beds or patios. Together they will look at what is possible given the existing shade trees and buildings, possibly laying brick for a new walkway or retaining wall. But when she wants to actually grow the plants, she needs to change scale and focus on the bed in front of her. She must select plants based on what already exists, looking at color and texture, and use a shovel or trowel. She might add some accent rocks or mulch to keep down the weeds, or work to ensure that the bed's edging doesn't get too weedy throughout the growing season. Yet the garden is fundamentally composed of plants and blossoms; ensuring their health requires working at yet another scale. Watering cans, pruning shears, antifungal treatments: all become important tools in helping to nurture healthy growth. A master gardener can work at one of these scales, while always remembering that changes at one level affect the other and, ultimately, the final result.

For those not metaphorically inclined, employment and training programs funded by the federal and state government provide a policy example. These programs are often carried out by local nonprofit organizations, accountable to local workforce development boards. Yet what directly shapes these service organizations' work are both federal rules and historically defined institutional roles within the policy field. Foundation-supported advocacy organizations might host conferences where good ideas can be shared and reinforced for adoption in the field. Particular organizations develop expertise working with certain populations, and some secure philanthropic dollars for low-income worker advancement programs not currently supported in federal or state law. As a result, some organizations develop more holistic service models, while others struggle to deliver basic service. Frontline practices such as competition or service referrals further influence program delivery because they shape both what clients receive and how neighboring nonprofits operate. These factors are all significant in the system and its results.

Policy fields are bounded networks among organizations carrying out a substantive policy or program in a particular place. In any jurisdiction, there is a potential pool of organizations composed of public agencies, interest or industry groups, professional associations, nonprofit service providers, or others that might participate in implementation because of their expertise or interests. When an institution actively engages in the policy field, it brings with it money, information, program knowledge, and other resources. These forces flow between organizations and create a structure that can shift and change as the tasks and issues of implementation shift over time. Thus, while the structure of the field is shaped by the form of public funding and availability of private resources, it is not determined by them. As a strategic action field, policy field structures and processes emerge from the interactions of people working within these institutions through their successes, partnerships, and battles over turf.

At the policy field level within implementation systems, certain implementation tasks are carried out. The various actors assemble policy tools and implementation resources that they believe are necessary for carrying out the program technology. Their interactions create the structure of the field. These interactions often involve significant negotiations because field actors come to implementation tasks with distinct understandings of the policy problem and potential solutions. However, it is through these negotiations—and how they reconcile differences in authority, culture, and resources—that the elements of program technology are set.

Many organizations exist within a policy field. Delving into the processes of certain key organizations is critical to understanding and improving policy and program implementation. Some organizations authorize the policy or program. Often this can be a state or regional public agency empowered through legislative authority to administer public programs. But private foundations that invest significant resources into a field can also play the role of authorizer, particularly in fields with limited public investment. Other organizations provide the public service. Their work directly influences the target population: the clients, citizens, or beneficiaries of the program. Although there are distinct roles, both authorizing and service organizations devise the program rules and structures enacted in implementation. They integrate ideas and opportunities from the field, either leveraging or ignoring the constraints and resources present.

At this scale, organizational actors attempt to reconcile the policy or program directives with existing organizational imperatives. They integrate these signals into existing organizational processes and expertise. The way this occurs is directly influenced by the sources of authority and culture within the organization, as well as the resources that exist or can be generated. All are combined to create the enacted program structure, the definitions of activities, and assignment of resources invested to carry out the program.

With our orientation to changes in target group behavior, the front lines of implementation systems are the final scale we see as critical. At this level, the system interacts directly with the target population to carry out the program. It is where larger directives are applied to particular situations. Sometimes the front lines involve face-to-face interactions between staff and the target group: think delivery of education, mental health counseling, or vocational rehabilitation.

Other times, the system and target group interact through other means, such as online registration for camping or call centers about Medicare claims. The decisions made at other levels in the implementation system about the contours of the program technology, as well as the professionalism and norms shared among staff and type of engagement required from the target group, all influence what occurs at this level.

One of the most troubling aspects of how policy and program implementation is often studied is how little attention is paid to understanding target groups' perspectives and behaviors.[29] Although public and private organizations frame problems, develop policies and program ideas, and attempt to implement them, the target group members themselves are often key problem solvers.[30] Whether they are drug users, students, ill elderly, or parents, the groups being targeted by the program or policy are the people who need to change in order for the intervention to be a success. The front lines are where the program is enacted for target group members. The decisions made by individual staff about how to carry out their work, or the ways in which the computer-based processes are assembled, facilitate or frustrate how target group members experience the public policy or program. At this level, public resources are delivered to real people who bring their own preferences and limitations to the task. They also assess quality and express feedback, either overtly or inadvertently.

Table 1.2 summarizes the key implementation activities accomplished at each level in an implementation system. It highlights the analytical focus, key roles, and types of implementation activities accomplished across any policy or program content area. In part 2, we explore each of these levels in detail and illustrate the more general concepts through our own analysis of two policy programs with which we are familiar.

Implementation as Policy Practice

With the devolution of much policy and program implementation from central government, we believe that people interested in improving policy and program implementation must learn about the various levels within these complex systems. Too often people believe policy activities are restricted to those advancing political positions or organizational interests during policy debates. Yet people with diverse job titles are involved in implementation: executive directors, board members, contract managers, program directors, funders, teachers, counselors, and volunteers. Whether they recognize it or not, they are all involved in implementation,

Table 1.2
Multiple Levels of the Implementation System

Level	Focus of Analysis at This Level	Key Role at This Level	Work Accomplished at This Level
Policy field	Bounded networks among organizations carrying out a substantive policy and program area in a particular place	Assemble policy tools and implementation resources; create field structure	Problems and solutions are negotiated; authority and resources are mobilized; coordinating structures are selected
Organization	Authorizing and service organizations that devise the program rules and structure	Integrate program with existing organizational processes; create program structure	Program is operationalized with defined activities; resources are secured and assigned to deliver program
Front lines	Workers or interfaces that directly interact with the target population to carry out the program	Enact program for target group; facilitate target group interactions with program	Resources and services are delivered; assessments of quality occur

and they all have a role in policy practice. In this book, we are inviting people in these diverse roles (or those aspiring to assume these types of roles in the future) to embrace, as one part of their professional identity, their abilities to affect policy outcomes through implementation.

In table 1.3 we summarize principles to keep in mind as you build your awareness of your own implementation practice and cultivate its effectiveness. It begins by understanding the larger systemic context of your work. Implementation activities are diverse: working with a network of agencies, replicating a new mental health service model, crafting new training programs for public health workers, or

> ## Table 1.3
> ### Principles for Cultivating Effective Implementation Practice
>
> Know the context where you can affect change: the participants and resources, sources of power, and cultural values.
>
> Unpack the core program (viable options, logic of change, and coordination), and identify changes to bring about public value results.
>
> Confront the technical and adaptive challenges necessary to create change, applying analytical inquiry and social skill.

monitoring factories' compliance with heath standards. Effective implementation requires people with many more diverse skills and orientations. As we will see, there are many different positions within implementation systems, many distinct actors playing different roles. Knowledge of the policy or program area and the target population attempting to be reached is essential. But so are tactical and managerial skills that allow one—regardless of official position—to mobilize resources and make change.

We have seen many managers, leaders, and staff spending considerable time complaining about conditions in the implementation system about which they can do little. State administrators blame the competing priorities of service providing organizations; frontline workers blame economic factors or lack of political support for their endeavor. They try to apply a tool that is inappropriate for the implementation problem they are confronting. We see these actors as suffering from *scale error*, a term from developmental psychology. In experiments, children introduced to a tool, such as a hammer, will try to use that same tool even when the physical task is altered. Much like these children, policy and program implementers regularly try to use tools that are familiar or ones they have seen other colleagues deploy regardless of the particular needs of the situation at hand. Improving implementation requires recognition and prevention of scale error.

As we walk through our multilevel understanding of implementation systems, we will dive into the social dynamics of each setting, emphasizing the unique elements of each strategic action field. This is because implementation practice occurs in a particular setting, often where you work or find yourself in the system. What needs to occur to implement the ACA at Connect with Health Colorado is different from careful explanations frontline staff must do with people signing up for their health insurance for the first time. Integrating the legislative priorities of the ACA into the strategic planning process of the Department of Health Care Policy and Financing is substantively different from the task of creating feasible staff assignments for exchange navigators in the service agency. Implementers must focus on improving implementation appropriate to the scale at which they work.

Significant impact can come from people who can operate effectively across levels and settings. These professionals are strategic in negotiating the power dynamics in the Department of Health Care Policy and Financing so that consistent rules and reporting requirements can be passed to service organizations. They position themselves as expert frontline workers who can provide formal testimony or informal information about frontline interactions with new insurers to the Connect with Health advisory committees. So while we focus on improving your understanding of differentiated levels within complex systems, we do not mean to imply that these levels are isolated from each other. As we will discuss in chapter 3, they are embedded and the boundaries between them are porous.

Second, our approach in this book bucks popular trends in management for a one-size-fits-all approach that tries to simplify the tasks, diverting attention away from the complex social processes at the heart of implementation, with the promise of more simplistic quick fixes. One management trend, called results-based accountability or "new public management," advocates not attending to implementation details at all. Significantly influenced by a private sector business orientation to financial results, advocates of this approach direct policymakers to merely specify results and trust that others will figure out the means. In this view, a shared focus on results will cause various implementers to select the appropriate technology needed to achieve the results—the details will work themselves out. While we certainly agree that performance measures and results-based management can be useful tools for improving implementation practice, many studies now document that they alone do not ensure effective change; measures can be merely used symbolically.[31] Other visible policy initiatives, such as the No Child Left Behind education reform, document that not understanding the means by which results are being pursued or providing inadequate resources to do so will create many unintended and detrimental consequences for implementation systems.[32] Understanding the means through which desired change is attempted in the target population – what we call the "core program"—and tending to the unintended consequences to bring about public value results is the central work of implementation.

The third principle for effective implementation practice requires confronting both technical and adaptive challenges, using inquiry into what is known and subtle social skill to engage others in determining what is not known. In some policy domains, there is a countervailing trend to results-based accountability that focuses on selecting program technology grounded in research evidence, evidence-based programs, or empirically supported treatments. In fact, as we will describe in the next chapter, a whole field of research called implementation science focuses on improving adoption and diffusion of such interventions by generating evidence about what activities have an impact on outcomes. Similarly, there has been a rise of small-scale randomized control trials to perfect technology in pursuit of cost-effective interventions. Federal and state governments are enthusiastically investing in research that makes such microadjustments in program technology to explore the impact on results and how to apply these findings in other settings.

We certainly support the use of research-based evidence to inform implementation activities; it is a large part of what motivates this book. However, we think it is shortsighted to reduce the application to merely perfecting program technology. Significant evidence documents that adoption of evidence-based interventions or behaviorally sound wording is not automatic. What is picked up is often a result of the skill of social actors within the particular setting, working with the power and values present to introduce technological elements that are viable while engaging others in participating in the suggested solution. In this book, we integrate research that helps us make sense of this process, attending to the social dynamics that occur in the strategic action fields that comprise implementation systems.

In coming to understand implementation as pragmatic policy practice, we have been influenced by many people who share our concern with professional problem solving. Nobel laureate Herbert A. Simon's *Science of the Artificial* established the idea that professions (in fields such as architecture, engineering, and management) share an essential trait: problem solving, or what he described as converting existing conditions into preferred ones. Eugene Bardach spent years at the Goldman School of Public Policy at the University of California Berkeley exploring how effective leaders develop practices that are influenced both by their context and what they are trying to accomplish.[33] Donald Schön, a professor at MIT, conducted extensive studies showing how practitioners think in action.[34] These three scholars share a common insight that we fully embrace here: professional effectiveness involves being able to describe a specific context, understand why it comes to operate that way, and act purposively using technical and social knowledge to solve problems. A multilevel framework for implementation analysis helps one to describe the context. Theories of social process, like strategic action fields, allow one to analytically explain what is occurring, and see patterns and underlying mechanisms that transcend the particular situation. When brought into use in a particular setting, this type of analysis opens the way for more skillful resolution of complex challenges. Said another way, it helps you understand who acts where, doing what, and how, and suggests what you might do to change those circumstances.

BRINGING THE ANALYSIS TO LIFE

Implementation practice is fundamentally about attending to details—about getting them right in order to make the change in your context. To help inspire your own analysis and illustrate our general concepts, we focus on particular illustrations of program implementation throughout part 2 of this book. We selected these examples because they are ones we know well from our own areas of expertise and experience. Both of us have worked at the frontline, organizational, and policy field levels of these implementation systems; our tacit knowledge of these levels helps us understand important implementation details. But, significantly, these examples are smaller initiatives than the monumental ACA. They evolved out of collective efforts to respond to public problems.

We suggest that the best way to learn to do implementation analysis is to pick a policy or program area of your own. It can be a large federal policy like the ACA or something more modest such as a targeted program or state-based initiative. Applying the steps in our analysis to an actual case will illuminate the potential for this analysis to point the way to more effective and strategic practice; the appendixes at the end of this book provide tools that allow you to easily translate the ideas of this analysis and apply them to your own cases.

The Hardest Hit Fund (HHF) was a program undertaken to respond to the foreclosure crisis of the Great Recession, an outgrowth of the Troubled Asset Relief Program (TARP). As box 1.2 describes, it concentrated on assistance to eighteen states particularly hard hit by the crisis, enabling them to offer mortgage assistance to unemployed or underemployed homeowners at risk of foreclosure. It is a redistributive program, reallocating resources from the government to assist homeowners in need.[35] The Quality Rating and Improvement System (QRS) is a program designed to improve early childhood education settings. As box 1.3 describes, rather than being initiated by the federal government, the program idea has spread from its initial development in Oklahoma in 1998 to forty-three states currently running pilot, regional, or statewide programs, with another six in planning stages.[36] QRS is a regulatory program, using a voluntary process to assess early childhood setting quality so as to improve services and provide information to parents.

Box 1.2
Introduction to the Hardest Hit Fund Program

The US financial crisis of 2007–2008 has been labeled the worst financial crisis since the Great Depression of the 1930s.[a] The crisis resulted in failures or near failures of some of the largest financial institutions in the country and led to record levels of unemployment and foreclosures for individual households.[b] The federal government stepped in with various initiatives to stem the potential collapse of financial markets, stabilize housing markets, and boost the economy. One of these initiatives was the Troubled Asset Relief Program, also known as TARP, administered by the US Department of Treasury.[c] The Hardest Hit Fund (HHF) program was one of the foreclosure prevention initiatives under TARP.

The HHF initiative was in part a response to previous federal foreclosure initiatives that fell short of expectations. While prior programs provided federal funding for mortgage assistance, the funds flowed through private lenders that determined borrower eligibility. Among other barriers, capacity and compliance issues with private lenders limited the success of these programs. The HHF program provided a new vehicle, state housing finance agencies (HFAs), to deliver assistance directly to homeowners.

Beginning in 2010, the US Department of Treasury allocated federal funds to states deemed to be hardest hit by the foreclosure crisis through the HHF program. Eighteen eligible states, including Ohio, received a total allocation of $7.6 billion under the HHF initiative.[d] The program required states to target funds to unemployed or underemployed homeowners, thereby serving a growing (critical) population of potentially distressed homeowners.[e] In each state, HFAs worked within federal guidelines to tailor their programs to the needs of homeowners in their individual states. While states had discretion in how they designed their programs, most structured their programs to provide mortgage assistance to homeowners through participating private lenders. Ohio

(continued)

(Continued)

was awarded $570.4 million under HHF, the third largest allocation among the eighteen states.

a. Miguel Almunia, Agustin Benetrix, Barry Eichengreen, Kevin H. O'Rourke, and Gisela Rua, "From Great Depression to Great Credit Crisis: Similarities, Differences and Lessons," *Economic Policy* 25, no. 62 (2010): 219–65.

b. Michael D. Hurd and Susann Rohwedder, *Effects of the Financial Crisis and Great Recession on American Households* (Washington, DC: National Bureau of Economic Research, 2010).

c. For more information, see the most recent financial report on TARP: http://www .treasury.gov/initiatives/financial-stability/reports/Documents/AFR_FY2013_TARP-12– 11–13_Final.pdf.

d. Much of the background information about the program is from the information on the program website: http://www.treasury.gov/initiatives/financial-stability/TARP-Programs/housing/hhf/Pages/default.aspx.

e. SIGTARP report 2012: http://www.sigtarp.gov/audit%20reports/sigtarp_hhf_audit.pdf.

Box 1.3
Introduction to the Quality Rating and Improvement Systems Program

Quality Rating and Improvement Systems (QRS) are programs adopted by states to bolster the quality of early childhood programs and improve parental access to high-quality services for their children. The supply of quality early childhood education is not provided by typical market dynamics, rather public provision of service is targeted through subsidies for low-income parents and their children. The QRS program provides parents with information about the early childhood education services and creates incentives for service providers to improve their quality through tying access to quality improvements or subsidy payments to higher ratings. Stated another way, it is a systemic approach to assess, improve, and communicate the level of quality in early childhood education programs. As such it is part of creating, as one report noted, "a decision support data system"[a] for early childhood education and is a programmatic strategy for solving a long-standing problem of market misalignment in early childhood education.

Early childhood education is largely a state-based public service. While private national accreditation and national Head Start program rules exist to define quality settings, the majority of settings are not covered by these requirements. State governments also have licensing systems, which establish the basic floor of health and safety for regulated settings.[b] QRSs are a means for states to assess setting quality, tie public investments to incentivizing quality improvement, and offer parents a way to access information about quality ratings of early education settings.

Between 1998 and 2005, ten states adopted the program and fourteen others, including Minnesota, embarked on planning. Virtually all offer QRS as a voluntary system for providers, and in those settings, about 30 percent of providers participate.[c] As of 2010, twenty-six states had implemented QRS, with others under development.[d] As is true for most other state-based education programs, there is significant variation in implementation across the states.

---

a. Kathryn Tout and K. Maxwell, "Quality Rating and Improvement Systems: Achieving the Promise for Programs, Parents, Children and Early Childhood Systems," *The Quest for Quality: Promising Innovations for Early Childhood Programs,* ed. P. W. Wesley and V. Buysse (Baltimore, MD: Brookes Publishing, 2010).
b. A portion of the early childhood education market is provided by legally unregulated providers, such as family, friends, and neighbors, who care for small numbers of children. If the children's parents are eligible for subsidies, these providers are able to receive public funds.
c. Kathryn Tout, personal communication (November 2, 2013).
d. An assessment done in February 2014 by the QRIS National Learning Network revealed that forty-five states and territories implemented a statewide, regional, or pilot QRS program, with an additional eight in planning stages. Only Missouri was not pursuing a program.

These two illustrative cases vary on a number of dimensions (see table 1.4): they were initiated at different times and have distinct scopes, they are different policy types and have distinct target populations, and each has distinct desired results. Yet as we will show in part 2, they allow us to discuss the details of implementation in practice and demonstrate how a consistent analytical framework can help uncover the dynamics that are at the heart of the implementation process. The cases help us illustrate how the general dynamics of strategic action fields operate and how a multilevel implementation analysis can proceed. We share them here to show how to undertake such analysis in your own policy or program area, to improve your understanding of implementation and identify points of intervention in your particular system.

We have taken this practical, applied approach because, as practitioners and scholars, we know only too well how difficult it is to understand and act strategically to improve policy and program implementation. We also are inspired to pursue this type of engaged scholarship by colleagues who have worked on these

Table 1.4
Comparison of Illustrative Cases

	Hardest Hit Fund (HHF)	Quality Rating and Improvement System (QRS)
Policy domain	Housing	Early childhood education
Initiation	Federal government in response to housing crisis (2010)	State government and diffusion of idea (starting in 1998)
Scope	Eighteen states	Approximately forty-three states
Policy type	Income transfer	Regulatory
Targets	Unemployed and underemployed homeowners	Early child education providers, parents
Service organizations	Nonprofit housing counseling agencies, lenders	Nonprofits supporting quality enhancement in early childhood education sites
Frontline staff	Housing counselors	Coaches
Desired outcomes	Homeowner stability (decrease in foreclosures)	Promotion of quality early childhood settings and enhanced information to consumers

important topics for a long time. As Lawrence O'Toole noted, "To establish as a goal that the field of . . . implementation should be able to assist practitioners does not oblige researchers to develop a single predictive theory which will then be employed by actors in the policy implementation process . . . Just as with other varieties of social science, implementation research can serve practical purposes by highlighting a problem, sensitizing others to it, and calling attention to consistently important clusters of variables and relationships."[37] This, then, is our intent.

To cultivate effective implementation we want to shine light on the problems confronted in the execution of implementation and sensitize others to them. We begin by recounting, in chapter 2, the three perspectives scholars have taken to understanding policy and program implementation in the past half-century. Then, in chapter 3, we integrate these perspectives, bringing into focus our approach that explores the social dynamics surrounding the program at the heart of an implementation process. By unpacking the dynamics of strategic action fields found throughout implementation systems, we provide language and concepts that bolster our analysis of the complex process.

In part 2, we explore how implementation works at various levels in an implementation system, providing helpful ways to describe key factors at each level and tools that can be used with others to appreciate the significant elements of implementation decided at that level. In part 3, we begin by illustrating a multi-level implementation analysis through the Hardest Hit Fund and early childhood Quality Rating and Improvement System programs. In this way, you will better understand how to analyze the structure and processes of implementation systems in your own situations.

We finish, in chapter 8, by laying out a practical approach to improving implementation that is possible with a thorough understanding of the system. We also provide helpful tools for improving implementation conditions in your own context. Rather than promoting the notion that implementation conditions should be predicted and controlled, our approach focuses on reflection and analysis to enable more strategic action in particular contexts. Thus, rather than providing a ten-step guide, we enable our readers to see things more clearly and equip them with helpful resources to cultivate their own gardens where public policy and program implementation occurs.

Conventional Perspectives on Policy and Program Implementation

chapter
TWO

In this book, we offer a new way to think about implementation, but the implementation challenges we explore are not new. For decades, policymakers, practitioners, and scholars have wrestled with the complexities of policy and program implementation and have offered various ways of making sense of what they observe. Significant contributions have been made along the way, helping to reveal the elements that make up the broader implementation system. Understandably these contributions tend to be made from the perspective and background of the observer. Those with a background in politics or political science tend to approach implementation challenges by thinking about the sources and structures of political authority that may lead to intended—and unintended—outcomes. By contrast, those with a management or administration mind-set tend to see implementation challenges through the lens of governance and coordination. Finally, those with training in clinical settings or behavioral sciences tend to focus on the intervention itself and the characteristics of the treatment more likely to lead to successful implementation.

These are not mutually exclusive perspectives; often observers from each of the three perspectives tip their hats to the other elements. Yet it is sometimes difficult to see the proverbial forest when focusing so intently on individual trees. One of our primary aims in this book is to provide a fuller picture of the forest within which implementation challenges emerge. This aim requires us to be pragmatic—moving across schools of thought and units of analysis

35

without getting bogged down in any one particular way of thinking. We will turn to this integration in our discussion of strategic action fields in chapter 3, but before pushing forward, it is helpful to review the insights that have evolved over time within each perspective. We expect that some of our readers will be more familiar with one perspective or another and may find the review within their perspective to be a bit superficial. Our aim is not to provide a comprehensive literature review of implementation-relevant scholarship within each perspective, but rather to introduce readers to all three perspectives to help ground our integration and application, thereby motivating our approach toward integration.

In the sections that follow, we group prior scholarship into three categories: political processes and authority, governance and management, and policy and program evaluations. Yet they don't operate in isolation; research focused on political processes contributes to understandings of governance and vice versa. However, there are general emphases and foci within each perspective that are distinct. Table 2.1 summarizes some of the key attributes of each perspective. We briefly review the development of each perspective and highlight some of the literature that has shaped its evolution.

Table 2.1
Three Traditional Perspectives on Implementation

Perspective	Unit of Analysis	Dominant Disciplines	Focus of Implementation
Political processes and authority	Public policies or policy problem areas	Political science	Power dynamics: top-down authority; bottom-up influences
Governance and management	Organizations or networks	Public administration; organizational science	Coordination: multilevel; multiactor; governance tools
Policy and program evaluations	Interventions	Economics and behavioral sciences	Change processes: impact analysis; innovation diffusion; behavioral change

POLITICAL PROCESSES AND AUTHORITY

In the 1960s, political scientist David Easton called attention to implementation as an important, distinct component of the larger policy system—the "throughput" between inputs and outputs.[1] His contributions pushed political scientists to move beyond a focus on particular political actions, such as the passage of a piece of legislation by Congress or executive orders issued by the president, toward a focus on policy outcomes that result from the broader political system—conceptualized as a series of stages rather than a one-time event.[2] Classic textbooks on the policy process built on this work and proposed more formal, discrete stages, including problem identification, agenda setting, adoption, implementation, and policy evaluation.[3] This perspective spawned a body of literature focused explicitly on policy implementation, initially favoring a linear top-down model of political control, followed by more organic bottom-up approaches, and finally integrative frameworks. The central thread through each of these approaches is the emphasis on political control, power, and authority that contribute to implementation success or failure.

Top-Down Authority

Initial studies of implementation assumed that the appropriate lever of change to improve policy outcomes was the design of the policy itself. Failures in implementation occurred because the policy put in place through legislation or executive orders either lacked sufficient clarity or did not match the context or policy problem it was intended to address. The first generation of implementation research in this vein was predominantly case studies of implementation failures evolving out of frustrations with the Great Society programs of the 1960s and 1970s. The 1973 book by Pressman and Wildavsky, *Implementation: How Great Expectations in Washington Are Dashed in Oakland or Why It's Amazing That Federal Programs Work at All*, is the classic study often credited with launching this stream of research.[4]

In their book, Pressman and Wildavsky unpack the apparent failure of a federal economic development initiative targeting resources to boost the economy and minority employment in Oakland, California. Their main premise is that the inability of the federal initiative to reach its intended goals was due to the disconnection of policy design and policy implementation. They counter the notion that policy designs are prescriptive plans that simply need to be executed; rather, they espouse that policies are hypotheses based on a theory about a chain of causation between "initial conditions" and "predicted consequences." Sometimes the chain is relatively simple, but more often the chain is complex, with numerous links that need to be in place to achieve the intended outcomes. Implementation is about forging the links in the causal chain; if the intended outcome is not realized, it could be that the links were not feasible to create or that the theory of change was incorrect in the first place. Essentially, perceived failures in policy may occur because of faulty policy design in crafting the theory of change—a mismatch between means and ends.

Applied to the economic development programs, Pressman and Wildavsky purport that policy actors in Washington, DC, crafted an initiative to boost the economy based on a theory of change that did not reflect reality or what was actually feasible to bring about change in the city of Oakland. They lay out the complexity of the hypothesis underlying the federal policy: if the federal government provides more than $20 million in funding through a new entity, the Economic Development Administration, to private businesses in Oakland and the funded businesses agree to hire minorities after spending the money at some point in the future, then new jobs will be created that will hire minorities, thereby reducing minority unemployment in the region. According to Pressman and Wildavsky, this policy design was based on too many indirect assumptions. To be successful, the policy needed to target resources in a more direct way toward the intended problem. Rather than subsidizing the general capital development of businesses, hoping they would hire minority personnel, the policy could have been designed to offer companies direct wage subsidies after they had hired minority personnel. In this way, the policy design could circumvent some of the difficulties of implementation by reducing the necessary causal linkages.

Pressman and Wildavsky's analysis has been criticized for being too rational and placing too much responsibility on implementation at the top during the design phase of the policy process.[5] However, in subsequent editions of their book, they clarify that they were in fact responding against the rational planning-and-control model of implementation. They were challenging that policy design should not be treated as a separate process, divorced from implementation, but rather that implementation is an evolutionary and adaptive process stemming from and building on the initial policy intent. Nonetheless, they continued to assert the importance of formal policy; they saw their approach as distinct from subsequent theorists who focused on interactions on the ground without substantial attention to the intended policy outcomes. Perhaps their key insight relates to the complexity of joint action—that the multitude of actors with different missions and time lines create implementation challenges. They stress that joint action is more difficult if the program or policy is complex, requiring multiple decision points to transform inputs into outcomes. In other words, the underlying core program and assumptions are critical to implementation success, a premise we agree with and discuss in more detail in chapter 3.

Following Pressman and Wildavsky, a strain of research continued to focus on policy design. Some offered more prescriptive recommendations, admonishing policymakers to take responsibility to set the stage or "fix the game" for success.[6] Other researchers began to move away from case studies and prescriptions toward empirical models and the identification of variables that affect implementation success—still from a top-down perspective.[7] For example, in the 1980s, Daniel Mazmanian and Paul Sabatier sought to identify important variables that influence the achievement of legal objectives throughout the implementation process. Their resulting model had seventeen important variables, categorized into three groups, measuring the tractability of the problem, the ability of the policy statute to structure implementation, and nonstatutory factors affecting implementation.[8] In general, the implementation studies in this approach—whether prescriptive case studies or empirical models—emphasize identifying levers of change in a mechanistic way that can be manipulated by policymakers to improve implementation and policy outcomes. The illustrations of machine-like contraptions on the cover and throughout Pressman and Wildavsky's book offer a case in point.

Bottom-Up Authority

As might be expected, other scholars pushed back against the top-down approach, emphasizing that it was not technically feasible or politically viable for policymakers to comprehensively structure implementation.[9] For example, RAND policy analyst Paul Berman observed wide variation in the same policy being carried out in different local environments. According to Berman, it is the interaction of policy with its implementation setting that creates implementation challenges. He concluded that policy designs were required that could be adapted to local conditions to prevent policy failure, particularly for unclear technologies.[10] These "bottom-up" scholars often called for a mapping of the local implementation context and relationships between actors that could then describe the incentive structures and behaviors on the ground. For example, European scholar Benny Hjern and his colleagues coined the term *implementation structures* to represent the self-organized, interconnected clusters of government agencies, organizations, and private businesses that carry out policies and programs at the local level.[11] Rather than focusing on a single policy, Hjern's approach was to start with a policy problem, identifying the multiple institutions and policies that affect the problem. Whereas the top-down approach was deductive, offering formal models and specifying variables that could predict implementation outcomes, the bottom-up approach was more inductive, identifying conditions on the ground to inform a descriptive (rather than predictive) account of the implementation process.

However, it is not just the institutions in the local implementation environment that matter, but also the individuals carrying out policies within institutions. Perhaps one of the best-known scholars to make this point is political scientist Michael Lipsky, who wrote the 1980 book *Street Level Bureaucracy: Dilemmas on the Individual in Public Services*. We will revisit Lipsky's seminal contributions in chapter 6, but some background is helpful here. Lipsky offered a sympathetic explanation for the actions of "street-level bureaucrats," the people who work on the front lines of public service provision. Whether they were police officers, social workers, teachers, or lawyers, these frontline agents often faced criticism for making decisions about individual cases that at times appeared capricious and insensitive to client needs. According to Lipsky, the solution is not to reduce the discretion of frontline workers, which is often infeasible and even undesirable. Instead, effective implementation requires attention to the experiences of frontline workers and adequate support to equip them to facilitate the desired policy outcomes. Other scholars have reached similar conclusions, stressing the need to engage street-level workers in the policy design process, empowering them to create the conditions that will lead to successful outcomes.[12] We agree, and highlight the front line as one of the three critical levels in our multilevel model of implementation.

Implied in Lipsky's analysis is the idea that behaviors and behavioral responses matter as much as or more than formal rules and procedures. This important assumption also underlies the work of Richard Elmore, who introduced the concept of backward mapping to understand implementation outcomes.[13] Unlike some of the other early approaches, Elmore's backward mapping offers a tool that can be used to unpack implementation and inform policy design rather than a theory to predict implementation outcomes. His approach considers the behaviors of the target population and their likely responses to the initiatives being implemented. It also takes seriously the behaviors of the street-level workers administering the program and how incentive structures might affect interactions between workers and the target population. Rather than a top-down approach to designing policy, Elmore suggests that policy instruments should be selected based on the behaviors to be changed at the lowest levels and the necessary incentive structures to bring about that change. This focus mirrors the behavioral economics approach that we think is essential to improving implementation practice, and we discuss it later in this chapter and throughout this book.

Integration and Frameworks

By the late 1980s, political scientists had identified a plethora of variables and contextual factors that might affect implementation outcomes; however, there was no comprehensive theoretical approach, perspective, or framework by which to make sense of them.[14] The title of a 1986 article by scholar Malcolm Goggin described the situation as the "Too Few Cases/Too Many Variables Problem in Implementation Research."[15] Rather than identifying new factors that might affect implementation outcomes, these scholars and others offered theoretical perspectives and frameworks toward integration.[16] For example, Goggin put forth a behavioral theory of implementation, focusing on the form and content of the policy, the capacity of implementing organizations, and the skills of people responsible for implementation. Under the behavioral theory, the primary measure of success for implementation is the integration of the new policy into the standard operating practices and procedures of implementing organizations and individuals. Later Goggin and his colleagues extended the theoretical approach to include an explicit focus on intergovernmental communications in the implementation process, unpacking the transmission of messages between the federal level (often in the form of policies) and local-level implementers.[17]

Another important theoretical contribution from political science that integrates implementation is the advocacy coalition framework (ACF), initially put forth by Paul Sabatier in the 1980s and generating a large body of research that continues today.[18] The ACF combines Sabatier and Mazmanian's prior emphasis on legal instruments that constrain behavior, but with particular attention to the context of implementation and actors at various levels of the policy process. One of the unique aspects of the ACF is the focus on the system affecting the policy problem over a substantial period of time—in cycles of ten years or more. Another is the focus on coalitions of "subsystem actors" that form over time in response to a problem, with different coalitions representing the varied belief systems operating in the policy environment. According to the ACF, these coalitions offer a more appropriate focus than institutions for understanding political dynamics and authority in implementation analysis. Actors who share common beliefs about the policy problem, its causes and the preferred solutions, coordinate together to advocate for their positions in a policy field over time. Multiple coalitions not only compete for power and dominance but also engage in policy-oriented learning, where coalition members gather information and analysis that helps support their beliefs and policy positions. Changing the outcomes of a policy subsystem, including those associated with implementation, thus entails shifting the beliefs or power dynamics of the dominant coalitions.[19]

While it offers a big-picture perspective for making sense of policy changes observed over time, the ACF has been criticized for providing limited insights for day-to-day implementation—failing to describe how policy changes resulting from coalition beliefs are carried out at the operational level or how implementation dynamics feed back into subsequent policy-oriented learning.[20] We agree with these limitations. However, we appreciate the ACF's attention to power dynamics within a policy subsystem and the coalitions that form and learning that occurs around particular belief systems to reinforce or challenge existing practices. Power dynamics, belief systems, and policy learning at the field level, but also at the organizational and frontline levels, are important components of our approach in this book.

Whereas the ACF offers a framework that is characterized by attributes of the policy environment, other scholars have offered frameworks that are characterized by attributes of the policies themselves. For example, beginning in the late 1980s and early 1990s, Patricia Ingraham, Helen Ingram, Anne Schneider, and other scholars began to call for a shift in perspective away from implementation generically toward understanding specific policy characteristics that might shape implementation and design choices.[21] Rather than treating all policies as equal, these scholars noted that some policies lend themselves more readily to easy implementation, whereas others have considerable diversity of stakeholders and complexity that might prevent strict policy design. Motivated by this perspective, Richard Matland proposed a framework for conditions affecting implementation success.[22] Depending on the levels of ambiguity and conflict, success for some policies would be more readily achieved through a top-down fidelity to the policy design—with the most important factors being those that would affect such adherence, and success for other policies would necessarily evolve through a more bottom-up implementation process—with the most important factors being the conditions on the ground that might affect policy learning and improvement.

Matland's framework, along with other implementation frameworks stemming from political science, offers a potentially useful heuristic to describe how policy environments and policies themselves may vary in systematic ways. However, most of these frameworks reflect a mechanistic view of implementation, seeking to find the right levers that can be adjusted at the top (policy design) or bottom (implementation settings) to improve outcomes. And with the exception of the ACF, the unit of analysis tends to be a single, clearly identified policy. In reality, implementation challenges are likely affected by more than one formal policy—and each policy may differ substantially. Even within the same policy, there may be variation at different levels of government and across implementation sites. The next perspective reviewed here, governance and management, is in a sense a reaction against this policy-centric view of implementation, favoring instead a focus on the structure and coordination of the broader implementation system.

GOVERNANCE AND MANAGEMENT

While the study of policy implementation was relatively new to political science in the 1960s, the study of implementation systems more broadly can be traced back to the beginnings of public administration. In his 1887 essay, "The State of Public Administration," Woodrow Wilson suggested that it was "becoming more difficult to run a constitution than to write one" and that serious focus needed to be placed on administration, as distinct from politics.[23] This was reinforced by Frank Goodnow's classic text in 1900, *Politics and Administration*. Their primary objective was to call attention to the study of administration and management and the need to acknowledge the complexities of carrying out policies in public agencies. In this regard, they drew a line between political processes needed to pass legislation and the administrative processes necessary to make government function. While some scholars critiqued Wilson and Goodnow as promoting an artificial dichotomy between policy and administration,[24] others suggested that if taken in historical context, they were primarily advocating the study of administration as distinct, but not separate, from the study of politics.[25] Indeed, the study of public administration and management has a robust and growing scholarship, a review of which is beyond the scope of this book.[26]

The focus of public administration is not explicitly on implementation; however, the study of the coordination systems to carry out government actions is inextricably linked to implementation challenges. One of the predominant themes in this perspective today is the multiactor, multilevel nature of the system in which policy and management take place. *Governance* is an umbrella term that scholars have used to describe this broader system.[27] Since the mid-1970s, when Harland Cleveland coined the governance terminology, researchers have grappled with how to describe and make sense of systems of "interlaced webs of tension in which control is loose, power diffused, and centers of decision plural."[28] Whereas traditional studies of public administration and political science tend to focus on governmental actors and political factors that affect outcomes, the study of governance implies a more comprehensive approach that includes nongovernmental actors and other factors that interact in a decentralized, often networked structure.

While governance includes much more than implementation, the concepts of multilevel and multiactor systems of action are fundamental to understanding implementation. Some scholars, such as Michael Hill and Peter Hupe, place the study of implementation within the governance framework.[29] Yet the challenge with a governance approach is that it is defined too broadly to be of much use—it has become everything and the "kitchen sink." The term is used to refer to organizational structure, managerial approaches, systems of incentives, market-based approaches, citizen participation, public sector performance, globalization, contracting out and devolution, corporate transparency, international independence, or a new approach to managerialism.[30] While research in each of these areas is critical to informing implementation, we join other scholars to assert that there is still a significant need to focus on implementation—that which occurs at the intersection between these governance and management practices, and policy-related inputs and outcomes.[31] We highlight some of the themes from governance research that have importance for understanding implementation.

Multilevel

To help make sense of the complexity of governance systems, many scholars have situated the diverse public (and private) actors and sources of authority for decisions in hierarchical, multilevel frameworks.[32] This is not a new concept; for decades, sociologists and institutional scholars have described organizations in a similar fashion, with each individual organization (or organized group of actors) nested within a broader organizational or institutional field.[33] From a public administration perspective, this sort of multilevel framework provides a way to think about how policy decisions made in the federal government resonate down to lower levels of state agencies, service providers, and eventually target populations receiving services.

Perhaps one of the best examples of this approach is the "logic of governance" framework articulated by public affairs scholars Lawrence Lynn, Carolyn Heinrich, and Carolyn Hill. For them, the central question of governance is, "How can public sector regimes, agencies, programs, and activities be organized and managed to achieve public purposes?"[34] The logic of governance framework hierarchically links the preferences of citizens, enacted laws and rules of policymakers, and decisions of bureaucratic agencies to outputs and outcomes. They describe a hierarchy of relationships found in modern governance between institutions, management, and operations.[35] While the levels of relationships are situated hierarchically, the system incorporates feedback mechanisms, where outputs and outcomes observed by citizens in turn affect preferences, and thus political choices at the top.

One of the important contributions of this framework is that it describes public policy outputs and outcomes as a function of formal and informal authority, including both legislation and rules as well as agency discretion and the actions of frontline workers. They correctly observe that researchers often model policy outcomes or outputs as a function of formal policy, ignoring many of the potentially important managerial and operational factors, many of which are particularly critical for implementation. In contrast, public management scholars tend to concentrate on the managerial and operational levels, which often overlook some important policy variables. However, by situating implementation questions within a multilevel logic, there is a general recognition that institutional factors at higher levels also affect the outputs and outcomes that are of importance to implementation.

This framework has spurred a robust body of research that approaches policy problems more comprehensively. For example, Ken Meier, Laurence O'Toole, and colleagues have conceptualized outcomes for school districts as being affected by four governance levels: the school board setting general policy, the superintendent who is responsible for overall management, the principals and central office administrators who manage the day-to-day affairs of the school, and teachers carrying out programs at the street level.[36] Others have applied the governance logic to health care delivery outputs and outcomes with three levels: the institutional level of Medicare and Medicaid policy, the public management level with physicians who have managerial responsibilities, and the service delivery level incorporating nurses' beliefs and values.[37]

While multilevel governance research is not specifically limited to analyses of implementation, it is easy to see why implementation questions might fit well within this sort of structure. In a sense, the multilevel framework provides an alternative to the stages heuristic of the policy process—where implementation is viewed as a stage after policy formulation and adoption. The multilevel framework does not require discrete stages but rather allows for nesting of "lower levels" that include implementation within higher levels of policymaking. Still, the division between levels can sometimes be arbitrary—like the divisions between stages—and thus it is important to think of this sort of logic as a heuristic device rather than a predictive theory.[38]

Others also have conceptualized policy systems following a multilevel approach. Most notably, the institutional analysis and development (IAD) framework developed by political scientists Elinor and Vincent Ostrom offers relevance for implementation.[39] The IAD framework helps make sense of the policy process by identifying the underlying institutions operating at multiple levels that govern decisions and thus affect policy outcomes.[40] In the IAD framework, collective decisions regarding policy problems are made and carried out in an "action arena." Decisions made in action arenas are affected by institutions, collective characteristics, and environmental factors. For the purposes of policy analysis and design, specific attention is paid to role of institutions, which they characterize as rules, norms, and shared strategies that constrain and enable collective action taken by individuals within the action arena. Similar to the logic of governance framework's operational, managerial, and institutional levels, the IAD framework has three levels of institutions that affect outcomes within any given action arena: operational, collective choice, and constitutional.[41]

Scholars have borrowed from both the logic of governance and IAD frameworks to make sense of implementation questions. For example, Michael Hill and Peter Hupe have proposed a "multiple governance framework" that combines the IAD framework's constitutive, directional (collective-choice), and operational levels, with actions taking place at three scales: system, organizational, and individual.[42] According to Hill and Hupe, implementation takes place at the operational governance level—what they suggest is the focus of implementation analysis. While the operational governance level is the focus of implementation, the operational level is nested within the other levels, and thus actions taken at the higher levels affect implementation.

One of the benefits of viewing implementation as part of a multilevel framework is that it forces the analyst to think about the level (or scale) on which action is taking place and to think about how other levels of action might also influence the outcomes of interest. A limitation of this approach is that it can again lead to the kind of isolation of implementation that was endemic to the stages approach to the policy process, particularly if implementation is restricted to occurring only at a specific level (e.g., the level of operational governance). To help address this potential limitation, we recognize in our approach that implementation occurs across multiple levels connected in a larger system rather than segregating it to lower levels of governance. We view all implementation action as occurring within policy fields, organizations, and the frontline levels within an implementation system.

Multiactor Networks

While multilevel frameworks provide one way to portray the interactions of participants involved in governance, multiple actors are also implicitly or explicitly embedded in interorganizational networks. Networks can be defined as "multiple organizations that are legally autonomous," linked through relationships "based on cooperation and coordination."[43] There are at least two fundamental contributions of conceptualizing governance from a network perspective. First, network terminology provides a way to describe governance structures, shifting the unit of analysis away from a single organization toward a set of actors with various roles and responsibilities. In this regard, simply mapping the different organizations involved in a particular policy area can help illuminate the relationships and linkages necessary to create policy or program change. This is similar to how Benny Hjern and his colleagues mapped various organizations involved in the implementation process on the ground to identify the "implementation structures," as described earlier.[44]

In sociology, an entire methodology, social network analysis, equips analysts with tools and terminology to map networks of individuals or organizations and their relationships.[45] It allows researchers to visualize the structural relationships (ties) between organizations, identifying network characteristics such as clusters of organizations, overall network density, and the centrality of key organizations.

Rather than viewing each organization engaged in policy implementation as an isolated, independent decision maker, mapping the network structure informs how an organization's relative position within a network influences the decisions it makes.

In addition, networks provide a way to describe the coordination of actors operating in a given situation, often juxtaposed against market mechanisms or hierarchical controls. In markets, exchange benefits are understood, legal sanctions can be evoked, and trust is not necessary. Prices simplify relationships by mediating between supply and demand. In hierarchies, interactions are structured by the nature of employment and, specifically, the authority provided through organizational position and past actions. In networks, however, transactions are reciprocal and relationships are the main modes of communication. It is always possible for people or institutions to exit, so priority lies in achieving mutual benefit. Since the 1980s, social scientists, including many public affairs researchers, have investigated the characteristics of networks in this light.[46]

A growing body of literature in public affairs applies the network perspective to help make sense of multiactor, multisector governance. The majority of these studies are descriptive, generating best practices for public officials and managers. For example, public management scholars often distinguish network or collaborative management from traditional bureaucratic management.[47] Many papers describe the requisite skills of network managers, such as activating resources, arranging structures, guiding interactions, and focusing on goals,[48] recognizing that the means for doing such things may differ when people are focused on interactions among network members or the entire network structure. In their extensive studies of local economic development, Robert Agranoff and Michael McGuire highlight a range of collaborative activities undertaken by local public officials to glean information, make adjustments in policy mandates, develop strategy, exchange resources, and engage in project-based work.[49] Not surprisingly, they discovered that the use of such practices varies by city, depending on the economic development needs and capacities of the local actors engaged.

Another way to think about differences in networks is to examine the purpose for which the network has evolved. For example, scholars Brint Milward and Keith Provan draw from nearly three decades of research on public networks to identify four primary types of networks engaged in public service activities: service implementation networks, information diffusion networks, problem-solving networks, and community capacity-building networks. These network purposes are not mutually exclusive; however, effective strategies for network coordination depend in part on the network purpose at hand. For example, service provision networks may require formal funding contracts and coordination agreements in place to govern participant interactions, whereas more organic information diffusion networks may lack formal agreements and rely more heavily on the voluntary participation of member organizations.

Not only are there differences by purpose, but networks also exhibit different structures. Considerable public affairs research employs social network analysis techniques to help describe the structures of public networks.[50] One of the most substantial contributions in this regard is Milward and Provan's study of mental health networks beginning in the 1990s.[51] Motivated by the deinstitutionalization and decentralization of services provided to the mentally ill, they sought to examine how differences in coordination of various agencies engaged in providing diverse services to clients—from counseling and medical assistance to housing and employment—might affect client outcomes. They collected extensive data from agencies, clients, and their caregivers in four cities across the United States, each with unique service network structures. The network structure in Tucson, Arizona, was highly decentralized, with funding flowing from a nonprofit in the city to other recipients providing diverse services. In contrast, the network structure in Providence, Rhode Island, was centralized and bureaucratic, with one central agency receiving all funding and providing services directly to clients, controlling referrals and services offered by other community agencies. Which network structure would be better for implementation? For client outcomes? Interestingly, Milward and Provan found that while the participating agencies reported higher satisfaction with the decentralized network structure (as was present in Tucson, Arizona), the clients and their caregivers reported higher satisfaction and better mental health outcomes with the centralized network structure. Why? Milward and Provan suggest that the clear roles and relationships between different organizations in the centralized structure, as well as the stability of the formalized model, provided more predictability and reliability for clients, thus enhancing their experience and outcomes.[52]

Ideas generated from the network perspective are particularly important for understanding policy and program implementation. One of the early critiques of implementation scholarship was that it often ignored the multiactor reality of implementation and assumed a single implementing organization with clear lines of operational authority and institutional boundaries.[53] Even with national legislation, where executive agencies are often tasked with carrying out a specific policy, multiple actors are frequently implicated. Researchers Thad Hall and Larry O'Toole make this point through an analysis of the implementation structures arranged by national legislation at two very different times (1965–1966 and 1993–1994). They find that in both time periods, nearly thirty years apart, legislation formally stipulated multiactor arrangements for implementation more than 80 percent of the time. In the more recent period, 55 percent of these configurations were intergovernmental, 27.5 percent included private business, and 10 percent included nonprofit organizations. They further classified the types of coordinated activities required by legislation and found that nearly one in four required joint or pooled production of the service underlying the legislation, while about one-third required sequential production and another one-third required reciprocal production. They key lesson here is that while we know that informal implementation often implicates multiple actors (as described previously by Benny Hjern and his colleagues), even in formal legislation, multiactor networks are implicated for producing the core program defined by policy.

Governance Tools

A final theme in governance research that has importance for implementation is the focus on coordinating mechanisms, or policy tools. Policy tools have been defined as "an identifiable method through which collective action is structured to address a policy problem."[54] In 1981, Lester Salamon called for a movement of attention away from agencies and programs involved in policy design or implementation to a focus on the distinct tools that are used to achieve public objectives.[55] Other scholars at the time echoed this movement as a necessity of decentralized government action. For example, in 1990, policy design scholars Helen Ingram and Anne Schneider asserted that core elements of policy included objectives, agents responsible for carrying out objectives, and target populations—linked together by policy tools, rules, and theories. In their conceptualization, policy tools are instruments that "are intended to motivate implementing agencies and target populations to make decisions and take actions consistent with policy objectives."[56]

Policy tools include grants, contracts, regulatory mechanisms, and other formal instructions intended to coordinate and guide the behavior of implementers and clients targeted for services. This underlies one of the foundations of governance—that authority is not centralized in government hierarchies but is dispersed through decentralized governing mechanisms.[57] These different structures for expending public resources likely have different implications for creating and managing policy change. One of the purported benefits of the tools approach is that while there are numerous federal and state programs, there is a more limited set of underlying tools employed across diverse programs.[58] Thus, developing a typology or classification system for common tools can help analysts and managers identify the reoccurring implementation challenges and factors that are likely to be important. We revisit the tools approach in chapter 4 when we discuss coordinating mechanisms in the policy field. However, it is important to consider the ways in which it has been used to help understand policy implementation, as well as the limitations of this approach.

Research employing a tools perspective tends to focus on the outcomes associated with a particular government tool, addressing questions about efficiency, equity, manageability, and legitimacy.[59] For example, research about grants tends to focus at the macrolevel, considering the prevalence of grant-in-aid from the federal to state and local governments and its consequence.[60] Research about contracts is often concerned with how these tools alter market-based dynamics or are affected by political concerns.[61] There is also extensive exploration of how contracting has altered public management; rather than managing service providers, public managers now focus more exclusively on developing contracts, monitoring service levels, and assessing performance rather than managing service provision.[62] Extensive research about vouchers explores implementation in particular policy domains, such as health, education, or housing, and the impact on market concerns, such as consumer incentives and restrictions of choice.[63]

On the plus side, an analytical focus on policy tools more appropriately captures the reality of public service provision today and the structures by which public authority and resources are used to deliver public programs. And research on these instruments demonstrates there are often different implementation considerations when political authority and resources are structured in a certain way. Direct subsidies distributed to end users require different administrative structures and technological processes than contracts awarded to nonprofit organizations to carry out a service program.

Understanding the different policy tools in use in a particular implementation context is certainly an important part of understanding implementation dynamics. In fact, we suggest that an inventory of tools in use in a particular policy field is an important step in understanding the current conditions, something we discuss in more detail in chapter 4. However, focusing on policy tools alone is insufficient to truly grasp implementation dynamics and improve implementation outcomes. While it is helpful heuristically to identify the commonalities and differences between different types of policy tools, in reality, it is often insufficient to sort specific programs that way. Policy and program implementation in a particular area often leverages multiple policy tools simultaneously to coordinate activities. And rather than a rational process of defining the policy problem and selecting the tool to fit the problem, policy tools tend to develop and evolve throughout the implementation process, often in response to political pressures and existing practices.

In practice, government tools come to resemble hybrids of the ideal-type policy tools described in the literature. For example, in the Hardest Hit Fund case we describe in detail throughout the book, competitive federal block grants were awarded to state agencies that provided services directly to homeowners in need, distributed grants to local nonprofits, contracted with private companies to develop intake infrastructure, and financed subsidies to homeowners—where the ultimate recipient of the funding was a private mortgage company. It is difficult to compare the policy tools in use in this particular program to the use of similar policy tools in other programs. What matters for implementation outcomes are not primarily the individual tools but the interactions of the multiple tools in use and the capacities and structures in place at the multiple levels of the implementation system.

POLICY AND PROGRAM EVALUATION

A third perspective of implementation shifts the focus away from the political processes or the governance system toward the characteristics of the intervention itself. We group together three distinct but complementary movements under the heading of "policy and program evaluation." Unlike the other two perspectives that grew largely out of academic disciplines, policy and program evaluation grew from practice and the desire to demonstrate the impact of social programming and government-funded policy interventions.

In the United States, the first federally required and funded program evaluation was initiated in 1962 alongside the launch of a new juvenile delinquency intervention. President Lyndon B. Johnson's Great Society programs of the 1960s and subsequent War on Poverty interventions were designed to be more systematically evaluated than prior government interventions, with the hope that rational analysis would provide objective evidence of what works beyond political jockeying. Social scientists were contracted to conduct large-scale evaluations of programs ranging from preschool under Head Start to housing assistance. Federally funded social experiments were undertaken in an effort to identify the causal impact of a particular initiative. For example, under the Moving to Opportunity (MTO) demonstration, poor people were randomly assigned housing vouchers to pay for an apartment in the open market rather than being assigned to live in public housing developments. By evaluating MTO, policymakers could learn about the impact of choice-based vouchers versus concentrated public housing on outcomes such as poverty, education, and even health.[64]

Many of the early evaluations of the antipoverty programs yielded depressing results. Head Start programs did not lead to the education outcomes that were intended, community action agencies made little impact on eradicating homelessness, and even the MTO demonstration yielded mixed findings.[65] However, while lack of findings fueled conservative critiques of social programs, null findings did not end evaluation research. Rather, the field of systematic program evaluation was born and developed to support the use of applied social science in policymaking and assessment. Along with this came the focused interest in implementation and the growth of implementation studies reviewed earlier. But to a large extent, implementation analysis largely was separate from program evaluation, and evaluation funding often did not include implementation analysis. In the late 1980s, Harvard professor and experienced evaluator Carol Weiss called for more integration of implementation insights into evaluations and policy analyses, which we view as a continuing need today and in part the charge of this book.[66]

In the sections that follow, we review three approaches in policy and program evaluation: policy analysis, implementation science, and behavioral economics. Most of our readers are probably most familiar with policy analysis, which is more closely intertwined with political science and public administration. However, there have been important movements outside the conventional approaches that contribute to understanding implementation as part of a broader evaluation framework. Within health sciences and clinical practice, implementation scientists seek to understand how new practices and innovations can become embedded in standard operating procedures. Behavioral economists combine insights from psychology and economics to understand human biases and motivations that contribute to (or detract from) implementation effectiveness.

All three of these approaches share a central focus on the characteristics of the "treatment," or intervention itself.

Policy Analysis

In 1951, political scientist Harold Lasswell called for a "policy orientation" to help address some of the most vexing social problems of the time.[67] On the heels of World War II and the Great Depression, traditional studies of political science were not well equipped to inform government's responses to the most fundamental problems of society, including national security and unemployment. According to Lasswell, a policy orientation would combine knowledge of the policy process with contextual understanding of specific policies and underlying problems. By employing scientific methods and theoretically based models, policy science could produce useful knowledge to improve policies and thereby better address public problems.

While questions relevant to policy implementation had been previously explored in other fields, the Great Society programs and growth of government interventions in the 1960s and 1970s spawned increasing attention on the study of policy explicitly. Policy analyses were launched in an effort to document the effectiveness (or ineffectiveness) of government interventions to secure (or eliminate) continued funding. In the process of conducting policy analyses, scholars realized that solutions needed to be implemented and thus investigated how such implementation occurred.[68] This shift both altered the unit of analysis and signified an important normative change. Conventional public administration was criticized for focusing on bureau politics and process without offering much relevance to public service delivery being carried out by different instruments and through an array of institutions.[69] Political scientists also weathered their share of critique from the emerging policy scholars. Sequential linear approaches that depicted implementation as merely a phase in the policy process were challenged.[70] And the appropriateness of rational systems models for policy decision making was questioned, such as the planning, programming, and budgeting system introduced in the Department of Defense in the 1960s.[71] As traditional public administration, political science, and econometric approaches were questioned, new schools of public policy and public affairs were launched in many major universities with new attention to policy and program implementation.[72]

Trained policy analysts began to occupy major positions in government in the 1970s, with offices of policy analysis created within departments at the federal and state levels.[73] Independent think tanks were formed to serve as evaluation and analysis contractors to government, employing cadres of policy analysts trained in economics and statistics. As with program evaluation more generally, randomized controlled trials and experimentation have often been upheld as the gold standard in policy analysis research. However, there tends to be recognition that the sort of experimentation that is feasible in the real-world policy environment is much different from the type of experimentation that would take place in a laboratory setting. For policy analysis, there is a preference for field experiments and what leading policy scholar Alice Rivlin terms "random innovation," whereby innovations are introduced systematically over time, perhaps within random subsets of the population.[74]

The initial promise was that policy analysis would directly inform government decision making by providing objective evidence to cut through political struggles.[75] However, it was soon realized that there is no single source of objective evidence and that politics is always part of decision making. In a classic textbook on policy evaluation, scholars David Braybrooke and Charles Lindbom positioned policy analysis as a part of the social process of political decision making, taking place in an incremental and exploratory fashion rather than as a definitive tool to determine political decisions.[76] Policy analysis is as much an art as it is a science. In his book paradoxically titled *Speaking Truth to Power*, Aaron Wildavsky cautions that there is no single truth to be uncovered through analysis and that the highest form of policy analysis is to use "intellect to aid interactions between people," to help promote discussion and deliberation on the problems to be solved and potential alternatives.[77]

Viewing policy analysis as part of a social process requires an understanding of implementation dynamics. Unfortunately, most of the evaluation models and econometric methods employed in policy analyses favor simplicity and precision at the cost of contextual integration.[78] For example, there tends to be a dominance of welfare economics, which uses microeconomic techniques at the individual level to evaluate well-being at the societal level in policy analyses of government programs. On the one hand, this offers a way to think about and monetize complex social problems, and thus evaluate the impact of specific interventions. On the other hand, there are many components of social problems that escape easy measurement, thus potentially compromising the validity of analytical findings. A number of critics of the technocratic approach to policy analysis have encouraged a more qualitative, reflective approach.[79] Sometimes these softer analytical techniques make their way into practice; however, most policy analyses today still tend to favor econometric models and experimental methods in an attempt to quantify policy impact.

On the plus side, by focusing on policy impact, policy analysis tends to call attention to the target population and potential shifts in the behavior and outcomes of the targeted recipients of programs. However, rather than operationalizing implementation as a process that takes place within a broader governance system, policy analysts tend to treat implementation factors as variables that can be identified and therefore taken into account in policy design or controlled for after the fact to achieve desired outcomes.[80] In our approach, we emphasize the importance of behavioral change in the target population as the end outcome, similar to policy analysts. However, as described in chapter 1, we also emphasize the importance of creating change in the implementation system as an equally important outcome for sustainable results. Identifying changes in operating systems is the dominant focus in the implementation science approach.

Implementation Science

A parallel yet independent trend in the study of implementation is the blossoming of implementation science in other research fields.[81] Although it is not explicitly linked to public policy, implementation scientists in fields such as medicine and community psychology develop models and methods to study the implementation of specific interventions and programs. These interventions are often funded, carried out, or authorized by public agencies and policies. In 2006, a scholarly journal, *Implementation Science,* was established to provide a publishing venue for this research. In the introductory volume, the editors clarified the intent: "Implementation research is the scientific study of methods to promote the systematic uptake of research findings and other evidence-based practices into routine practice, and, hence, to improve the quality and effectiveness of health services and care."[82] Since then, the approach increasingly has been seen in education and other human services fields, such as early childhood development, youth development, and employment.

Most broadly, implementation science posits that creating evidence-based interventions will affect results only if there is research examining implementation processes. The research tradition underpinning implementation science originates from medicine, where there was concern with promoting evidence-informed care at scale. As a result, implementation science scholars often anchored their approach to lessons about innovation diffusion and dissemination. In 1995, Everett Rogers, a rural sociologist, developed diffusion theory to explain how innovative ideas spread among farmers, largely through imitation.[83] This foundational, often cited theory suggests that innovations that present clear advantages (in effectiveness or cost savings) are more easily adopted or implemented. Those that align with the values or needs of the implementing group, are easily understood and visible, have low risk, and are brought in for time-limited experimentation or adaption are more seamlessly adopted in new settings.[84] This frame of innovation diffusion highlights the significance of behavioral change in individuals and organizations as a key part of implementation processes more clearly than much of the earlier research we have discussed.

In this field, the innovations are empirically supported interventions—what are referred to with many signifiers, including *evidence-informed practice (EIP), evidence-based practice (EBP), empirically supported treatments (EST),* and *empirically supported interventions (ESIs).* While increased internal validity for program evaluation is now achievable through a range of research approaches, the research designs do little to help investigators identify what elements of an intervention are causal. What really creates the effect? What is the factor that drives positive results when they are documented? And how do we scale these factors to realize this effect in other settings? Implementation science emerged to discover answers to these questions. Most often the work focuses on what it takes to inspire the people who deliver services, such as the doctors, nurses, teachers, or counselors, to embrace the evidence from program evaluations. Yet there is no magic bullet. Research clearly documents challenges in persuading these people to embrace evidence-based interventions and abandon the service models they are familiar and comfortable with.[85] Much like the implementation studies focused on political process and authority, there is a fundamental quandary: how to best realize the potential suggested by diffusion theory to promote successful interventions by convincing implementing actors working in existing systems.

Carl May and colleagues are focused on building a grounded theory to provide answers to this quandary. They investigate what promotes the take-up of new ideas in complex interventions, particularly increasing staff interest in integrating the novel into practice.[86] Like other implementation science scholars, they begin with an interest in medical interventions. Yet their normalization process theory focuses on better describing how practices are made coherent and meaningful to clinicians, how this inspires commitment, how specific actions are adapted and contextualized, and how activities continue to be actively appraised. Fundamentally they are interested in the social organization of work or how changes become normalized, transformed into everyday tasks that are sustained by implementers. By drawing attention to key capabilities and capacities, their work is focused on promoting more skillful implementation practice. We return to these ideas in part 3.

The growth of implementation science studies taking place has led to a call for integrative frameworks, not unlike the frameworks developed by policy implementation scholars.[87] For example, Trisha Greenhalgh and colleagues synthesized nearly five hundred published sources across thirteen health care fields to develop a model that predicts successful innovation implementation in health care. Their model identified more than fifty seemingly important variables to predict implementation success.[88] In its complexity, this effort resembles the multivariate models created by Mazmanian and Sabatier and other top-down implementation scholars already discussed to be similarly focused on predicting results.

In fact, a 2012 review in the *American Journal of Preventative Medicine* identified sixty-one models available for researchers exploring dissemination and implementation.[89] Virtually all of the models focus on identifying determinants of implementation behavior in relation to the core intervention.[90] Ironically, the effect seems to hinge on how the efforts are implemented. There are no magic tactics for changing service providers' behavior. This finding highlights a challenge with the implementation science reductionist analysis: researchers equate strategies to overcome implementation barriers to those helping doctors tailor clinical treatment for medical diagnosis.[91] As a result, scholars promote standardized assessment tools for program managers interested in objectively assessing their organizational capacity to successfully implement a new program or intervention. Duncan Meyers and colleagues attempt to integrate twenty-five implementation frameworks that ostensibly focus on the how-to of implementation to create what they term the "quality implementation framework" with an accompanying standardized rating tool.[92] In this effort, the implementation process is represented in fourteen steps to be used across settings. Beginning with assessing initial conditions and creating structures for implementation, to providing ongoing support and learning from experience, this framework—although built to align with the research findings—strongly resembles conventional strategic planning models.

In this expanding area of research, scant attention is paid to the policy environment. While it is repeatedly recognized as significant in both initial program delivery and dissemination of evidence-based interventions, only a small proportion of the models and frameworks incorporated policy activities.[93] While significant attention is focused on developing and sharing consistent measures of implementation, policy context is often seen as merely a few control variables. In the widely used CFIR (Consolidated Framework for Implementation Research), the policy environment is conceptualized as the "outer setting," highlighting that the technological intervention itself is what is most important in implementation activity.[94] Among health implementation studies published in the past ten years, fully one-quarter employ an experimental design that by definition is focused on internal reliability rather than external generalizability relevant to policy concerns.[95]

On the positive side, implementation science takes seriously the need to account for factors associated with innovation diffusion and dissemination when introducing a new intervention or making changes to an existing program. Too often, however, the approach starts from a blank slate or list of factors without a systematic way to make sense of the implementation system. By drawing from insights from multiple perspectives, our approach in this book allows us to position insights about innovation diffusion within a complex system. Rather than creating tools intent on trying to reduce implementation complexity, we think it is more practically useful and intellectually hopeful to generate ways of systematically investigating the complexity of implementation systems. Part of the complexity is the nature of human behavior—inherent in both the target population and the system engaged in implementation. To shed light on the human side of policy interventions and implementation, we find some insights in recent scholarship from psychologists and behavioral economists.

Behavioral Economics

A final current trend in our review of relevant scholarship is the use of behavioral sciences, particularly psychology and behavioral economics, to inform policy design and implementation.[96] Often the outcomes of policies and programs involve targeting the behavior of individuals. However, the natural or impulsive behaviors of individuals do not always fit with the assumptions of policymakers and program managers. Together, psychologists and behavioral economists identify and analyze such biases and heuristics that shape individual behaviors.

The insights revealed help inform how users experience programs, allowing implementers to design interventions that increase take-up and maximize behavioral change, often at less cost.

This less invasive behavioral approach to creating positive change has been popularized by the best-selling book *Nudge,* written by economist Richard Thaler and law professor Cass Sunstein.[97] Their book opens with a fictitious story about Carolyn, the director of food services for a large public school system. Carolyn identified a creative way to encourage children to eat healthier by simply restructuring the food line in the school cafeterias. By putting the healthier foods first, she can increase the likelihood that children in her school system eat better. Thaler and Sunstein refer to Carolyn as a "choice architect." Choice architects are people who create the environment in which others make decisions. Simple changes, or "nudges," can profoundly affect the behaviors of participants, such as children making healthier food choices because of a food presentation in the lunch line. Borrowing from their terminology, policy and program implementers can most certainly be defined as choice architects. Whether they intend to or not, implementers make decisions every day that constrain or shape the experiences of participants.

Despite its recent increase in popularity, behavioral economics is not new. Insights regarding the take-up of public benefit programs or food choices in the lunchroom are supported by decades of research from psychology about the limitations of individual decision making. Behavioral scientists and economists have challenged the assumptions of the purely rational decision maker for decades. Nobel laureate Herbert Simon articulated this critique in the 1940s with his conceptualization of bounded rationality.[98] In the 1970s, psychologists launched a new branch of behavioral decision-making research demonstrating the limits of human rationality and the power of social and contextual factors over human behavior. These limits were demonstrated most profoundly with the infamous experiments of psychologist Stanley Milgram in the 1960s. Following the Holocaust, Milgram sought to understand how Nazi soldiers could commit such horrific acts of torture against other human beings. Through laboratory experiments, he found that human subjects were willing to inflict what appeared to be high levels of painful electric shocks on other subjects when commanded to do so by the head researcher. His experiments revealed the social power of obedience to orders, even when it required inflicting irrational pain and suffering on other human beings.[99]

Aside from obedience to social orders, further research in this area sought to identify perhaps more subtle factors limiting human decision making. Psychologists Amos Tversky and Daniel Kahneman led the research in the 1970s with a series of articles outlining common heuristics and biases constraining decisions and the conditions under which such constraints are more likely to come into play.[100] In their 1974 article in the journal *Science*, they demonstrate that people are more likely to fall back on heuristics, such as recalling recent similar experiences, when they face an unfamiliar situation. Relying on heuristics might help individuals make decisions in these situations, but they may also lead to less-rational decisions than individuals would have made if they fully understood the context.

By identifying common heuristics and biases at play, researchers argue that such less-than-optimal decisions can be predicted and perhaps even corrected. Psychologists' work in this area drew the attention of other social scientists, particularly economists whose theories are based on individuals' interest in maximizing their own economic position. Understood this way, the behavioral insights from psychology are not at odds with economic theories and models but complement them, helping to explain and predict observed behaviors.[101]

Behavioral insights improve not only research but also implementation. Policies and programs can be designed and implemented in such a way that they recognize and even leverage common heuristics and biases to be more effective. Over the past few decades, dozens of studies have been conducted to identify these behavioral factors and test the effectiveness of different types of behaviorally based interventions on outcomes ranging from individual savings behaviors to corporate environmental practices. Typically these interventions are tested through randomized controlled trials, where some users are randomly selected to receive the new intervention and others receive the status quo.

One common example is testing of interventions that change the default options in a particular policy context. For example, in the area of organ donation, researchers have observed that the proportion of the population consenting to donate their organs on death varies greatly by country, with only 12 percent consenting in Germany compared to 42 percent consenting in the United States and a whopping 99 percent consenting in Austria.[102] Through surveys and lab experiments, researchers have found that one of the primary differences in consent rates is the way in which citizens were presented with the decision.[103] Specifically, if the default in a particular country (such as Austria) was to be automatically registered as a donor and the person had to explicitly opt out to not be registered, the registration rates were very high compared with a country like the United States, where citizens are typically given the option to opt in and become a donor when registering for a driver's license. Other researchers have extended this observation to test default options in other contexts, such as automatic enrollment for employee retirement savings.[104]

Behavioral economics is not just a trendy subject being discussed by researchers. Policymakers and foundation executives in the United States and abroad are beginning to emphasize the importance of incorporating behavioral aspects in policy and program decisions, engaging the expertise of behavioral scientists.[105] Typically economists have played a dominant role in advising policy decisions. For economists, government intervention is typically viewed as justified when markets fail to provide important services or do so in a way that is inefficient or ineffective. They help inform conditions under which information asymmetries between consumers and suppliers might create the need for disclosure on products or even signed releases acknowledging risk before making a purchase. However, a behavioral understanding of decision making demonstrates that not only is much information often imperfect, but it is also difficult to present information in a way that is unbiased. The font size on a disclosure or the phrasing of the costs and benefits as a loss or a gain can substantially affect the choices people make. To the extent that "mistakes" made regarding these choices have societal consequences, behavioral insights can help enable policy design and implementation effectiveness. To inform our purpose here, we will revisit some of the findings of this research—particularly some of the most common behavioral limitations and tested interventions—in part 3.

While policymakers and public officials across the globe are increasingly embracing the insights of behavioral economics, some are less optimistic about the potential for this movement to lead to better societal outcomes. The primary concern is that policymakers and program managers are people too—affected by some of the same biases as the target population. What makes implementers better decision makers than the target population that they are trying to serve? One well-known economist suggests that the realization that there are flaws in how humans make decisions should make us more hesitant for government to intervene, to try to manipulate human behavior in less easily observed ways.[106] Because it is often more difficult to observe behaviorally targeted interventions, such as subtle changes to wording in messaging campaigns or mandatory disclosures, public accountability may actually be reduced.

However, others will contend that for public interventions to be effective, they need to be able to match the messaging and sophistication used by the private sector to target consumers. Private firms have leveraged these sorts of insights for years in marketing campaigns and product messaging. As we discuss in chapter 6, rarely will a private firm develop a new product or services without testing the user perceptions and experiences. And smart firms know that they can exploit behavioral biases to increase profitability. Of course, the same incentives that lead firms to apply behavioral insights for profitability can have positive societal consequences.[107] For example, a private insurance firm interested in increasing the contributions of employees to their retirement savings might leverage behavioral insights to make it easier for people to save more; this helps the firm, but it also addresses the policy issue of undersaving for retirement. Sometimes, however, public and private interests conflict. It is possible, of course, that policies or programs designed to increase the positive behaviors of individuals could be undermined by marketing campaigns that play on their vices. It is important for implementers to be aware of the potential for signals to conflict.

Whether intentional or unintentional, there are components of policies and programs that evoke particular behavioral responses and affect policy outcomes. A simple opt-out check box for organ donation at the bureau of vehicle registration will lead more people to register as donors than an opt-in check box. It may be by chance that the implementer initially designed the form with an opt-in rather than opt-out. Nonetheless, this design dramatically affects the policy outcome. The question for policy and program implementation is whether we identify that these effects exist and use that information to improve the intended outcomes of the program or policy. This is a subject to which we return in chapter 8.

While behavioral economics contributes significantly to the way we think about program components, there are limits to a strict adoption of this approach to improve implementation. Most of the interventions designed using behavioral insights are tested through randomized controlled trials. Just as is true in implementation science research in health care, this approach allows an evaluator to zero in on the effect of the intervention without worrying about all of the other factors that could influence intervention effectiveness. However, testing interventions in controlled settings does not take into account the contextual factors that often are difficult, and perhaps undesirable, to control in the real world.[108] Furthermore, behavioral economics rarely accounts for the significance of the institutions that will ultimately carry out the interventions and bring them to scale.[109] Too often the hopes for an intervention to be designed, tested, and then replicated en masse in the real world are dashed when the complexities outside of the laboratory come into play.

CONCLUSION

This chapter provides a broad landscape of prior perspectives that inform policy and program implementation. Understandably researchers and practitioners with different backgrounds tend to focus on different aspects of the implementation system. Traditional policy implementation scholarship has been predominantly associated with political science, categorizing implementation as a stage in the process of policymaking. Classic studies of policy implementation tend to take either a top-down or bottom-up approach. From a top-down approach, implementation is viewed as directed by legislation and political officials and recommendations for improvement begin with policy design at the top. Those taking a bottom-up approach acknowledge the organic nature of the implementation system operating on the ground and recommend strategies to provide discretion to microimplementers. In the end, the classic literature provides a list of factors that can influence implementation outcomes, paying particular attention to political authority and power dynamics. But this scholarship struggles to make sense of this complexity to improve implementation results. Several frameworks have been proposed to organize the complexity, but these frameworks serve more as heuristics for research than practical ways to make sense of and manage within the complexity that is policy and program implementation to desired ends.

Rather than being situated abstractly within the policy process, alternative perspectives are grounded in either the governance system or the interventions being carried out. In public administration and management, the study of multilevel, multiactor governance has become the dominant approach. There is much to learn from this approach, particularly when thinking about the structure of implementation settings and the ways in which activities are coordinated between diverse actors. However, by focusing on the system, this approach tends to downplay the importance of the intervention being implemented. Instead, the intervention is often left to technical policy experts.

By contrast, the third perspective reviewed here is grounded firmly in the interventions underlying policies or programs. Beginning with policy analyses of the Great Society programs in the 1960s, the key objective guiding this perspective is to evaluate the impact of given interventions on desired outcomes. Researchers and practitioners in this perspective often start with technical policy or program expertise. Policy analysts tend to favor cost-benefit analysis and econometric models that can be used to support or refute specific policy proposals. Implementation scientists seek to identify the ideal intervention that can be easily replicated across settings. Evidence-based practices become the gold standard, creating a proliferation of program evaluations testing the effectiveness of specific interventions in one particular context but offering little generalizability to a broader understanding of implementation effectiveness. Behavior economists zero in at an even more granular level, at the interactions between target participants and specific interventions. They also prefer randomized controlled trials to identify behaviorally informed modifications to existing interventions. While their work calls attention to the importance of user experiences and interactions with the intervention, it tends to brush aside the importance of the implementation settings that are so critical to bringing new policy or program ideas into reality.

While we borrow and integrate learnings from all three perspectives, our commitment to developing a practically relevant approach to supporting more skillful implementation practice causes us to part ways with these traditions. As described in chapter 3, rather than understanding implementation as activities undertaken in regard to a particular intervention, our approach conceptualizes implementation as interactions within various strategic action fields in a multilayered system. Thinking about implementation as taking place within strategic action fields allows us to take into account politics and power dynamics, multilevel governance, and important attributes of the core intervention. Rather than starting from the question of what works, this approach explores how programs work[110] and considers opportunities to make improvements to the system that support achievements of desirable results.

A New Perspective for Implementation

Strategic Action Fields

As our review of prior perspectives has made clear, there are many approaches to describe and analyze policy and program implementation. Without a doubt, implementing program change is difficult because of the many players and the inevitable significant limitations in available resources. Yet within these constraints, those charged with managing public and nonprofit organizations, carrying out public policy, and developing innovative solutions do make progress on implementing such changes. Unfortunately, most of the literature does little to provide such professionals with a way to talk about the challenges they encounter, analyze the barriers, or develop more skillful responses to those conditions.

When we set out to write this book on implementation, we realized that one of the primary factors contributing to the gap between research and practice is the artificial division created in the current study of public affairs. As described in chapter 2, political scientists tend to focus on political authority and politics, management or administration scholars focus on coordination and governance, and other behavioral science specialists focus on the intervention or treatment. These divisions between the policy context, institutions, and interventions might be useful to organize scholarship; however, such divisions do not exist in the real world of practice.

The analytical approach we describe is relevant for either understanding implementation dynamics after they have occurred or assessing new initiatives that must be planned. We aim here to help those doing such work (or those who aspire to!) more clearly understand the implementation dynamics where policy solutions and systems' response intersect. Rarely are implementation systems built from the ground up with new institutions, agencies, and staff; instead, they almost always require working with existing entities or established market patterns. As a result, it requires convincing people that the change envisioned by policy or program parameters is justifiable to achieve different results.

While we are informed by the traditions of implementation scholarship, we are explicitly turning to new theoretical frameworks and pushing for a deeper level of integration and application. Our thinking about how to proceed is informed by an array of developments in the natural and social sciences. Most broadly, from the natural sciences, we can learn much from the operation of complex, adaptive systems.[1] In complex systems, factors are interrelated in nonlinear ways and it is difficult to anticipate the consequences of particular strategies or action. Our emphasis on complexity contrasts with prior studies that view implementation as complicated but predictable, categorizing successful implementation strategies a priori based on characteristics of the policy environment or intervention.[2] In complex systems, rather than identifying all possible factors that might predict implementation outcomes, the focus shifts toward understanding system dynamics and equipping managers with the skills needed to probe and respond to them.

When thinking about the complexity of the system, we have found it helpful to view implementation from the perspective of multiple levels, bringing essential parts of the system into focus for detailed exploration. As in an environmental ecosystem, the different levels of the implementation process at the policy field, organization, and front lines are not independent of one another but are embedded and interrelated. In part 2, we spend considerable time exploring the multiple levels within these complex systems where particularly important decisions often get decided. It is important to probe and understand dynamics at each scale. However, we cannot forget that they are intimately connected. Activities and constraints in the policy field ripple down and affect the organization and front lines. And innovations at the front lines or organizational levels emanate out to affect ideas in the policy field.

Analyzing implementation requires special emphasis on the intervention or core program. Across all levels of the system, the core program defines what is being done to whom under what conditions. Except in completely routinized and centralized implementation systems, the programmatic details are shaped by social dynamics in the policy field, organization, and front lines. Understanding implementation hinges on paying particular attention to the core program and how it develops and changes at different levels in the implementation system.

In practice, the importance of the program is so self-evident that it is often not even acknowledged. Professionals engaged in implementation often seek to increase their knowledge of the substantive content of the intervention and the characteristics of the target groups—they compare different models of mental health interventions and what research reveals about changes in emotional and social functioning; they assess educational curricula and consider how to intervene in children's lives characterized by many factors that predict their academic challenges; they review the engineering of energy transmission lines to improve throughput and output. Even if they work at different scales in an implementation, at different levels, and in various organizations, professionals who care about implementation care about programmatic elements.

One of the challenges in taking a more complex approach to understanding implementation is that it may begin to appear as if everything matters and therefore nothing is important. This was a problem with some of the earlier implementation studies that provided lists of literally hundreds of variables that might affect implementation outcomes.[3] Rather than equipping implementers with tools to increase implementation effectiveness, we end up overwhelmed and immobilized, with paralysis by analysis. Fortunately, we think that there is a practical way to think about the parts of the implementation system that can help prevent this sort of "everything and the kitchen sink" pitfall: strategic action fields.

INTRODUCING STRATEGIC ACTION FIELDS

Borrowing from sociology and organizational theory, we can think of each level within the implementation system—the policy field, individual organizations, and the front lines within organizations—as a unique institutional setting or strategic action field.[4] Strategic action fields are settings where collective action takes place; participants working together in that context have a general understanding about their purpose, their relationships, and the spoken and unspoken rules that guide their actions.[5] While different activities take place at distinct levels and policy areas, participants, resources, and program technologies are present in each implementation setting. In fact, as strategic action fields, each setting within the implementation system has a unique social structure that enables participants to work together toward a common purpose. By definition, social structures provide frameworks around how participants interact and make decisions within their group and create a boundary around what takes place.[6]

It is perhaps helpful to think back to the gardening and ecosystem metaphor to illustrate our meaning. Within the same ecosystem, multiple habitats exist simultaneously on different scales. Each habitat could be described in terms of plant and animal life, natural resources, and climate. Rather than existing independently, each habitat is embedded within a larger ecosystem—a forest, for example. While each habitat is affected by and affects the overall characteristics of the forest, each could also be described as its own subsystem; the plant and animal life, resources, and climate can be described and compared. Near a stream, the habitat may be very different from that found in a cave even when they are in the same forest. Importantly, the subsystem around the stream or cave has a natural boundary that in part determines what takes place within it.

Although people construct them, strategic action fields are like these habitats. At each level of the implementation system, there are social structures, formal and informal, that act as permeable boundaries, limiting the alternatives that actors within the setting consider when they are making decisions. These social structures could include formal regulations, funder expectations, or even norms about what is viewed as an acceptable practice. Rather than being predetermined, social structures emerge from the choices and dynamics among people as they work on shared concerns. Although in a strict sense, social structure is "made up" by people, it is very real, shaping the minds and actions of people who work within it. The social structure often creates the very terms that must be navigated to make change. As such, it is both a blessing and a curse. On the plus side, people have limited capacity and ability to consider all possible alternatives—the social structure operating at each level of an implementation system makes more manageable the number of participants involved, the ideas considered, and the resources deployed to tackle a specific problem. On the negative side, the social structures may constrain peoples' abilities to develop the most creative or innovative solution to the problem at hand. There is often some degree of what scholars call *path dependence,* where the same idea or resource is applied repetitively even if it is no longer effective.

Analyzing implementation to improve process and results requires unpacking the social dynamics and constraints operating at each level of the system. If we develop clearer descriptive analytics—just as we have developed ways of understanding that rocks are different from plant matter and that rocks in streams play different roles from those in caves—we will be able to better describe the patterns and compare them with what exists in other social systems,. For example, we will see that decisions made by networks of organizations combating hunger to increase availability of fresh produce in the field are related but distinct from the negotiations between food bank and food shelf managers about distribution methods. We will see how preferences for fresh produce in the policy field are unlikely to be reflected in discussions that food shelf volunteers have with clients as they put together their monthly food boxes, unless it is explicitly required, rewarded, or reinforced.

Often, improving implementation outcomes requires knowledge of the policy content (local food systems), skillful management of programs (efficient distribution practices), and knowledge of the social system (what people who work at the food shelf value and believe). It is relatively easy to develop knowledge of policy content because it is often written and retrievable. Management tactics can be developed and technical tools deployed. But understanding how social systems operate requires cultivating a more subtle understanding. Some scholars are interested in the functioning and development of strategic action fields more generally.[7] Yet, we think the concept is particularly useful for helping us think about how policy and program outcomes are shaped by the social structures in the implementation system. Because these social structures are not fixed, it is possible through analysis to discover their parameters and change them through purposive, strategic action in order to improve implementation effectiveness.

Let us think again about the core program. While it is critical to bring the best program knowledge to a problem, such expertise is insufficient to guarantee effective implementation. You are probably familiar with complaints such as, "The idea was good but . . . ," or, "The system is broken," or "This program would have worked perfectly if it weren't for all of those damn people!" Many technical experts who have identified, tested, and refined ideal interventions become frustrated when attempts to replicate and scale the interventions are thwarted in the field. Yet from another vantage point, program managers and directors who are skilled in navigating the system often cringe when they hear of the newest "evidence-based practice" that they now have to somehow integrate into their already complicated program design. While the idea might be good in theory, managers often develop an uncanny ability to tell if an idea will actually work in practice given the resource constraints, staffing, and structural dynamics operating in their setting

By thinking about implementation as taking place within strategic action fields, we are able to combine attention to core program technology with an understanding of social structures and dynamics. Each level of the implementation system has a distinct social structure guiding the coordination of participants, resources, and technologies. This social structure includes formal coordinating mechanisms such as hierarchical chains of command, contracts, rules, and information technology systems, but also more informal cultural beliefs and norms that shape the way a specific program is interpreted and carried out. And because the core program is embedded across multiple levels, each with its own social structures, what programmatic elements are actually brought into practice is the result of dynamics within and between the policy field, organizations, and front lines of the implementation system.

To illustrate this important concept, we turn back to an analogy from nature. Figure 3.1 provides a simplified visualization. As might be observed in how water flows through the natural water filtration system in a pond, a core program flows through multiple levels in an implementation process. Water circulates through

Figure 3.1
Illustration of a Multilevel System with Common and Distinct Elements

Source: Sook Jin Ong.

layered mini-ecosystems, each with its own plant, rock, and animal composition. Each layer is uniquely equipped to filter out particular types of debris and add important minerals to the water. And water circulates through the layers of the filtration system from all directions. A change to the composition of one of the layered ecosystems will affect the output and quality of the water in the larger pond.

The three-layered ecosystems in figure 3.1 represent the three strategic action fields operating at the level of the policy field, organization, and front lines in our framework. While they are sequentially layered, the boundaries around each are organic and porous.[8] In this sense, each level has its own unique social structure, but it is also embedded within the context of other levels. The social structure at each level acts as a filter, shaping the core program as it passes through. Some social structures are dense, substantially altering what passes through, while others are loose, affecting very little. Similarly, some programmatic ideas are impervious, pushing through almost any boundary relatively intact, while others are pliant, vulnerable to being significantly shaped by the power and cultural meaning of a social system.

This illustration is necessarily simplistic. In most policy fields, more than one organization is engaged in implementation, some taking the roles of primarily authorizing organizations, others taking the roles of service providers. The outcomes will likely vary depending on the organizations involved and their various social structures, which shape the core program. For example, it is no surprise that one food shelf might have different client satisfaction and overall volume of food distributed to needy families than another. Our explanation hinges on the unique strategic action fields operating within each organization that shape how the program ideas are implemented in that context.

Thinking about implementation as taking place within strategic action fields offers a useful starting point for creating effective change. Consider, for example, a policy problem of unemployed single mothers. The actual ideas about what could be done to address the problem are nearly endless—ranging from direct financial subsidies, to education and training, to support groups, to abstinence education. A variety of entities are potentially interested in addressing the problem, including private sector employers, nonprofit social service organizations, and churches. Sometimes people from across those institutions work together to figure out what to do, pulling together shared resources, participants, and technologies. Each entity also has its own social structure, with a unique set of resources, participants, and programmatic experience that shape their ideas about what could be done to address the problem. The program that is ultimately developed is the result of negotiations at the policy field, organization, and front lines. How does one wishing to improve outcomes for unemployed single moms proceed to make change in such a system? We suggest that this is both a technical and an adaptive challenge, requiring an understanding of the current conditions in the implementation system and acquiring skills to affect behavioral and social change. We will return to these challenges and what can be done about them later in the book. But for now, we focus on enabling implementers to better analyze how that process unfolds in the system.

An essential first step in implementation analysis is unpacking the core program.

CORE PROGRAMS

As mentioned in chapter 1, we believe a central, defining question for implementation is: How do we create desired change in the target population? The answer to this question is reflected in the operational elements developed by actors in the strategic action field to carry out a program, here referred to as the "core program."[9] It focuses on developing the means to accomplish desired ends, or the "throughput" that links together inputs and outputs. Program managers might call this a logic model, a work flow, or a program plan. But even if they don't use consistent language, they understand the core program to be the way activities and resources are applied to change current conditions into subsequent results.

From the beginning, implementation scholars drew attention to program technology as a critical part of understanding implementation outcomes. For example, in the 1983 revision to their classic book on implementation, Jeffrey Pressman and Aaron Wildavsky stress, "The ability of a policy to effect change in behavioral, organizational, or environmental conditions is dependent on the technology required to effect that change, which itself may be unsatisfactory, and the size of the problem, including the extent of the population and the degree of change required."[10] While they and others acknowledged the importance of program technology, they often simplified variation to one dimension in an effort to categorize variables and develop typologies for predicting implementation conditions.[11]

Rather than categorizing a particular program technology as "higher" or "lower" on a particular scale, it is perhaps more useful to think about how it is assembled and shaped by people in the strategic action field.[12] This provides some explanation for why the same program might look very different in different settings. And it helps highlight how strategic action by those same people could improve implementation. Core programs are not static but shaped by the implementation process. Here we unpack three important activities in that process: establishing viable options, identifying the logic of change, and coordinating activities to bring about results.

Establishing Viable Options

Establishing viable options involves developing or selecting an appropriate program approach, consistent with the policy or program purpose and contextual conditions.[13] What is the problem to be addressed? What do we want to accomplish? What is the range of activities considered appropriate to address this problem? While occasionally this is a technical process—satisfied by merely reviewing and faithfully adopting the practices outlined in legislation or replicating an intervention model proven empirically to work—it is often more an adaptive challenge. Often, establishing the technological core of implementation—the "how to" of attempting to achieve our desired impact—is negotiated among various parties within the strategic action field. The core program is defined, refined, and modified as the policy or program is examined and interpreted at the policy field, organization, and frontline levels in the implementation system.

Disagreement about domain, appropriate tools, and target groups served creates some of this dynamism. The higher the consensus is about what is viable, the easier it is for routine transactions to occur because less negotiation and bargaining are required. When there is dissension, some actors must lay down their first assumptions about what is desirable and feasible even before the program can be developed. In these cases, it is a process of negotiation and developing enough shared understanding about what is possible to warrant moving forward. The process of establishing agreement reflects a lot about collective purpose and how it should be pursued.

Within strategic action fields, not all potential program options are possible. Political ideology shapes understanding of the public problem and potential interventions. Experience and existing infrastructure within or between organizations also influence what actors believe they know about problems and solutions, as well as what is viable given resource constraints. There are many costs associated with developing a new infrastructure, and often this is not a possibility. In addition, implementers' assumptions about the target groups, their knowledge and abilities, all shape what actors consider to be a viable way of creating effective interventions. And rather than being fixed, these assumptions change over time.

The topic of housing is illustrative of this point. For fifty years, many debates ensued about the most effective way to improve housing affordability in the United States. Publicly run housing was developed at the end of the World War II as the most desirable, direct way to create shelter for large numbers of citizens. But this approach created many unintended consequences, including profound economic and racial segregation in some communities. Instead of direct government provision, the trend turned to favor market-based technologies; both demand-side subsidies to low-income families and supply-side subsidies to developers grew in popularity. On the demand side, Section 8 vouchers targeted low-income families, enabling them to rent housing on the open market. Recipients could choose where they want to live rather than concentrating them in particular neighborhoods with public housing. Yet because the market did not operate freely—not all landlords accepted vouchers—problems were encountered in implementing that approach as well. On the supply side, tax credits offered to housing developers to construct affordable housing units operated more smoothly in most policy fields.

This example highlights a general feature. Viability of a program is not objectively assessed and adopted once and for all. What is understood to be feasible changes over time with learning and shifting ideologies. When applied to analyzing programs in implementation, this insight helps provide some understanding of why certain means are assumed to be appropriate ways to attack a particular public problem and others are not even considered. Different ideologies come into fashion and often set the terms considered legitimate when implementation approaches are being established.

Identifying the Logic of Change

Another important element of the core program is the underlying logic of change that links inputs and activities with outputs and outcomes, sometimes referred to as the *causal logic*.[14] There are several important questions to be asked. How will the program bring about change in the target population? What assumptions are being made about the behavior of the target group? What assumptions are being made about the efficacy of the activities that have been selected and the workers implementing those activities?

For some program technologies, the link is rather clear: if you enroll a single mother in a food stamp program, she will be able to purchase additional food and her children will be less likely to be hungry. There are still assumptions being made—for example, that the mother will use the supplemental food assistance to purchase food for her children and not give the food away or hoard it for herself. However, the causal logic is pretty clear. For other program technologies, the causal logic is less clear. For example, rather than providing the single mother with a subsidy, you enroll her in a class to teach her how to grow her own vegetables. While one could still suggest that the purpose of the program is to decrease the probability that her children will be hungry (and perhaps increase the probability that they will eat healthy food), the garden education program makes assumptions about the single mom's desire, time, and ability to grow vegetables and assumptions that the garden will yield sufficient food to meet her family's food needs. Furthermore, the program of delivering the education class is more complex than processing eligibility for a subsidy. While eligibility can largely be automated with little variation across different implementation sites, the quality, content, and scope of the education class will likely vary significantly across implementation sites, potentially affecting the outcomes.

Previous implementation scholars often assumed that the nature of the policy problem or the intent of the policy objective would drive the complexity of the program technology and implementation conditions.[15] However, this simple example highlights how that is not always true. For the same policy problem—in this case, reducing food insecurity for a single mother and her family—two very different programs are implemented. Several important factors affect the logic of change.

First, program technologies that require changing behavior tend to be more complex than program technologies that process people. While many public programs, particularly human service programs, require some element of behavioral change, others focus primarily on people processing.[16] For example, the Social Security for the Aged program operates routinely across the country; eligibility criteria are established by policy, assessed through paperwork documentation, and verified through computerized systems. Certainly some individuals in the target group fall outside the norm—they have unique work experiences or react harshly when notified that their benefits are being changed. But these exceptions can be anticipated and alternative program processes developed. Overall, a people-processing technology is fairly standard. It focuses on controlling access to public benefits.

There are many instances when the policy or program is focused on changing people. In mental health, early childhood education, health care, environmental protection, and program technologies attempt to alter peoples' physical, psychological, social, or cultural attributes or actions. This is complex work and depends on the frontline staff—counselors, teachers, medical professionals, environmental educators—to customize existing procedures to the needs, circumstances, and even worldview of a particular client. Together, service provider and recipient coproduce the actual enacted program because it requires that the client engage in what is offered. In such cases, the moral categorization of both staff and clients may shape what is implemented, creating even more variation in the service as actually implemented. This complex programmatic form is customized through moral assessment, professional judgment, and engagement. In such people-changing technologies, it is impossible to predict or standardize activities in a routine way. This complexity can make it more difficult to develop standardized processes and procedures—and in fact, standardization might reduce the effectiveness of interventions targeting behavioral change.

Second, the policy problem does not completely determine the program selected. Sometimes complexity is inherent in the type of problem being addressed. Prior implementation scholars have referred to this as the "tractability of the problem."[17] Problems are more tractable when there is minimal variation in behaviors that cause the problem, the target group is an easily identified small group, and the amount of behavior change required is modest. Sometimes a policy problem—like food insecurity—can be made more tractable by reducing the assumptions about behavioral change. Providing food stamps relies on fewer assumptions about changed behaviors than an education class. Therefore, some might prefer food stamps as a more efficient or direct approach to addressing the problem.

For many policy problems, however, the desired change is more indeterminate and complex. In these settings, it is difficult for policy to simplify the means by which desired results should be achieved. This is understandable, and perhaps even desirable. An individual seeking counseling for a drug addiction would likely prefer an individualized approach rather than a one-size-fits-all treatment—if such treatment could even be identified. Often both service providers and target recipients have diverse characteristics and motivations, and it is impossible to predict how they might react to any intervention. For more complex problems, resources are often directed toward increasing the quality of the interaction at the time of service—ensuring services that are more likely to lead to positive behavioral change, and therefore the effectiveness of the intervention.

Coordinating Activities

A final process that shapes the core program in strategic action fields is activity coordination. How will the activities be coordinated to accomplish the objectives? Will all services be provided or technology be produced in-house, or will we work with partner organizations or contracted providers for some of the interventions? How will the work flow be structured for coordination and communication among participants? To some extent, the complexity of the structure to produce the program is directly related to the complexity of the program itself. Organizational scholars refer to this as contingency theory, proposing that the structure that develops within an organization is contingent on the type of work being performed and the conditions necessary to accomplish the tasks.[18] Programs that can be easily standardized may require fewer layers of specialization and supervision of program staff than those that require specialized expertise or individualized interactions.

A classic example is a city's implementation of garbage collection compared with a city's community programming for elderly residents. Garbage collection is a relatively simple program technology—the logic of change is relatively clear—and weekly collection of trash at individual residences will reduce the probability that waste will collect on the streets or in yards. The program technology for garbage collection can thus be routinized in a formal process that could be carried out by almost anyone who has the required materials (e.g., a garbage truck). Coordination is an easy technical task. We also can easily observe if the program technology is not working: residents will likely complain if their garbage is not picked up, and a quick stroll through the neighborhood can confirm this allegation.

The city's community programming for senior citizens, however, is more complex; perhaps the objective is to provide a safe place for residents to socialize and engage, thereby increasing their overall well-being. While certain aspects of the programming can likely be routinized, there is less standardization of services offered—an art class will likely be very different from a bingo game or a yoga class, which requires different rules and unique staff expertise, introducing more complexity in scheduling and coordinating services for seniors. It also is more difficult to observe whether the program is working. Measuring concepts like well-being is much more difficult to do than measuring whether trash is being picked up. Perhaps the seniors will complain if the programming is not entertaining or appropriate, but they may be less equipped to assess the key objectives of providing safe and engaging programs. Grandma might enjoy the challenge of the Flying Crow yoga pose, but it takes a different type of analysis to determine whether it is being taught in a way that is safe for her.

This example brings up two characteristics of program technology that can influence coordinating structures. Scholars use the term *asset specificity* to refer to the degree of technical expertise and material investment needed to produce the technology or provide the service. Programs also differ in terms of the ease of measurement of outcomes or the ability to monitor results. Public affairs scholars have used these two characteristics to suggest conditions under which contracting out is more or less advantageous.[19] Program technologies that have high asset specificity or have outcomes that are difficult to measure will likely require increased monitoring, or what economists call transaction costs, that make them more costly to contract out to external providers. In these cases, decisions to contract out are not easily justified on grounds of cost savings or efficiency, but might still be justifiable for other reasons such as technical expertise or political feasibility.

Contracting out versus in-house production is not the only consideration for coordinating activities. Decisions are also made about the sequencing of activities or work flow. How many different steps are involved in the process of transforming inputs into outputs? Where do these steps take place? Some programs are pooled, structured so that everything is completed in one step, with one worker (or department or organization) responsible for the full process. Others are sequential, structured so that there are multiple steps; different workers (or departments) have specialized knowledge and therefore are responsible for different activities. Once they complete their activity, they hand off the client or product to the next worker or department, similar to an assembly line. Finally, in what is called intensive technology, different workers or departments with unique expertise work together on the problem simultaneously, as would be found in an operating room of a hospital.

Beyond the physical structuring of activities, there also are differences in how information about the activities is transmitted as they are being carried out. Communication channels, including information technology platforms and regularized face-to-face meetings, must be developed to ensure implementation can occur. Operating rules must be negotiated and alignment between activities managed. Staff schedules must be aligned. In fact, the many details of program management often hinge on the aptitude actors have in these important, tangible skills for coordinating the necessary program activities. Activity coordination can also be shaped by the feedback mechanisms built into the program. Sometimes performance measures are established at one level of the implementation system and imposed on or shared with another. Formal program evaluation can also provide valuable information about how the program can be honed or more effectively aligned.

Bringing Core Programs Together

These three processes of core programs—establishing viable options, identifying the logic of change, and coordinating activities—directly influence the variation we see in policy and program implementation within different strategic action fields. Fundamentally, there are different understandings of what is going on and what is at stake in any particular moment. Routine and frequent program technologies are more easily implemented the same way across multiple sites. When there is more consensus about the nature of the problem and effective interventions, the implementation process is more likely to flow as designed. More complex programs are much less likely to be implemented consistently. There is no way to assume the nature of target groups will be consistent. In addition, because of the customization of activities required, program directives will not be interpreted in the same way across settings. Because more judgment is involved, there is likely to be less agreement among implementers. These characteristics affect the strategies implementers can take to be effective.

There is an important caveat to our discussion of core programs so far. It might make sense to assume that programs are developed in a rational, linear way, where the three activities we have described are viewed as the "three steps to successful implementation." First, establish viable options, or the objective to be accomplished within constraints. Second, identify the logic of change, based on the desired change in the target population within the parameters identified in "step 1." Third, taking into account the activities needed to bring about the desired change ("step 2"), design a coordinating structure that will most efficiently and effectively achieve the program results. If only it were that simple! In fact, if the program truly proceeded in this way, we would have no reason to write this book.

Occasionally problems, solutions, and participants come together in a linear, top-down way as envisioned by traditional implementation scholars. Legislation is passed that formalizes an approach (core program) to address a public problem through policy. A process is put into place and organizations are selected to carry out the policy in line with legislative intent. Sometimes the decision authority to shape the core program is centralized in one agency or task force. In those cases, once a core program is selected, implementers merely create appropriate communication channels to share the process flow and use feedback mechanisms to adjust processes when needed.

This notion of a rational approach to decision making is quite compelling because it conforms to conventional beliefs of what is involved in implementation—merely following a preestablished plan. Yet more often there are significant political compromises between competing ideologies when legislation is enacted. In these cases, there are significant incentives for leaving the specification of programs up to implementing agencies. Many more times, public issues are responded to through what scholars refer to as the garbage can model of decision making, where streams of problems, solutions, and participants come together around choice opportunities.[20] Even if legislation suggests how a program is to be carried out, identifying and selecting an approach is more like an artistic process of *bricolage*—a French word for tinkering. It refers to the particular ability some people have to use things that happen to be available in order to create or construct something new. In our notion, the core program technology is further developed as it comes into contact with existing organizational programs and frontline conditions, both of which are also strategic action fields.

While the core program is at the center of implementation analysis, the social structure of each strategic action field helps to explain how programs are developed and changed. Some aspects of the social structure are easy to understand—the formal rules and tangible resources. Yet the informal aspects of a social system, the understanding and values held by participants, are more difficult to define from outside the system. Let's consider these important factors in turn.

UNPACKING SOCIAL STRUCTURES AND DYNAMICS

Imagine that you are in the process of purchasing a home for the first time. A friend told you about a state program that provides down payment assistance to first-time home buyers like yourself. "Free money?" you think, "Sure, sign me up!" To qualify for the program, you have to purchase a home using one of the participating lenders—which means you cannot use your local bank. It just so happens that none of the participating lenders are located nearby, so you need to complete an application online or over the phone. After completing the paperwork, following a series of e-mails, phone calls, and even fax correspondence (you didn't even know people still use fax machines!), you learn that you must complete an eight-hour, in-person education class about the home-buying process before you can receive final approval for the loan. You have already found your home, been preapproved by a lender, and have signed paperwork with a realtor, so most of the content of the class does not really apply to you anymore. And the nearest education class is sixty minutes away, and the next class does not start until next month. At this point, you throw your hands up in the air and say, "Forget it!" Could they have made the process more complicated? Why would *anyone* design a program like this?

The reality is that this program, like many others, was not designed to be inefficient or ineffective. It is not that the policymakers or staff persons involved in the implementation of the program are ignorant or careless. Sometimes program practices that are viewed as cumbersome or ineffective exist because they have become embedded, or institutionalized, within the existing system. Some practices can be clearly traced to funder or policy requirements; however, the sources of other practices may be less clear. Perhaps they were a response to competitive pressures at one time to differentiate services from other providers. Or perhaps the practices were included as part of an ideal model in industry standards or as described at local conferences. Or perhaps the decision to include certain practices originated from frontline workers who needed an efficient way to keep track of everyone receiving services.

While the practices may have become ingrained in the program, it does not mean that implementation cannot be improved. Yet making improvements to a process like this requires more than an awareness of the problem or even good ideas about how the process could be restructured. Change requires an understanding of the constraints operating at each level that led to the current design. Recall that the fundamental definition of effective policy and program implementation is pursuit of changes that are *institutionally sanctioned*. By definition, this means that it is change that participants at the frontline, organization, and policy fields perceive to be legitimate and have requisitioned the requisite resources necessary to carry it out. In other words, in order for change to become lasting, it must have buy-in and sufficient resources in the implementation system.

In complex policy and program areas, obtaining buy-in and adequate resources for program change can be challenging. Many participants are interested in trying to ensure that their needs are met by the proposed change, even at the expense of its overall effectiveness. Within the same initiative, some of the practices may be more or less contested. For example, criteria to determine who is eligible to receive services or the geographic area to be targeted may be controversial, while the wording on the intake form is less subject to controversy. Yet this is not always the case. Power and cultural dynamics operating in the strategic action field determine what is understood to be controversial and who gets to influence which decisions. Scholars refer to this as *legitimate authority*—an actor is perceived to have a legitimate right to make decisions on someone else's behalf.[21] Depending on the power and cultural dynamics, this authority could stem from the ability to control resources, a formal or informal position within a hierarchy or chain of command, or a shared understanding.

Sometimes changing implementation practices requires shifting the power and cultural dynamics to allow new ideas and practices to be accepted and perceived as legitimate. Since these dynamics are unique to each setting, they are difficult to describe generally. However, drawing from and integrating prior theories, we broadly categorize common influences that operate within implementation systems in terms of authority and culture.

In this notion, we depart from constrained notions of political authority common in early studies of policy implementation, which located it strictly in legislation or formalized roles.[22] Instead, all of the elements of a core program, including the objectives to be accomplished and general ideas about how to accomplish those objectives, are influenced by a variety of factors. Some are external to the implementation setting, while others are created within it. They include formal legislation or policy but also market conditions, legitimizing practices, and individual values. For each, they help to provide means for answering the key questions in policy and program implementation about the viable program options, preferred logic of change, and feasible means for activity coordination. In any particular social system, one or more of these social constraints might be deterministic for shaping how the parameters and activities of implementation unfold in that context. Table 3.1 provides a summary.

Political and Economic Authority: Coercion and Competition

Almost by definition, forces in the external environment constrain the activities that take place within the strategic action fields important to policy and program implementation. Scholars often use the terms *political authority* and *economic authority* to reflect the extent to which behavior is influenced by the public

Table 3.1
Power and Culture in Strategic Action Fields

	Establishing Viable Options	Identifying the Logic of Change	Coordinating Activities
Overarching question	What do we want to accomplish? What is the range of activities considered appropriate to address the problem?	How will we bring about change in the target population?	How will activities be coordinated to accomplish the objectives? How is work structured to allow for communication?
Political and economic authority			
Laws and regulations	Defines legally permissible activities and scope of interventions	Requires certain processes and procedures	Stipulates who is involved and who is in charge, who has political authority
Market conditions	Justifies need for public inter-vention-based market feasibility or market failure	Incentivizes processes that increase efficiency and profitability	Affects willingness to collaborate based on degree of competition
Culture			
Legitimizing practices	Problems and solutions are approached in ways that have been previously accepted	Reduces uncertainty by adopting processes and procedures that fit with what others are doing	Affects willingness to collaborate based on reputation, trust, or repeated interactions
Beliefs and values	Interventions are selected based on values or beliefs	Base processes on assumptions about target group behavior	Affects willingness to collaborate based on shared goals and values

Note: While Fligstein and McAdams's formal articulation of field theory establishes some mechanisms, we delved more deeply into a wide base of social science theory to identify these formal and informal mechanisms of social structure as they relate to policy and program implementation. Neil Fligstein and Doug McAdams, "Toward a General Theory of Strategic Action Fields," *Sociological Theory* 29, no. 1 (2011): 1–26.

interests, most commonly through government, or by private interests, realized through a competitive market.[23] For example, an organization receiving a large federal grant must abide by the federal regulations regarding accounting, procurement, and hiring practices if it wants to receive the award. This is the influence of the political authority that accompanies the public funding. Public funding isn't the only source of political authority: regulations, authorizing statutes, and even citizen participatory processes also can be sources of political authority. Each provides a defensible basis for decision making in the public arena. A corporation selling goods or services in an open market has economic authority about what to produce and what price to charge the consumers who purchase the services, as well as the suppliers, competitors, and investors. By meeting the demands of the market and honoring the terms of economic authority, the corporation is rewarded with increased profits.

While corporate firms may be more strongly influenced by economic authority and government agencies may be more constrained and enabled by political authority, all organizations are to some extent constrained and enabled by both types. In his seminal book on the topic, public affairs scholar Barry Bozeman coined the term *dimensional publicness* to reflect this reality.[24] Regardless of sector, all organizations are public to some extent. Corporate firms must abide by regulations pertaining to environmental emissions, occupational safety, and minimum wages. In varying degrees, most public organizations also have an element of economic authority. When public agencies use market mechanisms to allocate goods and services, such as fee-for-services, vouchers, and competitive contracts, they draw on this authority. When nonprofit agencies establish social enterprises to raise funds through renting housing, selling coffee, or operating transit, they are leveraging economic authority.

The concepts of political and economic authority have traditionally been applied to organizational behaviors; however, it is reasonable to expect that political and economic authority would also affect behavior in policy fields or at the front lines. To understand how authority may influence policy and program implementation, let's explore two common sources: the legal and regulatory environment and market conditions.

Legal and Regulatory Environment

The legal and regulatory environment is the most commonly studied mechanism of influence in prior implementation literature. In particular, top-down approaches emphasized the importance of establishing clear objectives that delineate tasks and resources needed to achieve desired results. As we have discussed, there are often pragmatic reasons that few policies include this level of specificity. And any particular program that is being implemented may not have a direct link to a particular piece of legislation; rather, many programs are influenced by multiple policies, sometimes conflicting ones. These policies include not only formal legislation passed in Congress but also administrative rules issued by public agencies or regulations and requirements accompanying public funding.

This does not mean that legislative and regulatory influences are not important. Quite to the contrary, one of the critical features distinguishing policy and program implementation from other types of change is that it is backed by some form of political authority. This also is an important feature distinguishing the study of implementation in public affairs from other related topics such as operations research or intervention science more generally. In public affairs, we are not particularly concerned with whether a private hospital can integrate a new practice into its patient care system. Hospitals adopt new practices every day—from a new charting system to a new treatment for certain types of conditions. However, to the extent that the new practice to be integrated has grounding in political authority—legislation, administrative rules, or public funding regulations—it is now within the purview of public affairs.

While the legal and regulatory environment is not completely determinative of outcomes, it is a necessary influencing shaping the scope and approach of the core program. For one, laws and regulations bound the domain for the program by defining legally permissible activities. There is broad variation in the extent to which formal political authority spells out the specific activities that can or cannot be undertaken in the implementation of a program. And to make matters more complicated, the permissible scope of interventions is often subjective, requiring interpretation by legal experts who have a sense of the policy intent based on historical legal precedence (think, for example, of the Supreme Court ruling in the Affordable Care Act or more common court judgments).

It is typically the task of what we refer to as authorizing organizations in an implementation system to interpret legal requirements and then to issue additional rules or formal guidance for other actors in policy fields to ensure compliance with political authority. These agencies frequently rely on staff to scan the policy field for legislation, regulations, or court rulings that might have an impact on the way in which a program can be carried out. This review is not limited to the initiation of a new program; in contrast, any changes or improvements to the way in which a program is carried out must conform to legal requirements. Sometimes the need for legal review gives authorizing organizations or other entities in the policy environment possessing legal expertise considerable power over implementation decisions. And because the interpretation of legal requirements is subjective, different actors within a strategic action field can renegotiate the scope of permissible activities.

By constraining permissible activities, the legal environment can play a direct role in facilitating or impeding the logic of change that links inputs to outputs and outcomes. Sometimes well-intentioned rules and requirements can make it difficult for the target population to access the program or persist through the process. Even if the general program idea is good—for example, providing supplemental food assistance to low-income workers—the program itself will not achieve its desired results if the requirements are too onerous. Part of the task for skilled implementation practitioners is to weed through the various program rules and requirements to determine which are legitimately essential to maintain political compliance and which are no longer relevant or necessary. Others have referred to this as cutting through the red tape to streamline processes.[25]

But this oversimplifies the challenge. It takes skill to identify which requirements are in place to protect important public values such as equity or service quality and which serve little public purpose. Public affairs scholar Leisha DeHart-Davis refers to "green tape" as written rules and regulations in place that help facilitate the intended public objectives, perhaps preventing otherwise arbitrary and capricious practices. In her interviews with city employees, one code inspector described it this way: "Laws make it easier to do our job. The city's adopted the codes so I can show I'm not making up the rules. In most cases I can say 'I don't have any leeway.' It provides me with an out if someone wants to argue with me—Fire Codes Inspector."[26]

In addition to bounding permissible activities, the legal environment delineates the participants who are involved in carrying out the activities. Rarely do laws and regulations define all participants who should be involved in the implementation process, clarifying specific roles and accountability mechanisms. Sometimes authorizing agencies are identified in legislation, and funding tools such as competitive grants, contracts, or block funding are stipulated a priori for a particular program. However, this is not the case in many situations, and even if it is, there is still considerable latitude about the range of participants involved and how work is coordinated during implementation.

Nonetheless, government funding arrangements and legal expertise can concentrate power in particular organizations in a given policy field. Certain lead agencies may be endowed with political authority, thereby giving them a central role in coordinating the program, regardless of their technical expertise or experience in the given policy area. And once present, government funding within a policy field is quite durable. Once legislation has established a tradition of providing subsidies to farmers or supplemental nutrition for low-income families, the political forces ensure that these program elements are features of the field. A regular way of doing things gets established around public funding streams that ensure roads are maintained, schools are operating, and mental health services are provided.

Market Conditions

Often markets are juxtaposed against political authority as a way to regulate activities. Rather than relying on laws or rules, the market allows people to vote with their dollars. Drawing from the principles of supply and demand, programs offer services or interventions that match the needs or interests of those consuming the services. To the extent that the services are valued in the market, they will continue to be provided. If services are no longer valued, then resources are no longer expended to support the program, sending a strong signal that something needs to be changed. Markets tend to be more nimble than legislation. While it might take months or years for legislation or public funding to adapt to the preferences of constituents, signals from markets are received continuously and shift more quickly as preferences shift.

It is no surprise, then, that in countries like the United States, there tends to be a general preference to engage market mechanisms during policy and program implementation. While there may be market failures that prevent the good or service from being provided entirely by the market, policymakers and practitioners often look for ways to privatize particular activities or engage market mechanisms for certain aspects of the implementation process. Often this preference for engaging markets shapes the very domain of activities that are considered as on the table during implementation. And in many policy fields, markets are already functioning as part of the policy area. For example, in our illustration above, the program you were going to use as a first-time home buyer leverages the existing mortgage market infrastructure of banks and investors. However, reliance on market infrastructure can also constrain programs; at the very least, interventions developed cannot create uncompensated costs to market participants and on average should help improve profitability.

Market conditions therefore bound the activities integrated as part of the logic of change, perhaps as much as or more than the legal environment in many policy areas. This is not necessarily good or bad, but it is reality. For some programs, the target population also pays directly for the services or products as a customer. This is the case for many health care services or our illustration of low-income mothers receiving supplemental nutrition assistance. While customers may receive government subsidies through health insurance or a debit card, they choose where to spend those subsidies. Housing and child care subsidies are provided in similar ways; the individuals who receive subsidies can spend the vouchers directly on services or goods they choose. The decision to structure the program using a target population subsidy rather than a subsidy to the provider likely came from a policy decision in legislation or agency rules. It may or may not be the most effective way to create change in the target population (e.g., enable housing stability or ensure quality child care). But it bounds what is considered possible when trying to improve the effectiveness of implementation outcomes.

Market conditions in the strategic action field often affect the willingness of participants to collaborate in the implementation process and the terms of the collaboration. An important aspect of this is the degree of competition between the field actors. Competition is a function of both supply and demand; limited resources can increase competition, particularly if multiple providers can supply the same services. When there are multiple providers, increased competition can be a way to reduce the cost of providing certain program activities. In order to win a grant or contract, providers might reduce their costs, thereby driving down the overall cost of services. However, there is a trade-off to increased competition because it directly influences the willingness of providers to collaborate on other issues. Conditions for collaboration are more favorable when resources are plentiful and predictable, enabling actors to make autonomous choices about participation in collaborative ventures.[27]

In settings with flexible resources, there is often less competition and more overall field development. Private philanthropic investment can be an important ingredient in such a context for improving policy or program implementation effectiveness. The financial resources present in a philanthropic grant can unleash creativity that allows new solutions to be developed. Beyond direct financial support, philanthropic funding can bring providers together to generate new resources such as shared program knowledge, which in turn might be able to be developed into tool kits or helpful practical strategies. If stable over time, such financial investments can capitalize the development of valuable implementation resources within a policy field or organization.[28]

Interestingly, financial resources without that level of flexibility often do not enable the generation of new resources through cooperation. In strategic action fields where resource endowments are low, where the financial sources are unstable or inadequate, competition is more likely to result. Actors are focused on basic organizational survival rather than thinking creatively about ways to address complex problems. When resources are in short supply, the knowledge relevant to improving implementation is often sparse and not easily shared. Competition for money, talent, ideas, and connections becomes embedded in the setting as the only way of accomplishing tasks. Competition can exist at all levels of implementation systems. At the policy field level, different organizations might compete for contracts or grants to provide certain program activities. At the organizational level, different programs might compete for limited budget or staff time allocations. And frontline workers might compete for bonuses or clients.

Cultural Norms and Values: Legitimacy and Imitation

While external factors like political authority and market conditions certainly bound implementation activities, it is not uncommon to hear program managers explain: "While this is what is supposed to happen, let me tell you how things *really* work." How it "really works" is often reflective of the culture found in the setting. Culture, so critical to implementation success, is hard to identify or describe without experiencing implementation processes firsthand. It requires a qualitative felt understanding of the dynamics on the ground, or what anthropologist Clifford Geertz called the "webs of significance spun by humans."[29]

Unlike rules or mandates that are imposed through hierarchical authority, the roots of culture grow from the informal ways that tasks, resources, and environment intertwine.[30] It is both a result of and a cause of the core program. A strong culture creates shared understanding of what to do and how it should be done. It offers a means for sense making, providing a way to think about a problem to be solved in light of what is understood about the past.[31] In this way, culture helps a group define success and failure in that context, and it also helps assign value to what results from their activities. By attending to culture in our analysis of implementation, we are acknowledging that getting people to work together toward a common goal is not just about formal inducements such as paychecks and contracts but often more significantly about developing shared commitments. Such commitments can be a powerful motivator in shaping what and how people work to accomplish policy and program implementation.[32]

Although intangible, culture is often influential in how implementation unfolds. An interesting study by Ann Chih Lin of US prisons implementing rehabilitation programs is illustrative here. Rather than formal program evaluation sites or tightly controlled experiments, she investigated the everyday world of programs in five prisons.[33] Each of the medium-security prison settings was charged to carry out education, job training, and drug treatment programs. In some, the interventions were merely a way to keep prisoners occupied, to "keep the peace." In other prisons, the interventions had a transformative impact on the prisoner population. Conventional factors such as size, the nature of prisoners' crimes or disciplinary reports, or overcrowding did not predict the implementation variation. Instead, staff and leaders' understanding of the programs in the context of the rest of their work, their struggles and successes, directly shaped their activities, which supported, subverted, or aborted formal intent. In the prisons with successful programs, staff believed in the importance of rehabilitation beyond the mere custodial purpose; they told stories about its transformative power in accreditation visits and received accolades for their involvement from their supervisors. In prisons with no such programs, there was no commitment to even the idea of rehabilitation. In her analysis, Chih Lin highlights the significance of alignment between the program's rehabilitation goals with the prison's larger values. She concludes, "When policies are bent to purposes other than those that policymakers anticipated it is not because staff do not understand their work. Instead it is precisely because they try to make sense of their work . . . This naturally leads them to refer each new policy to the values that are most salient in their organization."[34] In this case, like others, cultural beliefs influence what and how implementation activities are carried out. While there are numerous ways one could unpack the sources of culture, here we focus on two broad mechanisms: legitimizing practices, and shared beliefs and values.

Legitimizing Practices   Recall the homeownership program example described at the beginning of this section. This example is based on a true case. The state agency adopted a program rule requiring home buyers to complete eight hours of in-person classroom education prior to receiving down payment assistance. Why? This decision was not grounded in legislation; Congress had authorized the agency to fund down payment assistance but made no provision requiring education. The decision was certainly not driven by market conditions; in fact, the private lenders who worked with the program expressed frustration about the requirement because they were losing borrowers due to it. Borrowers would rather purchase a home with another lender than meet the education requirements. The driving force behind the eight hours of classroom education was that the model was held up as a "national industry standard."[35] The state agency wanted to emulate best practices in the field and thus adopted the standard to demonstrate commitment to high-quality programming.

Industry standards or widely heralded "best practices" can be an important tool for ensuring quality and consistency in the delivery of programs. Prior to the adoption of the industry standards in home buyer education, there was no general rule to evaluate "good" home buyer education: everything from a thirty-minute phone call to a month-long intensive course was given the same label. Participants in the policy field across nonprofit, private, and public sectors joined together to establish national industry standards that could serve as a guidepost for effective practice. The challenge is that while industry standards can provide legitimacy and credibility, they do not necessarily ensure an effective program.

There are other normative influences that create binding expectations regarding appropriate practice. Think of the professional codes of behavior in nursing or social work, nonprofit agencies' adoption of management standards to achieve positive reviews from charity watchdog groups, or program ideas that are shared through a policy field. When the domain for a program is being established, legitimizing influences tend to approach problems and solutions in ways that have been previously accepted. They can offer some justification to the public and funders for why the program is being carried out in a particular way.

Legitimizing influences are particularly important when there is a lot of uncertainty about the logic of change underlying a program—where the link between means and ends is unclear. Organizational scholars have referred to this phenomenon as isomorphism: organizations in a particular field look more and more alike over time, adopting similar practices and structures to reduce uncertainty.[36] The challenge is that structures and practices that may be very effective in one context may be inefficient and even ineffective in another context. Even "evidence-based practices" often upheld as the gold standard are based on assumptions that may not hold when applied in different settings. It takes some astute analysis to identify the elements of program implementation that can be borrowed from other successful applications and require unique adaptation to the particular circumstances.

Legitimizing practices can also help facilitate coordination, as professionals sharing the same standards or certifications may have a higher degree of trust in each other. This can create a sense of moral responsibility for following through with tasks assigned and executing them according to the agreed-on standards. Sometimes these moral obligations are viewed as more effective at regulating behaviors than formal regulations grounded in political authority. In fact, in some areas, there is a push for industry self-regulation to reduce the need for government regulation. In these areas, there is often an umbrella organization, such as a nonprofit membership association, that certifies that organizations or programs are in compliance with agreed-on standards. For example, in the area of substance abuse treatment, programs can receive multiple certifications and accreditations to demonstrate their legitimacy. Funders may even require evidence of certification before awarding grants or contracts. However, there can also be conflicts regarding which standard to follow because the professional norms or certifications can conflict with formal authority of public funding.

Shared Beliefs and Values   The final mechanism important for understanding the social structure and dynamics in the strategic action field is shared beliefs, the crux of culture. Scholars often differentiate between the intensity of these beliefs, classifying some as norms, others as values, still others as underlying assumptions.[37] But the key idea for our purposes is that shared beliefs often operate as a cognitive framework, a means of sense making, of reducing ambiguity and making the world intelligible. These shared beliefs have an impact on the program during implementation. Agency leaders, program managers, and frontline workers throughout implementation systems often base decisions about implementation in their understandings of the target population, how the program operates, and their perceptions of other participants.

For example, consider a new teacher who works in a school where people believe they are playing essential roles in society, educating students with untapped potential, where he regularly interacts with other colleagues constantly striving to improve their teaching. In the same district, another new teacher is placed in a school in which students are perceived to be unmotivated and the public criticism of public education is believed to be true. She sees how others ostracize a colleague who stays late to learn new lecture-capture processes. The collective beliefs in each setting inform people's actions and the interpretations they see as valid. These beliefs, taught to these new teachers, then support their own behavior consistent with them. In the first instance, because education is essential and rewarding, it is expected that the new teacher will explore new pedagogical options. In the latter, because K–12 education is understood to be fundamentally broken and students are unmotivated, there is little incentive for a novice instructor to try new techniques in the classroom. The shared beliefs support actions that over time create a taken-for-granted reality in each school. And when the school district adopts a new math curriculum, this aspect of culture in each school shapes teachers' understanding of the program as well as the viability of its desired outcomes.

In terms of determining the viability of the core program, beliefs about human behavior are paramount in shaping the logic of change. Are people fundamentally trustworthy and motivated, or selfish and lazy? Will the manager or staff adhere to program mandates or do everything to shirk responsibilities? Are target groups worthy of respect and high-quality service or undeserving of the support being offered? The answers to such questions directly shape the formalization of the program design. Fewer formal means of control, such as rules or sanctions, are necessary if there is a shared belief that people in the implementation system, either those providing public programs or those receiving them, are worthy of respect.

Similarly, the way in which implementers approach the logic of change is often grounded in their beliefs about effective interventions. Sometimes these beliefs come from professional socialization: doctors who learn to see their skills as distinct from nurses; early childhood educators who differentiate themselves from child care providers; engineers who distinguish themselves from technicians. Each has a unique way of diagnosing a problem and recommending a solution, sometimes resulting in different preferences for program design. For example, an after-school program staffed by social workers may be implemented very differently from an after-school program staffed by educators. But beliefs about effective programs also can emerge from experience as actors make sense of what happens to them each day or listen to the stories others share about battling with the legislature or working with clients. This sense making creates a schema that often provides powerful mental shortcuts that influence how implementers interpret and act on program or policy ideas.[38]

Finally, shared beliefs can be an important part of coordinating activities around the core program. The degree of alignment or divergence among the actors' understanding of shared beliefs, particularly about what should be done and how it should be accomplished, varies across implementation settings; a strong culture provides a collective interpretation of the problems to be solved, develops definitions of success and failure along the way, and assigns value to what results. It reduces ambiguity. Shared beliefs about agency reputation can also directly influence organizations' willingness to coordinate their activities at the policy field, organizational, or frontline levels.[39]

Many scholars emphasize the stabilizing function of culture in studies of organization, highlighting the way it works as glue that holds groups of people together.[40] In this research, culture is particularly significant during times when a group is confronting change because of the potential for what Christopher Ansell calls a "resonant collective identity."[41] Yet more often while there are dominant cultural signifiers, countercultures often develop, creating opportunities for those without as much power in the social system to come together. As alternative stories and metaphors are used and alternative beliefs offered as interpretation, the dominant culture is weakened. This fuels new understandings and interpretations that in turn create more opportunities for unpredictable action and innovation. When there is divergence among beliefs and values in strategic action fields, various coalitions can form that assemble their own resources and build authority to push forward their own collective beliefs about the nature of the problem or present viable solutions.[42] The very terms of culture can be contested as different actors make competing interpretive claims about events and appropriate action. This dynamism creates some of the unpredictable nature of implementation processes in strategic action fields.

CONCLUSION

This chapter has provided a new way to understand policy and program implementation. Thinking about implementation activities as clustered in interrelated yet distinct strategic action fields provides new analytical tools. By focusing on the core program, we see how establishing viable options, identifying the logic of change, and coordinating activities are critical tasks that occur in implementation. The core program is shaped across levels of the implementation system by authority found in the legal environment and market conditions and in culture reflected in legitimizing practices and shared beliefs and values. Recognizing the mechanisms that shape how programs are defined and shaped throughout the implementation process opens up new opportunities for intervention across an implementation system.

In practice, these forces all come together within a setting and are felt most acutely when an individual changes roles or enters a new implementation system. Someone who has worked for a mental health advocacy group in one state will feel a significant shift when she moves to another state and starts a job at the state-level mental health department. Although the content area is consistent, different core programs likely exist even when funded by the same federal program. As significant, because of the change in the mental health worker's role, her knowledge of relevant sources of authority and cultural values will be brought into question: advocacy organizations work in the networks of policy fields where these forces combine dynamically, whereas public administrative agencies are more directly focused on enacting their political authority. Understanding each context is essential for being an effective professional. And yet there is often not a common language for this person to examine the change or the differences between the settings until she makes a mistake.

In writing this conceptual chapter, we are attempting to introduce a language you can use to describe the influences present in most strategic action fields that shape program components in implementation systems. This is an important first step, but it is only the first step. The next task is to consider the various scales of activity within an implementation system—the policy field, the organization, or the front lines. For the mental health advocate moving to another state, she considered jobs only at the policy field level. But she obviously knows that important implementation activities happen elsewhere and that participants and resources significantly shape the core program. In the next three chapters, we explore to implementation systems at each of these levels, providing both a general landscape and unpacking how authority and culture might shape programs. Then, in chapter 7, we put the system back together to explore how implementation across the whole system works together to affect public value outcomes. We present our case studies of the Hardest Hit Fund and Quality Rating System to provide illustrations of the general concepts introduced in this chapter about core programs and the significance of social structure in shaping what actually occurs in policy and program implementation.

In this way, our approach is different from the advice given in guides or "best practices" workshops to improve policy outcomes. For people interested in improving implementation, it is conventional to identify a particular practice found to be effective in other settings and emphasize its replication as a way of improving effectiveness. The practice is like a magic fertilizer found to be effective for growing beautiful, fragrant flowers in a full-sun rose garden. It is upheld as the ideal method for improving flower growth—even though the flowers that you trying to grow happen to be located in a rock garden underneath a large oak tree. Our approach suggests that failed attempts to get the fertilizer to work properly may not be the fault of lack of skills, or commitment to fertilizer use, or even faulty fertilizer—it may simply be that the fertilizer is not the right concoction for the particular plants and parameters of your garden. Throughout part 2, we explore approaches you can take to understand the ecosystem, plot, and flower bed where you are growing flowers. In this way, we are framing the task of improving implementation as an endeavor focused first on cultivating understanding of your context so you can develop a more subtle and skillful intervention.

PART TWO

The Implementation System at Multiple Levels

Context is the set of beliefs, at times ones that we are unaware of, that dictate how we think, how we frame the world, what we pay attention to, and consequently how we behave. It is sometimes called a worldview.[1]

Nothing undermines the creative process more than the naive belief that once the vision is clear, it's just a matter of "implementation." In fact, moving from concept to manifestation is the heart of creating—which literally means "bringing into existence."[2]

In the chapters in part 2, we apply our multilevel framework to help describe policy and program implementation systems. We begin by considering each of the major levels in these systems. Before we can improve implementation to be more effective, we need to first understand the existing structures and constraints at each level. We want to emphasize the significance of this contextual analysis. In public affairs professional circles today, there is a lot of talk about the importance of "moving the needle," making "systems change," and improving "collective impact." Conferences, training sessions, and professional publications all reflect a larger yearning for being able to make large-scale systems' change on persistent public challenges that transcend a particular organization's or party's narrow self-interest. Cases of success are lauded and attempts made to replicate the efforts in other communities.

While the last part of the book will help professionals deliver on the promised transformation, suffice it to say now that typically reductionist models or simplistic solutions are the norm. When they are applied, they often fail to deliver on the large-scale change envisioned. And implementation can actually be made worse if people become disengaged when they see that so little resulted from their efforts. Improving collective impact is really an effort to hone the operation of policy and program implementation systems. Ambitious ideas—how to engage a community in improving children's educational attainment, reduce a town's carbon footprint, or bolster immigrant-owned small businesses—cannot be realized without significant alterations to existing systems.

We believe that the ability to make significant system change starts from a thorough analysis of its conditions. That is what motivates our multilevel analysis and has sent us to the social science literature to excavate useful concepts and tools relevant to policy or program implementation.

In chapter 4, we first focus on policy fields, the networks of public and private organizations with an interest in the implementation process in a particular place. The organizations involved in a policy field possess knowledge, funding, and opinions about implementation and can be activated to participate in the various tasks of enacting the core program. Their existing relationships can be an asset or a hindrance to smooth implementation. But each participating entity in the policy field is part of the structure and process of implementation—just like plants and weeds which make up a garden—enabling and constraining how the policy or program unfolds.

Yet there are other analytical levels to understand. Organizations themselves have their own structure and processes that further refine the program, and we explore this setting in chapter 5. Their existing technical competencies, staffing, and structure directly influence how programs are implemented. The need to learn new means of accomplishing the desired end might be rejected, embraced, or modified. At the front lines, other issues come into focus, and we turn to this level in chapter 6. Here, target populations, with their various motivations and incentives, become forces to be reckoned with. The degree of desired behavioral change in the target group also directly influences the tasks that need to be carried out.

At each of these levels, we include analytical tools that can help you conduct your own implementation analysis and include them in appendixes. By presenting ways to technically describe the important factors for implementation in these contexts, we hope to enable new understanding and ways of talking with colleagues about implementation in a multilevel system. We also draw on our two cases to illustrate the immediate application of the conceptual ideas to implementation projects.

Policy Fields

In conversations about many public issues—health care reform, homeland security, food assistance for the needy—most people, after expressing their opinions about the substantive issue, shake their head at the operations of "the system." Allusions are made to politics, bureaucratic processes that impede quick actions, or incentives that don't seem aligned. But rarely do they actually know very much about the specifics of "the system." Who is involved? What are their motivations and desired results? What are their accountabilities and incentives? What important relationships could be leveraged to exert influence to improve things? As suggested by the issues confronted by the various actors in Colorado's Affordable Care Act (ACA) implementation, such questions move front and center into our awareness in implementation analysis. They are essential for understanding implementation problems and potential solutions. Yet in implementation analysis, you must move beyond a general sense of "the system" to better understand how the existing health care institutions and markets worked together before the passage of the ACA, how the federal government works with states to carry out the various programs involved in homeland security, how the networks of food banks and food shelves help ensure an adequate supply of emergency food. As suggested in the Introduction, there is a multilevel implementation system to be explored. Our investigation begins at the macrolevel with policy fields.

Policy fields are bounded networks among organizations carrying out a substantive policy and program area such as homeland security, health care, or food assistance that emerges in a particular place and time. In practice, they reflect the core elements of policy environments in a geographic area. Because the governments and the jurisdictions they cover are involved at least in some way in policy and program implementation, the geographic bounds of policy fields are often significant. The state, county, and even school district can bound a policy field, creating unique social and political dynamics within that particular strategic action field. Obviously policy fields do not exist in isolation. The Colorado policy field, which shaped that state's implementation of the ACA, was directly influenced by the national policy domain where the law emerged through negotiation and compromise between industry, nonprofit advocacy groups, and lawmakers. The national politicization of the act, its moniker of "Obamacare," and subsequent legislative attempts to repeal it directly shaped the environment in Colorado. But the way these national forces influenced the implementation decisions within the policy field actors is not predetermined. In this state, legislative leaders moved forward with law to create their own health care exchange even before the political controversy died down. Private foundations invested in studies of consumer engagement and education to help provide needed evidence during implementation planning. The Connect with Health Colorado exchange organization convened groups of stakeholders in important areas like small business and health plans to develop work plans. These same actions did not occur in neighboring Kansas or Nebraska.

More generally, as a strategic action field, the social structure of the policy field shapes how federal laws are administered, whether privately funded programs contribute to field development and whether collaborative programs develop to address pressing community problems. While some political scientists use the term *policy subsystems*,[1] as scholars influenced by organizational studies, we use the terminology *policy fields*.[2] This more intuitively reflects that people and institutions working together create these networks. Because the interested parties have a history and work together on the public problem in the context, they bring these experiences to the implementation of a policy or program change. Policy fields provide the arena in which implementation of a particular policy or program unfolds.

Policy fields are formed by a number of forces. They can be initiated in response to a national crisis or historic event. In the mid-1960s, when the national government embarked on the War on Poverty, it expanded its role considerably, creating new responsibilities at each level of government and founding new nonprofit organizations that came to arrange themselves in policy fields. Similarly, the 2001 terrorist attacks on the United States created new needs for enhanced homeland security with a fundamental reorientation of existing institutions. New organizations developed and new relationships were forged among existing ones to better respond to the national need. This top-down orientation is common to how national policymakers and some researchers conceptualize implementation, seeing it merely as the development of a service network to carry out policy mandates.

However, many more times, policy fields are not created new out of whole cloth in response to an event. Rather, they evolve over time, shaped by experiences organizations share as they work on public problems. In fact, to understand the more common development of policy fields, it is helpful to think in a more bottom-up way. As we learned in chapter 2, Benny Hjern and David Porter described local implementation structures. In their conception, this structure is formed from the pool of organizations with potential interests in any public issue that can be found in a particular place.[3] It is difficult to predict the actual involvement of a particular organization from that pool in the field when a new policy or program comes into focus. The decision to engage is just that—a decision to step into the action arena offered by the field. It can be influenced by reputation—the organization has a history of being involved in this type of initiative. It can be shaped by leadership or staff expertise—people have professional knowledge that will be germane to shaping implementation. It can be motivated by board priorities or the potential availability of new funding. There are many motivations for stepping out of the potential pool into active engagement in implementation. But from outside the strategic action field, it is difficult to predict.

In many ways, this fluidity is by design. In any largely decentralized government such as that found in the United States, fields evolve in relation to unique local and state conditions as people in organizations respond to opportunities and constraints. It is the promise of federalism. Policy fields provide the setting in which people in local institutions can engage in issue-specific implementation disputes and grapple with competing values. How can the right people be brought together in Colorado to design the state's health care exchange? How can a police department share data with their local health department to better monitor homeland security? How can food shelves overcome their history of mistrust to develop processes that allow low-income people to access food support but not take advantage of the services? The answers to these questions emerge from the social structure of policy fields.

These fields are complex. It is essential for professionals interested in making policy change to develop a language for understanding their dynamics as the precondition to improving implementation. In fact, in our own practice, research, and teaching, we have come to see policy fields as equivalent to how particular markets operate within private sector industries.[4] Markets vary in form, scale, and the goods or services exchanged, as well as participants and location. They facilitate trade and enable distribution and allocations of resources in society. They can be constructed deliberately, but more often than not, they emerge given local preferences, skills, and resources. A key business competency is market analysis; studying the particular dynamics of market informs firms' planning and strategy in relation to inventory, workforce talent, purchasing, and facilities. In the same way, a key public affairs competency is policy field analysis.

Yet although policy fields are fundamental structures to achieve public purposes, scholars do not understand their operation well; no studies yet systematically compare policy field development and results in one content domain across states.[5] In part, it is because the framework combines formal factors, such as laws, contracts, and performance measures, and the informal mechanisms, such as relationships, trust, and agreements, that are more elusive to systematic documentation. It is also because scholarly attention is often focused on understanding more general concepts, such as intergovernmental relations or policy networks. Yet although it has not been studied directly, it is clear from generations of policy implementation research that something important to implementation happens at this "macroscale" of the system. Practically, it is also evident that the same large public policy like the ACA produces very different results depending on the context within which it is implemented. While scholars might decry this complexity, it is a reality of public affairs worth probing to enlighten practice.

State-level public managers who issue requests for proposals and host technical assistance workshops for nonprofit agencies know the significance of effective policy field practice. So do private philanthropic funders, such as United Way or community foundations, that convene state-level actors for strategic planning conversations to move systems change forward. Staff in state legislatures, trying to navigate different interest group perspectives as they weigh how to improve the effectiveness of public investments, also can appreciate how policy field conditions both influence and are influenced by their actions. In fact, often individuals working within one of these institutions move in between them over the course of their career, taking up other roles within the same policy fields. Their expertise lies in their in-depth and nuanced understanding of the formal and informal mechanisms important for implementing change within their field. This competency is something to be developed and purposively reinforced.

In this chapter, we begin by bringing policy fields into focus, describing the field first as a whole and then the roles played by its interrelated parts. Too often, we rush to analyze the trees that are involved in implementation and lose sight of the forest. Here we provide the landscape of the forest. To heighten our analysis, we also probe how the core program is shaped at this level of the implementation system. We conclude by introducing helpful tools that implementers can use to describe and analyze policy fields.

POLICY FIELDS IN FOCUS

Policy fields are bounded networks among institutions and organizations carrying out a substantive policy and program area in a particular place.[6] They are made of up formal and informal relationships between various units of government, private corporations, and nonprofit agencies. Multiple government institutions at the national, state, and local levels engage in the same policy field at any given time, adding to the complexity.[7] At the beginning of the twenty-first century, there were approximately eighty-seven thousand governments in the United States.[8] While the US case is extreme, many other nations have developed similar administrative layers in federalist systems in which authority is divided between a centralized authority and regional and local entities with specified roles and responsibilities. Many assume there is a hierarchical relationship of national, state, and local governments. Yet researchers studying intergovernmental relationships clearly document a long tradition of considerable legal, fiscal, and political interdependence.[9]

Almost every policy field reflects significant intergovernmental negotiations and challenges. In the national health care reform case, for example, although all states were given the authority that Colorado took to develop their own health care exchanges, thirty-four states refused to do so for political reasons. Instead of seizing the prerogative, they defaulted to the federally administered system and waited for operational challenges to emerge. These political and administrative tensions are predictable, even enabled, in a federalist system. There are often competing needs for administrative centralization and geographic customization responding to political and regional conditions.[10] National laws and regulations are often impractical, either too grand to provide necessary guidance or mired in details that do not apply to particular places; there are disconnects between mandates and funding realities; and few incentives exist for national policymakers to prioritize decisions. Instead, they often pass legislation without consideration of the whole policy portfolio.[11]

In addition, private organizations, both corporations and nonprofits, play essential roles in policy fields—providing public services, brokering resources and information, educating the public, and facilitating policy and program evaluation.[12] While this has a long tradition within the United States, governments' changing roles in Europe, Australia, and Asia have created new roles for civil society organizations and public-private partnerships around the world. As noted in chapter 2, many researchers are concerned with the governance of these decentralized networks and the diverse tools that the public sector uses to implement public policy.[13] The tools approach emphasizes the formal exchange of political authority between a government agency and a private sector organization, such as a state agency contracting out employment placement services to a private firm. While understanding the formal sources of authority in a given field is certainly important, it is also important to understand the informal power and cultural dynamics that developed between institutions in a shared context. To do that requires stepping back to get a bigger picture of the field as a whole.

Policy Fields as Strategic Action Fields

Different perspectives help make sense of the interrelated sets of institutions operating within a given physical or technical space. For example, as described in chapter 2, the network perspective provides a language to think about how the different actors in the policy field work together and coordinate their activities. While network actors may not have formal lines of authority, like different units of an organization that are layered within a hierarchy, there are still institutional bonds, or "institutional glue," that tie them together.[14] Some of these ties are more formal, grounded in contracts or exchanges of financial resources, while others are less formal and based in trust and sharing of information. In contrast to just looking at the ties between two organizations, social network analysis maps out ties among multiple organizations at the same time.[15]

Perhaps closest to our notion of policy fields is sociologists' definition of organizational fields, the aggregate of organizations working in a recognized area of institutional life.[16] At base, this idea explores the significance of groups of organizations engaged in collaboration and competition for survival. These organizations, often geographically bounded, must interrelate because of shared functions or resource dependencies. For example, organizations providing public utilities would all be seen to exist within one field, similar to those working together to accomplish passage of new environmental protection provisions or those who all receive United Way grants supporting their work with the aged.

Organizations in the same fields often develop structures and ways of working together that are mutually beneficial. The organizational field begins to develop its own shared cultural rules and meaning, sometimes referred to as institutional logics. While particular organizations might not be linked together directly, the field creates common conditions within which they operate. Institutional logics provide members of the organizational field a sense of collective purpose that both helps explain their connections and guides their interactions. While multiple logics might exist, organizational fields often are thought to coalesce around dominant institutional logics.[17] Organizations working in the same field may even start to look alike, adopting similar policies, programs, and management techniques in an effort to appear legitimate to others in the field—a process referred to as isomorphism.

The benefit of the organizational field perspective is that it emphasizes the importance of institutional culture for policy and program implementation. Within a field, resources are frequently pooled to carry out activities, emphasizing the role of trust over formal contracts.[18] Trust is created through relationships, developed and nurtured, and earned rather than automatically granted through hierarchical position. Sometimes there are strategic attempts to manage ongoing interactions among the network actors through what some have termed metagovernance structures.[19] Yet the organizational field frame minimizes the formal influences of political authority that are typically inherent in policy and program implementation.

By defining policy fields as strategic action fields, our approach combines the structures and formal sources of authority inherent in intergovernmental relationships and networks with the culture and power dynamics of the organizational field. Understanding the influence of intergovernmental authority and its ability through policy tools to shape institutional relationships is essential; government retains power over some decisions, particularly those shaping public service roles. Economic authority through funding and competitive pressures for contracting may also be significant. However, the horizontal nature of network ties is consequential. Appreciating the significance of organic collaborations among public, nonprofit, and business organizations cannot be overlooked. All are important but not sufficiently integrated given our needs here. We needed an integrative, analytical approach to understand implementation systems, and policy fields provide that framework.[20]

Institutions within Policy Fields

In any setting, there are potential pools of institutions—governmental agencies, nonprofit organizations, and private firms—that might participate in implementing a program or policy because of their interests and expertise. Each institution has a role or set of roles to play that shape the dynamics of the policy field. Because there are always limited resources—staff, time, funding, expertise are rarely sufficient in the public arena—these field players must make choices about whether to engage and, if so, in what capacity. Organizations often are activated by function; some are brought in for planning or resource provision, service provision, or evaluation.[21] But the specific program or policy, or even the specific task at hand, motivates different organizations from the field to step into active roles in implementation. When they do so, they bring their staff expertise, their interests and ideas, and other important resources into the policy field. Yet stepping into active engagement with implementation clearly does not imply that the resources or actions are necessarily aligned with other field actors. There is a dynamic, social process of negotiation and meaning making at the heart of the policy and program implementation process.

When an agency steps into active engagement in the field around the implementation of a particular policy or program, significant relationships and resources accompany them. Money, information, and program knowledge all flow among the organizations, creating an implementation structure that might shift and change depending on the implementation tasks or project time line. The organizations act as nodes in a complex, emergent system. In this way, the shape and dynamics of policy fields are unique to that place and time, to the organizations and people involved at this level of the implementation system. Said another way, they are endogenous to the policy environment found in a particular place.

Many types of institutions operate in policy fields.[22] Each confronts a range of potential activities they could lead or participate in given their mission. There are conventional ways each is expected to contribute but also more active ones that leaders can pursue in a particular implementation project if they believe it is warranted. Table 4.1 provides general descriptions of the range of institutions that might be involved. Public agencies are important in structuring policy and program implementation. They respond to laws and administrative regulations, issuing rules and dedicating staff to public accountability mechanisms, such as open solicitation of public comment periods or structured grant review processes.

Table 4.1
Institutions Involved in Policy Fields

Type of Institution	Conventional Roles	Active Roles
Public agencies (national, regional/state, local)	Respond to federal, state, or local laws or administrative regulations Determine how to allocate public funds Determine rules and manage within those parameters	Policy field design
Philanthropies	Invest funds in priority areas	Commission studies Provide resources (convenings, network development) to support sharing of implementation knowledge Fund intermediary organizations to centralize field knowledge and build implementation capacity
Nonprofit, for-profit, and public service providers	Respond to contractual opportunities from public agencies	Attend field-level meetings and convenings to share and learn implementation lessons Participate in ongoing groups (communities of practice) focused on implementation Support implementation teams within organizations
Intermediary organizations or purveyors	Respond to requests for programmatic and management training	Develop field networks through convening Enable coordination, collaboration, and partnership development Provide financial resources Share implementation resources (reports, convenings, Internet communication platforms) *(continued)*

Table 4.1

Institutions Involved in Policy Fields (Continued)

Type of Institution	Conventional Roles	Active Roles
Research and evaluation organizations	Respond to requests for formal studies	Provide technical assistance materials to support implementation
Nonprofit membership and advocacy associations	Represent members and constituent interests on official bodies and policy position statements	Share implementation resources (reports, convenings, Internet communication platforms) Provide information from field experiences to public policymakers

They determine how to allocate public funds and generally operate in regard to other governments in a federalist system. Yet Stephen Goldsmith and William Eggers showcase in their book *Governing by Network*[23] what years of consulting practice taught them—how public agencies sometimes assume a more active role in designing network relationships within a policy field.

Private philanthropies also can play important roles as sources of private capital to smooth implementation challenges caused by inadequate funding. These organizations play more active roles when commissioning relevant research, supporting convenings and other means of sharing relevant knowledge, or funding particular entities that centralize technical knowledge in the implementation network. In the implementation of the ACA, the state of Colorado and others benefited directly from these types of investments from private foundations. In the Quality Rating and Improvement System (QRS) case, they were similarly significant.

Intermediaries as well can be essential entities within a field.[24] They garner information and resources to decrease transaction costs between two parties, thereby increasing operational efficiencies and program effectiveness. Highly developed in policy domains such as mental health, community economic development, and affordable housing, these organizations can play essential roles in policy fields. Most basic, they can offer management or program-specific training in innovative approaches or evidence-based models. More actively, though, they develop relationships among organizations by convening organizations, providing financial resources, and developing implementation resources. They also can offer information to public decision makers about the successes and challenges of policy implementation visible from service agencies. By offering these types of supports, intermediaries buffer service-providing organizations from turbulence in the field. Often private funders, corporations, banks, or philanthropies support such activities because of their interests in implementation results. Where neither pure markets nor public provision operate effectively, intermediaries are one force in field building for enhancing systems' capacity and enabling the whole to operate more coherently.

In some fields, institutions referred to as purveyors have an interest in sharing innovations or evidence-based practices. Purveyors can be significant in some fields. For example, the Parents as Teachers model is an early childhood home-visiting program focused on increasing parents' knowledge about early childhood development, changing their parenting techniques, increasing early detection of developmental delays, and preventing child neglect. More than two thousand Parents as Teachers affiliates provide the service across all states and internationally. Like many other purveyors of proven interventions, this organization invests significantly in creating implementation support; the agency's website provides extensive resources, including an overview of the model, case studies about sites, and information about training opportunities, conferences, policy advocacy strategies, and speakers for implementation leaders operating in fields where the model is not yet present.[25] The core mission is to promote the intervention, which provides essential information to implementers looking for practices that are documented to have a desired impact.

Research and evaluation firms or professional membership associations are other organizations that can play important roles in policy fields. They can represent their narrow interests and respond to requests from public and private funders. More actively, they can initiate projects that share relevant information and knowledge throughout the field, such as providing evidence-based program models, developing resources to help implementation, or sharing implementation experience with policymakers. However, none of these activities can be systematically predicted; the roles that public and private organizations play depend completely on the context.

Sometimes policy fields reflect strong governance, and there is widespread clarity about who can do what to whom under what authority. In national security, for example, while there are multiple organizations involved in policy implementation—military bases, state-level national guards, training facilities, contractors supplying equipment—there are a clear hierarchy, deep socialization of members who support it, and explicit and agreed-on rules of operation. Sometimes service networks are purposively designed to carry out a new policy initiative. In the mental health networks that Milward and Provan studied,[26] one central organization was given the authority to both provide services and coordinate those among others. Centralized network structures facilitate the use of government tools like formal contracts.[27]

More often, though, policy fields reflect contested governance, especially when relationships between organizations are not designed but rather have emerged as people work together over time to solve implementation issues. In these situations, diverse organizational actors vie for authority to define problems and solutions in relation to a policy or program. There often are competing change strategies and conflicting professional norms.

We return here to the two cases described in chapter 1 that we use to illustrate implementation analysis throughout the book. The Hardest Hit Fund (HHF) is a policy focused on foreclosure prevention in states hardest hit by the housing crisis. Quality Rating and Improvement Systems (QRS) are programs designed to improve the quality of early childhood settings and provide better information to consumers. Box 4.1 explains some of the institutions important in the policy field implementing the HHF in Ohio. National public institutions and financial networks are important for structuring the implementation conditions; they shaped the guidelines and negotiated operating conditions of the policy. There was, for example, a summit which brought together large financial institutions, such as Chase and Bank of America, that needed to coordinate the HHF program across multiple states. The event, convened by the US Department of Treasury, clarified the rules and led to the design of common tools to use to process HHF loans in each state. Within this context, the state-level Ohio Housing Finance Agency played a central role and actively designed the field relationships through convening an interagency council for advice and contracting with housing counseling agencies.

Box 4.1
HHF Policy Field Actors

The HHF program is a federal initiative, administered by the US Department of Treasury and authorized under federal legislation. However, all of the eligible states created their own programs, creating unique policy fields within each state. This box describes of some of the important actors involved in the policy field for Ohio's HHF program.

National Actors

Public Agencies (US Department of Treasury)
The Emergency Economic Stabilization Act of 2008 (EESA) gave the US Department of Treasury the authority to distribute up to $700 billion in funds under the Troubled Asset Relief Program (TARP) as one of its financial stability initiatives. Under this program, Treasury allocated nearly $60 billion for foreclosure mitigation efforts, including $7.6 billion for the HHF program.[a] Treasury set the general guidelines for the program and approved program proposals from the eighteen eligible state housing finance agencies.[b]

Private Financial Institutions (Lenders)
Mortgages are legal obligations between homeowners (borrowers) and financial institutions (lenders), with specified procedures for collecting payments and pursuing foreclosure if payments are not made. Assistance provided to borrowers through the HHF program often requires a change in the terms of the mortgage, thus requiring the participation (and approval) of private lenders. HHF funds were typically paid to private lenders on behalf of borrowers.

National Intermediaries

Fannie Mae and Freddie Mac
Fannie Mae and Freddie Mac are national intermediaries in the United States, also known as government-sponsored entities (GSEs), that securitize private mortgages held by lenders, allowing the mortgages to be sold to investors on the secondary market. Many of the mortgages that lenders service are securitized by the GSEs, and therefore the lenders must make sure that any changes that they make to mortgages are acceptable to the GSEs. Lenders were hesitant to participate in the HHF program until they had the approval of the GSE from the Servicer Summit.

Other National Intermediaries
The Mortgage Bankers Association represents the interests of US financial institutions that originate mortgages. The National Council of State Housing Agencies represents the interests of the state housing finance agencies that administered the HHF program at the state level.

Other National Stakeholders
The HHF program was conceptualized in planning sessions with industry stakeholders, government agencies, and policymakers as an innovative strategy to

(continued)

(Continued)

address deficiencies of prior foreclosure prevention programs. Participants included the administration, the National Economic Council, the Council of Economic Advisers, the US Department of Housing and Urban Development, Treasury officials, housing and mortgage sector participants including the Mortgage Bankers Association, the National Council of State Housing Agencies, and HOPE NOW.[c]

State Actors

Public Agencies

As a quasi-governmental entity with a governor-appointed board, the Ohio Governor's Office had a significant voice at the table, ensuring that political interests across the state were represented

The Ohio Housing Finance Agency (OHFA) has been administering homeownership and rental housing programs since the 1980s. It has operated as an independent state agency since 2005, with a board of directors appointed by the governor. OHFA is the central agency for the HHF program in Ohio, responsible for the design and administration of the program.

OHFA convened an interagency council to help inform the design and administration of the state HHF program. Different state agencies participated, with varying degrees of power and authority depending in part on the expertise brought to the table. For example, the Ohio Department of Job and Family Services and the Ohio Department of Taxation were critical early on to identify the number of unemployed homeowners in the state who might be eligible for HHF assistance. The Ohio Department of Commerce was a critical participant to engage lenders and servicers in the program (particularly state institutions).

Nonprofit Support Organization: Ohio Capital Corporation for Housing

HHF federal program guidelines required that the recipient of HHF funds in each state be structured as a "financial institution." To meet this requirement, OHFA partnered with a local nonprofit organization, the Ohio Capital Corporation for Housing (OCCH), which subsequently formed Ohio Homeowner Assistance LLC (OHA), a wholly owned subsidiary, to serve as the eligible entity to receive funding from the HHF program. OHFA has been a longtime partner with OCCH on many housing programs and was instrumental in the creation of OCCH.

Statewide Foreclosure Prevention Network: Save the Dream Ohio

OHFA launched Save the Dream Ohio in 2008, two years prior to the HHF program, funded in part through the National Foreclosure Mitigating Counseling (NFMC) program.[d] OHFA served as the administrator of the Save the Dream NFMC program in Ohio, distributing more than $8 million in funding to twenty-one nonprofit counseling agencies to provide counseling to homeowners facing potential foreclosure. In addition to these agencies, the program brought together a network of agencies, including state agencies, legal aid societies, and pro bono attorneys. A toll-free hotline for homeowners in distress and a website were established.

Service Organizations: Nonprofit Housing Counseling Organizations

Like many other states, Ohio has a strong network of nonprofit organizations providing foreclosure counseling, as Department of Housing and Urban Development certified housing counseling organizations. In Ohio, these nonprofit organizations often work collaboratively with a strong advocacy voice. OHFA contracted with more than twenty nonprofit housing counseling organizations to conduct the initial intake screening for the HHF program. Organizations were reimbursed on a fee-for-service basis.

Research and Evaluation Organizations

OHFA partnered with the Ohio State University to form the Office of Affordable Housing Research (OAHR) in 2009, prior to the initiation of the HHF program. The OAHR engages research expertise from a variety of entities to guide and evaluate its programs, including the Ohio State University, Cleveland State University, the Federal Reserve Bank of Cleveland, Policy Matters Ohio, and Ohio Capital Corporation for Housing. In addition, in partnership with OSU, OHFA was recently awarded a grant from the John D. and Catherine T. MacArthur Foundation to evaluate the HHF program.

---

a. Much of the background information about the program is from information on the program website: http://www.treasury.gov/initiatives/financial-stability/TARP-Programs/housing/hhf/Pages/default.aspx.

b. http://www.sigtarp.gov/audit%20reports/sigtarp_hhf_audit.pdf.

c. http://www.sigtarp.gov/audit%20reports/sigtarp_hhf_audit.pdf.

d. NFMC provided funding for counseling to homeowners in foreclosure, not direct financial assistance. Homeowners receiving counseling were still dependent on financial institutions to work out a solution to their hardship (renegotiate mortgage payments, screen for eligibility for federal programs).

Box 4.2 provides an overview of some of the institutions important in Minnesota's early childhood education policy field focused on QRS implementation. Organizations from various intergovernmental levels are important in this policy field. Public organizations are joined by national intermediaries, as well as membership and research and evaluation firms, as operators in this policy field. As we will see as we explore these cases in more detail throughout this book, implementation unfolds as people from various institutions in policy fields learn from their efforts to make progress on collective problems.

Box 4.2
QRS Policy Field Actors

Although QRS are state-based programs, a number of important national agencies provide information and concrete implementation resources to states. Along with state and local organizations with formal authority and interest in the program, they operate in the policy field that shapes what is decided through the implementation process in Minnesota.

National Entities

Public Agency

The US Department of Health and Human Services, Office of Child Care and Office of Planning, Research and Evaluation support state implementation of QRS through funding both comparative descriptive research and the National Center on Child Care Quality Improvement that provides technical assistance to states.

Private Philanthropies

Since the late 1990s, national foundations have come together through the Early Childhood Funders Collaborative to share information and make pooled investments to improve early childhood education systems in states. One of the agreed-on policy strategies is supporting the development of QRS programs throughout the country.

Intermediary Organizations

The BUILD initiative receives funding from sixteen private philanthropies to provide a venue for convening, peer learning, and exposure to research among states. It operates the QRS National Learning Network, which provides technical assistance and facilitates information sharing among states around programming and research.

Research and Evaluation Entities

Child Trends, RAND, and Child Care Policy Research Consortium provide descriptive research and create valid assessment tools that states use to assess early childhood education quality. A number of states participate in research and technical assistance work groups that support state program design.

Nonprofit Membership Association

The National Association for the Education of Young Children is a professional association that promotes excellence in early childhood education through accreditation, conferences, and publications.

State and Local Entities

Public Agencies

The Minnesota Office of Early Learning is a new public office accountable to the state Departments of Education, Human Services, and Health. It administers QRS in Minnesota as part of federal grant requirements and convenes the Parent Aware Advisory Committee quarterly for information exchange.

The Early Learning Council, an appointed body, makes recommendations to the governor, Children's Cabinet, and legislature on "creating a high-quality early childhood system that ensures all children arrive at kindergarten school-ready." It has representatives from the state legislature, Federal Reserve Bank, intermediary agencies, and service-providing organizations.

Private Philanthropies

A number of groups were essential in the initiation of this program in the state. For example, the Minnesota Early Learning Foundation (2006–2011) raised capital ($20 million) for a pilot program and sponsored evaluation. Start Early Funders Coalition is a group of foundations investing in small parts of the implementation. Great Twin Cities United Way funded evaluation and projects to support quality enhancement.

Nonprofit Service Providers

Child Care Aware of Minnesota works through a network of local nonprofits to support providers in assessing programs and preparing for assessment. It also operates a statewide website to communicate with parents.

Nonprofit Advocacy Agency

Parent Aware for School Readiness is a group of business leaders (many previously involved in the Minnesota Early Learning Foundation) that publishes research findings, marketing materials for parents, and scorecards of QRS implementation.

Nonprofit Membership Association

The Minnesota Association for the Education of Young Children provides programming such as an accreditation facilitation project and professional development training that supports QRS implementation. Initial development of the Minnesota Center for Professional Development, the centralized registry of provider qualification and training, is now housed at a local public university.

Research and Evaluation Organizations

The Center for Early Education and Development, University of Minnesota, provides assessment of some child care settings used in the rating. A local office of the national group Child Trends provided early specification of assessment tools and ongoing evaluation of impact and implementation.

ANALYZING THE DEVELOPMENT OF THE CORE PROGRAM

The core program and results are the cornerstones of policy and program implementation. Core programs determine what gets done and how it is accomplished, defining how means are directed toward identified ends. As suggested in chapter 3, while occasionally programs are defined through legislation, more often they are defined and refined through field negotiations before being shared with organizations and frontline levels. The policy field is the place where the core program is assembled through interactions between field actors. Actors debate what they want to accomplish and how to approach it. They negotiate an underlying logic of how they might change conditions for the target population and determine how the various activities will be coordinated within or across agencies, securing the necessary authority and resources. It is within the field that policy problems, proposed solutions, and participants first come together.

Establishing Viable Options

How do policy field actors assemble the ideas that will become the core of a program? Sometimes these ideas evolve out of a formal legislative process, with clear policy mandates about a particular initiative to develop. But other times, ideas about how to tackle a public problem evolve more organically within the field, from a foundation proposal, an excited discussion at a task force meeting, or receipt of initial program evaluation results documenting intervention impact. Field actors with a sense of urgency to respond to a specific public problem may brainstorm alternative ideas about what could be done to address the problem. What aspect of the problem will be addressed? Who (or what) will be targeted for the intervention? While there are times when new ideas and creative solutions are selected, often the solutions selected resemble ways of doing work that already exist in the field; it is what scholars have called path dependence.[28] A solution seems salient not because it is the ideal strategy, not because it is most efficient or effective at achieving the desired ends, but because it is similar to what the field participants are already familiar with and have the capacity in place to carry out.

This process of considering activities that could be assembled together to achieve desired ends is a central focus at the policy field level in implementation systems. This does not mean that the process is always coordinated or structured; in some policy fields, there may be a formal planning process around one initiative, but in other fields, organizations working together in a similar problem area share ideas more informally—sometimes more or less successfully. The ease of this negotiation often depends on the degree of agreement in the domain about the significance of particular problems and the viability of particular approaches to address the problems. For example, as discussed in chapter 3, there is often significant disagreement about the viability and effectiveness of supply-side or demand-side interventions. Sometimes there is a strong preference toward providing services and funding directly to the target population. Other times there is a strong preference for providing subsidies directly to the child care providers, landlords, or educators who serve needy families.

One of the important activities in policy fields is collaboration to secure needed resources and authority to address a public problem. If current policies prohibit the types of interventions viewed as most beneficial, policy field actors may work together to lobby for a shift in legislation or administrative rules. Similarly, if resources are lacking to address the problem, policy field actors may coordinate to advocate for funding not only from government but also from nongovernmental actors like foundations and private sector investors. In the process of coordinating to garner authority and resources to address a public problem, policy field actors add definition to the problem and identify solutions that are perceived to be legitimate, thereby narrowing the domain of program technologies that will be viable in a policy field. Organizations operating in the policy field need to secure resources and authority to address the public problem and thus will be constrained in part by the decisions made at this level. This does not mean that the policy field is entirely deterministic. As a social structure, the dynamics of the policy field are in constant flux and the ideas that are perceived as legitimate shift over time.

Identifying the Logic of Change

In addition to assembling ideas about the public problem and general solutions that are perceived as legitimate within a policy field, policy field actors may contribute to the technical development of the solutions. For example, resources and authority may be secured for a general solution at the field level, such as providing funding directly to nonprofit organizations to support job training programs. However, the details of the types of services that job training participants will receive—the program technology that is intended to bring about behavioral change—also may be decided. Sometimes formal policies may have requirements for particular processes that constrain the options available in the policy field for bringing about change in the target population. There may also be best practices or program standards that are disseminated, encouraging organizations to structure their processes in one way.

To some degree, the extent to which field actors have influence over the specific interventions may be limited by the complexity of the problem and therefore what needs to be done to address it. Recall that complex program technologies have many varied steps between inputs and desired outcomes, and they require interventions that are often customized to meet the varied needs within the target population. In complex technologies, it may be possible (and desirable) only to make general suggestions from the policy field level rather than formulating a standardized intervention; the intervention must be customized given the needs of the target group understood at the organizational or frontline levels. Despite this reality, sometimes field actors spend considerable time detailing idealized activities without a real understanding of the target population. Activity requirements are adopted and specified for people receiving income support without adjustments for skill levels, training experience, or local labor market conditions. A more nuanced approach, informed by insights from the organizational and frontline levels, is needed to achieve the desired results. It is likely that in simple technologies—accessing universal programs like Social Security, rolling out smart electrical meters in homes, renewing automobile licenses—it is possible to specify the steps in the more routine processes. In these cases, the ideal flow of the technological steps can be described with fair amounts of detail from the policy field level. However, this is not the case with many of the more nuanced public problems that require individualized solutions.

Aside from stipulating certain practices, policy field actors can also facilitate shared learning about practices that can guide organizations as they flesh out their technologies. Intentionally or unintentionally, actors working together in the policy field often assemble nonfinancial implementation resources that others may look to as they integrate programs. As illustrated in table 4.2, different types of implementation resources may be present in policy fields, most of which we see working in the HHF and QRS cases. Professional gatherings such as conferences or events, research-based briefings or practical tools, marketing and communication resources, evaluation reports, and web-based platforms to support the exchange of emerging ideas can be essential to developing and sharing innovative ideas. Many times, these resources come from corporation- or foundation-funded projects at

Table 4.2
Examples of Implementation Resources

Common Nonmonetary Implementation Resources in Policy Fields	HHF	QRS
Professional convening among organizations or conferences	Interagency councils among state agencies, Save the Dream Ohio network of organizations	Gatherings among state administrators
Evidence-based program descriptions and tools to enable replication	Examples from other state HHF programs and other state foreclosure programs (like Pennsylvania's Homeowners' Emergency Mortgage Assistance Program)	Summary two-page documents
Communication tools such as branding, brochures, or websites	Save the Dream Ohio network includes a toll-free phone number, website, and branding	Posters for care providers following their ratings Marketing materials and websites providing ratings to parents
Policy research or evaluation reports	US Department of Treasury posting of state-by-state HHF performance data	State-by-state comparisons of QRS development
Virtual information-sharing platforms		QRS National Learning Network

national research or evaluation firms, intermediary, or membership organizations in the field.

From an in-depth study of community policing, Heather Hill suggests four mechanisms through which such implementation resources help identify the logic of change and support what is decided at the policy field level.[29] First, they help interpret the formal policy as written in law and regulation describing more accessibly what is desired. Community policing, for example, evolved out of discontent with traditional patrols and rapid call responses. When the federal Violent Crime Control and Law Enforcement Act passed in 1994, it included public funding for law enforcement officers to interact directly with community members in an effort oriented toward prevention. The legislation was vague, providing no clear definition of community policing or details about the nature of what was meant by the goal of "interacting directly with members of the community" described in the legislation. Hill's study revealed that rather than waiting for the government to clarify this intent, local officials consulted membership associations, consultants and scholars, and organizations such the National Center for Community Policing for training, basic principles, and practices and also attended professional conferences focused on the new direction.

Second, implementation resources suggest appropriate technologies—activities that a service organization might adopt—or other changes in professional activities consistent with policy. In the community policing training, for example, experts offered specific advice about job roles and responsibilities, technical changes in how to handle service calls and change what previously was routine practice. Third, they provide an opportunity to understand and learn new skills or develop new knowledge needed to implement a policy or program. In a community setting, suddenly officers needed to know how to build rapport and trust with community members. They needed to stop and consult other citizens before acting and be more transparent about what resulted from their actions. Through role playing and other interactive exercises at the training, officers learned how valuable community knowledge is in describing what is going on in the streets.

Finally, the existence of these implementation resources provides a reason to focus on the change at hand. As many studies have demonstrated, implementers at the organization and frontline levels have many directives given to them.[30] In the community policing case, while one of the police officers interviewed said the intervention was merely "common sense," he acknowledged that he didn't know much about it until a training and that afterward he was motivated to go and do his own research on the approach. Although this officer was skeptical of what he perceived as the "sell" from the consultant, he found the idea of community policing to be legitimate after doing his own investigating and drawing on other implementation resources he found. Implementation resources in the form of trainings, websites, and reports provide individuals, frontline staff, service organization leaders, private funders, and local authorities opportunities to engage themselves and others in learning about the new interventions.

Coordinating Activities

Other debates about the core program at the field level involve decisions about how activities among actors should be coordinated. At the field level, which entities are involved in the provision of services? How is communication facilitated among these entities? And perhaps more fundamental, how are authority and resources structured to carry out the program technologies? In chapter 3, we discussed the importance of laws, regulations, and market conditions for constraining implementation. These sources of authority are assembled at the policy field level of the implementation system. They are not typically isolated to any one organization but cut across actors in the policy field—although organizations can respond to these influences in different ways, more or less strategically, which we discuss in chapter 5.

Practically, many policy problems are messy and fall outside the scope of one organization. Thus, it is necessary to engage multiple organizations in providing the technical elements of the intervention. At the policy field level, decisions are typically made about which organizations will be involved with various aspects of the program. For example, are service organizations providing all aspects of the program? Or is the program broken into distinct components that are then distributed across a number of agencies? In the QRS case, one organizational network stepped forward to provide coaching to the early childhood setting, while another hosted the professional development registry and still another provided an objective assessment of providers' quality. Infrastructure can also be developed at the field level to support information sharing and feedback throughout the implementation process. Sometimes software or database systems are developed by lead organizations in the field to facilitate information sharing between organizations.

Sometimes coordination is achieved informally through repeated interactions that generate trust. As research on policy networks reveals, trust can be a defining feature in unpredictable and risky settings.[31] In policy fields, trust—the belief that another actor will take both parties' interests into account—is developed from lived experience, formations of coalitions, and frustrations of past plans stalled.[32] When present, it allows others to assume good intentions and makes them comfortable with assuming risk. In a network with diffuse authority, trust also helps motivate different organizations to invest their resources such as knowledge, time, and money into the field, increasing stability in the field. Trust in networks also helps facilitate learning and innovation because actors do not second-guess events in terms of opportunistic behavior but rather invest in collective problem solving. In chapter 7, we explore in great detail how the differences in power and interpretation are important to policy implementation in the HHF and QRS cases. Furthermore improving implementation systems often requires close attention to these informal yet important aspects of interorganizational relationships in policy field.

While the coordination methods described so far are more informal, many times there also are formal coordinating mechanisms in a policy field that leverage the authority and resources of government. The policy tools approach offers a common language to describe the methods by which collective action is structured in a field around public problems.[33] There are many different types of policy tools. In his book, *The Tools of Government: A Guide to the New Governance*, policy scholar Lester Salamon provides a detailed review of common tools in use across different policy fields.[34] Table 4.3 summarizes some of the more common policy tools.

Although there are variations in policy contexts, the policy tools approach suggests that commonalities inherent in the use of a particular tool are not context dependent. For example, contracts are often used in public-private transit partnerships to establish terms of engagement—to specify the financial, technical, or operational risks and required results. These contracts are similar to those used by state education departments to authorize charter schools. Vouchers increase the purchasing power of individuals in the market, in housing, child care, and emergency food, in similar ways. Government-sponsored loans, be they for small businesses, individuals' higher education, or capital construction, have similar underlying principles. Focusing on generalizable characteristics of government tools helps to highlight important design choices during policy formation; for example, education tax credits can have a more positive impact on the behavior of low-income people if they are refundable, like the earned income tax credit, a highly effective thirty-five-year-old federal antipoverty initiative.

Table 4.3
Selected Government Tools Important to Implementation

Tool	Definition
Direct government provision	Direct delivery of goods and services, often focused on production or police functions.
Economic regulation	Specialized bureaucratic process that controls prices, output, and entry or exit of firms in an industry.
Social regulation	Rules, standards, and sanctions to mediate economic activities' impact on health, safety, or social welfare of citizens.
Contracts	Business arrangements between government and private agencies in which products or services are delivered to government or citizens in exchange for money. As a business arrangement, there is liability for nonperformance.
Grants	Payments from government to the recipient organization to stimulate or support the recipient's service or activity. Some grant amounts are determined by formula, others by specific need.
Loans and guarantees	Provision of credit by government to fund or encourage provision of capital for other important activities.
Tax expenditures	Provision in tax law to encourage certain behavior by deferring or reducing tax obligations.
Vouchers	Subsidy that improves the purchasing power of an individual to choose goods and services.
Corrective taxes and tradable permits	Prices and other market mechanisms that create financial incentives for behavioral change.

Source: Adapted from the ideas presented by Lester Salamon, *The Tools of Government: A Guide to the New Governance* (Oxford: Oxford University Press, 2002).

While the actual tools in use may be diverse, there are some key dimensions on which the tools vary that can provide insight into the social structure operating in a given policy field. Salamon describes how policy tools vary on four key dimensions: coerciveness, directness, automaticity, and visibility. For example, economic and social regulations are more coercive than tax expenditures, which are often voluntarily taken as credits or deductions when individuals complete their annual tax returns. Tools also vary in their directness: grants, loan guarantees, and contracts are indirect because the entity authorizing and financing the activities is not involved in carrying it out. In contrast, economic regulation imposed by government on private industry is very direct. Tools vary in their automaticity, the extent to which they use an existing administrative structure rather than creating a special new infrastructure. Finally, each tool varies in its visibility. Some are very visible in the political process—direct government subsidies, direct loans, and grants. Others are more invisible and as a result more politically popular at adoption. For example, tools like regulations or tax incentives do not show up in normal budgeting and policy review processes and thus may be subject to less review and controversy.

A purely rational approach to policy implementation would suggest that the policy problem and intervention should drive the selection of the coordinating mechanism, including the policy tool. Different policy tools are associated with different outcomes, and ideally, a tool would be selected that is most likely to be associated with the desired outcomes. However, rather than thinking about tool construction from scratch, policy field actors tend to adopt what they are already familiar with or already have an administrative apparatus in place to support. Their selection is typically not based on a rational analysis put forth by policy analysts but on the existing assumptions and power dynamics in the policy field. As a strategic action field, the policy tools in use are more often coordinating mechanisms that reflect different understandings of the compromises required in a particular policy field. As such, they tend to reflect and reinforce the political and economic authority that shapes the core program.

Given these limitations, we do not employ the policy tool approach to drive implementation analysis. However, we do find this approach to be helpful in classifying the wide range of coordinating mechanisms that might be in use in a policy field, especially those leveraging government authority or resources. We return to a practical application of a policy tools analysis in the next section.

Illustrating How Core Programs Come Together

These aspects of the core program—the viability, logic of change, and coordination of activities—come together first at the policy field level. Boxes 4.3 and 4.4 illustrate how these elements appear, respectively, in the HHF program in Ohio and in the QRS program in Minnesota. When one is first trying to understand and unpack the details of policy or program implementation, it is helpful to try and describe what core program exists.

Box 4.3
Ohio's HHF Program

While each state had the discretion to propose its own programs for how it would use HHF funds, federal regulations specified that the funds could not be used for counseling, legal aid, or job training. Some of these restricted technologies, particularly counseling and legal aid, were a core part of the existing technology that was being used in many states to address foreclosure problems.

The US Department of Treasury did not require states to adopt particular technologies but did provide a list of "sample program interventions" that it would approve. Each HFA had the discretion to propose other strategies; however, most states proposed programs that closely resembled one or more of the sample interventions. Ohio's HHF program followed Treasury's examples, with several options for homeowners:

(1) Mortgage payment assistance covering mortgage payments for unemployed homeowners while they searched for a job
(2) Rescue payment assistance, structured as a one-time payment to bring homeowners current on their mortgage
(3) Principal reduction to pay down the mortgage balance for homeowners underwater on their mortgages (owing more on their mortgage than the house could sell for)
(4) Transition assistance to help homeowners exit homeownership (e.g., give their home back to the bank and move while avoiding foreclosure)

To be eligible for assistance, homeowners had to meet certain income requirements and had to be able to demonstrate a hardship that put them at risk of not being able to make their mortgage payments, such as unemployment. Unlike other federal foreclosure programs, homeowners did not have to be behind on their mortgage payments in order to qualify for assistance. Most homeowners who received assistance through the program received mortgage payment assistance, whereby the HHF program paid their monthly mortgage payments (directly to their lender) while they were unemployed, for up to fifteen months.

Box 4.4
Minnesota's QRS Program

While states' early childhood education QRS programs vary significantly, they have five common elements:

(1) Standards are developed to assess quality.
(2) Early childhood settings are assigned ratings based on these standards.
(3) Quality improvement services are offered to settings.
(4) Policy is developed to offer financial incentives to improve quality, such as increased rates for highly rated providers serving low-income children.
(5) The ratings are disseminated to parents and consumers.

National research reveals significant differences in how each element is defined in each state context.[a] For example, there are differences in how standards are defined and how assessments are conducted; in some places, observations are conducted, while in others, assessments hinge on provider self-reports. In addition, states vary in how the individual assessment variables are combined into one overall quality rating score.

In Minnesota, all of these elements were implemented in the QRS program, Parent Aware. Parent Aware was instituted in 2007 as a pilot program funded by private philanthropies and targeted in five localities. In the four-year pilot program, early childhood settings were assessed on four categories: family partnerships, teaching materials and strategies, tracking learning, and teacher training. Each received a rating of one to four stars, with four stars designating the highest-quality program.

At the end of the pilot program, state funding was not initially forthcoming, but Minnesota received an award from the federal government's multimillion-dollar Race to the Top–Early Learning Challenge. The state's application was strengthened by the pilot program experience, as all states receiving the grant had the QRS program as one strategy in improving the early learning system. Among other things, this federal grant funded QRS implementation statewide from January 2012 through 2015, with a goal of voluntarily enrolling thirty-seven hundred programs during that period.

---

a. Diane Paulsell, Kathryn Tout, and Kelly Maxwell, "Evaluating Implementation of Quality Rating and Improvement Systems," in *Applying Implementation Science in Early Childhood Programs and Systems*, ed. Tamara Halle, Allison Metz, and Ivelisse Martinez-Beck (Baltimore, MD: Brookes Publishing, 2013); Kathryn Tout and Kelly Maxwell, "Quality Rating and Improvement Systems: Achieving the Promise for Programs, Parents, Children and Early Childhood Systems," in *The Quest for Quality: Promising Innovations for Early Childhood Programs*, ed. Patricia. M. Wesley and Virginia Buysse (Baltimore, MD: Brookes Publishing, 2010).

Yet this often provides a description at just one moment in the overall implementation process. Rather than being definitively decided, discussions of the domain, logic of change, and coordination of activities usually continue. As we illustrate in chapter 7, they are resolved over time. Field actors meet to discuss the appropriate actions; funders bring financial resources and program accountability measures; others bring insights from comparative policy reports, knowledge of the surrounding environment, and opportunities that emerge. Organizations and frontline staff try to work with decisions made at the policy field level and call for further refinement. This dynamic process of the entire implementation system is important to recognize, even while one is trying to document what is occuring at a particular moment in the implementation process.

APPLYING POLICY FIELD ANALYSIS

Implementers at all levels in the system benefit from understanding the structure of the fields they operate within and appreciating how their position within the field shapes the dynamics of power, culture, and strategic action. Policy field analysis can be used to uncover the institutions involved in the policy field and articulate the important relationships and resources. This is a systematic way to describe the structures of the context that shapes how a policy or program is implemented. It is much like a landscape architect who needs to site the building and must consider the slopes in part of the yard, the placement of large trees that influence how the lawn and garden are related, and where the microclimates might exist. These tools provide a way for leaders to describe the important aspects that structure a field so that others can understand the significance and limitations of the current system.[35]

Policy Field Audit

It is best to begin with an audit of the field. (Appendix A provides step-by-step instructions.) After identifying the substantive policy or program of interest, one then moves on to identifying the institutions engaged in a designated policy field, the significant laws and fund streams, and a description of the policy tools and implementation resources that help structure implementation.

Identifying participants with a stake in a policy field can begin with an informal brainstorming of the organizations in the field that have knowledge of or interest in the program, its staff, and target group. In most locales there is a significant, although limited, number of institutions engaged in work with an explicit interest in it. Consider those with intergovernmental authority and those whose influence is felt more horizontally through networks' resources. This exercise really focuses on identifying the players in the policy field (those with power and interest) and their organizational affiliation.[36] Not all organizations, though, have equal power. Some possess interest but lack power. Others possess power, such as legislative authority, but have low interest. For professionals actively engaged in the policy field, such brainstorming is easy. It draws on their knowledge developed through work experiences, connections made on the job, or simple professional networking. For those entering a new field, brainstorming often inspires phone calls or meetings to develop a more complete list of organizations working on an issue. This is a more refined, focused approach to conventional networking.[37]

The second analytical step is to understand the laws, public funding streams, and other implementation resources that shape the structure of the field and the implementation conditions of the program of interest. Cataloguing the policy tools in use is one important way to describe existing coordinating mechanisms being employed in the field. It can also help unearth why organizations in different parts of the field are used to different funding relationships. In the early childhood case, Head Start organizations receive grants that include funding for family support workers, health services, and management training. Other service providers receive contracts or vouchers that specify the rate of care without providing funding for any such supplemental services. And nongovernmental financing mechanisms are important to identify as well. Fees from target groups, sponsorships of private corporations, grants from philanthropies, and individual charitable contributions all exist within the field, usually coming to rest in organizations that are playing identified roles in the implementation system. Other nonfinancial implementation resources are also present in policy fields and can be invested to yield other implementation resources for the field.

Taking the time to understand the operative policy tools and implementation resources is important for understanding the policy field. This is because in an implementation system, many different policy tools often are applied toward achieving the same policy outcome, and sometimes they work at cross-purposes. For example, in providing K–12 education, federal and state officials use an array of tools: direct government provision through school districts, contracts with chartering entities operating charter schools, grants to disadvantaged areas, social regulation to ensure that children with special needs receive adequate services, and tax credits to defray costs for some parents. All of these tools are in use in the educational policy field found in, for example, California and Texas. In the early childhood case, we see grants, contracts, and vouchers all operating as funding mechanisms in the Minnesota field. The QRS program itself is a regulatory tool, albeit a voluntary one.

Policy Field Map

Policy field maps are visual illustrations of the institutions and relationships in a field. Often many organizations have an interest in a particular policy or program implementation in a particular locale, and the relationships can be multidimensional. A visual diagram, even sketched informally, can be a helpful communication tool when trying to share policy field analysis with others. (Appendix B provides step-by-step instructions.)

The first step in visualizing a policy field is to identify the relationships among the institutions in the field. There are several types of relationships, some of which can be directly linked to policy tools or implementation resources. Funding relationships are obviously important, but there are other important ones too. Legal accountability may accompany funding but can also be created through regulatory or other legal mechanisms; these types of relationships often constrain an organization's ability to creatively respond to a challenge, so it is useful to identify these forces early in your field analysis. Finally, service linkages are important. They can relate to referral of clients or patients through the network or instances in which organizations work together to coproduce services through formal partnerships. Certainly many other significant types of relationships might exist in policy fields. Organizations work together all of the time to plan new efforts, have significant conversations, or conduct evaluations. They share locations or work with similar lobbyists or management consultants. In analysis, think carefully about the types of relationships that are important to understanding the program of interest. How do organizations work together to craft and carry out the key program elements?

Just as sketching an organizational chart improves understanding of organizational roles and relationships, a visual representation of the field can help represent the interplay between these structures and institutional actors.[38] When fully developed, these word-and-arrow diagrams illustrate the institutional relationships, the vertical and horizontal influence, and relationships within the policy field. Figure 4.1 is such a map, representing the early childhood policy field

Figure 4.1

Early Childhood Education Policy Field in Minnesota, 2012

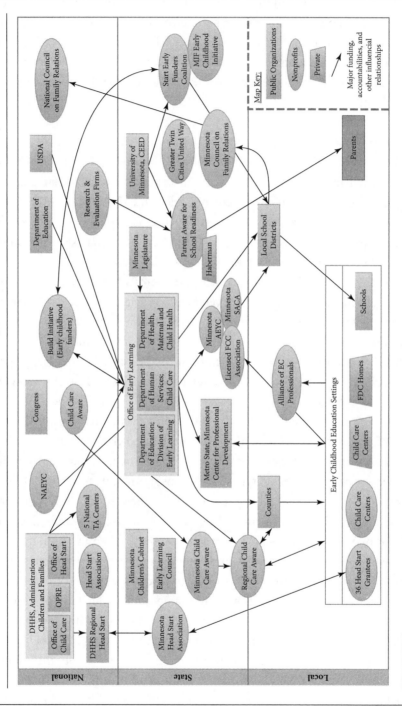

National institutions: OPRE = Office of Planning, Research & Evaluation; DHHS = US Department of Health and Human Services; TA = technical assistance; NAEYC = National Association for the Education of Young Children; USDA = US Department of Agriculture.

State: MN AEYC = Minnesota Association for the Education of Young Children; MN SACA = Minnesota School Age Child Care Association; CEED = Center for Early Education and Development; MIF = Minnesota Initiative Foundations.

Local: EC = Early Childhood.

in Minnesota in which the QRS program developed and was implemented. Like many other policy environments, many entities are involved. They correspond to the major institutions described earlier as playing essential roles (summarized in box 4.2).

The leader who created this map drew it to emphasize the significance of public funding streams in shaping institutional relationships in this field. This was important because she wanted to highlight that the QRS program cut across the historic silos in the field created by these distinct public investment approaches that had evolved since the mid-1960s: Head Start, child care, and school-based preschool. In the negotiations at the start of QRS, both Head Start and school-based preschool representatives were able to ensure their programs automatically received the highest four-star QRS rating without any outside validation. This argument held because of the belief that Head Start programs and schools provide high-quality services because of their own accountability systems. This created two paths to QRS enrollment and reflected the power of Head Start and schools in the field.

This complex figure also suggests the interests of a large number of nonprofit agencies in QRS implementation. The Minnesota Child Care Aware network is embedded in its own national and state professional network that supplies parents with information and offers training to child care providers. When QRS was launched statewide, the service organizations that had been working with providers were most interested in voluntarily going through assessment; the state's Department of Human Services regarded these regional nonprofits as critical partners in improving the early childhood market. A number of nonprofit advocacy groups in this field have an interest in QRS, and the Office of Early Learning needed to take them into account in crafting its QRS working groups. Other organizations provide important resources in the field. The University of Minnesota's Center for Early Education and Development carries out the independent observation of the child care center's pursuing three- or four-star QRS ratings. The Greater Twin Cities United Way and Head Start Early Funders collaborative significantly influence what happens through their provision of private grant dollars; both, for example, have invested in program evaluation and marketing for parents that are essential for understanding implementation dynamics at the front lines.[39] Private foundations' investments also enabled a Minnesota team of nonprofit, private, and public sector leaders to participate in a national peer learning effort coordinated by the Build Initiative.

The policy field analysis process provides a way to describe how policy implementation interacts with the mix of public, private, and nonprofit leaders and institutions in a particular context. Through this process, valuable information is created that can be shared with others in the field to help bring into focus the way in which field conditions both support and hinder effective implementation. The written materials can help brief field actors about the state of the field. The maps can create a visual to better orient others to the state of the field. As we discuss in chapter 8, both can be used as what scholars have called boundary objects—artifacts that allow you to communicate effectively with others across differences. They can be used to build knowledge within an organization and bring more knowledge and awareness to the field itself. Just like the proverbial blind man feeling the elephant, policy field actors can often lose sight of the larger institutional context and resources that shape so much of what occurs in complex implementation systems. The constraints, opportunities, and relationships among actors become more objective when seen through an analytical lens.

CONCLUSION

Policy fields are a critical part of the implementation process. They are where professionals articulate and interrogate their desired collective ideas about how to approach a public problem. Sometimes these ideas are articulated through formal public policy requiring particular targets, such as the expectation of ninety-day retention in jobs after employment training or minimum percentages of children passing standardized tests in schools. And certainly there are many times that people and institutions disagree about the adequacy or scope of these targets, feeling that only employment with adequate wages is sufficient or debating the validity of standardized tests. The diversity of policy field actors can create challenges in public understanding.

Policy fields are also sites where resources, always seemingly inadequate to respond to the challenge at hand, are generated and shared. Devolution in health and human services, for example, has led to significant variations in funding for early childhood, employment, and public health systems from state to state. Federal block grants and states' own decisions about investing state revenue lead to significantly different funding and regulatory approaches. The absence or presence of private resources found in philanthropic institutions, intermediary organizations, or professional associations shapes the contours of the policy field. When they are present, they can provide valuable resources that aid implementation through sponsoring conferences, blogs, or training programs. Privately funded coalitions allow knowledge to be shared and efficiencies to be developed.

Finally, information about programs or services is shared in policy fields. Sometimes there is pressure within the field to offer similar service mixes. Some theories suggest this pressure comes from a need to legitimize themselves within the policy field with private funders or other institutional leaders.[40] As we discussed in chapter 2, the rise of evidence-based program models creates additional pressure from funders to adopt what is documented to work. Others suggest that organizations learn from each other, offering insight and practices in the spirit of diffusing innovations.[41] And certainly mandates can be written into public policy, focusing attention on information about implementation approaches and strategies to the mandated model.

As strategic action fields, policy fields are significant for effective implementation. They are settings where implementation problems can be identified and either resolved or intensified through the actions of actors at the field level. Through interactions and negotiations, they often define the issues to be resolved at other levels of the implementation system. They also assemble the authority and resources that can be drawn on in the implementation process. In this chapter, we have described policy field analysis as a practical tool to help unpack some of these dynamics.

Organizations

magine that you are a program manager for a midsize nonprofit organization that provides job training services to the unemployed. Although you receive funding from the state to provide the services, you have considerable latitude about the way you structure those services. You recently attended a conference where you learned about a new evidence-based model for job training services that several other nonprofits have adopted. Should you adopt a similar model for your organization? You are an astute manager, and several questions come to mind. Would implementation of the new model require additional capacity, technology, or programming, or can you leverage and expand your existing program? Is expansion of your program in this way a priority for your organization, likely to garner the support of the chief executive officer and board of directors? How might other funders and stakeholders respond to your pursuit of this new model? In a nutshell, how does the new model fit within your existing organization? Organizational factors constrain and enable your decision about whether to pursue the new employment training model and, if pursued, how to design and integrate it within your own structures and processes.

If implementation practice is like gardening, organizations are the potting shed. They operate as integrators, interpreting signals from the policy field about effective practices, creating actionable objectives grounded in legitimate authority, and assigning resources to carry out the objectives. Decisions made by organizations at each stage in the process have the power to dramatically shape the outcomes achieved—intentionally and unintentionally. Rarely is a new organization formed to carry out a specific program or policy initiative. Rather, new programs and policy ideas are implemented within existing organizations with preestablished structures, resources, and cultures. The ideal plans of policy and program designers may be thwarted if they are not well integrated into the existing organizational system.

139

Borrowing from the language learned in chapter 3, two organizations operating within the same policy field may have very different social structures that influence their approach to creating change in the target population. Even if the organizations are operating under the same set of legislative policies and regulatory rules, they likely differ in the participants and resources that they are willing or able to devote to a specific program.

Understanding how organizations affect processes and outcomes is the subject of a large body of literature. In fact, entire disciplines in sociology, business management, and economics study organizational behavior. In public affairs, the design and management of public and nonprofit organizations—"public management" and "nonprofit management"—have become their own subfields, with textbooks and courses devoted to the topic.[1] The primary aim of this scholarship is to better understand the structures and processes of organizations broadly—public, nonprofit, and private—that interact in the public sphere. For example, public affairs scholar Robert Behn identified three big questions for public management: the micromanagement question, or how to manage in light of bureaucracy and procedural rules; the motivation question, or how to motivate workers toward public purposes; and the measurement question, or how to use performance information to manage toward effectiveness and increase accountability to stakeholders.[2] Exploring such questions can equip public and nonprofit managers with the tools needed to manage day-to-day operations and create effective organizational change in a complex environment.

For policy and program implementation, we care about organizations to the extent that they affect program formation and delivery. Studies of organizations and management can provide useful insights for identifying factors that may be at play, how they constrain and enable decisions made regarding a particular program within a specific policy context, and how they might affect outcomes. One of the criticisms of political science approaches to implementation is that the administrative processes critical to shaping programs at the organizational level are often overlooked.[3] Programs are not designed or implemented on a blank slate. The priorities and resources of the organization within which a program operates shape the contours of the program, for better and worse.

The ability—and willingness—of an organization to adopt a new program or to make changes to an existing one is constrained by the strategic action field. We've all heard stories of overly bureaucratic public agencies that are impossible for clients to navigate (maybe you work for one). If you are a student in a university, perhaps you've encountered this difficulty when trying to make a change to your schedule, purchase a parking permit, or even ask a question about your tuition payments. Now think about a program manager within that same bureaucratic organization who wants to make a change to an existing program or adopt an entirely new one. Perhaps she lacks the discretion to make the change and must secure buy-in from the agency director before proceeding. Difficulties in coordination stemming from the existing organization may not only delay the process but may make certain changes infeasible altogether. Navigating (and perhaps even altering) the strategic action field at the organizational level becomes a prerequisite to program success.

We begin this chapter by describing organizations as integrators for implementation, combining ideas and resources from the policy field together with the existing organization to assemble an operational program. We narrow in on two specific roles that organizations play for implementation: authorizers and service providers. In playing these roles, organizations bring together the authority, resources, and technology necessary to make a program function on a day-to-day basis. Rather than viewing this as a mechanical process, with inputs engineered to produce desired outcomes, we describe how the strategic action field at the organizational level creates the social structures that are observed. We show how these processes at the organizational level shape the core program. To conclude, this chapter ends with descriptions of tools that implementers can use to better understand the dynamics taking place at the organizational level.

ORGANIZATIONS IN FOCUS

In our multilevel framework of policy implementation, organizations occupy a critical middle position in the system between policy fields and the front lines. Organizations can be defined as "social structures created by individuals to support the collaborative pursuit of specified goals."[4] As social structures, they are strategic action fields, coordinating the contributions of individuals toward a common purpose. In the pursuit of shared goals, organizations provide a boundary for decisions, including decisions made regarding policy and program implementation.[5] They can create boundaries for making important program decisions by specifying goals, rules, and routine processes. For policy and program implementation, they play a pivotal role in filtering all of the possible problems and solutions in the policy field and integrating the structure and resources necessary to create an executable program.

Put yourself back in the shoes of the program manager considering a new job-training model. The organization where you work sets parameters that will shape your decision, such as alignment with your organization's mission, technological capacity, existing program priorities, and stakeholder interests. Sometimes the parameters are clear: goals are precise, technology is certain, and priorities are agreed on. Often, however, goals are vague, technology is uncertain, and there is little agreement about priorities. In these cases, the organization serves as a "garbage can" for making program decisions. In the garbage can model, organizations act as a conduit, bringing together the independent streams flowing through the policy field: problems, solutions, participants, and choice opportunities. Organizational decision makers attach solutions (programs or interventions) to problems in part by chance, depending on what and who happen to be in the field at the moment. As noted at the start of this book, implementers are more often institutional gardeners than engineers.[6]

In addition to facilitating the integration of problems and solutions, organizations act as assemblers, assigning resources and inducing the participation of staff persons, volunteers, contractors, and others to accomplish the key tasks. Certain types of functional expertise are required for the implementation of almost any program, including legal services and human resources, information technology, financial management, fund-raising and marketing, and research and development. In very small organizations, one or two key staff persons may perform these functions. Sometimes these services are contracted to experts outside the organization. Given that organizations often implement multiple programs at any given time, resources for any given program are often contested. Like any other strategic action field, the way in which the focal program in implementation analysis is situated within the organization relative to other programs, including formal allocation of staff persons and resources, affects the degree and type of attention given to it.

While organizations in the policy field are involved in all aspects of implementation, they play two critical roles essential for making a program operational: authorizing and service delivery. The literature on implementation tends to place the focus on one role or the other; however, both are equally important to effective implementation.

Authorizing and Service Delivery Roles

Policy fields are composed of numerous organizations, all contributing in different ways to a policy problem and its solution. However, there are two organizational roles highlighted here because of their pivotal importance in shaping implementation across implementation contexts: (1) authorizing roles, or organizations that devise accountability rules, funding instruments, and performance definitions, and (2) service delivery roles, or organizations where the target population experiences the policy or program. In some policy fields, a single organization may play both roles, and in other fields, distinct organizations may carry them out.

This distinction of these roles expands on the classic policy implementation literature. RAND analyst Paul Berman called attention to the local organizational context for implementation, or those organizations carrying out the programs on the ground, which he refers to as "microimplementation."[7] He views this level of organization as distinct from macroimplementation, where centrally located government agencies devise program parameters, similar to our concept of authorizing organizations. Local organizations, as microimplementers, respond by integrating the macroimplementation parameters into their own program, similar to our concept of service delivery.[8] This distinction of roles is also found in the multilevel logic of governance framework, where activities at the public management level include executive government agencies acting on formal political authority, and activities at the service delivery level are conceptualized as public agencies conducting primary work.[9]

The authorizing role is a distinguishing feature of implementation in a public context, as opposed to implementation of private sector initiatives. While public implementation may not begin with an official policy mandate or legislative directive, as was assumed under a top-down approach to implementation, implementation of public programs must demonstrate compliance with political authority, often leveraging formal political authority to bring about significant system change. The authorizing organization's responsibility is to identify and interpret the laws, regulations, and funding mechanisms in a policy field that pertains to a specific program. This process is not deterministic; different authorizing organizations interpret and integrate the same laws, regulations, and mandates in very different ways, depending on the dynamics within their own strategic action field.

For example, as authorizing organizations, state agencies have historically taken very different approaches to their interpretation and integration of federal

Temporary Assistance for Needy Families (TANF) block grant legislation into their own state welfare programs. Depending on structural, cultural, and political dynamics, some states have adopted "get tough" program rules, viewing recipients as deviants in need of social control, while other states have adopted more generous program rules that provide assistance to all eligible recipients without additional stipulations.[10] Differences among state agencies, as organizations with unique strategic action fields, affect how policies and programs are authorized. Authorizing organizations play a critical middle ground between policy fields and front lines in interpreting and structuring how implementation unfolds.

Organizations play an equally important service delivery role in the implementation process. Whereas authorizing organizations interpret signals from the policy field to create administrative and program rules, service delivery organizations translate such rules and signals into operational processes that are then enacted by the front lines of the system. In fact, the front lines of the implementation system are typically located within the service delivery organization. But it is not sufficient to skip over the service delivery organization as a whole and move directly to the frontline workers. As a strategic action field, dynamics within the service delivery organization significantly shape the way that programs are carried out, including the resources directed toward (or withheld from) particular programs. Variations in organizational priorities, structures, and processes can cause two organizations to deliver the same program in very different ways, likely with impacts on the ultimate outcomes.

At a most basic level, service provision quality can be influenced by organizational sector. For example, an entire body of literature considers the differences in service provision between public, nonprofit, and for-profit providers that implement the same programs, in areas such as education, mental health services, substance abuse treatment, and nursing home care.[11] One of the key findings from this research is that while for-profit providers may be more efficient at processing patients or paperwork, they may produce poorer results on process quality results that are less easy to measure, such as quality of care. This makes sense if one thinks about the accountability of for-profit firms to shareholders and the need to demonstrate profitability and performance on measurable targets.

In our minds, it is not sufficient to attribute service quality differences to a sector; in fact, some for-profit firms may provide higher-quality services than nonprofit or public providers. Other influences in the organization's strategic action field, such as funding, accreditations, affiliations, trainings, and even organizational culture, can lead organizations to implement programs in different ways, some more (or less) in line with public values.[12]

Authorizing and service provision roles are analytically distinct in an implementation system. Yet sometimes these roles are performed by the same organization. For example, in the Hardest Hit Fund (HHF) program, the state housing agency takes the role of the authorizing organization by designing eligibility criteria, setting funding parameters, and establishing criteria for evaluating performance. Local nonprofit organizations contracting with the state housing finance agency to screen applicants take the role of service providers. However, to help meet program demand across the state, the state housing also has in-house employees who take on the same role as the nonprofit organizations—screening applicants for eligibility. Thus, in some cases, the state agency assumes the role of both authorizer and servicer provider. In fact, this practice may allow an authorizing agency to be more aware of implementation challenges on the ground, seeing how authorizing rules and processes can impede or enable successful service provision. It can reduce what researchers refer to as information asymmetries, where service providers may have more information about the program than the authorizing agency, potentially leading service providers to have power over authorizing agencies in contract negotiations or administrative rule making.[13]

As should be evident from the discussion thus far, the roles that organizations play in an implementation are not formulaic or determined, but rather are evolutionary and adaptive, based on the logic that has arisen in the policy field. Therefore, while the policy field is a strategic action field, each organization is also its own strategic action field, with structure, power, and cultural dynamics that shape important decisions affecting implementation.

Organizations as Strategic Action Fields

Organizations are strategic action fields, with multiple programs and priorities competing for limited time and attention. Which programs get priority? What resources are devoted to important tasks? Where is the program located within the organization's formal structure, and how much supervision is required? These important questions are often the subject of negotiation between internal and external stakeholders. Effective implementers understand organizational constraints and priorities and can navigate these boundaries to create program change.

Some of these constraints are internal to the organization. For example, the needs of the program manager for a specific program may conflict with the overall needs perceived by the executive director for the organization. Certain functional experts may hold more power over program decisions, particularly if they have important skills and are in high demand from multiple initiatives within the organization. While the organizational chart may not list information technology (IT) staff at the top of the decision hierarchy, given our reliance on information technology infrastructure to execute programs today, they often hold considerable power over implementation processes; programs are often subject to the time lines and skills (or skill limitations) of IT personnel. Effective implementation management often requires skillful navigation to obtain needed organizational resources, a topic we return to in part 3.

In addition to constraints imposed internally, the external environment shapes and constrains what happens inside organizations. Organizational theorists often describe organizations as open systems.[14] As systems, organizations align participants, structures, and technology to accomplish tasks. As open systems, they survive and improve by obtaining needed resources from the environment. In an implementation context, the choices organizations make about programs are not only constrained by the people within the organization but are shaped by the entities in the organization's environment—particularly those that the organization depends on for resources. In this regard, the policy field provides not only resources for organizations but also expectations that shape the organization's selection of activities.

Organizations are embedded within policy fields, and the resources, regulations, and coordinating structures of the policy field directly affect organizations. Some of the factors that might be attributed to people or processes within the organization actually stem from constraints imposed by the external environment. Consider the example of the overly bureaucratic department within your university. Some of the bureaucratic constraints may be the result of internal structural decisions, but some of the red tape may stem from external regulations—for example, federal guidelines requiring specific documentation in order to be eligible to receive financial aid. In order for the university to remain eligible to process students receiving federal student aid, it must require a specific set of forms to be completed. In organizations less constrained by government regulations, other funders often have written or unwritten requirements about how an organization should implement a specific program. To the extent that the organization is substantially dependent on them for resources, it is likely to comply with the requirements, even if they make the implementation process more complicated or less effective than it would be otherwise.

For policy implementation, top-down directives in legislation or agency rules may prescribe that implementing organizations carry out the program or intervention in a specific way. These prescriptions may be based on political feasibility and a desire for public accountability rather than program effectiveness. But different actors in the policy field, governmental and nongovernmental, may hold conflicting expectations for the implementation of a particular policy or program. In their foundational book, *The External Control of Organizations*, sociologists Jeffrey Pfeffer and Gerald Salancik proposed that organizations seek to meet the demands of those entities on which they are most dependent for resources, referred to as resource dependence theory.[15] Thus, rather than making decisions about programs based on empirical evidence or even random chance, organizational actors may select the interventions most valued by their primary funders. This is commonly observed in practice. Often funders can have considerable influence over how an organization carries out a program. Even if they do not require a particular practice, their stated preferences will likely be influential with organizations that rely on them for important resources. The influence of every funder may not be the same—those supplying a larger portion of the resources or more critically needed resources may have more potential for influence. And funding sources that are more reliable are also likely to be perceived as more valuable, such as a government grant that is renewed year after year.

In addition to financial resources, organizations need legitimacy. They may adopt certain practices not because of regulations, funding requirements, or even evidence of effectiveness but to appear legitimate. As discussed in chapter 3, pressures for legitimacy can cause organizations working in a similar geographic or policy area to adopt similar practices. Specifically, under conditions of uncertainty, organizations may mimic the practices of other organizations in the field that are deemed to be "successful."[16] This helps explain why programs implemented by different organizations in a policy area may all look alike, even if the model underlying the program is perhaps not the most effective or efficient. This insight suggests that understanding implementation dynamics requires looking not only at funding sources but also at other organizations providing similar programs or services in the policy field.

As strategic action fields, organizations do not simply conform to the expectations and requirements of their external environment. If they want to be successful, they monitor and strategically respond to changing circumstances. You may be familiar with the parable of the boiled frog. According to the parable, if you put a frog in a pot of boiling water, it immediately senses the hot temperature and jumps out. However, if you put a frog in a pot of lukewarm water and slowly turn up the temperature, the frog will not jump out. Instead, it will adjust to the warmer temperatures until it is eventually cooked all of the way through! This parable has been used to describe the need for organizations to respond strategically to their rapidly changing environments.[17] If organizations simply adapt and conform to changes in the environment without taking stock of their own condition, they eventually may end up "cooked" like a boiled frog. To the extent that a program within the organization simply conforms to the way things are without strategically negotiating changes that lead to improvement, the program may also fall victim to boiled frog syndrome. In the next section, we describe how a core program is shaped (or potentially boiled) at the organizational level.

ANALYZING THE INTEGRATION OF THE CORE PROGRAM

As we mentioned at the outset of this chapter, we are interested in organizations to the extent that they contribute to the integration and functioning of a core program related to larger public policy issues. At the organizational level, this core program is significantly shaped by the rules and processes put in place in both authorizers and service providers—intentionally and unintentionally. Consider the take-up of Medicaid benefits by eligible clients in a particular state. While states' Medicaid policies are typically evaluated based on their generosity with eligibility requirements, a recent study of Wisconsin's system found that administrative processes significantly affected the extent to which eligible beneficiaries enrolled in benefits.[18] A change to Wisconsin's Medicaid processing system that required beneficiaries to document their employment status using a paper form, completed and signed by their employer and then mailed to a third-party verification center, was associated with a 20 percent decline in Medicaid enrollment among children and a 17.6 decline in parent enrollment in the state.[19] When Wisconsin subsequently moved to a technology-driven process that placed the administrative burden on the authorizing organization rather than the beneficiary, the number of eligible beneficiaries enrolling in the program dramatically increased.

Making a change to Wisconsin's Medicaid process was not a formal legislative decision, made at the level of the policy field. Nor did frontline workers who processed applicants on a day-to-day basis make the change. Certainly feedback from both the policy field and the front lines likely informed the problem and the solutions ultimately adopted. However, it was the authorizing organization—in this case, the state Medicaid agency—that ultimately made the programmatic changes that substantially affected implementation outcomes in Wisconsin's program. In the sections that follow, we explore more generally how programs are shaped at the organizational level.

Establishing Viable Options

According to the top-down policy implementation literature, the idea for program change originates in legislation and is then assigned to an organization for execution. In fact, program changes rarely come into being in this way. More often, an existing organization—an authorizing organization or even a service provider organization—brings a new program idea into being by pulling together the needed political authority, resources, and participants from the policy field. In this way, we see organizations in implementation as integrators rather than executors.

Sometimes the organization may be mobilized to take action by the passage of legislation or the decisions of executive agencies. The HHF program provides an example of this. Federal legislation, combined with a call for proposals from the US Department of Treasury, mobilized eligible state housing finance agencies to seek program funding. However, the decisions regarding the domain of the actual program, including the specification of the program technology and the target population, were left to the state agency to develop within the federal guidelines.

At other times there is no such impetus. In the Quality Rating and Improvement System (QRS) example, increasing pressures from the external environment built up as more states adopted a voluntary regulatory program; policy field leaders and foundations assembled resources first to explore program viability through pilot initiatives carried out by service organizations. As commitment to the program intensified, it was revised and ultimately came under the auspices of the authorizing organization, the Office of Early Learning in Minnesota's Department of Education.

Most typically programs are created within existing organizations. For public programs, decision makers must act within the boundaries of formal policies and mandates in any given area. However, as discussed in chapter 3, formal laws and regulations are only one set of influences that affect organizational decision making. Other influences include the market environment in which the organization is situated, the desire to affirm their legitimacy to important stakeholders, and the beliefs and values that make up the internal culture of the organization.

Organizations face what strategic management scholars have referred to as an entrepreneurial problem when exploring whether or not a program is viable in their context.[20] Managers make decisions to expand or maintain the organization's existing target market and programming. New program ideas will either be molded to fit with the existing program capacity and target market, or the organization will make a decision to expand one or the other. Market signals such as the profitability of new markets and potential demand for new technologies can play an important role in this decision. However, organizational decisions about viability are also bounded by a need for legitimacy. Sometimes organizations decide to enter new markets or design a program in a particular way not because it is profitable but because they are mimicking the practices of other organizations in the policy field that are perceived as legitimate. Some organizations may have a culture that is risk averse, causing them to stick with the status quo, while others may be more open to new ideas even if the ideas might fail. An organization that has been implementing the same program in the same way for twenty years may have difficulty shifting strategies. This does not mean that a new domain cannot be introduced within the organization; however, as a strategic action field, power and cultural dynamics have to shift as well to support the new endeavor. This often requires social skill on the part of implementers, a point to which we return in chapter 8.

Identifying the Logic of Change

Establishing viability options is only one program component to be decided. Programs must also be operationalized in a way that links together inputs and outputs to produce outcomes—what we define here as the desired change in the target population. Organizations act as integrators for this process, bringing together ideas and authority for effective practices from the policy field, combined with existing organizational capabilities, to create a program. From a rational perspective, an organization would select the intervention that best fits the problem and has been proven to be most effective at achieving the desired outcomes in the target population. In both authorizing and service organizations, managers often attend workshops, trainings, and networking events where they learn new models to improve outcomes for their target groups. And some astute managers subscribe to industry publications or electronic mailing lists that disseminate the results of research around evidence-based practices in their program area. They may even hire a consultant to conduct a program evaluation, identifying specific mechanisms that could be improved to lead to better outcomes. But how does a manager ultimately make a decision about whether to adopt or change an intervention within their organization?

For better and worse, the decision is often influenced as much by the constraints operating in the strategic action field and the capabilities internal to the organization as it is by the effectiveness of the intervention for the target population. For example, the administrators of a local school district may attend a national training where they learn about a new model to teach reading skills to kindergartners that has been proven to increase reading outcomes in prior trial studies. A purely rational administrator would do some additional research to see if this model is truly "the best" one, perhaps even convening focus groups of technical experts to debate the pros and cons. However, if you have experience with local school boards and the environment surrounding school district decision making, you might darkly respond, "It's all political." Both responses are partially correct, but they are also partially shortsighted.

On one hand, administrators need to ensure that the new model does not violate any laws or regulations regarding reading instruction at the state and national levels. Although official policies related to reading education may establish certain curricular requirements that require slight modifications to the "ideal" model, it is unlikely that the requirements are so specific that they would completely negate the model's adoption. However, administrators must also consider the capacity of their local schools and their capability for integrating the new model into their existing programs for reading instruction. Because programs are operationally housed within an organization or set of organizations, the interventions must either fit with the organization's existing capabilities or there must be the will to expand its current capabilities. This assessment of fit includes availability of resources and staff persons, but also the willingness and skill of program staff, including frontline staff, to integrate the new model. In the school example, there must be sufficient funding and technical support, as well as the ability to cultivate buy-in from the teachers for the model to be integrated successfully.

Typically program technologies that are more similar to the technologies already being employed within an organization have a higher probability of successful integration. This does not mean that such programs will necessarily lead to better outcomes for the target population; it simply means that they have a higher likelihood of being operationalized because of the resources the organization has already invested. And while perhaps discouraging from an innovation perspective, the reasons make sense. Organizations are often path dependent; once the authority, resources, legitimacy, and buy-in for an existing program exist, there are additional costs for introducing something new. This does not mean that program improvements that lead to more effective outcomes cannot occur. In part 3, we discuss strategies for implementation redesign that can increase behavioral change in the target population while at the same time acknowledging and leveraging the existing constraints and opportunities within strategic action fields, including those at an organizational level.

Coordinating Activities

While all levels of the implementation system involve coordination, organizations by definition are formally established entities for coordination. Through formal and informal structures, organizations provide a mechanism to coordinate joint action toward common goals. Figure 5.1 provides a broad overview of different means that organizations can employ to coordinate implementation activities,

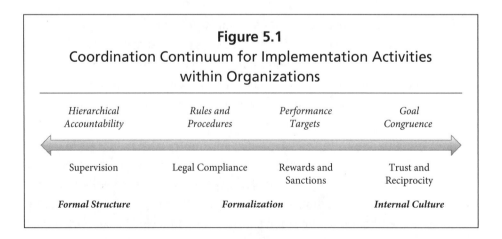

Figure 5.1
Coordination Continuum for Implementation Activities within Organizations

Hierarchical Accountability	Rules and Procedures	Performance Targets	Goal Congruence
Supervision	Legal Compliance	Rewards and Sanctions	Trust and Reciprocity
Formal Structure	*Formalization*		*Internal Culture*

ranging from hierarchical control associated with formal organizational design structures to goal congruence associated with internal organizational culture.

On the far left side, implementation activities can be coordinated through the formal structure of the organization. For example, by locating a program within a particular department, the head of the department becomes responsible for ensuring that the activities are carried out. The number of layers of supervision between the department head and the frontline staff carrying out the program can affect the ease of coordination. Programs with multiple layers of supervision may have greater difficulty with communication and feedback.

Coordination can also be accomplished through formalization, or the extent to which organizations have written rules or established procedures to use when making decisions. Rather than relying on the functional structure of the organization to coordinate tasks, written processes can be specified that provide the boundaries around decisions for specific tasks. This may actually give program managers more discretion over program design if they can innovate or adopt programs that do not violate existing protocols. There is a fine distinction between the presence of written rules and instructions and the extent to which employees actually refer to them when they make decisions. The former is more likely to be associated with needless red tape, whereas the latter is more likely to improve coordination.[21]

Another approach to coordination is through performance measurement and management. In their book *Reinventing Government: How the Entrepreneurial Spirit Is Transforming Government*, David Osborne and Ted Gaebler describe how government bureaucracy can be made more efficient by holding agencies accountable for results and outcomes.[22] Performance measures are defined as "objective, quantitative indicators of various aspects of the performance of public programs or agencies."[23] Organizational staff may be evaluated and even incentivized based on the extent to which their actions achieve the performance targets for a particular program rather than compliance with formal rules or procedures. By holding employees accountable for outcomes and performance targets, more discretion is granted to how the work is actually performed.

Finally, while formal structures, written rules, and performance targets can facilitate coordination, the informal structure of an organization can be equally important. Scholars have noted that goal congruence between employees and employers can substitute for formal structure and procedures.[24] Some describe this as a clan form of organizing, where the culture of the organization induces the workers to collaborate toward a shared purpose even if performance measures are ambiguous. This culture can be created through the socialization of newly employed workers or the selection of workers who share common motivations to join the organization. Public management scholars stress the importance of this sort of motivation for public and nonprofit organizations, where considerable ambiguity often surrounds performance targets.[25]

For program implementation, a rational approach would be to identify the coordination system that is best suited to the characteristics of the program technology at hand, in line with a contingency perspective.[26] According to this perspective, the type of coordination structure selected should fit with the uncertainty of the task and therefore the amount of communication and feedback that is required during the execution of the task. In general, if a task has low uncertainty, it can be "preprogrammed" using formal rules and procedures to coordinate completion.[27] As uncertainty increases, hierarchical supervision might be necessary to allow feedback about needed improvements or changes during task execution. Finally, when there is nearly complete uncertainty about the tasks or processes that are appropriate to achieve the desired outcomes, workers can be coordinated through compliance with performance targets or outcomes.

While allowing program technology to drive the coordination system makes sense in theory, organizations in practice are once again constrained by the strategic action field. How organizations coordinate program activities is a function not only of the type of program but also the guidelines present in laws and regulations, pressures for accountability and legitimacy, and internal culture. Rather than an organization having one system for coordinating a program, most programs are subject to all four types of coordinating systems to some degree: formal orders and procedures, legal requirements for democratic control, stakeholder expectations regarding responsiveness, and professional standards. In the public sector, scholar Barbara Romzek refers to this as the web of accountability that public managers must navigate when implementing public programs.[28]

This discussion demonstrates that the core program is substantially shaped by the organizations engaged in implementation. Improving implementation requires a grasp of the conditions present at the organizational level and how these conditions affect its viability, operationalization, and coordination within that setting. In the next section, we discuss some practical tools for assessing implementation at the organizational level.

APPLYING ORGANIZATIONAL ANALYSIS

Unlike the policy field and frontline levels of the implementation system, where we are charting relatively new territory, there are many existing tools to analyze different aspects of organizations and organization strategies. Rather than providing a laundry list, we focus here on those that are helpful in the context of policy or program implementation. For implementation, the purpose of analysis at the organizational level is to assess the fit between the program and organization, identifying specifically how the conditions at the organizational level may enable or constrain implementation. As we have discussed, the primary role of organizations in implementation is to integrate ideas and authority from the policy field together with participants, resources, and technologies. Both authorizing and service organizations perform this integrative function. In this section, we describe two sets of tools to help make sense of these factors at the organizational level of analysis: program process flow and an organization-program integration audit.

Program Process Flow Analysis

The program process flow analysis, a tool we have adapted from design and operations management in the private sector, is intended to aid in communication about technological processes.[29] It most often involves engaging others in assessing how a program is brought into operational reality in an organization. Because organizations are a repository for the group's intention and understanding, it is more efficient to undertake this analysis with others. However, the step-by-step instructions provided in appendix C can also be adapted for an individual to use alone. Since program operations happen in sequential fashion, it is often useful to begin by creating visual representations that capture the steps and sequences involved in a core program, a standard tool of project management. They can be crafted in various ways to illustrate the intensity of application, duration of interactions, and points of referral to outside services. They can reflect activities in one service organization or illustrate key activities carried out across multiple organizations or settings that must be coordinated to enact the overall program technology. They can be used in management and program refinement, as well as to build shared understanding and overall competency among a service team.

Figure 5.2 provides an illustration of a program process flow diagram of the activities and sequencing in our QRS case. It was created through interviews with frontline staff in a service organization and helps to identify where potential bottlenecks and challenges in activity coordination might arise. This core

Figure 5.2
QRS Program Process Flow

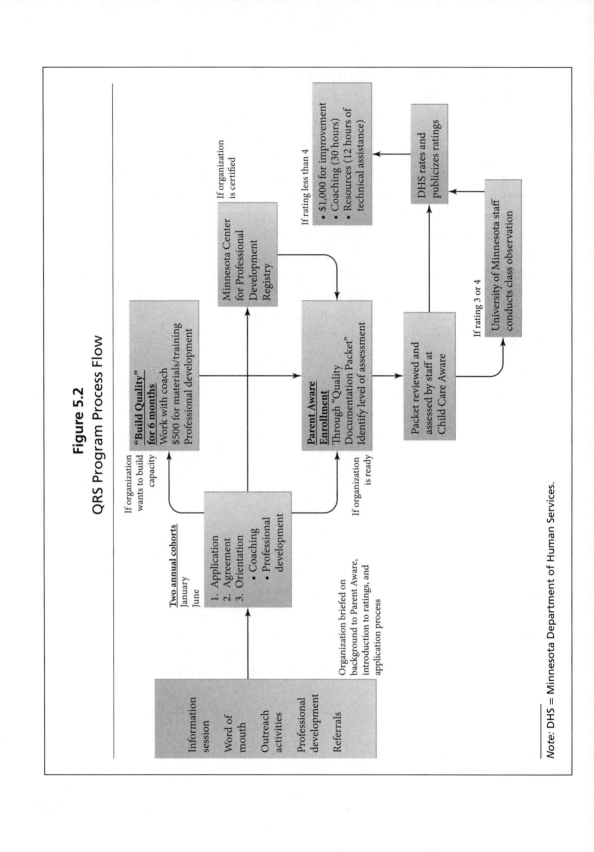

Note: DHS = Minnesota Department of Human Services.

program focuses on engaging early childhood education providers, both centers and family day care homes, in the voluntary assessment of their quality. It does not account for an important target group in the program, children's parents, who are making choices about the settings of early education for their child. Instead, this diagram illustrates frontline activities focused on engagement, enrollment, assessment, and remedial support of early childhood providers. Because it is a voluntary program, the service workers have developed an array of tactics to engage potential participants in an effort to bolster take-up rates.[30] They host orientations and direct potential participants either to enrollment or a remedial support initiative, "Build Quality." Providers choosing this option receive support from quality coaches, access to modest funds for materials or training expenses, and consultation with professional development coordinators for six months before actually enrolling in the QRS process. From frontline staff perspectives, the Build Quality route is significantly preferable because it allows them to work intensively with providers. In these coaching sessions, they can customize their intervention, suggesting alterations in physical environments and developmentally appropriate ways of interacting with children.[31] When providers enroll to be assessed in the program, they declare their desired level of assessment and complete a uniform quality documentation packet that lays out the standards needed to achieve each level in four dimensions: physical health and well-being, teaching and relationships, child assessment, and teacher training. Certain types of settings—child care centers desiring a three- or four-star rating—will have an independent observation of the facility conducted by the university's Center for Early Education and Development. The actual assessment of this document is made not from these frontline staff but by other managers in another nonprofit, Child Care Aware, and confirmed by the state-level manager. When a rating is completed, the relevant coach is notified. If a setting has not successfully achieved a four-star rating, they can continue to use the coach as a resource for quality improvement and access additional modest improvement funds for training or additional materials.

This diagram points to some important issues in organizational implementation of this program. Most significant, it reveals how the program logic is not at all focused on engaging parents, which seems to be a key implementation oversight. Parents weigh many factors when selecting care for their children: convenience to work or home, cost and payment details, as well as quality. The QRS program is premised on the notion that parents desire objective information about setting quality to inform their early childhood education selection. Yet as the program process flow diagram illustrates, interacting with the parent target group is not emphasized in the process used for statewide program expansion. To respond to this gap, a nonprofit supported with private funding hired a marketing firm to launch a digital advertising campaign focused on parents. But little is done to integrate these efforts into the core technological process; it was an afterthought triggered only when it came to the state's Department of Human Services to make the ratings public.

This diagram also helps make explicit the importance of attending to the transitions between activities to ensure seamless implementation. In a situation like this, where different employees and organizations have responsibilities for engagement, remedial support, and actual rating assessment, bottlenecks and miscommunication can result. In fact, as we discuss in more detail in chapter 7, implementation challenges could have been anticipated and managed more effectively if the various actors had understood more clearly their roles and interdependencies as illustrated in such a process flow.

Organization-Program Integration Audit

New organizations are rarely created to implement a program. Instead, most often programs are integrated and redesigned within the context of an existing organization. A tool we think is helpful for understanding implementation at the organizational level is an organization-program integration audit (OPIA). It provides a way for exploring how a program is situated within an existing organization. As should be clear by now, how a particular organization implements a particular program hinges on how the program relates to other key organizational operations and capabilities. An OPIA provides a concrete methodology for thinking through this relationship carefully. It provides a valuable snapshot for managers interested in making changes in implementation to more effectively achieve public value results.

Conducting the audit involves describing both the organization and program on some key dimensions. Then the fit or alignment is assessed and areas of potential conflict identified. Like many other analytical tools presented here, its use is often strengthened when it is done with a group because people can then offer various perspectives on organizational or program-level descriptors. However, it is possible for an analyst to work alone and use it to facilitate group deliberation about things enabling or constraining program implementation.

Appendix D provides step-by-step directions for the OPIA. After setting the scope of the analysis, it is useful to consider key factors from the research and theory discussed earlier in this chapter. It is often easiest to start by considering the target audience the organization serves. Sometimes organizations use different program technologies but concentrate all their attention on a specific target audience. For example, an organization targeting its services to a disadvantaged neighborhood may have deep knowledge of the needs in the community and tailor different programs to fit these needs. Other times, an organization may use the same technology across its programs targeting different groups. For example, a nonprofit organization may primarily run a soup kitchen to provide dinners to local homeless residents and use the same technology—the infrastructure and expertise for the soup kitchen—to start a for-profit catering business for private-paying customers. This can be an entrepreneurial social enterprise strategy for the nonprofit; however, it requires that the organization understand a new type of market demand and be willing (and able) to comply with those dynamics. Without proper management, this new demand might pull organizational attention from its core target audience, particularly if the new initiative is more financially lucrative in a cash-strapped nonprofit organization.

Given the prominent role of program technologies in implementation analysis, it is useful to describe the current organizational technologies in use. Each organization has a set of programs that build on existing technologies. When doing a program process flow analysis across the organization, there would likely be distinct visual diagrams for each of an organization's initiatives. OPIA draws attention to this comparison by encouraging analysts to identify how the technology of other organizational programs may constrain the technology of interest to this particular program. For example, if most of the programs administered by the organization use education classes as the primary mode of intervention, then the core program might also take the form of an education intervention—regardless of whether it is the most effective way to create change in the target population. Constraints in organizational resources might also influence how a program technology can be shaped; in agencies with robust information technology systems or skillful programmers, some tasks can be streamlined and more easily managed to ensure quality results. There often are incentives for organizations to filter new opportunities through their existing processes to capitalize on the investment already made in staff skill and infrastructure. If organizations seek to diversify or expand their technologies, they often must invest in this type of skill or infrastructure development.[32]

A third factor to describe in assessing organization-program integration is structure, including both the agency's formal structure and degree to which it typically relies on rules and written procedures to guide activities. Sometimes the location of a program within an organization can make it more or less able to access the needed authority and coordination to accomplish activities. For example, a program that reports directly to the executive director and has direct access to important support staff such as information technology or legal expertise may flow more smoothly than a program buried within a separate division of the organization with many layers between the program and the organizational decision makers and no direct access to needed support expertise. Furthermore, a tendency to rely on written rules and procedures for other programs within the organization may lead to increased formalization in the focal program, even if formalization is not desirable or even feasible. For example, a local public housing authority that typically processes rent payments for tenants may rely heavily on written rules and procedures. However, if the same housing authority also operates a program to provide supportive housing to adults with developmental disabilities, more flexible procedures may be necessary, a requirement that sometimes creates conflict between programs.

Financial resources are another critical factor in determining the alignment between the program and larger organization. Many private sector companies make decisions about expanding or contracting particular lines of business based almost entirely on the profitability of the business line to the organization. While profitability is not typically the primary motive for an organization's implementation of a public program, financial viability of a program is still important. Some operate at a net financial loss to the agency but are recognized as vital to the organization's mission so that resources from general revenues or other programs are used to cover some of the costs. Some programs generate significant revenue and can cross-subsidize other agency priorities if the revenue streams permit flexibility in the use of the funds.

This raises an important point. In public sector initiatives, dollars are not always equivalent.[33] Some funding streams come with few constraints, such as small charitable donations from individuals as a result of an appeal or block grants from national to state and local government. The funds can be applied to cover costs associated with program delivery, but the managers making those decisions have some autonomy. Some funding streams are consistent, with revenues that can be projected for years, while other streams are highly variable. In nonprofit organizations, these dimensions of funding—the autonomy and reliability of revenue—are significant because so often all of an agency's operating budget must be secured each year. More autonomous revenue streams that are stable from year to year are typically more desirable to organizations than restricted revenue streams with no guarantee of renewal or continued availability. If the program is profitable or has high revenue autonomy and stability, the program may be a higher priority for the organization because it either brings funding to pay for management or does not demand excessive management because of the stability. In addition, these overall characteristics of an organization's revenue can shape the agency's strategies and tolerance for experimentation or risk.

A fifth factor in the organization-program integration audit is culture, in particular the extent to which shared goals or values are an important part of coordination. In some organizations, a shared commitment to the mission and values is the primary force driving staff participation. New employees may be selected in part based on their alignment with the values of the organization, and workers may be socialized in line with the commitment to the mission and purpose of the organization. To the extent that a program aligns with this shared culture, it is more likely to be perceived as important to the organization and motivate participation; however, if the program does not embody the same values, integration may prove difficult. In agencies serving low-income people, for example, managers may ask staff to reflect on their perceptions of the causes of poverty during hiring interviews. Yet certainly not all organizations are bound together by a strong sense of culture or shared values, and workers may not be motivated to participate because of the organization's mission. This can also adversely influence program implementation because there are few shared values or motivations to tap into among staff members.

A final factor in an analysis of organization and program integration is the key external relationships important to the program being implemented. Obviously organizations have many relationships—with board members, funders, partner agencies, and competitors. From the vantage point of senior managers, certain relationships are essential. Sometimes these relationships are the same as those important to program implementation, such as large funders or legislative authorizers, but other times they might be quite different. Describing this alignment or disjuncture is another way to understand how day-to-day organizational operations are significant in shaping program implementation.

By exploring these factors, and engaging others in discussion of the OPIA as described in appendix D, implementers can better understand the significant strengths and constraints. Without sustained organizational commitment, the best-designed program with innovative strategies will not be able to create desired change in the target population.

CONCLUSION

In this chapter, we have described the role of organizations in the implementation process. Organizations act as integrators, bringing ideas and authority about practices that are perceived to be effective and legitimate together with organizational resources and structures to create an operational program. While there are many types of organizations in a given policy field, two roles are particularly important for program integration, authorizing and service delivery, although these roles are not necessarily mutually exclusive.

As strategic action fields, organizations have existing social structures that can significantly shape the core program. They tend to operate more than one program at a time and therefore must make decisions about where and how to direct limited resources. The focal program from an implementation perspective may or may not be the top agency priority. Decisions made regarding the viability, logic of change, and coordination structure for the focal program often take into account the organization's overall portfolio and existing social structure and dynamics within the agency. An understanding of the step-by-step operationalization of the core program and its fit within the larger organization can help implementers better understand why a given initiative is carried out in a particular way. In this chapter, we have described some tools to help facilitate this sort of analysis. Understanding the current conditions is the first step to creating lasting change.

chapter SIX

Front Lines

The front lines of policy and program implementation are quite important and distinct from the other levels in the system. Think about your own diverse experiences as someone who has benefited from public policy. What was it like to sit in an eighth-grade classroom in a public or a private school? Although you didn't know it then, if you were in a public school, public policies and programs shaped the math curriculum, size and condition of the classroom, teacher training, compensation, performance assessment, and availability of electives such as physical education and art. If you attended a private charter school, many of these elements were spelled out in a contract between the nonprofit chartered organization and the local school district. If you attended a private school, organizational leaders had more latitude but also received tax relief to support their operations.

As a student, you had little awareness of these larger forces. Certainly you didn't understand that to policy professionals, you were considered the "target population" of education policy. But by eighth grade, you might have understood that some schools, as organizations, had different resources than yours. When you talked with your cousins or went to event competitions, you could see that some schools were better kept and others a bit more ragged around the edges. You might have heard stories of better information technology resources—some classes had Smart boards, other kids had access to iPads. Because of the importance of standardized testing, you also likely understood that the annual achievement assessments were significant to your teacher and principal. But undoubtedly, you experienced these factors as secondary to your experience in the classroom. That reality was shaped by other things: your respect for the teacher, access to learning aids like special books, field trips, and a host of other things beyond the classroom—your friends, the extracurricular activities available, and the stability of your home.

Your experience as an eighth grader also was fundamentally different from your experience as a patient during a routine visit to the doctor's office, as a driver getting your automobile plates renewed, or as a student applying for federal loans. In all of these instances, though, you were the beneficiary of public policy, the target group of policy intervention. Your experience was directly and indirectly shaped by implementation decisions and structures at the policy field and organizational levels. Yet the particulars of what happened to you—did you really master basic geometry in eighth grade, wait through endless routine medical tests, quickly renew your plates, or experience frustration when the web-based loan application crashed—were more directly influenced by the unique implementation dynamics at the frontline level.

From a business orientation, implementation front lines are viewed as customer service. Analysts investigate the service encounter and consider how to best achieve the gold standard goal of flawless performance; in pursuit of this quality result, considerable management attention is often paid to equipping frontline employees with training, information, and tools to approach this goal.[1] Most generally, quality service is determined by the comparison customers make between their expectations and what actually happens. While many customers care about the technical quality (does the provider actually know the most effective means of dealing with the problem?), interestingly, they care as much about the functional quality (how the service is delivered). By learning more about customers' expectations and their overall satisfaction, managers seek to align frontline service delivery activities with these expectations.[2] As we will see, these assumptions are quite different from the ideology that is shaping directives given to frontline staff implementing many public programs. Although the rhetoric of customer service may be employed, the modification and customization of service interaction is not encouraged.

In the United States, a signature of the Clinton administration was the National Partnership for Reinventing Government, which focused on administrative reform throughout the national government to "work better and cost less." Two of their main strategies were to cut red tape and put customers first. This reframing of citizens as "customers" was bolstered by stories of local and state governments embracing this approach shared in popular books like *Reinventing Government*.[3] Positively, this turn emphasized that public services should focus on understanding, responding to, and providing high-quality interaction and service to target groups. Yet reducing citizens to "customers" creates practical challenges. As consumers, people possess no responsibilities other than contributing their financial resources in exchange for goods and services. When carried to its logical conclusion, seeing citizens as customers limits their sense of responsibility and makes it difficult for a vibrant public arena to thrive.[4] As the iconic business scholar Henry Mintzberg astutely noted: "I am not a mere customer of my government, thank you. I expect something more than arm's-length trading [controlled by the forces of supply and demand] and something less than the encouragement to consume . . . I am a citizen, with rights that go far beyond those of customers."[5]

The front lines of policy and program implementation play a more significant role than would be suggested by a customer service orientation. Frontline workers make decisions every day that have a direct impact on outcomes, often in fundamental ways. In 1980, Michael Lipsky drew attention to the people who work at the front lines of public services by labeling them "street-level bureaucrats."[6] The terminology has stuck. Street-level bureaucrats, employed by both public and private organizations, do the work of policy delivery. They provide immunizations, patrol national borders, educate children, and monitor the pollution of factories. Yet there are fundamental tensions inherent at this level of implementation systems. From Lipsky's study of teachers, welfare workers, and police officers, he concludes, "Street-level bureaucrats often spend their work lives in a corrupted world of service. They believe themselves to be doing the best they can under adverse circumstances, and they develop techniques to salvage service and decision-making values within the limits imposed upon them by the structure of the work."[7] They want to respond to clients', students', and patients' needs but face constraints.

And some public programs do not have people who work for public or nonprofit organizations at the street level. Instead, the target group interacts with online application forms or automated service lines or contracts directly with professionals who can help them with policy compliance, such as accountants at tax time. Analyzing implementation at the front lines requires bringing the specific context into focus and exploring the motivations and behaviors of the target group, the realities of frontline staff or design of alternative delivery methods, and the interactions that influence the achievement of policy or program goals.

In this chapter, we begin by describing frontline conditions and the necessary but sometimes contested nature of worker discretion. We then bring front lines into greater focus by situating the activity that takes place within the context of a strategic action field and describing how target groups are socially constructed by the implementation system. We move to the core of implementation analysis, unpacking how the program is shaped at the front lines of the implementation system. We conclude by describing helpful tools that implementers can use to make sense of frontline conditions in a particular policy or program.

FRONT LINES IN FOCUS

The front lines of implementation systems are where the program is enacted for the target population. Sometimes this occurs through direct interactions between frontline workers and target group members. At other times frontline workers operate behind the scenes, processing paperwork or carrying out organizational processes that affect the target population. From an implementation perspective, front lines are often described in terms of the amount of discretion, or independent judgment, that frontline workers have over program decisions.[8] Some frontline workers, such as post office employees delivering mail, have relatively routine, programmed tasks that may not require much independent judgment. Other frontline workers, such as guidance counselors in a school investigating potential child abuse, may have to use considerable judgment when making decisions related to their work. Discretion can apply to decision making about both process (what activities should be undertaken) and outcomes (what goals should be achieved).

As illustrated in table 6.1, for our purposes and interest in implementation, the predictability of tasks and means that supervisors use to direct frontline activities vary along a continuum. On one end are professionals who must exert considerable judgment in customizing technology to particular situations, such as mental health counselors and legal services lawyers; the range of their discretion can include both what is done (process) and what is achieved (outcome) in particular cases. At the other end are workers who carry out largely routinized tasks, such as clerks working at the motor vehicle or Social Security departments; their work is shaped by rules that seek to standardize their responses to target group circumstances. They rarely are given formal discretion in either process or results but sometimes exert discretion in choosing among the vast number of rules developed to guide their work.

Table 6.1
Variation in Illustrative Frontline Occupations

Doctor	Teachers	Forest rangers	Motor vehicle clerks
Mental health counselors	Financial counselors	Medical technicians	Social Security eligibility workers
Legal services lawyers	Patrol officers	Vocational rehabilitation counselors	911 operator

← ———————————————————————————————— →

Professional Judgment and Codes of Conduct   Rules and Standardized Protocols

Customized Tasks   Routine Tasks

From a traditional implementation perspective, frontline discretion posed a potential threat to democratic accountability. Deviation from elected officials' directions in implementation was troublesome because both administrators in executive agencies and the staff who worked for them—the teachers, doctors, park rangers—were not democratically elected by the people.[9] In this way of thinking, discretion was something to be minimized, most often through the development of elaborate rules to shape decision making, even in the face of complex tasks. This idea led to reliance on procedural due process to redress mistakes and enabled the proliferation of red tape as a means for controlling implementation in public bureaus. Recognized as administrative processes that create compliance burdens without advancing the legitimate purposes,[10] red tape became almost synonymous with public organizations in practice, as well as in the minds of citizens.

In addition, economists and political scientists who perceived frontline conditions as replete with principal-agent problems voiced similar concerns about discretion. Because street-level staff members always possess more information about policy requirements than citizens do, agency theory predicted they would squander it to reduce their own work responsibilities. As principals, their self-interest was focused on bolstering their own power, manipulating the citizen-agents to make them do what creates the least amount of work regardless of policy or program directives. Yet empirical investigations reveal that explanations that depend on rules to eliminate discretion or see frontline motivations as determined by shirking behavior are not complete.[11]

Michael Lipsky's articulation of street-level bureaucrats offered an alternative interpretation, challenging the presumptions of either hierarchical control or principal-agent dynamics. Discretion became understood as an inevitable reality of frontline work, a means employees use to try to manage the requirement of their responsibilities within the limited resources they are allotted. Yet a somewhat unintended consequence of these coping mechanisms is that through exerting their autonomy, street-level bureaucrats interpret and apply policy parameters in ways that are deterministic. As Lipsky wrote in the Introduction to his book, "The decisions of street-level bureaucrats, the routines they establish, and the devices they invent to cope with uncertainties and work pressures, effectively become the public policies they carry out."[12] To clearly reject the past frame within public administration, economics, and political science that discretion was problematic, some scholars even encouraged recognition that core values could legitimate "street-level leadership."[13]

Yet some of the concerns with democratic accountability and principal-agent tensions remain. For example, frontline workers who engage people in processing operations such as corrections, law enforcement, public welfare, disability services, or 911 operations leverage the power of the state to transform citizens into "other" through the application of policy-based categories such as prisoner, delinquent, or low-income parent.[14] If this power is abused, citizens may be unjustly subjected to discrimination or even inhumane treatment. To the extent that frontline workers are stretched thin with limited resources and capacity, they may be more likely to make decisions that cause harm, intentionally or unintentionally. Because of inadequate resources and institutional constraints, public service provision is inherently unequal. Frontline judgment can be used for the good by trying to salvage impractical social policy through a customized response to client circumstances. Or it can be used to exercise state power over those who are less powerful.[15] But it is not random. Discretion seems to be influenced by the task at hand, the organizational setting in which it is carried out, and even the larger political or social value attributed to the work.[16]

While frontline worker discretion is helpful in understanding some dynamics relevant to policy and program implementation, the picture is not complete. For one, the focus tends to be on the client interaction or staff member in isolation, divorced from the important ways that the structure and process of the context shape what occurs. Second, a focus on discretion necessarily calls attention to frontline workers, paying little attention to describing or analyzing the people with whom these policy implementers interact. In many instances, these target groups of the policy or program are highly significant in shaping what unfolds as a result of implementation processes. In the section that follows, we bring the front lines into clearer focus by first describing target groups—how the target group can be socially constructed during implementation. We then shine the light on the frontline level of activity as a strategic action field, with a unique social structure that forms during implementation and substantially shapes implementation outcomes.

Target Groups

Target groups are the intended beneficiaries of the implementation system operating in a particular policy or program context. The target population is often defined at the policy field level and refined through eligibility requirements and operational procedures at the organizational levels in an implementation system. In some instances, there is not much ambiguity in how the target group is conceptualized. In implementing federal tax reform, taxpayers are the target group. In educational initiatives operated in national parks, visitors are the program's target group. But in social, education, and health programs, the particular conception of a target group is significant because so much hinges on the understanding embedded at the front line.[17] For example, in a program designed to meet the needs of teenagers, there likely will be significant differences in the actual program activities adopted if frontline staff perceive them as students preparing for college, foster care children aging out of the system, potential summer employees, or runaway youths. And while in actuality, one teenager might fit into more than one of these categories, the resources brought to create the core program are directly shaped by how the target group is defined by these categories.[18]

These social constructions suggest some fundamentally different assumptions about target groups that are often embedded in implementation discussions. As noted earlier, in the past thirty years there has been a move in public service provision to conceptualize target groups as "customers," evoking images of private sector responsiveness and customized services. Yet this notion implies that all people can make choices among service providers, access information to inform those choices, exercise the principles of exit, or voice complaints when the quality of service is inferior. It also underemphasizes their responsibilities as citizens. There are other ways too in which a customer label is not really appropriate, because the recipients are truly "clients" who are dependent on the expertise of a particular public service provider. Think of low-income people seeking publicly funded legal services or homeowners' interactions with an electrical utility. At still other times, target groups are really "captives" who are mandated and often coerced into participation, such as people pulled over for traffic violations or a manufacturing plant that is deemed responsible for water contamination.[19]

A proverbial challenge for implementation is ensuring the compliance of target group participants with a particular intervention. If target group members fail to enroll in a program or follow through with program guidelines, they likely will not achieve the desired outcomes. However, the analyst's own approach to studying this problem shapes what type of investigation is undertaken to investigate the cause of this problem. An interpretivist approach directly asks participants about their experiences, with the intent of better understanding and appreciating the target group members' experiences. Describing the methodology used in his study comparing parents receiving Head Start and welfare programs, Joe Soss explicitly notes, "I asked why reasonable people found it sensible to choose and act as my interviewees did. I sought out clients' reasons for considering this action more appropriate than that one . . . for drawing particular conclusions from particular experiences."[20] Other frames are explicitly more paternalistic. For example, behavioral economists presume that science can help identify what happens behind individuals' conscious awareness. In exploring why many households are entering retirement age without sufficient savings, behavioral economists note both human tendencies to procrastinate and resistance to going without in the short term to save for something in the long term.[21]

One analytical frame privileges investigating what can be learned from examining target groups' conditions and asking them why they do what they do. The other seeks to discover what forces drive people even when they might not be conscious of it. For those interested in learning more about implementation at the front lines, either can yield important insights. Both address an oversight in many of the past studies of policy and program implementation that paid little attention to target groups. And yet program targets rarely act in the way that policymakers or program designers intend them to, even when it appears to be in their self-interest.[22] How this behavior is interpreted by the workers in the implementation system can also have a profound impact on the remedies taken to try to increase target group compliance. And this interpretation is often socially constructed in the strategic action field operating at the front lines.

Front Lines as Strategic Action Fields

When frontline conditions are analyzed primarily in terms of discretion, one might conclude that frontline conditions have more impact in situations when workers have more discretion, such as the left side of table 6.1, where professional judgment and codes of conduct are more prevalent. Indeed, that was the conclusion drawn by prior implementation researchers.[23] Frontline factors were thought to matter more when technology is complex and policies lack specificity. However, by thinking about the front lines as strategic action fields, even rule-based frontline systems can have tremendous impact on implementation. The way that rules are interpreted and applied can vary significantly. Our approach to implementation analysis draws attention to the strategic action fields developed by workers operating at the front lines: teachers sharing frustrations in their school's lounge about new curricular mandates; mental health professionals considering the relative costs and benefits of integrating a new service model just as a new billing practice is introduced; clerks interpreting new regulations in motor vehicle departments. While there are certainly many differences in the topics and tasks of these settings, there are also key dynamics relevant to implementation analysis. As frontline researchers Steven Maynard-Moody and Michael Musheno so aptly state, "Street-level work is, ironically, rule saturated but not rule bound."[24]

In their in-depth study of the stories told by police, teachers, and vocational rehabilitation counselors about their work, Maynard-Moody and Musheno provide up-close and personal accounts of frontline experiences. Developing a sense of social identity and relating with fellow frontline staff within and across agencies is a central, defining characteristic of the work. This social orientation provides frontline workers with a sense of belonging and helps them make sense of their work tasks. While there may be formal procedures and processes in place, frontline workers often learn how to do their jobs by consulting and observing their peers. From a study of activities taking place at the front lines of public welfare offices, Celeste Walkins-Hayes emphasizes the importance of social and professional identities in shaping implementation:

> Identities—both social and professional—are the missing pieces in the explanations of the implementation of . . . public policy more generally. Our limited attention to the evolution of professional self-conceptions has caused us to underestimate the degree to which *how* street-level bureaucrats think of themselves—as professionals, members of racial groups, women, men, and community residents—shapes what they value, what they emphasize, and how they negotiate distributing the resources of the state to clients.[25]

Occupational and social identities are essential for understanding what holds things together at the front lines and understanding the sources of discord and division that might unexpectedly influence policy and program implementation. Because resources and authority are rarely distributed equally, differentiation by race, professional training, class, or sexual orientation is not uncommon.

Occupational actions also are fundamentally shaped by both the nature of the work and time. The coercive powers held by police affect their sense of their responsibilities, both on and off duty. There is never enough time to follow up on all potential leads or engage with all potential community members. Urban teachers struggle with whether their role is to impart learning or discipline students—or attempt to accomplish both simultaneously. They must make choices between learning new teaching approaches and providing case management.[26] Vocational rehabilitation counselors who see themselves as advocates trying to change the system still have to take time to provide support so clients can access employment and needed benefits. Time spent on one detailed case is time not available to spend on another. Welfare workers can either shape their work identity so they are social workers consumed with resource brokering, or as efficiency engineers focused on paperwork accuracy and people processing.[27] In the resource-constrained realities of most frontline settings, professional identities shape decisions, but time is always a precious commodity that requires trade-offs between daily reality and abstract ideals.

Empirical investigations of Lipsky's original ideas are consistent: frontline workers are agents who determine how they will apply themselves and what responses they will give to the introduction of new ideas. A study of school-based mental health professionals, for example, highlights that staff assess the viability of evidence-based practices first and foremost around competing time demands and the relative benefits of participation.[28] Counselors consider what they understood to be viable in their particular school setting. Their peers' understanding also significantly influenced their own engagement with and understanding of the new ideas. Like others, this study shows that the mechanism of change at the front lines is as complex as that at other levels of the implementation system.[29]

It is not that regulations, supervisors, and standardized procedures are insignificant. At the front lines, these forces are ever present like the office furniture or telephone system. Yet across studies of worker behavior, these structures are not particularly significant in predicting worker behaviors or relevant to what staff recount as most important in shaping their work activities. In fact, for police, teachers, and vocational rehabilitation counselors, part of the glue that binds a strategic action field together is their never-ending conflict with what they refer to as "the system." In their stories, "the system" is an undifferentiated amalgamation of other departments, other organizations, public elected officials, and the media—forces that are recognized as having authority to shape their work tasks within adequate information. Street-level workers, say Maynard-Moody and Musheno, "see themselves as moral actors working in opposition to the system and rarely describe themselves as part of it."[30] Although policy field actors and organizational managers often see frontline staff as agents of the state, tasked to carry out policy mandates influenced by a chain of hierarchical influence, these staff more often experience themselves as citizen agents bound by their own moral code. They see themselves "as professionals who know what is best for citizens, clients, and kids."[31]

There is good reason to see social structures as the mediating forces that shape frontline workers' behaviors. Just as we have discussed at other levels of implementation systems, authority and culture interact to create dynamic and often contested strategic action fields. But the day-to-day experience of frontline work is also refreshingly pragmatic. While policy field actors and program managers can think abstractly about the policy principles, target group characteristics, or flaws, frontline daily activities and social interactions create a clear understanding of what is possible for individuals in that context. Maynard-Moody and Musheno conclude:

> Street-level work is not antiseptic but personal and close. The emotional space created in street-level work and stories is best described by three pairs of poles: deadening routine and moments of panic,

chaos, and violence; benevolence and revulsion; and hopelessness and accomplishment. These extremes describe the range of worker emotions . . . But more than marking emotional territory, street-level work often shifts abruptly from one pole to the other. These rapid, unpredictable shifts . . . highlight the undercurrent of tension and apprehension rife in street-level work, which is unsettled, always churning.[32]

There is an embodied reality at the front lines of most policy and implementation systems. Certainly there are times of deadening routine, but also moments of chaos. Emotion and judgment are always present, even in the most rule-bound systems. There are moments to feel success and moments for hopelessness. It is where the fundamental tensions between policy generalities and a real target group member's particular circumstances come into focus.

Heightened awareness of these frontline realities should not diminish our concerns about some significant normative questions about frontline workers' influence on implementation results: What should be done when frontline workers undermine democratic governance? What occurs when workers discriminate against certain members of target groups and exert power that inhibits people from accessing services to which they are entitled? What happens when their discretion is applied to craft responses that are not best suited for achieving policy goals?[33] These are significant questions, and implementation analysis of a particular policy and program must consider them squarely. But program managers or policy field actors' tactics to address these issues should not be pursued naively. Frontline workers are agents who make decisions because of their own occupational identities and the tasks they must accomplish in the time allocated to do so. Their peer groups and pragmatic assessments of what is possible shape their activities. Both understanding behavior and how technology is shaped at this level is critical for appreciating the implementation process.

ANALYZING THE APPLICATION OF THE CORE PROGRAM

The core programs at the heart of implementation are enacted at the frontline level of an implementation system. Be it a smartphone app designed by program staff, a one-time encounter around mandated paperwork, or a recurring face-to-face training or support group session, this is the moment where policy and programs are experienced. In his work on street-level bureaucrats, Lipsky talks about the front line as the "zone of control" because of the significance of these service interactions in shaping what a policy or program becomes. Since the publication of his work, the sites of this zone have proliferated. While interactions happen face-to-face in public organizations, now often these interactions are under the auspices of private nonprofit or businesses charged with delivering public services. They can be virtual, structured by a website or automated phone menu. But each activity imagined at the organizational or policy field level needs to be operationalized and coordinated if they are to become anything at all. Unintended problems with take-up rates or excessive demand for services need to be responded to. Interactions with the target group members create pressure for refinements. This is where the means to create the desired change is finally applied.

However, at the front lines, these interactions can illuminate the fundamental tension between general and abstract rules of policy or programs, on one hand, and specific situations presented by a target group member, on the other. An unpredictable and unintended consequence often can emerge from everyday interactions—a fifth-grade teacher whose curt treatment builds resentment in his student, an unintended loop in the automated phone menu that frustrates the citizen merely trying to renew her license plate, a technical bug in a web page that crashes the federal educational loan or health insurance application. Frontline interactions can build engagement or resentment, enabling the changes desired through policy or frustrating them.

Just as at other levels of the implementation system, we gain considerably by unpacking how the key elements of the core program are shaped at the front lines.

Adopting Viable Options

Throughout, we have stressed that strategic action fields are embedded in larger systems with permeable boundaries, much like habitats in ecosystems or microclimates in gardens. This interconnection is often significant for how the actors operating within the front lines answer the key questions of viability: What do we want to accomplish? What are the basic parameters for how it should be accomplished? At the front lines, the basic answers to these questions have already been crafted. The target group members are defined in categories, which determine the distribution of public services and benefits. Idealized plans of program processes are usually articulated, and often even standardized forms or computerized tracking systems are created. Yet there are always sites of conflict and potential change.

Often discussions about appropriate interventions at other levels in the system seem to influence what frontline staff consider to be legitimate work activities. There is growing research to document this fact, including a study by Eve Garrow and Oscar Grusky about HIV/AIDS counseling.[34] In this study, frontline staff working in organizations with a "medical logic" and a treatment focus were less likely to do comprehensive preventative counseling than those working at community-based organizations with a "social movement logic," even when implementing the same program. In fact, frontline counseling in settings where this social movement logic predominated covered 28 percent more topics. The authors suggest the mechanisms through which this occurs, echoing our notion of what establishes viability: "Institutional logics may influence policy implementation by providing cultural and material repertoires that shape workers' understandings of the means and ends of their interests."[35] These institutional logics might originate from the service organization, professional associations, training, or conferences held by other organizations in the policy field.

In fact, there is a range of means that can be deployed at the front lines to engage target groups and secure compliance with policy mandates. We have illustrated these options in figure 6.1 for better appreciation of the choices available. At the far end of a continuum, target groups are engaged through participatory means to

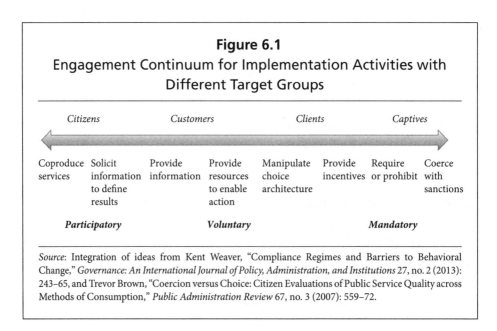

Figure 6.1
Engagement Continuum for Implementation Activities with Different Target Groups

Citizens	Customers	Clients	Captives

Coproduce services | Solicit information to define results | Provide information | Provide resources to enable action | Manipulate choice architecture | Provide incentives | Require or prohibit | Coerce with sanctions

Participatory | | *Voluntary* | | *Mandatory*

Source: Integration of ideas from Kent Weaver, "Compliance Regimes and Barriers to Behavioral Change," *Governance: An International Journal of Policy, Administration, and Institutions* 27, no. 2 (2013): 243–65, and Trevor Brown, "Coercion versus Choice: Citizen Evaluations of Public Service Quality across Methods of Consumption," *Public Administration Review* 67, no. 3 (2007): 559–72.

coproduce services and provide critical input to help define desirable results. This approach is common in local environmental assessment, transportation planning, and in some countries' social or health services.[36] In these areas, target groups are understood to be citizens with a legitimate stake in engaging to define policy or program activities and outcomes. As service users, they also might be engaged in long-term relationships with frontline staff as sources of substantial insight. At the opposite end of the continuum, target groups are engaged through requirements, prohibitions, or sanctions because the policy or program mandates changes they are expected to resist. Think about the arena of environmental protection, judicial actions, and public safety, where coercion of some is justified to provide safety or well-being to the larger public. In these instances, target groups are captives who are mandated to participate.

Between the two extremes is a full range of implementation activities. When target groups are engaged voluntarily, they can be given information and resources as customers who are able to choose the best option. Other times they are given actual incentives to induce compliance, such as quick refunds for filing taxes electronically or more graphically appealing automobile license plates for people donating to the state's natural resource fund. As behavioral economists suggest, policy rules can shape the choice architecture so that such options are the default rather than a choice.

The overall point of figure 6.1 is to stress that the concept of target groups and nature of engagement intersect to shape what are considered to be valid and appropriate from the front lines. It is not to suggest that decisions about activities along this continuum always are predetermined by decisions at the organization or policy field levels. Like all other implementation tasks, the decision about activities in a particular case can be negotiated between frontline staff and their supervisors. They can be resolved in how an intake process is carried out, directions on a form are worded, or designation of default options in a computerized form. Yet this continuum also illustrates how often activities considered in a particular case are limited by the way the program viability is assessed. Fundamental definitions of the target group and the nature of interaction shape what are considered legitimate possibilities in that situation.

Fundamental shifts in domain can sometimes alter the nature of frontline work. Consider, for example, transformations in the work and responsibilities of physicians. They are listed on the far left side of table 6.1 because their work requires years of specialized training in classrooms and clinical settings.

This background historically gave them unique authority to exert considerable professional judgment in determining the medical treatment of their patients. The variation in presenting conditions and patient needs required treatments to be customized. Yet the public health field has gone through incredible changes in the past fifty years: care facilities are more privatized and most are consolidated into large health systems; advances in science have created more pharmaceutical treatment options; physicians specialize in their training and are less able to comprehensively address patients' health concerns; and costs of care continue to skyrocket. In the larger policy field, the domain logic has shifted toward market principles in which physicians' judgments are curtailed by concerns about cost. Professional norms are being replaced by expectations of evidence-based treatments when dealing with patients' health concerns. This example illustrates how program viability at the front lines can be significantly influenced by trends, shifting authority, and culture in the larger implementation system.

Enacting a Change Process

In policies or programs where the behavior change among the target population is minimal, tasks can be standardized and routinized. Computerized templates can assist with structured decision making, and consistent forms can be used to document various steps in the process. At the front lines, though, a reality often becomes apparent. Implementation systems have a tendency to overspecify the change process through reliance on standardized processes and consistent formats, even when the process of actual change is difficult to predict. This leads to a disconnect in daily frontline tasks. What staff know from either experience or professional development is necessary to reach the target population is often not what is recognized in standardized forms and process steps. The entry of case records and completion of documentation is an administrative burden rather than something designed to support what is necessary to implement the spirit of the policy or program. In these situations, many of the critical decisions made by staff go unreported and thus are unknown to the larger implementation system.

Staff understanding of the logic of change can also be influenced by independent influences on their thinking. It goes without saying there are often people with diverse skills and educational backgrounds playing similar roles at the front lines. Formal education and training programs can establish professional standards and norms and reinforce moral codes of conduct. In medicine, doctors take the Hippocratic Oath. Psychologists and social workers' training programs stress research-based intervention models and standardized assessment tools, such as the *Diagnostic and Statistical Manual of Mental Disorders*. As we discussed, professional associations and purveyor organizations can play important roles providing implementation resources appropriate to frontline staff. Relevant new research, promising model programs, evaluations comparing treatment options: these resources can inspire and motivate professionally oriented frontline staff and be important sources of independent insight. Depending on the context, these resources can also be introduced to entry-level frontline staff to enhance the execution of their job duties. They might be shared informally or at scheduled staff meetings. However, what determines take-up of these ideas within the strategic action field is more unpredictable: it depends on the combination of authority, beliefs, and values operating within the front lines.

It is interesting how the relevant implementation indicators and challenges to be resolved and adjusted emerge from the particulars of an operation. In a voluntary program where intake does not happen seamlessly, there may be worries about take-up rates. As we will see in our discussion of the Hardest Hit Fund in chapter 7, initially low participation rates caused program implementers to adjust the intake processes to enable more people to access the program in Ohio. In programs where target group demand might exceed what is available, implementation activities often include careful screening to ensure that those receiving the program are indeed eligible. Additional steps might be created to actually increase the administrative burden to discourage some participants from engaging. This pattern is well documented in social welfare programs, such as Supplemental Social Insurance, unemployment insurance, and Medicaid, where the introduction of documentation or alteration in recertification processes directly affects program participation.[37] If key parts of a process are automated, then it is possible to more easily track time on task and monitor bottlenecks. Thus, the program parameters, tasks, and target group engagement all combine to create the issues that can be monitored, assessed, and adjusted at the front lines depending on how the change process is attempted.

Coordinating Activities

Finally, important decisions about activity coordination and sequencing come into focus at the front lines, again bringing a concreteness to implementation and showcasing how organizational management is very influential in shaping what actually is implemented. Does one staff member deliver the program in its entirety to one target group member, or do different staff members deliver different parts of the program in sequential steps? Does implementation involve coordinating among a multidisciplinary team that might not always agree about the problem or solution in a case? Are tasks distributed across multiple organizations so that information technology infrastructures must be in place or referral processes developed? The decisions on these questions of how tasks are sequenced and aligned is a central aspect of how the core program is applied at the front lines.

If the front line is found in one hierarchy, responsibility for answering these questions is in part resolved within the formal chain of command. Supervisors set up job responsibilities and accountability systems. Formalized rules and forms are developed, and automated systems for information sharing are created. In some interagency partnerships, similar tools can be deployed to help coordinate the activities of staff across various settings, even over great distances.

One common way to attempt to coordinate frontline work is through performance targets and incentives, crafting very specific measures that program managers or whole teams regularly assess. When staff are told their work is focused on achieving particular goals—helping job seekers find jobs, teaching so that children succeed at standardized tests, picking up the trash in public parks—it sends a strong signal about what is desired in implementation. In some fields, financial incentives are added to these goals. In police departments, officers are encouraged to meet targets for reduced crime in their precincts or geographic areas; in some school systems, teachers receive performance bonuses when their students do well on standardized tests. Yet considerable research questions the efficacy of these techniques because of the unintended consequences that often result.[38]

There are other questions raised about the challenges of relying too extensively on performance measures. Cream skimming is the incentive that frontline staff have to provide more help to those target group members who are most likely to be successful, to decrease the amount of effort required to effectively count someone a successful program recipient. In other words, frontline workers select the cream at the top of the milk bucket because they help satisfy the short-term requirements of performance measurement rather than the longer-term policy outcomes. Examples are teachers who concentrate their attention on the best students and workforce development programs moving easy-to-employ people into employment. "Gaming" refers to instances where frontline workers reactively subvert the desired intent of the measure because it goes against what they consider common sense.[39]

Gwny Bevan and Christopher Hood offer a chilling illustration of a performance management system gone awry in a graphic illustration from the British National Health Service.[40] In the early 2000s, the National Health Service adopted a goal to increase the percentage of patients waiting less than four hours for emergency room treatment. In quarterly reports, this performance target and similar ones showed dramatic improvement, presumably reflecting an increase in the responsiveness of frontline staff to emergencies. However, because of limited resources, there was little monitoring to understand what was actually showing up in the numbers. An independent study found that frontline staff were gaming the performance measurement system in many ways, depending on the construction of a particular measure. The most graphic example was the practice of having patients wait in queues of ambulances outside emergency departments so their case was not officially recorded until the hospital was convinced they had the capacity to respond to their needs within the four-hour target.

This example and many others demonstrate that incentivizing frontline workers to meet performance targets can sometimes inadvertently create implementation challenges. Adopting tactics to coordinate or incentivize frontline activities without appreciating the work being done and the context within which it is being carried out can actually undermine the program objectives. While coordination of tasks is fundamental to being able to implement program ideas, it is something that must be carefully designed in relation to the context and desired result. To provide concrete ways to apply these ideas to your situation, we turn to two analytical tools that help provide a concise snapshot of frontline implementation conditions.

APPLYING FRONTLINE ANALYSIS

The primary role at the front lines of implementation systems is to enact the program, providing the interface between the target population and the implementation system. While some of the details of the frontline interactions are programmed at the organizational level, they are experienced at the front lines of the system. This is where the rubber meets the road, so to speak. The intended target group finally experiences the processes and structures assembled and modified at the policy field and organization levels. The frontline is where all of the steps and processes of the core program—the throughput that transforms inputs into outputs—come into focus. Is frontline interaction consistent with the policy or program intent? Does it use available resources effectively and efficiently? What is the target group members' experience with the program? In our experience, we find that too often critical details are not thought through at the frontline level of implementation systems, leaving wide-open opportunities for misinterpretation and program subversion. In this section, we describe two types of tools that can be used to help make sense of the experiences and constraints at this level: the frontline interactions audit and target experiences analysis.

Frontline Interactions Audit

There are important differences across policy and programs in how target groups are described, engaged, formulate their own expectations, and conceptualize the overall significance of the public program to their lives. When describing implementation from the frontline level, it is important to clearly establish these characteristics and understand their implications. A frontline interactions audit provides a tool to systematically catalogue a particular policy or program along such dimensions. Appendix E provides a template and step-by-step directions for carrying out such an audit.

First, the audit requires that all assumptions and understandings about the target group are made explicit within the implementation system. Labels ascribed to the target group can influence how the system responds to their situation. The target group also has a degree of homogeneity or diversity relative to the policy or program intervention. All people receiving license plates have cars; all people buying lottery tickets are choosing to gamble money for the possibility (however remote) of winning. Contrast these examples with people who have lost their jobs and are searching for employment, with youth who are homeless and on the street, with young children in the public education system. People in these target groups have diverse skills, backgrounds, and orientations in relation to the policy or program objectives of finding work, locating permanent housing, or ensuring effective learning. Where there is greater diversity among a target group, it would be logical that the core program and frontline interactions will be more complicated than in cases like issuing license plates or lottery tickets.

The audit then considers how the implementation system has structured the interaction itself through platforms and intensity of communication. The medium of communication is important, whether or not there is a website application, a phone-automated information system, or a required face-to-face interview. The duration of the interaction is also important to understand to ensure that the contact is consistent with policy or program intention. Some programs require quick, routine interactions, while others are complex and occur over an extended period of time, such as daily connections among teachers and students who hope to yield generative learning environments. The nature of information and infrastructure to support communication also shapes interactions. Some policies mandate consistent information to be shared with all target group members, while others encourage customization to particular circumstances. Some programs require the sharing of technical information. Sometimes considerable documentation is developed to explain the program or provide assessments for target group members to reference it later. Think, for example, of colorful program brochures in early childhood programs or the technical documentation provided by city housing inspectors. These artifacts are tools that can shape the nature of frontline interactions. Cataloguing what exists and thinking about other tools that might be developed to improve communication can provide a more complete understanding of implementation dynamics at this level.

The audit also includes space to document target groups' expectations, since research suggests that while the technical and functional quality of the information provided is important, satisfaction with public service is significantly determined by it. In addition, because target group members do not always possess the ability to leave an unsatisfactory interaction in public service provision, we think it is important to understand how important the policy or program is in shaping target group members' lives. One way to explore this is to describe how information disparities between the system and target group are typically handled. The existence of the disparity is not a problem; in fact, it is to be expected as professionals work to deliver public services. For example, home energy auditors working on a conservation program clearly possess significant technical information about electricity, insulation, and water systems that homeowners do not need to know in detail. But because the program's intent hinges on its ability to translate information into actionable behavior, it is important that tools, such as a checklist the auditor can leave with the homeowner after the visit to prompt necessary home improvements, are operational to ensure effective program implementation.

The audit helps to bring into focus some of the key factors in frontline interactions that are often obscured. It also enables important conversations about how the key factors of interaction shape the target groups' experiences. It can highlight how subtle choices that frontline staff make are often quite significant in determining what occurs. In situations in which target groups expect transactional encounters, awareness of power differentials and modest adjustment can make a significant difference in exceeding expectations of customer service. A brief story illuminates this simply. One of Jodi's foreign-born graduate students recounted her experience of waiting to get her student visa renewed. Although there was a considerable wait time and significant consequences for the student, all was made better by the consular officer's manner in the short interview. The woman chatted with the student about her own child's study-abroad experience as she processed the routine paperwork. Although quick and transactional, this type of interaction was humanized by the officer's manner, which greatly exceeded the student's expectation. Although it could easily become routine for the frontline staff member given that she interacted each day with many student visa applicants, her efforts to be personable led to high-quality service interactions. It also supported the overall policy intent to engage foreign-born people pursuing higher education in this country.

The factors included in a frontline interactions audit—target group engagement, interaction structure, and social significance—shape frontline interactions in virtually all policy and programs. In the Hardest Hit Fund program described in box 6.1, we can see how they all come together in practice. The program is voluntary for homeowners at risk of foreclosure; this enables frontline staff to clearly see the services in a positive light, as part of a public effort to mitigate the significant problem of home loss among workers unpredictably hit by the Great Recession. The Ohio Housing Finance Agency (OHFA) invested in a standardized online registration system, the Restoring Stability System, which enabled homeowners to register for assistance online. Alternatively, homeowners could contact a toll-free telephone hotline to be connected with a housing counselor over the phone, who would initiate the online process. In either case, once the initial online process was complete, the homeowner was referred to a housing counselor over the telephone to complete the registration process, including the submission of documentation in person, by mail, or by fax.

While the initial registration online was rapid, the more prolonged interaction between counselor and homeowners to document the financial circumstances and ensure eligibility could take considerable time. In fact, there was often considerable drop-off between the number of homeowners registering online and those who completed the full application process with a housing counseling agency. The agency conducted an assessment of the reasons for the time delays at different points in the intake system and subsequently streamlined their system to improve the process flow.[41]

Box 6.1
Frontline Interactions in HHF

Target Group

Ohio homeowners who have experienced a hardship, such as loss of income, can voluntarily seek assistance from the HHF program. For reporting purposes, OHFA labels homeowners who simply enter intake information as "registrants," while those who go on to submit a complete application with verified supporting documents are called "applicants." This differentiation is important in regard to calculating the take-up rates of potential beneficiaries who sign up for the program. Not all registrants go on to complete a full application for assistance, so any take-up rate that considers the number of registrants who receive funding will be lower than the rate of applicants who receive aid, and both of these would be lower than the rate of all eligible individuals in the population unless all eligible households register.

Interaction Structure

To receive mortgage assistance through the Hardest Hit Fund, homeowners register online, over the phone through the Save the Dream hotline, or in person at a participating housing counseling agency (the vast majority of individuals registered online). Either the homeowner or the certified housing counselor initiates the registration process online through the Restoring Stability System (RSS). The RSS form is comprehensive in scope, with 175 fields covering borrower characteristics, finances, and loan information to be completed by the homeowner.

Once a homeowner is registered in the system, a housing counseling agency is automatically assigned to him or her, and a counselor is required to make contact within ten days. The homeowner and counselor then work together to develop an action plan that is submitted to OHFA for underwriting assessment. The housing counselor also verifies income, liquid assets, employment status, and loan status by gathering supportive documents and completing required paperwork. This documentation process can take significant additional time. If homeowners do not meet with counselors in person, they must transmit signed documents and extensive paperwork by fax or post. Together they create an action plan using a particular Restoring Stability program.

What is not immediately clear to the homeowner from these interactions is what happens next. Once the application is completed, the application is passed

(continued)

on to the underwriting department housed at OHFA, which provides a further check of adherence to eligibility requirements. The homeowner's mortgage servicer is contacted to arrange for payments or, in the case of some programs, to negotiate a matching principal reduction, lien cancellation, or loan modification. Once the loan servicer agrees to the plan, the reserved funds can be released for assistance. This verification and approval process can take several months.

Social Significance

Loss of employment and foreclosure can be a highly emotional experience for homeowners. Often homeowners develop a personal relationship with the housing counselors who assist them through the process. The economic value of the assistance is large, up to twenty-five thousand dollars in mortgage assistance. The homeowner likely weighs the potential value of the assistance against his or her perceived probability of being approved. Those who think they are not likely to be approved may not persist through the process. Although it is not the housing counselor who approves or denies assistance, homeowners may receive signals from the counselor that encourage or discourage them from continuing through the program.

This audit process provides a simple way that professionals within implementation can describe more fully the nature of how frontline interactions are structured. There is, though, another tool we developed to more fully describe and analyze current realities, pointing the way forward to implementation improvements.

Target Experiences Analysis

The profession of design specializes in improving users' experiences with products, buildings, physical settings, and systems. According to Nigel Cross, design thinking provides a process for tackling ill-defined problems creatively using problem-solving processes that are both solution focused and exploratory.[42] In this regard, it is often best applied when there is considerable diversity in the target group on factors relevant to their interaction with the program or a need to think outside the usual frameworks to conceive a new solution. Unlike many social science research methods that ask people to talk about their opinions in focus groups or interviews (such as what they like in their coffee), designers observe what people actually do (what they put in their coffee in the coffee shop) and put this experience at the heart of their understanding of the problems to be solved. This principle of user-centered design has motivated the development of a number of practical tools relevant to our interest in documenting conditions at the front lines of implementation systems. We have integrated the key ideas in the target experiences analysis (see appendix F for step-by-step directions).

The process begins with some systematic information collection from the target group using methods that probe their experiences. Because implementation is so often focused on operational concerns, there is a tendency to put all of the attention onto the point-of-system interaction. But there are often important things that happen before and after the actual service interaction. In the HHF example, people turning to the program had already lived through months of economic stress because of a job loss or reduction in hours. Many likely had used their savings, asked family and friends for loans, or made other lifestyle adjustments in order to make their mortgage payments. It was only after depleting all other potential sources that most people discovered this unusual public program. A target experiences analysis would begin by trying to understand the pathways that might lead someone to the program. It would showcase the significance of this context in shaping target group expectations of the program and highlight dynamics that might naturally evolve through frontline interactions.

The data collection approach taken should be informed by the heterogeneity or homogeneity of the group. Using the examples mentioned earlier, while all people receiving license plates have cars and all people buying lottery tickets are choosing to gamble, there might be important differences among those target groups relevant to a new policy being implemented—motivating larger numbers of people to contribute funds to natural resources preservation when renewing their tags, for example, or providing some citizen education during lottery ticket purchase. There is also clear diversity among the unemployed, homeless youth, and parents with school-aged children. In this first stage of analysis, implementers should familiarize themselves as completely as possible with the target group (and subsets within the target group) to understand their experience. Direct observation, interviews, and focus groups are all methods that can be applied. In addition, valuable information can be gleaned when an analyst poses as a member of the target group to experience the operation of the program from the recipients' perspective.

To share insights with others and set the stage for efforts to improve implementation conditions, personae can be developed to help illustrate key aspects of diversity in the target groups and how they experience each stage of the program.

It can be done in a just-in-time approach or varied under different economic or social conditions depending on the policy or program context. The intent of this exercise is to promote awareness of key aspects of the target group experiences that are obscured in typical daily operations of the implementation system. Promoting empathy for the target group can stimulate human ingenuity, and the implementers can begin to consider how irrational system dynamics can be addressed.

A frontline interactions audit and target experiences analysis provide concrete ways to apply the lessons from this overview of frontline conditions in implementation systems. The structured steps provide a way to document and share with others some of the important aspects of technology and resources that are present. This helps pragmatically to ensure that all important actors share consistent reference points about significant dimensions of implementation. This helps ground discussions and opens up the possibility for improvements in the system.

CONCLUSION

The front lines of implementation systems are critical because this is where the program comes to life and engages with the target population. In this chapter, we described the important role of enactment that takes place where processes and structures shaped at other levels of the implementation system are experienced by frontline workers and the target population. In the private sector, much more attention is given to this level of interaction, with a focus on customer service and satisfaction. Attempts made to apply these same customer service concepts to the public sector have been met with mixed reviews. Part of the challenge is that the customer-centric approach is not necessarily the answer; rather, there is a need to emphasize quality interactions across varied understandings of target groups—citizens, clients and customers.

In the public sector, there is significant debate about the amount of discretion that should be provided to frontline workers. Some view discretion among frontline workers as a threat to democratic accountability and equity in treatment. However, as Michael Lipsky noted, discretion is often inevitable in many policy areas, desired or not, as frontline workers cope with the inconsistencies between rules and procedures and the demands of day-to-day activities.[43] Rather than ignoring or suppressing this reality, effective implementation practice requires an understanding of the experiences of these frontline workers rather than assuming they can be completely determined by formal rules. In this chapter, we provide helpful ways to think about how frontline workers cope with their work situations, relying not only on organizational resources but also professional training and support from others.

Finally, we document how the core program continues to be shaped at the frontline level of implementation as strategic action fields with unique power and cultural dynamics. Beliefs and values about the target group, as well as pressures and incentives to meet performance targets, may shift the way in which frontline workers interact with the target population. Sometimes this leads to better outcomes, while at other times it may lead to unintended consequences. Astute implementers recognize that through system analysis, one can mitigate some of the places of tension and potential challenges to clear the way for system improvements.

PART THREE

The Practice of Effective Implementation

The problems of real-world practice do not present themselves to practitioners as well-formed structures. Indeed, they tend not to present themselves as problems at all but as messy, indeterminate situations[1]

[A] reliance on planning tends to promote strategies that are extrapolated from the past or copied from others. "In science as in love," someone once quipped, "'a concentration on technique is likely to lead to impotence."[2]

We stressed in part 2 that the existing roles, relationships, authority, and culture in networks and organizations fundamentally shape how implementation occurs. Our professional experiences working with public officials, nonprofit leaders, and philanthropic investors on dozens of projects have impressed on us the importance of understanding the context before developing new strategies.

When opportunities present themselves, though, one needs to have an explanation for why things exist the way they do and what might be done to shift important systems dynamics. "The way things are" is merely the way things are, not the way things need to remain. In terms we have used throughout this book, this shift of mind and skill comes through realizing that the existing dynamics within strategic action fields are malleable. The system evolved this way, sometimes through purposive design but more often through the accumulated consequences, intended and unintended, of past decisions. Implementers must appreciate what is but also consider what could be. There is a tension in holding these two realities at the same time. Peter Senge calls it a "creative tension," Parker Palmer the "tragic gap."[3] And you have a choice of whether to think of the tension or gap as an opportunity for problem solving or an excuse to descend into despair and cynicism because of all that lies between what is and what could be. This choice does not happen theoretically. It often happens in an instant when you recognize an opportunity for positive change and figure out whether you have the skills and passion to respond.

Part 3 describes the process of leading change in implementation systems. And as we will see, it is neither a linear nor fail-safe practice. The size of change need not determine its significance. Complexity theory stresses that small changes can be quite significant in altering system operations; eligibility criteria or program rules can be tweaked, websites can be rebuilt and promoted, and coordination procedures between two service programs can be improved. Astute observers also can identify more significant improvements: staff members agree to adopt an evidence-based program model and monitor whether it creates better results in a youth program; policy field actors solicit a local foundation to support network convenings to redesign service arrangements for people living with HIV/AIDS in light of changes created by the Affordable Care Act.[4] All and all, most implementation improvement comes through incremental adjustments and a commitment to continuous learning about what unfolds.

Once in a great while, though, there are large opportunities for change that disrupt the existing strategic action fields fundamentally.[5] Sometimes global crises call into question existing ways of doing business. The Great Recession required that new opportunities be developed and deployed to keep home owners in their homes; the Hardest Hit Fund is one of the programs that resulted from that crisis. At other times, a more localized event creates an opportunity: new evidence comes to light about racial disparities in children's educational outcomes, generating new interest among local foundations, and a new policy field is constituted to engage in conversations about what can be done. A new organizational configuration—a merger or partnership—enables leaders to reallocate staff and resources and adopt a fundamentally different program.

However, rarely do existing implementation systems naturally orient themselves toward change that better achieves the types of results desired by policy or a new program initiation. There are many competing institutional interests and established operational procedures that justify subversion of such action for more narrow ends. Short-term fixes and solutions that benefit a single organization or occupational group are compelling because they seem more practical, more immediate. Like proponents of collective impact, we know the only way this orientation will take root is if implementation actors recognize their own roles in creating the complex system and focus on the large results society needs. This shifts attention from concerns about self-interest and preservation of the status quo to a mind-set of problem exploration and learning anchored in a clear focus on the behavior change desired in both target groups and system operators.

We begin in chapter 7 with an illustration of how implementation change occurred in the Hardest Hit Fund housing program and the Quality Rating System early childhood programs. We describe implementation across the full system and use the interactions of power and culture within and across each strategic action field to explain what results. As we stressed earlier, the levels in an implementation are interconnected and interdependent, yet there are analytical gains made when we recognize the unique implementation work that occurs at each scale. While most people work at one level of the implementation system, these cases also showcase how helpful it can be to understand how the larger system functions. It allows one to recognize and be able to respond when opportunities present themselves to make systems change.

In chapter 8, we discuss the technical and adaptive components of leading change in implementation systems and focus on a number of critical questions:

What are the technical aspects to improve implementation? What is known and what needs to be learned about the desired behavioral change? How can activities best be aligned? Through consulting existing research and other investigations, this process is one of analytical inquiry into technical challenges. We also explore others: What are the adaptive challenges around improving the core program? How do we practice social skills to engage others? When can the culture and authority in the strategic action field help to achieve public value results rather than private aims? These questions are fundamentally about engaging others in adaptive challenges, in releasing the illusion of control and attending to what emerges from the complex system at work.

To be clear, effective implementation practice on the ground is not for generalists. While we have articulated concepts at a general level because of our desire to engage readers across all policy topics—environmental protection, public safety, social welfare, economic development, education—improving policy and program implementation requires particular expertise in the policy problem and in the settings involved in addressing it, which is why we must start with case-based illustrations of our multilevel analysis at work.

chapter SEVEN

Exploring Implementation in Practice

In part 2, we focused on describing what is taking place at each of the multiple levels of an implementation system. Within each level, there are multiple sites where people work together and shape what unfolds in the implementation process. And we described how the core program is often modified as it moves between and within these various settings and levels in the system. This descriptive analysis is important. It pragmatically helps describe who is doing what, and where, within an implementation system. But it does not assess what is expected nor reveal much about *why* activities unfold in these ways. Consequentially, it does not provide much insight into how one might intervene in these complex systems to improve implementation processes and results in line with public values.

For that, we must dig deeper still and consider the actual dynamics within the strategic action fields that comprise implementation systems. As discussed in chapter 3, we have come to understand that such analysis focuses on investigating how authority and culture influence and shape the technological core of a policy or program. In that chapter, we laid out our conception of these mechanisms, focusing on laws and regulations, market conditions, legitimizing practices, and beliefs and values. By definition, however, that discussion was somewhat abstract; a social system reflects particular conditions that are difficult to describe generally except in theoretical terms. Yet the interplay of these mechanisms of authority and culture within a particular context is easy to see in practice; these are the stories that are told all the time about how implementation plays out as people move the changes of implementation forward.

In this chapter, we illustrate these dynamics in particular instances, using the Hardest Hit Fund (HHF) and Quality Rating and Improvement System (QRS) cases. To do so, we pull from and expand on the case details provided throughout parts 1 and 2 and also extrapolate from the facts to add more life to the cases. As a result, it is important to point out that these descriptions are not research-based case studies or historical accounts (that would be rather boring!). Rather, we present them here as illustrative stories to help showcase how implementation dynamics unfold around attempts to address public problems.

To supplement these case descriptions, we also have developed a tool, implementation dynamics and outcomes analysis (appendix G), with a step-by-step process for applying these ideas to your own implementation case. Like the other appendixes, it provides a rigorous way to apply the analytical concepts to the actual situations you and others encounter. This is important. People working in different contexts or levels in an implementation system often have difficulty understanding what drives decisions at another level that have consequences within the whole system. Frontline workers do not understand what justification was used to create a form, brochure, or website in a particular way; managers in service organizations shake their head at the program rules embedded in a contract for services; policy field actors despair when learning that frontline workers have little belief in research-based programming ideas. Using implementation dynamics and outcomes analysis can improve understanding of what causes these events and lays the foundation for alignment and effectiveness improvements. Said another way, it helps to unearth the origins of significant management and programmatic decisions that are rational and salient in one strategic action field but may have unintended consequences in a different context.

In this chapter, we walk through each of our policy cases—first the HHF program in Ohio and then the QRS program in Minnesota. We start at the end of the story, with a snapshot of where the case is today. We then walk back in time, revealing how the core program was shaped by the implementation system to lead to the observed results. We wrap up each case with a summary of implementation challenges emerging along the way, assessing the extent to which the enacted system presented a threat to public value outcomes.

IMPLEMENTATION DYNAMICS: THE HARDEST HIT FUND

On April 12, 2012, not even two years after the launch of the HHF program, the *New York Times* ran an article about the program with the headline, "Treasury Faulted in Effort to Relieve Homeowners."[1] The article describes how at the end of the first year of the program, the HHF program across all eighteen states had only spent 3 percent of its budget, helping just over thirty thousand homeowners nationwide. Referencing a report commissioned by Congress, the article criticized the US Department of Treasury for a "lack of planning and leadership" and for failure to set "clear measures for the number of homeowners to be reached, and when." The report, conducted by the special inspector general for the Troubled Asset Relief Program (SIGTARP), was coincidentally titled, "Factors Affecting Implementation of the Hardest Hit Fund," citing challenges in TARP implementation, particularly at the federal level, that led to its apparent failure to deliver on its promises.[2] Even as of the second quarter of 2014, when the HHF program began to wind down, the number of homeowners assisted through the program nationwide was far lower than that which was originally projected. In Ohio, the initial target was to assist 63,485 homeowners; by the end of the second quarter of 2014, when the last homeowner was eligible to register for assistance, the program had served only about 20,000.

One could look at these numbers and surmise that once again, "great expectations in Washington" were dashed through implementation, similar to the assessment of Jeffrey Pressman and Aaron Wildavsky in the 1970s that launched the study of implementation.[3] And in fact, as the SIGTARP report demonstrates, many will come to this conclusion—just another federal program that failed to deliver on its promises because of faulty implementation. But we think that this is shortsighted. For many of the homeowners who received assistance, including those in Ohio, the program was a huge success.

Before the HHF program offered assistance, those who had lost their jobs were torn between making their mortgage payments and putting food on the table. Darren had been on time with his mortgage every month for the past five years since purchasing his home in Cleveland, Ohio. But when he was laid off, his bank told him that they could not talk with him about possible assistance programs until he was at least three months past due on his mortgage—at which point, he would accumulate additional interest and fees, not to mention ruining his credit record. Even if he waited until he was three months behind, there was no guarantee that he would be eligible for the mortgage assistance programs the bank could offer or that they would be willing to work with him. But Darren had heard about the HHF program through an advertisement on the radio. After completing the HHF application online and talking with a housing counselor over the telephone, a plan was in place with his bank to cover his mortgage payments while he looked for a job. No trade-off between paying for his mortgage and purchasing groceries. No need to pull his children out of school to move in with family to help make ends meet. No damage to his credit record that would prevent him from making purchases in the future. No foreclosure.

While Darren is not a real person, his case is illustrative of the many home buyers who received assistance. We understand that stories like Darren's cannot make up for the hard numbers that demonstrate a program that fell short of its initial targets. At the end of the day, public taxpayer dollars were invested in a program, and the public is entitled to know the results of how that money was spent. There should be accountability and when there is suspicion of fraud, investigations should take place to make sure that funds were not mismanaged. But if such an analysis is going to lead to improvements rather than finger pointing, it is important to understand how the implementation system operates at all levels—not just Treasury and the federal government, or the state agencies in Ohio and elsewhere, or even the interactions with individual homeowners. The results that we observe, for better or worse, are the outcomes of constraints and negotiations across all levels of the implementation system. Borrowing from the terminology that we have developed in this book, the core program and results are directly shaped by the dynamics taking place in the strategic action fields at the policy field, organization, and frontlines levels.

Indicators of Effectiveness: Results That Create Public Value

Before delving into the core program details and the dynamics of the implementation system, it is useful to first reflect on the initial intent of the program. In chapter 1, we defined effective implementation as deliberate, institutionally sanctioned change motivated by a policy or program, oriented toward creating public value results on purpose. But how do we identify whether the outcomes are oriented toward creating public value? As we noted in chapter 1, there is no single definition of *public value* that is universal across all policy and program areas. Rather, assessing public value is context specific, based on the public consensus about how a program ought to be carried out and desired changes that should result. Sometimes this is partially expressed in legislative intent. But many times the "public value consensus" for a specific policy or program is also shaped by interactions within the policy field.

The HHF program was authorized by legislation, the Emergency Economic Stabilization Act of 2008 (EESA). As with many other public programs, the legislative intent of EESA was not initially to create a program like HHF. In fact, EESA was initially enacted to stabilize the economy and housing markets by purchasing "troubled assets" from financial institutions in the United States that were at risk of going bankrupt during the Great Recession. In total, EESA authorized the expenditure of nearly $700 billion in federal funds; the HHF portion of the appropriations at its peak totaled only $7.6 billion, roughly 1 percent of the overall US budget.[4] Suffice it to say, establishing a precise policy intent for the HHF program was not the primary concern of EESA legislation. Related to HHF, the legislative intent for EESA was to "restore liquidity and stability to the financial system and to use Troubled Asset Relief Program (TARP) funds in a manner that, among other things protects home values, preserves homeownership and promotes jobs and economic growth, and provides public accountability for the exercises of such authority."[5]

The US Department of Treasury had broad discretion. In designing the HHF program, Treasury officials met with numerous policy field actors at the federal level to identify how a portion of the TARP funds could be used to directly assist homeowners at risk of foreclosure. In the end, Treasury's goals for the HHF program were intentionally broad: "to preserve homeownership and prevent foreclosure," thereby passing to states considerable authority in defining how to best use the funds to address the challenges in their communities. This lack of specificity in the federal program guidelines was later criticized as one of the factors that contributed to poor implementation.[6] However, the amount of flexibility was an intentional design; states were facing diverse challenges given variations in local economic circumstances and housing markets. In some states (e.g., Nevada), housing values had plummeted to nearly half of their peak amounts and were the primary cause of foreclosures. In other states, including Ohio, housing values did not drop nearly as substantially, but unemployment rates soared, contributing to large numbers of people losing their homes through foreclosures.[7] Given the nature of the problem, it was prudent to design a policy that gave states discretion in developing their own programs and allowing a more tailored solution.[8]

Therefore, to understand the public value consensus for the HHF program means moving from the federal-level policy field to the policy field within each of the individual states. States paid close attention to the signals from Treasury and federal legislation, but they also were charged with identifying their own public intent for their programs. As the recipient of the block grant funding from Treasury, the Ohio Housing Finance Agency (OHFA) led the way in setting the goals and targets for Ohio's HHF program. OHFA convened an interagency council to help inform the design of the state program. These agencies possessed expertise, which became sources of authority during the program design. For example, the Ohio Department of Job and Family Services with the Ohio Department of Taxation were able to provide data on the numbers and locations of unemployed homeowners in Ohio. These numbers were used to justify the amount and types of assistance proposed under Ohio's program.[9]

OHFA also convened a wider network of stakeholders, including political officials, financial institutions, and nonprofit housing and advocacy organizations, to help set the priorities for the program. In its formal proposal to Treasury, OHFA defined its objectives in this way: "Consistent with the purpose of EESA and TARP, Ohio's program, Restoring Stability, aims to protect home values, preserve homeownership, promote jobs and economic growth and provide public accountability."[10] Box 7.1 provides details about the program intent that were offered in the proposal, including guiding principles that were established and common themes emerging from stakeholder engagement.

Box 7.1
HHF Program Objectives

In Ohio, an interagency team was formed by OHFA to identify the strategy for responding to the HHF Request for Proposals (RFP). As specified in Ohio's proposal, the following guiding principles were identified:[a]

- Optimize the potential for sustainable results from HFA HHF.
- Use existing networks and infrastructure to promote and support programs developed with HFA HHF.
- Intervene as early as possible to increase the number of individuals who avoid unnecessary foreclosure.
- Maximize every dollar of Ohio HFA HHF by effective and efficient programming.
- Create a program that is transparent, and develop reporting and oversight that allow for public accountability.
- Disperse funds in a meaningful way, using data to support funding and eligibility decisions.

As noted in their proposal for funding, common themes that emerged from stakeholders included:[b]

- Create a comprehensive program that connects homeowners with resources such as job training and financial education to improve the potential for sustainable outcomes.
- Incorporate housing counselors and legal services into Ohio's program to help navigate homeowners through the foreclosure process and improve their chances of success.
- Provide assistance to unemployed homeowners through payment assistance.
- Make Ohio's program flexible to give counselors the ability to structure a tailored plan for each homeowner to increase the quality of individual solutions and improve the chance that the homeowner obtains a positive, sustainable outcome.

---

a. http://www.treasury.gov/initiatives/financial-stability/programs/housing-programs/hhf
   /Documents/HHFfinalproposal%204–11–2011.pdf.
b. Ibid.

One way to make sense of the varied public intent for the program is to think about how it situates on the dimensions of both system and target group change and on quality results and ultimate outcomes. Table 7.1 replicates the table that was provided in chapter 1 within the context of the public intent expressed for the HHF program. Interestingly, it spanned both system and target group change—both process quality and ultimate outcomes.

The ultimate change desired is both a fully integrated delivery system to help homeowners, particularly those who are unemployed, and significant reduction in foreclosure rates. These are ambitious outcomes for the implementation of a new program. In the next section, we consider how the core program was shaped in an attempt to bring them about.

Core Program in Action: How It Is Shaped by Social Structure and Dynamics

A variety of program technologies could be employed to prevent foreclosures, the ultimate desired change in the target population for Ohio's HHF program.

Table 7.1
Indicators of Effectiveness in the HHF Program

	Process Quality Results	Ultimate Outcomes
Change in systems operations	Program transparency and public account-ability; give counselors flexibility to tailor solutions	Use existing networks and infrastructure for HHF; incorporate existing housing counselors and legal services; maximize HHF funding with efficient programming; disburse funds in a meaningful way informed by data
Change in target groups	Early intervention and tailored plan to connect homeowners with resources	Assist unemployed homeowners in avoiding foreclosure; optimize potential for sustainable results

In fact, in response to the 2008 economic and housing crisis in the United States, many different programs were implemented at the national, state, and local levels to try to stem the rising tide of foreclosures. Some programs offered direct sub-sidies to homeowners in distress to help them make their mortgage payments. Other programs offered counseling and education so homeowners could better work with their lenders and navigate the mortgage system. And some programs funded demolition of foreclosed properties in communities, with the hope that it would stabilize housing values and prevent additional foreclosures. At the fed-eral level, financial incentives were offered to lending institutions in exchange for renegotiating mortgages for distressed homeowners.

Given all of these possibilities, Ohio, like most other states, centered its HHF program on providing direct mortgage subsidies to eligible homeowners. As delineated in box 4.3, Ohio's program initially offered four program options for homeowners, largely following examples provided by Treasury and also adopted by other states. Why was this so? Eligible states were given discretion through a block grant to design their own local program technologies, with ultimate approval or denial of state plans resting with the US Department of Treasury. This customization was a unique policy design element of the HHF program, distinguishing it from other federal foreclosure initiatives. While national policymakers rationally anticipated that technologies would be selected because of their effectiveness or efficiency at addressing the state-specific foreclosure problems, it did not always unfold that way in practice.

States certainly did take into consideration the underlying local problems to be addressed, but the proposals submitted to Treasury by states were not as different as one might expect. In total, more than sixty programs were approved across the eighteen states.[11] However, once the different program components are boiled down, there were really five different types of technologies proposed that were structured in slightly different ways across states, largely mirroring the technologies adopted in Ohio.[12] Part of this reflected the guidelines issued by Treasury, including examples of six possible types of technologies (not meant to be exhaustive). Part of this reflected restrictions on eligible uses of funds as interpreted by Treasury. For example, some states, including Ohio, proposed using the funds for housing counseling, job training, or legal assistance. However, Treasury determined that these uses fell outside the intent of the authorizing legislation.[13] Part of the reason also had to do with the states' desire to select interventions that had some track record of success or at least had been tried before. This sort of path dependence provided legitimacy and protection against future backlash if an intervention did not work as hoped. For example, prior to HHF, Pennsylvania had implemented a foreclosure program for unemployed homeowners (the Homeowner Emergency Mortgage Assistance Program) that states often referenced as a model for their programs. Thus, at the field level, constraints interpreted from legislation, sample guidelines promulgated by Treasury, and existing models of foreclosure interventions shaped the range of viable options that states like Ohio considered when implementing the HHF program.

By shaping the range of possible interventions, the policy field for the HHF program also simplified the complexity of the program to be implemented. Interventions intended to reduce foreclosures, the stated goal of the HHF program, vary significantly in complexity depending on what underlying behavior or problem is being targeted. For example, targeting the financial instability of individual homeowners may require individualized solutions and thus more steps between inputs and outcomes than interventions targeting the demolition of abandoned housing in a neighborhood. Both interventions may have the end goal of reducing foreclosures—the first by increasing the likelihood that the individual homeowner will be able to afford to make monthly mortgage payments and the second by increasing neighborhood property values and reducing the spread of foreclosures in a geographic area. However, it is likely more difficult, and perhaps less effective, to standardize and routinize processes for changing human behavior than targeting homes for demolition. In the HHF program, all of the initial programs approved by Treasury targeted the financial stability of individual homeowners. However, rather than starting from scratch with each homeowner to identify a tailored solution, each state identified a handful of different interventions in line with expectations from the policy field. In this regard, the process of working with Treasury to approve specific interventions reduced complexity and increased the standardization of interventions to be provided.

Complexity in the HHF program was further simplified by a field-level focus on outputs rather than outcomes. The goal of the HHF program is to prevent foreclosures; thus, the primary outcome is the number of foreclosures prevented. However, this outcome can be difficult to measure and is affected by numerous factors that may be outside the control of the HHF program. For example, if a homeowner receives assistance through the program and stabilizes her mortgage payments for two years but then forecloses in the third year, should her outcome be considered a success or a failure? Indeed, the issue of re-defaults among assisted borrowers has been a problem plaguing foreclosure interventions since the onset of the crisis. What re-default rate is permissible to still consider the program a success? What interventions are necessary to detect and prevent re-defaults?

Partly because of the complexity of measuring foreclosure outcomes and political pressure to spend down program funds, the output of the number of homeowners served and dollars spent has taken top priority in the HHF program. At the field level, Treasury required states to submit performance data quarterly. Quarterly performance reports primarily reflect outputs of funds spent and number of homeowners served, with some general statewide statistics on employment and foreclosure outcomes.[14] At the policy field level, other federal foreclosure initiatives were sharply criticized for assisting substantially fewer homeowners than projected. Thus, going into the HHF program, there was tremendous pressure to assist as many borrowers as quickly as possible. Treasury was under pressure to spend TARP funds before its authority expired in October 2010. The focus on getting funds out and spent took central focus as the key indicator of success for the program. Although this simplified the complexity of measuring outcomes such as re-defaults and foreclosure rates, there is likely a trade-off between interventions designed to provide the most assistance to the maximum number of borrowers as quickly as possible and interventions designed to reduce foreclosures and increase long-term housing stability. In summary, preventing foreclosures is a complex outcome requiring complex technologies. The complexity of the HHF program at the policy field level was reduced through standardization of interventions and a shorter-term focus on outputs—maximizing the number of homeowners served and funds expended—rather than on reducing long-term rates of foreclosure.

The core program for HHF was further shaped at the organization level of the implementation system within the authorizing organization (OHFA), within the service provider nonprofit housing counseling organizations conducting intake, and within the service provider private lending institutions that ultimately accepted (or denied) the mortgage assistance plans for the homeowners. The role of OHFA as an authorizing organization for the HHF program was not new. OHFA, like most other state housing finance agencies, had already been playing a central role coordinating actors in the state around solutions to the foreclosure crisis. OHFA had coordinated other similar initiatives previously and was seen by other actors in the state as having legitimate authority for the program.

The existing structure that OHFA had put in place for the early initiative, entitled Save the Dream Ohio, was both enabling and constraining for the HHF program. On one hand, it created a ready-made infrastructure within which to launch the HHF program. The agency funded nonprofit housing organizations across the state to provide counseling and legal services to homeowners facing foreclosure. An existing reporting and IT infrastructure for this initiative was already in place with OHFA's subgrantees, facilitating coordination and commu-nication among the parties. And the local nonprofit service organizations already had networks that enabled them to reach out to the target population. Therefore, although the core program provided through the Save the Dream Ohio initiative was different from that to be provided through the HHF program, the target population was the same: homeowners at risk of foreclosure. As noted in box 7.1, there was a strong sense among OHFA's stakeholders that the HHF program should leverage this existing infrastructure, funding the same housing counseling organizations to provide the HHF intake services and activating the same networks to engage the target population. Indeed, without this infrastructure already in place, it was unlikely that Ohio would have been able to pull off the HHF program under the short time frame of the federal government. In this regard, the existing infrastructure was critical to feasibility.

On the other hand, working within the Save the Dream Ohio infrastructure constrained the options for the HHF program, perhaps resulting in a program process flow that was not as ideal or behaviorally sound as it would have been if designed on a blank slate. The Save the Dream Ohio infrastructure was designed to provide counseling to troubled homeowners, not direct financial assistance. By legislation, the HHF program was restricted from using HHF funds to pay for counseling or legal services. Despite OHFA's efforts to obtain an exemption for this restriction, counseling services were not part of the HHF program. So while the HHF program provided services to the same target population, it engaged a fundamentally different logic of change.

This created a challenge within the service organizations as well. While their core expertise was in housing counseling, they were not allowed to provide that service to clients funded through the HHF program. Whereas housing counseling is more of a people-changing technology, the HHF program they were to implement (client intake) was more of a people-processing technology—collecting paperwork, verifying eligibility, and following up to make sure all necessary documentation was complete. Some of the counseling organizations lacked the infrastructure to process volumes of paperwork, creating backlogs and time delays for the target population. In many cases, it also created a tension between the program and organizational goals. To the extent that the HHF program did not make up a large proportion of the client volume for a given service organization, some service organizations were resistant to investing time and resources in a new program requiring more paperwork and less skill.

The lending institutions can also be viewed as service organizations for the HHF program, subject to substantial degrees of market authority. The decisions of lenders to participate in the program could not compromise their profitability or position in the market. Although the lenders had little interaction with HHF participants, they had to agree to any mortgage assistance that was provided through the HHF program. Mortgages are legal obligations between homeowners (borrowers) and financial institutions (lenders), with specified procedures for collecting payments and pursuing foreclosure if payments are not made. Because assistance provided to borrowers through the HHF program could require a change in the terms of the mortgage or servicing guidelines with investors, lenders had to agree to participate, so the program had to be structured in a way deemed acceptable to them. This was one of the problems encountered by previous federal foreclosure programs—it was difficult to get the participation and compliance of private lenders. Under the HHF program, working through state agencies was intended to help facilitate this coordination.

The large national lenders that service the majority of loans in each state have significant market authority over the implementation of the program, so there would be no program without their participation. National lenders preferred standardization, with clear guidelines to determine eligibility and available assistance, not eighteen different state programs, each with different technologies. After several months of individual states unsuccessfully attempting to recruit the participation of national lenders in their programs, a more standardized national strategy was developed, facilitated by Treasury. Thus, the reliance on existing infrastructure to implement the HHF program, through both the Save the Dream Ohio network and the national lending system, necessitated a more standardized approach to the program than was initially intended with the localized design of the HHF program.

Aside from the structures and processes put in place at the organizational level, the program is ultimately shaped as it is enacted at the front lines of the implementation system. For the HHF program, the target population, homeowners at risk of foreclosure, interacted directly with the program through a combination of an online registration portal set up and administered by OHFA and intake services provided by a housing counselor, typically over the telephone. The homeowner typically initiates the process by filling out a registration form (with 177 fields) on the online portal or calling an agent at a toll-free hotline who will complete the online portal fields on behalf of the homeowner. This is undoubtedly a charged conversation at first. The homeowners have been wrestling for months with the reality that they might lose their home. Somehow they heard about this program and with excitement began to explore the requirements—only to face a complex application process. After completing the application, though, homeowners are automatically referred (through the information technology system) to a housing counselor tasked to follow up with homeowners within a set number of days. The housing counselor then reviews the information submitted online either over the phone or in person and collects hard copies of documentation to back up the material submitted online, such as tax returns, paycheck stubs, and verification of unemployment or other hardships. The housing counselor then submits the completed packet to OHFA, which internally processes the application for eligibility. Finally, once a client is determined to be eligible, OHFA contacts the lender to seek its approval of the assistance.[15]

This is the frontline reality of the people process technology at the heart of HHF. The process can take anywhere from several weeks to several months. It is perhaps no surprise that many homeowners, even if they may be eligible for assistance, did not persist through the entire process. During the first eighteen months of the program, fifty thousand Ohio homeowners initiated the process online of registering for HHF assistance and about twenty-eight thousand appeared to be eligible. Yet only about ten thousand submitted a complete application.[16] This low rate of take-up was a significant concern for HHF program administrators across the country. OHFA made several improvements throughout the process to reduce the number of steps and amount of paperwork required from homeowners, even engaging external consultants.[17] It is difficult to achieve the ultimate goal of behavioral change, reducing foreclosures, if homeowners fail to take up the services in the first place. The application complexity was not a result of a desire to curb applications. Rather, it was an unintended consequence of the need to launch the program quickly with existing infrastructure.

In addition to the interactions with the paperwork and processing systems, the target population ultimately interacted with a housing counselor during the intake process. It was the role of the housing counselor to document the homeowner's eligibility for the program and to facilitate an action plan around the type of mortgage assistance most appropriate for the homeowner. Recall that one of the quality outcomes desired for the HHF program was to allow counselor discretion in designing tailored solutions for homeowners. However, given the need for standardization, some of this discretion was limited. A set menu of program options was identified (box 4.3), and eligibility criteria were established.

Despite this standardization, as frontline workers, housing counselors could still nudge homeowners toward options counselors felt were most appropriate for their particular situation. It is likely that the experiences of housing counselors in dealing with borrowers facing foreclosures—hearing their stories about lenders who were unresponsive to their needs and the impending loss of their home—may have fueled housing counselors to become advocates on behalf of homeowners. While the counselors' official role for the HHF program was one of an intake specialist, not a counselor or advocate, the target population was the same, and they heard the same stories from the homeowners. This could potentially influence their recommendations to clients. For example, while one of the four program options was transition assistance to allow a homeowner to give his or her home back to the bank without facing foreclosure, this option seemed like the last resort to many. Even if the homeowner was not likely to be able to resume making mortgage payments after assistance from the HHF program expired, they might as well benefit from the assistance while it was available and buy themselves more time in their homes. This strong belief could have contributed to the very low take-up of transition assistance among homeowners, causing funding for that option to be substantially reduced.

Finally, as frontline workers, housing counselors could be more or less helpful in facilitating the documentation of eligibility for a homeowner. Given that counseling agencies were reimbursed at a higher rate for homeowners who submitted applications and were determined eligible, there could be internal pressure within a counseling agency to serve clients who would be more likely to be determined eligible. An unintended consequence could be for counselors to be less responsive to homeowners they thought were not as likely to be eligible for the program, inadvertently discouraging them from persisting through the process. There is no documentation of this occurring in Ohio's program; however, it is important to think about how incentives and internal pressures could affect the behavior of frontline workers. Although the ultimate change desired in the target population was people changing, the task for frontline workers in the HHF program was people processing. This role potentially conflicted with their frontline role as housing counselors in other programs and could affect their interactions with the target population.

Implementation Challenges: Potential Threats to Public Value

The program components in the HHF program were not cooked up in a back room by naive bureaucrats who thought that they had devised the best possible scheme to deliver the desired outcomes. Rather, the program developed across levels of the policy field as opportunities and constraints were encountered. There were challenges along the way that significantly shaped the implementation of Ohio's HHF program and ultimately the observed results. An important final step in reflecting on the HHF case is to consider the public value outcomes desired for the program, as summarized in table 7.1, and the extent to which the implementation system presented threats to achieving the outcomes.

First, in terms of program quality, there was an initial desire for counseling agency flexibility and discretion to tailor assistance options for homeowners. Given the complexities of foreclosure processes, individualized interventions were viewed as important. However, characteristics of the implementation system led to a more standardized approach to interventions. In order to gain the participation of private lenders, the sheer number of assistance options provided to homeowners needed to be narrowed. The pressure for standardization was reinforced by a need for legitimacy from the states. Rather than create their own program models from scratch, it was technically more feasible to adopt similar models across states that closely mirrored the examples provided by Treasury. Although standardization reduced flexibility, it allowed increased reporting transparency, which was also valued for the HHF program. This reflects the trade-off that sometimes occurs between creating systems that allow easy measurement and transparency and creating systems that foster tailored interventions.

The second public value outcome was to create a sustainable system that leveraged the existing capacity and infrastructure in the state. In many ways, the HHF program successfully achieved this result. Working within the existing infrastructure of the Save the Dream Ohio initiative was important for being able to launch the HHF program quickly, within the limited time frame set by Treasury. However, the logic of change underlying Save the Dream Ohio was fundamentally different from the logic of change required for the HHF program. Reliance on the existing infrastructure reduced consideration of other alternatives for coordination that may have been more closely matched to the tasks to be performed: screening applicants for eligibility. A challenge moving forward will be to determine how, if at all, this network can be mobilized to help homeowners after the receipt of assistance ends.

Third, the public value of the HHF program depended in part on client take-up, with all eligible homeowners given equal access to assistance. The lengthy processing time was a significant barrier to program accessibility. Many homeowners started the application process but never finished it—some reporting that they became frustrated with the time-intensive process. This was made worse by the limited capacity of some housing agencies to respond to clients and geographic barriers, like driving distance to office locations, to providing required documentation. OHFA made continual changes to its intake system to try to reduce processing time, even waiving documentation of certain items. However, such a tactic can reduce the ability to appropriately screen clients for eligibility. Developing programs that increase accessibility and maintain eligibility standards is an ongoing challenge for public assistance programs like HHF.

Finally, and perhaps most critical for the public value of the program, the structure of the change logic in the HHF program as people processing may not have addressed the fundamental people-changing aspect of preventing foreclosures. Providing financial assistance to a struggling homeowner is not the same as providing a monthly Social Security check to seniors. When seniors are provided with a monthly income, it is relatively clear that they will have greater financial stability than they did before receiving the check. However, with mortgage assistance, it is unclear whether the money provided will be sufficient to prevent foreclosures over the longer term. Sometimes more substantial changes are needed. For example, one approach is to provide additional financial coaching or counseling to help prepare homeowners to resume making payments before the mortgage payment assistance ends. Unfortunately, resources were not available to invest in this sort of longer-term follow-up given the restrictions in the federal policy for eligible uses of funds and incentives across all levels of the system to process as many eligible applicants as possible in the short term. This remains an ongoing threat to the perceived public value of the program.

IMPLEMENTATION DYNAMICS: THE QUALITY RATING AND IMPROVEMENT SYSTEM

Unlike the HHF case, there was no prominent press story to draw the public's attention to implementation issues in the early childhood systems improvement using Quality Rating and Information Systems (QRS). Rather, implementation of this program built over time as knowledge about the importance of early brain development and concerns about setting quality grew. In Minnesota, when it came to securing federal grants and new state investments in early childhood education, it was important that the fledgling QRS program existed. Fiscal conservatives touted it as a way to bring accountability to the child care and early education market, as a way to "prove to taxpayers and parents that they are using the best practice for preparing children for kindergarten."[18]

Yet in reality, the operation of the QRS provided much more than public accountability to people engaged in the program. Sylvia, a child care center teacher in rural Minnesota, accessed new training through the program that altered how she worked with three-year-olds in her classroom each day. Liatt, a recent refugee from Somalia, had little understanding of the operation of K–12 education in her new country but wanted to help prepare children for school. The program provided her access to modest financial resources and coaching about how she might carry out developmentally appropriate activities in her family child care home.

Thousands of parents could now consult the Parent Aware website to learn the ratings of the settings as they considered where their children might be cared for while they were at work, helping to reduce their stress during this important family transition. Fundamentally, this was a program focused on changing people: how providers worked with children, how parents selected early care and education, and what children would experience in their first educational settings.

The program's promise depended on the voluntary participation of over twelve thousand providers of early childhood education in the state. Although it was billed by advocates as a significant change in Minnesota's early learning system, the reality was that far fewer numbers of providers signed up to participate in the first years of statewide expansion than state administers had promised in their application for the federal Race to the Top–Early Learning Challenge grant. In the application, they had planned to voluntarily enroll thirty-seven hundred programs over four years. Yet take-up in the first two years was slow, particularly among private home-based providers or child care centers, settings in which it was believed quality was the most variable. Across the state, only 5 percent of the eligible programs had received ratings through the QRS program. To improve take-up, policy field actors successfully lobbied to create more financial incentives to participate. At the beginning of the third year, the legislature passed a measure enabling highly rated settings to receive bonus payments if they served children receiving public subsidies. In addition, new public investments in early learning scholarships created requirements that they be used in settings highly rated by QRS.

Much like the HHF case, the QRS implementation could initially be viewed as feeble because of a failure to meet targets for enrollment. But this overlooks the reality that enrollment targets are just that—projected metrics that help focus an implementation system on key activities related to program implementation. Their intent is to provide some short-term indicators to help motivate continued adjustments within the implementation system—such as what policy field actors did when they advocated for financial incentives to improve program participation. As we will see, program implementation in this case reflected negotiation and adjustment, progress and some dead ends, as various levels of the implementation system interact in determining what the QRS program becomes in daily practice.

Indicators of Effectiveness: Results That Create Public Value

Before diving into these implementation details and how they came to be, let's step back and consider the desired results of implementation. As should be clear

Table 7.2

Indicators of Effectiveness in the QRS Program

	Process Quality Results	Ultimate Outcomes
Change in systems operations	Increase in the number of early education providers assessed and accessing high-quality training and coaching	More high-quality early childhood settings operating (as measured by three or four stars)
Change in target group	Parents access valid ratings to inform their care and education choices	Increase in children's preparation for kindergarten

by now, it is important to think about what results from implementation in terms of the public value being created. Just as is true in the HHF case, there is not one indicator of the public value desired in implementation. And unlike the implementation of HHF in Ohio, none of the field actors stopped to identify ahead of time the desired results of QRS implementation. Nonetheless, table 7.2 applies the framework from chapter 1 to identify relevant indicators of effective implementation of the QRS program.

The most self-evident indicators of implementation effectiveness in this case are changes in the results of the early childhood system, increasing the number of providers participating in the program; these are the targets identified in the federal grant application. This is one necessary step that represents a change in the system, where early education providers understand their roles and access resources to improve the quality of their educational environment. The other implementation outcomes involve creating changes in both the system (improving setting quality throughout the early education market) and the target population (children's preparation for kindergarten because of their early education). As we will see, the service organizations in this implementation system focus exclusively on recruiting and supporting participating early education providers; implementation activities did not focus much on engaging children's parents. This oversight is a direct consequence of how the core program was shaped as QRS was implemented.

Core Program in Action: How It Is Shaped by Social Structure and Dynamics

Many different approaches could be used to achieve the ultimate outcomes of improving the quality of early education settings to support children's development and ensure they are ready for kindergarten. Regulations could impose mandatory standards, such as the standards that are used to ensure the safety of highway bridges or to ensure that disabled people have access to public buildings. The government could develop and run high-quality programs and require all young children to enroll, much as we do for the education of children after age five. Before becoming parents, adults could be required to attend instructional programs and lay out a plan for educating their babies in the first years of life.

In this policy domain, the viability of any approach is set by public willingness to allow government to shape what happens within their families. In the United States, there is limited political tolerance. In addition, when the idea of a national early childhood education strategy was rejected in the early 1970s, the states became the arenas in which changes occur. Across the country, a patchwork of policy initiatives was initiated, some focused on improving affordability, others trying to improve access to care for low-income and other special populations, and still others focusing on quality improvement in this underresourced field.[19] Because early education is carried out in a variety of settings—individuals develop family child care businesses in their homes; child care centers operate as small businesses or nonprofits; churches, schools, and community centers host early education classrooms—these policies and programs require implementation across public, nonprofit, and for-profit settings.

In this context, states began to learn about and adopt QRS because of the successful Oklahoma initiative in the early 2000s that showed early educational settings could improve quality through a voluntary regulatory effort. As they learned that the idea was being adopted in many other states, early childhood policy field actors in Minnesota began researching options. Because no definitive standards were yet in use nationally, they began by raising funds from local foundations to carry out a field test of potential assessment tools to develop valid indicators for program quality assessment. Among these policy field actors, this seemed to be the logical first step because many believed that any public investment would require a solid social science research base. A task force of diverse field actors convened to oversee the process and results of the field test.

Although not all field actors agreed with the importance of this activity, the real controversy did not occur until the results of the field test were used to help shape the pilot program. While policy field actors agreed to name QRS in Minnesota "Parent Aware" because of how they intended to emphasize one of the key target groups of the program, there was no initial agreement over how the other program elements should be structured. The organizations advocating for business interests believed it was important to create a competitive market for early childhood care as "purely" as possible. That meant focusing investment in both the rating system and in marketing information to parents to influence the demand. In contrast, those rooted in early childhood education pointed to considerable evidence of market failure; the costs associated with providing high-quality early education and care in the market exceeded parents' abilities to pay. Research documented that this failure was particularly acute in the care of low-income children who had the most to gain in terms of educational preparation. They noted that in virtually all states, supply-side supports—in the form of reduced-cost training, financial incentives, and grants—were necessary to create incentives for early educators to participate in the voluntary program. To bolster this evidence, field actors drew on detailed experiences in other states. This was easy to access through the Build Initiative, an intermediary supported by national philanthropies, which hosted the QRS national learning network that brought together state leaders for peer learning, research briefs, and tools that translated ideas into potential practices. These implementation resources were important in Minnesota as policy field actors debated the logic of change in the core program. Ultimately consensus emerged that the demand-side objective assessments and parent information should be accompanied by adequate supply-side program support.

To launch a pilot program in five communities during 2007, many other details needed to be worked out at the policy field level. Roles needed to be negotiated across the network: some service organizations needed to be identified to recruit and provide coaching and training to providers interested in going through the program; a centralized registry needed to be created to facilitate access and document participation to professional development training; marketing materials for providers and parents were developed—and each needed to be coordinated and aligned with the other.

It was not self-evident how to do this. Because program implementation evolved from a larger movement in the national field, Minnesota's program started without a centralized authority. Task forces and work groups of policy field actors made many decisions. And private philanthropic organizations played a pivotal role in this early phase of implementation. Coordinated through their own formal collaborative, these entities invested millions of dollars to support activities important to successful pilot program launch: staffing, information infrastructure, marketing, network facilitation, convening, and evaluation all were supported through private investment.

By all accounts, the pilot program was modestly successful. It rated 144 early childhood programs through a process that involved application, coaching, assessment, and rating on a four-level score across four types of activities: family partnerships, teaching materials and strategies, child learning assessment, and teacher education. An additional 244 programs in the communities automatically received the highest level rating (four stars) because of national accreditation or compliance with federal standards.[20] Overall, 28 percent of the eligible providers in the five pilot project communities participated. Although the concern of parents were not really driving the initial program design, private business interests in the field nevertheless wanted to ensure that parents' perspectives were not lost. They commissioned some research during the pilot phase about ethnic minority parents to document key issues for them in selecting early childhood programs.[21] It revealed that parents strongly felt it was essential for caregivers to understand the values and traditions of the parents' cultural communities and establish trust.

Even before the results of the program implementation were shared, the philanthropic partners drew public attention to the significance of the QRS program. During the 2010 legislative session, the United Way and other prominent funders held a press conference at the state capitol calling for more effective early childhood policy, stressing the essential role of the program in improving accountability.[22] This action effectively drew the attention of state policymakers, bolstered by the perceived neutrality of the private foundations' voices on the issue. Ultimately the newly elected governor created a new cabinet-level Office of Early Learning and charged it with carrying out a plan reflecting many of the recommendations made by the funders' group, including exploration of how to expand the QRS program statewide. This move set the stage for the state to respond to an opportunity when the Obama administration called for proposals for the Race to the Top–Early Learning Challenge application.

Before moving to how implementation dynamics shifted with the award of this grant, it is useful to summarize what this case illuminates to this point. Improving quality in the early childhood market and improving children's preparation for school is complex. Some of the interventions necessary, such as mandating that parents develop an educational plan for their children, lay outside the bounds of the publicly acceptable. Instead, QRS developed in response to a need to improve educational quality in the formal market; the specifics of program implementation were shaped by the actions, resources, and understanding that emerged among policy field actors over time. Among these actors, participation in these activities was voluntary, fueled by a commitment to try to intervene with a public program that could operate at some scale. Resources from private sources were essential for enabling implementation activities at this level.

When awarded, the federal grant fundamentally changed the dynamics in the policy field. No longer was QRS merely a program advocated by nonprofit service organizations, business interest groups, and private foundations. It had become a federally funded initiative administered by the new state Office of Early Learning. This authorizing organization developed service directives that flowed through contracts to nonprofit service organizations. The state convened advisory committees of policy field actors, which ensured that lessons from the field test and pilot program were incorporated into continued implementation refinement. In carrying out its operations oversight, program activities scheduling, and refinement processes, the Office of Early Learning acted primarily in relation to their accountability for administering the $45 million, four-year Race to the Top grant.

Yet this accountability also was influenced by the Office of Early Learning's position in state government. When established, the vision was for the office to cut across the state departments of education, health, and human services because of each agency's role in administering early childhood programs. But operationally these seemed difficult to accomplish. Each agency had its own mission, and early childhood education was difficult for the Department of Education, used to working with school districts, or the Department of Public Health, used to working with county health departments, to prioritize. While an Office of Early Learning director was appointed and worked with the governor's appointed Early Learning Council, QRS implementation was one of eleven projects instituted as part of the Race to the Top grant. And it was not immediately integrated into ongoing activities in the departments. To get early education licensing, staff from the Department of Human Services and food program (Department of Education) who worked regularly with the same target group of providers to promote Parent Aware in the course of their work, required stern memos from each agency's commissioner. The day-to-day administration of the Parent Aware program came to rest with a coordinator in the Department of Human Services.

In addition, while there were financial resources to scale the pilot program, it became clear there would need to be a number of changes in the core program. Some assessment processes needed to move to self-reporting because of limited funding for direct observation. The intensity of the coaching and financial incentives decreased. Some of the research-based indicators were altered. In consultation with working group members, the Department of Human Services created a number of manuals, documents, and forms to standardize what potential participants learned about the program. They also entered into contracts with new statewide entities for training and assessment accountability. They adopted a new process that specified that new participants could begin the program twice a year, in January and July, and provided training to frontline staff in service organizations about these and other parameters. They also needed to establish a process for how coordination among these various entities would occur. What was instituted is reflected in figure 5.2, developed to illustrate the program process flow tool.

In spite of these efforts to standardize the program, there remained significant variation in how the fourteen service organizations provided Parent Aware with providers. One service organization, Child Care Resources, provides an illustration of how organizational-level forces continued to refine the core program. As a visible and long-established organization in the metropolitan area, the agency ran a number of initiatives relevant to QRS implementation within its $9 million budget. Its extensive cadre of professional development programs, experience working with low-income parents administering subsidies, and experience in the Parent Aware pilot program were valuable.

As the parameters of the QRS program changed to accommodate a statewide focus, they needed to reassess how the activities of recruiting and supporting early education settings were carried out. All of the forms changed. Some of the key program elements, such as direct observation of classroom settings, were curtailed for many settings. And the expanded scale of the program caused managers to rethink how to staff organizations' activities of recruiting and supporting early education providers through the process. Luckily, the agency had already established the New American Provider Project, focused on encouraging the creation of new educational settings in refugee communities. It provided customized coaching and technical assistance to help establish this program. The private funding for the project was decreasing just at the time the new contract for Parent Aware was issued, so the manager just shifted some of staff costs to the new contract and told staff they would help the organization realize its goal of providing ethnically appropriate coaching.

Because of its investment in Parent Aware's mission and its own business interest, the agency's leadership decided to invest managers' time in the field-level committees convened by the Department of Human Services. The agency's program manager participated in a number of retreats and working meetings as ongoing refinement in the forms and process used statewide occurred. The organization's president filled a coveted position on the Governor's Early Learning Council, drawing on the experience within her agency to suggest modifications in policy and implementation activities. Yet these investments and external engagements came at a cost. Although the organization operated many other programs relevant to QRS implementation, there rarely was time to work across the internal organizational silos to have staff learn from each other and align their activities.

Thus, implementation decisions within both authorizing and service organizations were directly shaped by their institutional context. Accountability structures, funding formats, standard operating procedures, and external engagement influence how the details of program implementation appear at the organizational level.

The state contract specified specific roles for frontline workers in the program—coaches, trainers, and professional development coordinators in local agencies—all focused on working with the early childhood providers and supporting them through the assessment process. While the ultimate rating occurred by review from the authorizing organization, these frontline workers focused their attention on recruiting providers and motivating the behavioral change imagined by the program. Through this work, they often felt hampered by the standardized processes that seemed more focused on processing than changing participants. Their experience was echoed in program evaluation reports; throughout the state, while coaches appeared successful in establishing positive relationships and customizing engagement in the first year, they were hampered by limited face-to-face contact, changing paperwork, and inconsistent processes.[23]

At Child Care Resources, the frontline staff who worked on the New American Provider Project had expertise providing outreach to the Latina/o, Hmong, Oromo, and Somali communities and brought it to Parent Aware implementation. Their experience impressed on them the importance of their one-on-one relationships with providers. Often they would receive word-of-mouth referrals to other potential program participants. In a voluntary program, it was important to follow up on these leads. Yet the agency's contract limited the time they could devote to outreach, necessitating that some of it happened after formal work hours on their own time. Each worker developed preferred ways of bringing potential participants into the program, and they shared ideas with each other about what seemed to work. The contract procedures also specified that new participants could come into the program only at two specified times in a year, creating a quandary. When someone wanted to enroll in Parent Aware, it seemed important to be responsive right away. As a result, staff developed alternatives to formal enrollment that enabled them to maintain contact and start to build the coaching relationship. After program enrollment and initial assessment, the coaches continued to work with participants to increase their star rating, providing access to free training, modest funds for materials, and, very important to frontline staff, authorization for one-on-one technical assistance and support.

This hand-holding is necessary given what is required of early education providers to participate in the voluntary program. They must first submit an application and attend an orientation, enroll in a professional development registry that tracks all training and professional development, and submit an extensive documentation packet reporting everything from curriculum to materials, child assessment to food practices. The overall process can take two to eight months. Although marketing materials laud the many benefits of having quality recognized and access to free supports, the costs in terms of time and risk seemed considerable. It is not surprising that target numbers under the Race to the Top grant were not initially realized. Thus, considerable programmatic supports were developed to support early education providers' participation in the program. However, the top-down desire for standardization created barriers for frontline staff and early education providers for efficient and effective engagement in the program. Pressures to reduce this initiative to a people-processing technology were mediated at the front lines through the relationships between staff and early education providers.

Implementation Challenges: Potential Threats to Public Value

This account highlights how the core program in the QRS initiative evolved over time, across various levels in the implementation system. The challenges faced in reaching the numbers of participants noted in the federal grant application highlight only one element in the implementation story, and perhaps an element that is not the most important in ultimate implementation success. As indicated in table 7.2, success indicators for the public value of QRS included not only participation of providers but also a sustainable infrastructure of high-quality child care, engagement of parents with the system, and ultimately an increase in children's readiness for kindergarten.

The creation of a sustainable statewide infrastructure for QRS was a significant challenge that was resolved for the most part. While the federal investment provided a much-needed influx of financial resources into the implementation system, the administration of those funds gave rise to some issues. The administrative disconnect between the program and other activities of the Office for Early Learning decreased its perceived importance in the larger early childhood policy field. While the state government now had clear accountability, the top-down manner and reliance on contracts to coordinate activities across the policy field decreased involvement. Only through the continuation of working groups and committees was the valuable pilot program experience not lost. While the initiative was more firmly established in state policy priorities, with a plan to make the program available throughout the state, the process of standardizing program process flow created barriers for engaging some participants. In addition, statewide implementation and standardization reduced some of the higher-touch monitoring associated with the pilot program. Rather than conducting on-site assessments to confirm practices, early child care providers have been taken at their word to establish the QRS ratings. This could potentially create a threat to the program's public value if child care providers' self-reports of their practices do not match what they are doing in practice.

Perhaps of greater concern to the program's public value is the lack of parental engagement with the QRS process. Although the Minnesota QRS program was titled "Parent Aware," virtually none of the statewide implementation activities focused on engaging parents. Although surveys of the target group revealed that the overwhelming majority thought a community-based quality rating system would be helpful and identified high-quality ratings as a very important factor in selecting care,[24] virtually no public money was invested in reaching them. The state contracted out the creation and maintenance of a website. But other marketing depended on the modest activities of a nonprofit advocacy organization supported by private funding.

Finally, the ability of QRS to achieve its ultimate outcome, increasing children's readiness for kindergarten, is still unknown. There are numerous factors outside the scope of the core program for QRS that could certainly impede readiness, such as poor child nutrition, inadequate family support, or community violence. However, it is important to caution that the logic of change in the QRS system was not designed to target these sorts of issues. QRS is an information-sharing technology designed to increase parent information about child care providers. To the extent that parents use this information to place their children in higher-quality child care and that this higher-quality child care is associated with increased readiness for kindergarten, then the QRS logic is sound. Ongoing monitoring of use of the QRS system by parents and the quality of care associated with providers will demonstrate the continued value of the program.

This case is a work in progress. At this writing, financial bonuses and unique access to scholarships for highly rated programs are still at early stages of rollout. These financial incentives might, in the end, overcome the barriers to enrollment in this voluntary program. Examining implementation dynamics through formal evaluation and attentive management will continue to reveal elements of the system to be aligned, refined, and improved. Yet continuing to overlook one of the program's primary target groups, parents who are the decision makers for their children's early education, artificially curtails the range of activities included in the program. This is unfortunate because stimulating the demand side of the market is necessary to institutionalize the program beyond the four-year federal grant. It is also essential to ensuring that the program realizes its ultimate public value of creating more high-quality supply that supports children's early education.

OPPORTUNITIES FOR CHANGE

The two cases in this chapter illustrate the complexity of implementation systems and provide insights as to why the core programs unfolded in particular ways in the HHF and QRS contexts. In both cases, we started at the end of the story. A quick glance at program numbers or skim of a headline news story might lead one to believe that the program is yet another example of implementation failure. We would take issue with this shortsighted assessment. Not only is it likely inaccurate, it diminishes the value of the important and hard work taking place at all levels of the implementation system to bring a program into reality. It is easy to point fingers and find flaws after the fact; it is more difficult to engage in the process and truly understand the constraints and social structures that led to the observed reality.

We hope that the stories do not end there. Implementation is a process of learning and continual modification of ideas when new information is available. As we mentioned at the outset of this book, effective implementation is fundamentally about creating change in systems and in target populations, pursuing public value outcomes on purpose. This is difficult to do. It is easy to get lulled into accepting how a program operates, whether or not it is actually connected to desired results. Adept policy and program implementers learn how to become reflective and strategic actors within the system, leading both technical and adaptive processes to create change. We turn to this discussion in chapter 8.

In appendix G, we provide a tool to assist with the assessment of implementation dynamics and outcomes applied to your own case. The purpose of this exercise is to move beyond identification of system components toward integration of system dynamics. To do this, in-depth understanding of the power and culture at play in a given system is needed through direct experience, observation, or interviews with key stakeholders. Through this learning, we hope to take the analysis beyond a place where many people get stuck—being frustrated by parts of the system that are "wrong," that don't seem to "make sense"—and begin to identify opportunities for change within a particular implementation system.

chapter EIGHT

Leading Learning in Implementation Systems

A s we have discussed throughout, effective implementation creates deliberate change—in the target group and in the system—to better achieve public value results. It is not merely arguing for particular government tools because of an ideological position, or making modest adjustments to existing organizational operations in order to receive additional funding. It is not pursuing change for change's stake. Instead, effective implementation requires leadership invested in improving the operations of the system so that it facilitates positive change in the behavior or conditions of the target group, consistent with public values. It requires skillful management practices to embed the new approach into the daily operations of an implementation system. These are the ultimate outcomes of implementation effectiveness that we discussed in this book's Introduction and applied to the cases in chapter 7.

As we have seen through taking a systems approach and applying the multilevel implementation analysis to the Hardest Hit Fund (HHF) and Quality Rating and Improvement System (QRS) examples, many challenges are revealed when we pursue these results. If you are systematically doing your own application using the book's appendixes, you also have discovered much more than you knew before about the implementation conditions surrounding your policy or program of interest. This analysis sets the stage for being a force for positive change in improving implementation because you can proceed with a clear understanding of the constraints operating at each level. But understanding is not doing. Leading change requires courage and perseverance because ideas that other people involved in the implementation process hold dear are often challenged. It also requires realistic assessment of what is possible to accomplish with the existing resources, time, and talent.

To support your ability to respond, we turn in this chapter to an insight about leadership offered by Ron Heifetz and Marty Linsky: many problems come bundled with technical and adaptive components.[1] Technical challenges are those for which cause and effect can be described, solutions are known, and tactics for adoption can be shared and replicated from setting to setting. They are problems for which either people have the know-how to solve or such information can be discovered with some basic research. They require analytical investigation. Adaptive challenges are those requiring more astute attention because they are more ambiguous and involve values and power, beliefs and authority, the very issues we explored in chapter 7 as so critical in what actually occurs in implementation processes. To move beyond adaptive challenges, people need to engage in experimentation, integration, and risk taking, learning new things and often moving beyond their comfort zones. These challenges require social skill.

The distinction between technical and adaptive challenges is useful to organize this chapter as we tease apart the key elements of leading improvements in implementation. But as Heifetz and Linksy write, "Most problems come bundled with both technical and adaptive aspects. Before making an intervention, you need to distinguish between them in order to decide which to tackle first and with what strategy."[2] This helps one to be practical when moving to address the parts of the system that are particularly significant in public value failure. It is important to note that people occupying very different roles in implementation systems can lead change: nonprofit leaders, program coordinators, private funders, public managers, and frontline service professionals. While each individual possesses distinct capabilities and resources, each has a role to play in system change.

The actual technical and adaptive challenges in implementation are shaped by the policy issue and the complexity of the core program being deployed to address it. They are influenced by the unique mechanisms of authority and culture in the strategic action field and related fields. They are formed by your own role in the implementation system. And it is important to start from where you sit; use the knowledge of your own strategic action field to identify practical strategies of change. Effective implementation practice also requires leadership that crosses the boundaries of your immediate context and identifies other participants and resources that help propel larger change.

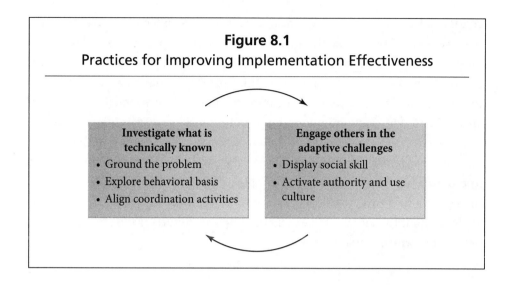

Figure 8.1
Practices for Improving Implementation Effectiveness

Investigate what is technically known
- Ground the problem
- Explore behavioral basis
- Align coordination activities

Engage others in the adaptive challenges
- Display social skill
- Activate authority and use culture

In this chapter, we discuss practices for cultivating more skillful implementation, as summarized in figure 8.1. Making changes to the core program is as much a social process as it is a technical process. Following the lead of philosopher and pragmatist John Dewey, it is about creating opportunities for social exchange and shared learning that advance understanding beyond any one individual.[3] Armed with open minds, participants can bring new ideas and evidence to the table that can shift the way things have "always been done." Of course, it is important to get the technical details right about the intervention or core program: investigate the problem in relation to concerns about public value shortfalls, investigate what is known about the behavior of target group and frontline staff, and align and coordinate activities. But it is also just as important to engage others, applying knowledge about the strategic action fields and exerting what academics call situated or practical judgment.[4] People need to be brought along in the change process. This is done by displaying social skill, activating existing sources of authority, and using sources that legitimate the change and resonate with field values.

In this chapter, we describe these professional competencies and suggest that during times of implementing change, they need to be regularly practiced. This is because progress is unpredictable, or what systems theorists recognize as emergent; strategies cannot be planned and documented in detail in work plans. Instead, effective practice requires competencies, commitment, discipline, and continual learning from what unexpectedly occurs. Effective implementation practice is about being a tactician and an artist, relying on analysis and intuition, direction and reflection. To help in building these skills, we also share some practical resources we have found useful. To help document your application to a particular project, we offer an implementation improvement blueprint in appendix H that poses questions for you to consider relevant to each of the elements discussed in this chapter. It also provides a simple mechanism to highlight particular elements to focus your attention on as you identify ways to improve the implementation in the complex system. Throughout, it is important to keep in mind what you've already come to understand from your multilevel analysis about the authority mechanisms and the culture of the strategic action field within which you find yourself.

INVESTIGATING TECHNICAL CHALLENGES

Given the complexity in implementation systems, it is easy to point to many things that could occupy implementation reformers' attention. Perhaps computer systems could be upgraded, staff could be better trained, performance measures adopted, or work teams reorganized. Many managers pursue such initiatives in their larger efforts to improve organizational effectiveness. In fact, in public agencies where political appointees are given administrative authority, employees come to expect these types of managerial changes when a new administration takes office; change for change's sake often seems more the rule than the exception. Certainly managerial reforms to modernize public sector human resources practices or improve information technology or transparency are important. But managerial change for its own sake does not necessarily improve implementation results.

Policy analysis also is concerned with problem definition, often consulting social science research before providing advice or recommendations about policy alternatives.[5] Because many policy problems are merely symptoms of a much deeper cause, this process often begins with problem analysis. If low numbers of young people are completing high school, policy analysis seeks to first identify the potential causes of the problem—family income, parental education levels, poor-quality schools. Policy interventions addressing these factors are weighed in relation to their constraints, and some are recommended because of their potential for intervening in the causal relationship. In the same vein, factors not substantiated by empirical research—racially segregated housing promoted to improve high school graduation rates—create policy problems or failures. These are most often thought to be a concern of those engaged in policy design or reform. But this overlooks how policy problems get embedded in the assumptions of policy fields, the operating procedures of organizations, and the mind-sets of frontline staff.

Too often management reforms are divorced from policy concerns, and policy failures are attempted without adjusting the network or organizational context. Effective implementation involves trying to address policy concerns with relevant management practice. It requires integrating technical knowledge from both. Yet frequently professional training in public affairs artificially divorces the two, training people to think about managerial challenges divorced from policy problems. If policies are poorly specified and the program's logic of change does not reflect what is known about how best to address the problem, implementers' activities in service organizations and front lines are focused on ineffective means. If management reform is pursued for its own sake, it might lead to conditions that do not reinforce the quality interactions necessary to engage the target group. Effective implementation fundamentally requires focusing on changes in the core program that contribute to the program's public value.

While there are potentially endless things that could be changed about a program, we believe it is helpful to think about the changes in light of the three processes of the core program that we have woven throughout this book: establishing viable options, identifying the logic of change, and coordinating activities. Each of these processes encompasses a set of assumptions that shape the way the core program is being implemented in practice. To make change in the program, these assumptions must be reviewed—an activity that we refer to as technical analysis. First, with regard to viable options, it is important to spend time grounding the problem. What is already known that can be used to maximize an initiative's chance of creating results that the public values? What is known includes both evidence about technical effectiveness and insights about the public value desired and potential threats to public value. Next, to better understand assumptions about the logic of change, we think it is essential to investigate what is known about its behavioral basis. As we discussed, a range of factors often influences the logic of change that is adopted when shaping the core program. To lead change, it is important to step back from this context and examine what is known from research or common sense about the behavioral basis of the program. Finally, it is prudent to ensure that there is a coordinating structure that aligns with and reinforces the program activities most important in generating results. We understand that coordinating structures are not always as malleable as some management textbooks might have us believe; we often can't change the hierarchical structure of the organization or the formal contracts with shared providers. However, effective implementers can find ways to work within existing structures to facilitate coordination that creates public value. Taken together, attending to these technical elements raises confidence that improvement strategies are pursued in relation to publicly desired results rather than more instrumental interests.

Many tools and tactics are available to support the analysis of technical challenges. Table 8.1 describes a few basic management and policy analysis tactics and tools that can be applied to help uncover what is known about an implementation challenge. These tactics and tools range from schematics that describe management roles, to statistical techniques that summarize best practices, to standardized approaches for assessing program impact. Rather than viewing these as stand-alone fixes to program challenges, it is perhaps better to think of each as one tool in a tool kit of resources that may lend insights for particular challenges. For example, policy research, program evaluation, and cost-benefit analysis may be helpful for grounding the problem, whereas operations analysis may lend insights into the behavioral logic and coordination challenges. We will refer back to some of the tactics and tools in table 8.1 as appropriate within each area of technical analysis.

Grounding the Problem

At their core, all program technologies are intended to address a problem. Food pantries distribute food to address hunger needs, after-school youth programs structure activities for teenagers to keep them safe and off the streets, and free income-tax-return preparation services work to improve the financial well-being of vulnerable groups. The types of problems we are interested in here are those that are public problems—problems that affect not only individual interests but have a collective impact on society. Most of these problems are messy problems, where the boundaries and solutions are not well defined. There is no one best way to address these problems, and there is not even always agreement about what it is that needs to be addressed. As we have described throughout this book, viable options to address the problem and the logic of change to be employed are often

Table 8.1
Tactics and Tools for Technical Change in Implementation Systems

Tactics and Tools	Types of Technical Challenges Suited to Solve	Examples
Strategic management Alignment of staffing, structure, and environment to maximize results	Improve capacity and professional development of actors	Balanced scorecard, manager's competing values model[a]
Project management Tactical activity of organizing resources to achieve specific objectives	Alignment and delivery	Practical organization tools, GANTT charts, cloud-based software (Basecamp)[b]
Cost-benefit analysis Technique estimating the strengths and weaknesses of alternatives in monetary terms	Control costs and need to maximize benefits	Cost-benefit studies; social return on investment models[c]
Policy and program research Systematic approach to selecting and synthesizing high-quality, relevant research evidence	Document what is known from existing formal research; identify evidence-based practices	Academic research and policy briefs; systematic review or meta-analysis[d]
Operations analysis Continuous improvement techniques applied to specific organizational processes	Improve process efficiency; identify and eliminate bottlenecks	Total Quality Management, Six Sigma, kaizen, Lean[e]

(continued)

Table 8.1
Tactics and Tools for Technical Change in
Implementation Systems *(Continued)*

Tactics and Tools	Types of Technical Challenges Suited to Solve	Examples
Program evaluation Systematic approach to collecting and analyzing information about programs and their impact	Assess program delivery, its progress, adjustments, and consequences	Impact evaluation and randomized controlled trials; opportunistic experiments; formative or process evaluation[f]

[a] Robert E. Quinn and Sue R. Faerman, *Becoming a Master Manager: A Competing Values Approach,* 5th ed. (San Francisco: Jossey-Bass, 2010).

[b] *HBR Guide to Project Management* (Cambridge, MA: Harvard Business Review Press, 2013).

[c] For an overview of cost-benefit analysis, see Edward J. Mishan and Euston Quah, *Cost-Benefit Analysis* (London: Routledge, 2007). For examples of social return on investment, see Andrew Flockhart, "Raising the Profile of Social Enterprises: The Use of Social Return on Investment (SROI) and Investment Ready Tools (IRT) to Bridge the Financial Credibility Gap," *Social Enterprise Journal* 1, no. 1 (2005): 29–42.

[d] For an overview of meta-analysis in policy research, see Evan Ringquist, *Meta-Analysis for Public Management and Policy* (San Francisco: Jossey-Bass, 2013).

[e] For an overview of Six Sigma, see Mikel Harry and Richard Schroeder, *Six Sigma: The Breakthrough Management Strategy Revolutionizing the World's Top Corporations* (New York: Random House, 2005). For an overview of continuous improvement approaches applied to the public sector, see Karen J. Fryer, Jiju Antony, and Alex Douglas, "Critical Success Factors of Continuous Improvement in the Public Sector: A Literature Review and Some Key Findings," *TQM Magazine* 19, no. 5 (2007): 497–517.

[f] For example, see Laura I. Langbein, *Public Program Evaluation: A Statistical Guide* (London: M. E. Sharpe, 2012).

contested and established through social dynamics operating at the policy field, organization, and frontline levels of implementation.

While we will return to the social processes in the next section of this chapter, we also know that meaningful social interactions about the program are enhanced through information. What more can be learned about the needs or constraints of the target population? What have others found to be most effective at creating the types of process and outcome changes desired by the program? What are the potential threats to creating public value associated with existing or proposed changes to the program? To help inform these questions, we suggest grounding the problem in both scientific inquiry and public values. We use the term *grounding* intentionally, as it suggests the need to enhance one's own understanding with additional knowledge. There are many ways to acquire this additional knowledge. For public policy and program problems, we think that the key is to balance the knowledge obtained from scientific evidence with an understanding and assessment of public values in context.

First, one must investigate what is known more broadly about the population, the systems' operations, and the interaction between the two. For example, if there is an interest in improving consumers' use of smart appliances, it is useful to consult the emerging literature about customer preferences and behavior. It also is useful to understand what types of meters are currently available and being developed. If working to improve low-income women's chances of sustainable employment, it is important to explore what is known about the population, the volatility of the low-wage labor market, and documented barriers. It also is useful to harvest information about frontline activities or interventions that seem to be effective in supporting the move to employment from evaluation research.

Policy analysts and researchers often assume actors in the implementation system are well versed in such research. Or they decry the failure to not bring research to practice. But it all depends on how the implementation issues were framed in the strategic action field. For example, in some policy fields, like that found in Washington State around smart appliances, there is an expectation that all actors are well versed in technological advances and customer preferences. The policy research is a valued resource in the field and provides a source used to influence debates about how to implement more effective consumer education programs. In the policy field focused on low-income women's employment in Arkansas, in contrast, the principal decisions around the core program have reflected past institutional practices rather than research about target-group conditions or program evaluation about interventions.

When stepping into leading improvements in policy or program implementation, it is important to challenge both assumptions and research alternatives. Often resources are too limited and institutional interests too vested in the status quo to invest in substantive change. However, by building up a repertoire of resources about innovative practices and new techniques, astute implementers will be ready to seize opportunities for change when they arise. Sometimes this information can be acquired through policy and program research, as referenced in table 8.1.

Industry gatherings like national conferences and online e-mail lists provide the opportunity to engage with new insights on evidence-based practices. From our own experience as practitioners, we have come to learn that effective implementers are not generalists; rather, they become context experts in the problem area in which their work is invested.

But policy context knowledge about the problem is not sufficient. The second element of grounding the problem involves probing public values. To enable implementation that creates public value, one must have a sense of the public values—or threats to public values—in the current domain. In chapter 1, we provided a framework to identify indicators of implementation effectiveness, drawing from a multidimensional perspective of public value creation. However, these indicators alone are not sufficient to determine if a program is creating public value. Many times the sorts of results and outcomes desired by a particular program do not lend themselves readily to quantifiable measures. And even if there are numerical outcomes, how does one determine if a particular measure is at a threshold where it achieves public value?

A variety of approaches have been designed to help practitioners manage for public value. Some, like Mark Moore's book *Creating Public Value*, place the emphasis on the individual manager to analyze the values at stake in a particular domain.[6] The challenge is that this approach assumes that the manager has knowledge of the important values. Critics worry that this sort of approach might lead to a manager's perception of the public good to be held up as the gold standard but not really do anything to further the common good.[7] An alternative approach is to elicit the public values at play in a domain though the direct engagement of clients and stakeholders. These participatory processes can be effective at not only generating insights about public values; they can also help facilitate the sort of deliberative learning processes that are often necessary to shift system thinking. Indeed, citizen engagement strategies are an important adaptive tool that we discuss in more detail in the next section.

Here, we suggest an additional tool that offers a middle ground between the all-knowing manager and direct citizen engagement. While it may be difficult (and perhaps undesirable) for implementers to unilaterally identify the public values at play in a given domain, with some specific criteria to use as a guide, reflective practitioners can identify potential threats to public values. Armed with the contextual knowledge of the implementation system and the core program components, potential barriers can be identified that may reduce the public value of the program.

This approach follows the lead of public affairs scholar Barry Bozeman and his articulation of "public value failure" criteria.[8] One of the challenges to using the concept of public values to drive decisions in practice is that they are often contested and diffuse. There is no singular public value to be maximized at all times in all contexts and no well-defined set of public values. Fortunately, Bozeman offers an alternative. He suggests applying a set of diagnostic criteria to identify public value failure, similar to criteria of market failure. They can be used to help evaluate situations where public values may be at risk and signal opportunities for intervention.

Following this approach, we identify criteria that may indicate public value failure with respect to a particular result or outcome. Table 8.2 provides a summary of the criteria, aligned along the same dimensions for assessing implementation effectiveness. In identifying our criteria, we draw from the eight public value failure criteria that Bozeman originally proposed.[9] Like Bozeman's original work, we are not implying that the criteria we identify in each quadrant are exhaustive because there may certainly be reason to add (or delete) a particular criterion. Yet this set offers a helpful starting place to identify potential threats to public value in a given domain.

Starting with the upper-left quadrant in table 8.2, low-quality program delivery that threatens basic human rights is an indicator of an initiative not achieving its public value. Defining *low quality* is context dependent. However, program

---

Table 8.2
Indicators of Public Value Failure for Implementation

	Process Quality Results	Ultimate Outcomes
Change in systems operations	Low-quality program delivery that threatens basic human rights	Lack of collective capability or infrastructure
Change in target groups	Lack of due consideration of target group needs or interests	Lack of desired change in target group due to short-term focus

delivery that violates basic human rights would likely be considered a threat to public value regardless of the context.[10] This is one of the primary reasons that scholars evaluating the effectiveness of particular policy interventions must comply with standards for the protection of human subjects. It would be considered unethical to deny a group of sick patients a known medical treatment so that researchers could have a valid "control group."[11] Less extreme examples of unethical practice can occur every day, threatening the public value of a program. For example, in the HHF program, we would likely consider it a violation of privacy and threat to human dignity if confidential information about homeowners facing foreclosure were to be disclosed publicly (intentionally or unintentionally) without homeowner consent. Safeguarding the public value in this program requires attention to the protection of confidential client information.

Moving to the far right quadrant of table 8.2, lack of collective capability or infrastructure is also considered a threat to public value. We have stressed throughout this book that successful implementation by definition will create change in the implementation system. If this system change is not achieved, then the public value pursued by the program is likely not going to be sustained. System change requires attention to collective action in the policy field, ensuring available capability and infrastructure for the delivery of all aspects of the core program, where diverse institutions work together to build a common pool of resources and information.[12] On the contrary, public value failure may occur when organizational leaders in the policy field neglect or refuse to invest in the system, prioritizing the survival or status of their organization at the expense of the collective program objectives.[13] For example, if the QRS program were to set standards in such a way that only certain private providers could qualify (e.g., only nonprofit educators), there would likely be a public value threat to the sustainability of the system. While this could occur through intentional "collusion" of certain providers, it might also occur unintentionally if certain providers dominate the market simply based on their size or capacity.

Another indicator of public value failure in implementation is lack of due consideration of target group needs or interests. In a democratic society, there is an expectation that the needs and interests of target group members will be given due consideration.[14] The way this will be manifest will vary depending on the context. In some settings, it may be appropriate to provide targeted groups an active voice in programmatic decisions, and failure to provide such an opportunity may itself be indicative of a public value failure. The case of QRS is illustrative of this failure, where the primary target group, parents, was not engaged or consulted in programmatic discussions. In other settings, however, target groups may not be willing or able to represent themselves, such as when services are provided to those with mental illness. In these situations, implementers may identify and address target group needs by engaging the insights of professional experts and caregivers. As we have stressed from the beginning of this book, there is no one public value or a single mutually agreed-on definition of the desired public outcome in a particular context. Failure to continually engage with the population for whom the program is being implemented and make adjustments in response can lead to a carefully executed program that achieves no public purpose at all.[15]

A final dimension of public value failure in policy and program implementation is lack of desired change in the target population due to short-term focus, reflected in the bottom-right quadrant of table 8.2. Certainly change in target group behavior or condition is dependent on numerous factors outside the scope or control of implementers. However, implementation systems that emphasize short-term results over long-term outcomes may be less likely to invest in the type of program needed to bring about the ultimate desired change. This can be a significant challenge for implementation in public settings, where pressure for accountability and measurable results may shift the focus toward short-term outputs that can be measured rather than longer-term change in the target population that may be less easy to measure. In the HHF case, pressure to spend federal funds prioritized a short-term focus on the number served at the expense of longer-term strategies to address the underlying issues that cause foreclosures. Pressure for measurable results can also lead implementers to intentionally engage in gaming behaviors to boost performance metrics without actually improving outcomes.[16] Whether intentional or unintentional, short-term thinking can be subversive to the often long-term change desired in the behavior or condition of the target population.

The first technical step in leading learning in implementation systems is grounding the problem. Effective grounding requires scientific inquiry and consideration of public value. Both are context dependent; however, as we have described, there are resources and tools that can be analytically helpful.

Exploring the Behavioral Base

Obviously program technologies seek to create change—changes in systems and ultimately changes in human behavior. While a program process flow might depict change as a mechanical process of linking inputs and outputs, it might also reflect underlying assumptions about how people will respond. Sometimes exploring more deeply the behaviors of system participants provides invaluable insight that can shape the strategies for improving implementation.

This idea is not new. As discussed elsewhere in this book, scholar Richard Elmore proposed a backward-mapping approach to implementation that essentially starts with people interacting at the front lines of system operations. Policy and program implementation tends to occur in complex rather than merely complicated systems.[17] In these systems, because factors are interrelated in nonlinear ways, it is important to ground technical research in the behaviors that a policy or program most seeks to address at the implementation front lines.[18] This backward mapping begins at the point in the implementation system in which "administrative actions intersect private choices."[19] Then it looks into the implementation system to consider what part of the system has the greatest likelihood of changing that behavior. Is a teacher's subtle interaction with the troubled student what is needed to motivate her new learning? Are there economic incentives that can be altered in the policy field that can have almost immediate effects? Can the framing adopted by a service organization create consequences for noncompliance? A backward-mapping logic orients one to the behavior needing to be changed and draws on various sources of information to understand that behavior.

In some fields, this frontline behavior is investigated through applied social science. As we discussed in chapter 2, behavioral economics is a robust area of scholarship that bridges psychology and economics. It focuses on exploring and identifying the many systematic biases and heuristics that influence individuals' decision making, including those that occur in policy implementation systems. Researchers have investigated human behavior in a range of settings—African farmers' use of fertilizer, police lineups, stock trading—and have generated some significant and often counterintuitive insights about the psychology of decisions.[20] The impulsive decisions individuals make every day often do not align with the rational assumptions made by program designers or implementers or even what they might choose with full, unbiased information.

Rather than chastising program participants for not behaving more rationally, behavioral economists challenge that the behavior observed may indeed be rational—or at least not unexpected—given the design of the system and common behavioral responses. Following this logic, implementation systems create a choice architecture around which people make decisions. It is what target group members face when interacting with the policy system, and research documents that it influences how they respond.

Intentionally and unintentionally, implementers become choice architects when they carry out or make changes to core programs. Decisions made in passing about how to enroll participants in a program or how to design an intervention can have profound impacts on the ultimate behavioral change in the target group. Kent Weaver recounts a graphic illustration when he describes how first responders working in two communities around Hurricane Katrina developed a powerful frame of choice. Evacuation holdouts were instructed to write their Social Security numbers somewhere on their bodies with a permanent marker to increase the ease of identifying their corpses. This frame, which helped people realize the authorities were considering it quite likely that they could die, worked well in convincing people the threat was significant and they should leave.[21]

Taking some time to think through how relatively small details of implementation—like the arrangement of food, the construction of a default option, or framing of choices—that create a structure privileging some types of choices is worthwhile when trying to investigate the technical sources of implementation problems. It can help uncover assumptions about target group behavior that might exist within a particular strategic action field or implementation system that might be creating unintended consequences.

A key insight of behavioral economics is proper diagnosis of the behaviors underlying the problem being addressed. Richard Thaler and Shlomo Benartzi provide an example of the applicability of this sort of approach in their work on employee retirement plan contributions, motivated by the societal concern that many households in the United States are entering into retirement without sufficient savings.[22] Part of the problem is caused by a shift in policy for employer retirement plans over the past few decades. Previously most companies administered a defined benefit plan: employees paid a fixed amount of money into their plans out of their paychecks each month and were guaranteed a set benefit amount on retirement. However, corporations today predominantly structure retirement plans based on a defined contribution, where employees choose how much to put aside each month, with no guarantee of a set amount on retirement. Employees systematically are less likely to participate in voluntary employer retirement plans and deposit less money each month than they "should" to have enough funds to live on when they retire. Assuming that this is a poor decision or "mistake," how can this be corrected?

Traditional approaches are to provide employees with additional education about the importance of retirement savings and even to offer individualized tools to help calculate how much money needs to be set aside each month today to have a sufficient income in the future. While these educational and planning interventions have had some success, they can be costly and do not substantially move the needle on the problem. One problem is procrastination and self-control. We might say we will review or increase our retirement plan contributions, but then we get busy and never make the change. In these situations, simply changing the default for participation in the employee retirement plan or the amount contributed each month can be effective. One study found that increasing the default to be automatic enrollment of employees in the retirement plan (with an option to opt out) increased participation among newly eligible workers from 49 percent to 86 percent, the majority of whom elected to keep the default monthly contribution amount set by the company at the time of enrollment.[23] Thaler and Benartzi point out that it is not necessarily that employees don't know what they should do. Rather, behaviorally, it is difficult to reduce the amount of take-home pay you receive today in order to save for an event in the distant future.

In this research, they draw from Kahneman and Tversky's research on prospect theory and loss aversion, noting that individuals are less likely to make decisions that they perceive to result in a net loss (for example, a reduction in the amount of take-home pay), particularly under conditions of uncertainty (like retirement planning).[24] Their solution? Benartzi and Shlomo have developed and tested an intervention they call "Save More Tomorrow," whereby employees agree to increase the amount of money they save for retirement with their next pay raise. Essentially, the next time they get a pay raise, employees agree to have an automatic increase in their retirement plan contributions by a set portion of the pay raise. In this way, there is no reduction in take-home pay, but monthly contributions would increase. In a randomized field experiment, they find that not only do more than 80 percent of employees agree to this sort of plan, but that the majority of those agreeing stay with the plan for the entire four years of the study period—automatically increasing their retirement contributions with each subsequent pay raise.[25]

This is just one example of interventions that have been behaviorally targeted and tested to increase policy outcomes. Drawing from the broader literature, table 8.3 provides a summary of five common behavioral biases from this research, as well as examples of how programs could be arranged to account

Table 8.3
Common Behavioral Biases

Common Bias	Description	Alternatives	Example
Rules of thumb	People tend to rely on past or familiar experiences when faced with a new decision.	Present anchor choice sets to individuals with an example of a recent experience.	Provide a suggested amount to deposit into a savings account from income tax return to encourage savings.
Loss/risk aversion	People tend to avoid losses more than they seek out gains; e.g., they would rather not lose $100 than gain $100.	Frame the benefits of participation as a loss rather than as a gain.	Encourage participants to join the program now or they will lose benefits, rather than providing an incentive if they sign up.
Status quo bias	People tend to go with the default option; they often forget to make changes to the default later (even if desired).	Set the default to be something that is most likely to lead to positive change for the participant.	Make the default option on an application to opt in to beneficial programs or services, giving the choice of opting out.
Future discounting	People tend to make decisions that benefit themselves today and worry less about costs in the future.	Set up commitment devices today for future behaviors.	Encourage participants to make a commitment today for some action that they will take later, such as setting aside money from future pay increases.

(continued)

Table 8.3
Common Behavioral Biases *(Continued)*

Common Bias	Description	Alternatives	Example
Too many choices	People tend to be overwhelmed by too many choices and may not make a decision or fall back on a default.	Limit the number of choices or create a default option that will be most likely to lead to positive change.	Provide participants with a short list of easy-to-understand options and select a default that is most beneficial to the participant.

for these biases. This list is illustrative of the types of insights that behavioral economics can provide to policy and program implementation.

Other professionals have developed tools useful for discovering more about the behavioral interactions at the front line of implementation systems. Designers have adopted a user-centered design principle that has led to the development of many relevant and creative innovations. In chapter 6 we applied some of these ideas to understand frontline realities, such as interviews to shape development of personas. Designers trying to understand what shapes frontline behavior also use other methods, such as shadowing and secret shopper types of methods. For example, in trying to understand the challenges of emergency room operation, a design team sent in someone feigning a foot injury. When he was admitted, he experienced how frustrating and bewildering hospital admission was for new patients.[26] When analyzing video taken during the experience, the design team realized that the conditions in the space—featureless waiting rooms, acoustic ceiling tiles visible from a gurney, an endless hallway—created a mix of boredom and anxiety that shaped the patient's experience more than the quality of care did. This awareness of frontline conditions allowed the design team to make recommendations for improving service quality based on the frontline experience.

Considering either the choice architecture or behavioral biases existing in implementation interactions or learning from observing target group members provides important technical information in efforts to make changes. In the daily operation of implementation systems, these realities often get obscured by all of the other factors of people and power, rules and tools. Before turning to these types of adaptive challenges, let's consider one final element of the technical challenge.

Aligning Coordination Activities

One of the key processes of programs is assembling the various institutions and activities to accomplish desired goals. This process of structuring is fundamental to implementation, as people and institutions with different self-interests are coordinated to accomplish collective action. Yet as we have seen, rarely is a coordination system for a program designed from scratch; rather, the coordination process is shaped by the existing structures, rules, performance expectations, and goals at each level of the implementation system. To make matters more complex, coordination spans strategic action fields. While there is coordination taking place within each level, there is also coordination taking place across levels, linking together actors at the front lines, organizations, and policy fields to accomplish important tasks.

Given this complexity, coordination is both a technical and an adaptive challenge. Ultimately coordination is about inducing people to work together toward a common goal, which often requires considerable social skill, particularly in decentralized implementation systems where formal mechanisms for control may be lacking. However, coordination problems often result from technical challenges as well, where the processes employed to coordinate action end up being the wrong tools for the task at hand. There is no one-size-fits-all coordination process that is optimal. Rather, organizational theorists have emphasized that coordinating mechanisms should fit the task or technology being carried out.[27] For example, when the logic of change is clear and results are easily measured, tasks can be more readily coordinated through formalized processes, well-specified contracts, and hierarchical chains of command. However, when tasks are uncertain and the logic linking means and ends is unclear, more discretion of system actors is often needed and trust and goal alignment may play a more important role. This contingency approach to coordination makes sense in theory; however, in implementation practice, there are at least three technical challenges to keep in mind.

First, coordination systems are often inherited from the strategic action fields in which programs are embedded. In a hierarchical policy field, where organizational relationships are specified with formal contracts and written procedures, it may not be feasible to structure an entire program with less formality and more discretion even if the core program has significant uncertainty that could benefit from a more flexible approach. However, astute implementers look for opportunities to create flexibility and enable just-in-time learning, even within the hierarchical control. Meetings among contractors, virtual learning communities, or an explicit expectation of sharing implementation insights can be quite useful in improving alignment. Sometimes programs may be separated into distinct components, where some aspects of the process are formalized and other aspects are flexible.

A second technical challenge for coordination is improper diagnosis of the coordination problem. There are two broad types of problems: inefficiencies, where desired ends are being achieved but the process to get there is not smooth (e.g., it takes too long or is too expensive), and ineffectiveness, where the desired ends are not being achieved. Many popular management tools, such as Six Sigma and Kaizen, target inefficiencies in processes.[28] These tools are borrowed from private industry, similar to the Total Quality Management movement of the 1980s, and applied in public and nonprofit settings with the promise of reducing waste and improving program performance.[29] To the extent that the coordination problem to be solved is related to inefficiency, these tools may indeed have their promised impact.

For example, one of the challenges in the implementation of the HHF program was lack of follow-through with the application process, contributing to low take-up of the program. Homeowners would start the process but then fail to follow through. Why? In part, the process was too time-consuming and laborious, indicative of a potential problem with efficiency. Ohio's HHF team brought in government consultants from a management reform initiative.[30] For the HHF program, this management intervention reported simplifying the intake process to be nine times faster, eliminating fifty-six unnecessary steps in the intake process.[31] To the extent that the slow application process contributed to low take-up, this change to the coordination system may improve intended results.

However, this sort of process is not intended to address problems with effectiveness. If the problem is related to ineffectiveness, where the desired outcomes are not being achieved, streamlining the process to address inefficiencies is likely the wrong fix. At best, it achieves no purpose, like organizing deck chairs on a sinking ship. At worst, it could actually make the problem worse, particularly when opportunities for communication and feedback during the coordination process are eliminated in an effort to improve efficiency.

A final technical challenge to coordination is appropriate use of performance information. In an era of accountability, actors engaged in implementation are often required to track and report performance metrics, ranging from data on inputs, to outputs, to outcomes. While on one hand, this performance information may simply be used to promote transparency, often it is also used for coordination.[32] Sometimes performance measures are tied to rewards and sanctions. Target metrics may be specified in formal contracts between providers engaged in joint service provision in a policy field, in a program manager's annual performance review evaluation, or in a frontline worker's quarterly assessment for additional incentive pay.[33] This can be a very effective approach for coordination when the logic between inputs and the measured outputs (or outcomes) is clear. For example, for post office workers delivering mail, it might make sense to evaluate performance and reward (or sanction) a worker based on the number of routes completed.

However, when the logic is less clear, coordination based on rewards and sanctions tied to performance metrics can have unintended negative consequences. When there is no one proven logic and learning what works (and what does not work) is valued, it may be counterproductive to tie rewards and sanctions to performance targets. No one wants to admit that something is not working or that the hard effort to create change failed. And when an organization's reimbursement from a funder is on the line or a manager's reputation on the job is at stake, it is even more unlikely that the organization (or manager) will report poor performance metrics. Sharing complete and unbiased performance metrics, the type of information needed for system learning under uncertainty, requires trust. In these situations, effective coordination may be best accomplished through ensuring goal congruence and appealing to intrinsic rewards.[34]

Most implementation challenges involve some elements of the program that are relatively clear and other elements of the program that are ambiguous. And most strategic action fields include coordinating mechanisms that are formal, sometimes linked to rewards and sanctions, and other mechanisms that are informal, with shared goals and reciprocity. Effective implementers learn how to manage coordination systems so that they are not constantly reinventing the wheel for something that could be more efficiently programmed into a contract or formal process or are not efficiently reproducing a failed program with misaligned incentives that impede learning. There is no magic bullet. But there are better ways to learn and improve.

ENGAGING OTHERS IN ADAPTIVE CHALLENGES

While it is essential to investigate the contours of the core program adopted by a system, examining the articulation of the problem, its behavioral basis, and the coordination of tasks, these technical issues go only so far in addressing implementation challenges. It is equally important to engage others on the more intractable, adaptive issues, which involve less rational concerns such as norms, values, and worldviews. These are what we have emphasized throughout the book as the social structure and dynamics of strategic action fields. It is what was so significant in actually determining what unfolded during implementation in the HHF and QRS cases, as described in chapter 6. These forces are potent and present when desires to improve implementation effectiveness surface. And since part of policy and program implementation success is measured by the degree to which it gets incorporated into daily work, change efforts must engage others in the system in ways that they understand to be legitimate.

Leading such change requires the use of social skills that both demonstrate one's knowledge of the existing social structure and point a way toward change. It also requires activating the existing resources present in the field, both authority sources and cultural values. Sometimes the formal authority mechanisms already salient in the field—tools of political influence like regulations or economic influence like contracts or grants—can be used to address public value failure. Yet these tools can sometimes backfire because they do not activate deeper commitment. These situations require the use of cultural values to encourage people to engage in the change in terms and values that they find salient. If the cultural dimensions are not addressed, sometimes people can respond by subverting or aborting the intent of the program because they do not feel what they value is taken seriously.[35]

Unlike the analytical inquiry used to address technical challenges, adaptive challenges require a more iterative approach: acting, waiting to see what happens, reflecting, and then making plans for the next action step. It is really engaging with continuous learning about how a complex system operates. Opportunities emerge and must be responded to flexibly to account for the unexpected ways that others react to change.[36] To support this type of work, a whole industry of consultants exists, each with its own frameworks and assessment tools. And while there is variation in quality, we have found that some tools can be very helpful for improving implementation practice. Table 8.4 highlights some of the tools, tactics, and resources potentially useful for effectively engaging others, with purposes ranging from improving group effectiveness to assessing systems dynamics, and

Table 8.4
Tactics and Tools for Adaptive Change in Implementation Systems

Tactics and Tools	Types of Adaptive Challenges Suited to Solve	Examples
Facilitation Design and running of meetings and workshops	Improve group effectiveness	*The Skilled Facilitator*; International Association of Facilitators[a]
Negotiation Dialogue intended to resolve points of difference	Reconciliation of competing positions	*Getting to Yes*[b]
Focus groups or interviews Systematic research method for gathering qualitative data to document understanding and meaning making	Need for systematic assessment of values or understanding of people about a topic	Reference books by SAGE publications; analysis software such as NVivo and Atlas.ti[c]
Whole systems analysis and engagement Understanding of relationships and effects of interacting factors by engaging those affected by or interested in an issue	Create understanding of complex problem, cocreate viable solutions, and build goodwill	Future search, scenario planning, IAP2 spectrum, *Art of Hosting*[d]
Storytelling Use of narrative arts to engage others in understanding problem and solutions	Motivate others to engage in situation; share lessons about successes and failures	TED, *The Story Factor*[e]

(continued)

Table 8.4
Tactics and Tools for Adaptive Change in Implementation Systems *(Continued)*

Tactics and Tools	Types of Adaptive Challenges Suited to Solve	Examples
Strategic planning Process of defining direction and making decisions about resource allocations for pursuing it	Build goodwill for collective action to achieve shared goals	*Strategic Planning for Public and Nonprofit Organizations*[f]

[a]Roger Schwarz, *The Skilled Facilitator: A Comprehensive Resource for Consultants, Facilitators, Managers, Trainers, and Coaches,* 2nd ed. (San Francisco: Jossey-Bass, 2002).

[b]Roger Fisher, William L. Ury, and Bruce Patton, *Getting to Yes: Negotiating Agreement without Giving In* (New York: Penguin Books, 1991).

[c]Richard Krueger and Mary Anne Casey, *Focus Groups: A Practical Guide for Applied Research,* 4th ed. (Thousand Oaks, CA: SAGE, 2008); Herbert J. Rubin and Irene S. Rubin, *Qualitative Interviewing: The Art of Hearing Data,* 3rd ed. (Thousand Oaks, CA: SAGE, 2011).

[d]There is a range of approaches. For a helpful orienting framework in relation to purpose for public policy, see International Association for Public Participation: http://c.ymcdn.com/sites/www.iap2.org/resource/resmgr/imported/IAP2%20Spectrum_vertical.pdf. For processes focused on systems' wide engagement, see Marvin Weisbord and Sandra Janoff, *Future Search: Getting the Whole System in the Room for Vision, Commitment, and Action,* 3rd ed. (San Francisco: Berrett-Koehler, 2010); Peter Schwartz, *The Art of the Long View: Planning for the Future in an Uncertain World* (New York: Currency/Doubleday, 1996); art of hosting: http://www.artofhosting.org; Leah Lundquist, Jodi Sandfort, Cris Lopez, Marcela Sotela Odor, Karen Seashore, Jen Mein, and Myron Lowe, *Cultivating Change in the Academy: Practicing the Art of Hosting Conversations That Matter within the University of Minnesota* (Minneapolis: University of Minnesota, 2013), http://conservancy.umn.edu/handle/155523.

[e]Technology, Entertainment, and Design conferences: www.ted.com; Annette Simmons and Doug Lipman, *The Story Factor,* 2nd ed. (New York: Basic Books, 2006).

[f]John Bryson, *Strategic Planning for Public and Nonprofit Organizations: A Guide to Strengthening and Sustaining Organizational Achievement* (San Francisco: Jossey-Bass, 2011).

from gathering information systematically to cocreating solutions. By building comfort with these approaches, implementers can become more adept in working through the adaptive challenges found in implementation improvement. For example, negotiation is often required when facilitation breaks down as a way to move a group forward. Focus groups and storytelling are tools that engage people's hearts and values, but in very different ways; the first unearths them for scrutiny and consideration, while the latter leverages them to motivate commitment to a change direction.

In complex systems, sustainable change is not cultivated with control or mandates. It begins with actors demonstrating subtle skill, planting seeds, and creating conditions so that others can integrate the new ideas or techniques into the way they accomplish work together. One must develop skills in reading and shaping social interactions, including informal conversations, planning sessions, conference addresses, and team meetings. One must be constantly engaged in reflection, analyzing what is unfolding in the social dynamic and making adjustments. And one must leverage simple tools to communicate meaning and engage others, displaying social skill.

Display Social Skill

As we look around the fields where we work, we both are struck again and again by the subtle social skill of people who lead others in making changes. They work hard, often for modest pay. They occupy various roles, leading small agencies formed to support a nonprofit network, acting as program managers in larger agencies, providing consulting services, or staffing large bureaucracies. Their formal position is not what is most striking about them. It is their self-awareness and understanding of other people, their ability to assess a situation and know exactly how to meet people where they are so that they can become positive participants in change. They also reflect on events and make seemingly midcourse corrections when things are not unfolding as planned. Finally, they create or leverage heuristics—abstract representations of complex things—in engaging others. We have found three concepts helpful in deepening our understanding of these dimensions of social skill.

First, management books and training programs describe self-awareness and the ability to understand others as emotional and social intelligence, stressing its equivalence to other forms of intelligence. Daniel Goleman, a psychologist writing for the *New York Times,* popularized the emotional intelligence concept.[37] In his consideration of scientific evidence, he uncovered that unlike some other innate personality traits, emotional intelligence can be learned and developed. The brain's ability to grow and change alters in response to stimuli and enables us to become more skilled at building durable relationships with others. In his conceptualization, emotional intelligence begins by developing more self-awareness of one's own emotions, including what triggers intense fight-or-flight experiences. This self-awareness enables us to engage in self-management—knowing that going for a walk or working out can bring us back after such intense experiences. It also opens up the possibility for grounded and reflective social awareness. Social awareness is the foundation of our ability to connect effectively with others, to understand how their emotions may drive their actions and ideas and may significantly shape what happens in groups.

Goleman's model suggests that when individuals develop more awareness of self and others, they are able to more effectively manage relationships. Because this ability builds on social awareness, it is not primarily about assessing and using authority to direct others. Rather it hinges on the ability to put ourselves in someone else's shoes, to appreciate the concerns and possibilities that someone else might have, and craft a response to those concerns accordingly. Philosophers and psychologists talk about this as intersubjectivity—the shared understanding that develops between people as they engage with each other from different perspectives.

Individuals interested in improving policy and program effectiveness must demonstrate such emotional intelligence. Tuning into the realities of others, understanding how they think of themselves, their work and priorities, provides essential insights. It helps them anticipate how to frame new ideas, adjust plans to be more feasible, and build rapport that inspires others to commit the resources they have to the change effort. This social skill is essential even for those who possess some resources or authority by virtue of a position in the strategic action field. Everyone likes to be consulted and engaged rather than being told what to do; while this is not always possible, those who spend time learning about the other important actors in their setting can increase the likelihood that their change ideas will be received more openly.

A second competency in social skill is the ability to reflect on and reflect during action. Over thirty years ago, pioneering MIT professor Donald Schön embarked on a series of in-depth studies of professionals, revealing that often they know more about their work than they can say, and that through practice, they develop the capacity to act and adjust their actions depending on what unfolds. Ultimately this inquiry resulted in the publication of two important books: *The Reflective Practitioner* and *Education of a Reflective Practitioner*.[38] In developing his ideas, Schön did extensive studies of different professionals—an architect, psychologist, engineer, urban planner, and business manager—as they were going about their day-to-day work. He realized that all developed a know-how in carrying out their work responsibilities, be it creating three-dimensional building models, holding therapy sessions, or running community meetings. They drew on technical knowledge from their profession that provided a reference point, but they also improvised when the unexpected occurred. This improvisation he equated to what a jazz musician does; in a set, the musician draws on her technical knowledge of chords and tempo, but also spontaneously creates something new within the structure provided by music fundamentals. Schön noted that a similar type of improvisation occurred among other professionals when encountering something unexpected, a surprise. It prompted what he came to term "reflection in action."[39]

Since then, many scholars and educators have focused on better understanding this professional competency that, like emotional intelligence, seems able to be learned.[40] But there are two aspects to this capacity. First is taking time to reflect on events after they have occurred. Given that socially skilled actors know more about their strategic action fields than they can typically articulate, it involves paying attention to moments of surprise. When do things not go as you expect? When does someone else have an unexpected reaction to an announcement or event? When are there unintended consequences from a new program idea? Often as one mulls over the events on the drive home from work or the next day while exercising, one tends to focus on the outcome, the action itself, or the intuitive assumptions in the situation. Taking these times for diagnosis is essential. It is reflection in action. And it helps provide insight about strategic action field dynamics to inform a socially skillful response.

There also is the practice of reflection-in-action, when one doesn't have or can't take the time away but must be noticing surprises and making adjustments in real time. In his analysis of architects and psychotherapists, Schön saw professionals who engaged in on-the-spot experiments; they hit the unexpected, adjusted their frame of the problem, and proceeded with a new understanding, often continuing this cycle of noticing, adjusting, and acting throughout the encounter. The same was said of engineers, planners, and managers. In his mind, this dynamic process revealed the "art of their practice."[41] Others describe this ability as "going up on the balcony" to better observe the "dance floor" of social interaction, understanding it more completely before rejoining the dance with a new awareness.[42] Regardless of the metaphor, this ability to sense and adjust is a skill of effective social actors. Rather than feeling just-in-time adjustments are arbitrary, this evidence helps us appreciate the significance of the skill.

We do not mean to imply that reflection about or in action is a solo event. Oftentimes it can be enabled through a community—other strategic actors in your work, people all practicing a type of engagement technique, others in your spiritual community also engaged in discernment. As humans, we inherently want to make meaning about complexity with others. This truth is the heart of dialogue and discussion that is so essential in adaptive change making.

A third and final competence that socially skillful actors demonstrate is the purposive use of heuristics and diagrams to bring abstract ideas to life and make them concrete for others. This seems to have particularly strong impact at the policy field and organizational levels, where the work hinges on motivating and directing others in carrying out program ideas. Some people naturally create a sketch or diagram to communicate an idea and share it with others. But such a skill can be developed even among those who don't naturally possess much artistic or design ability. With a little practice and humility, anyone can create visual representations of ideas through rough sketches. Similarly, designers create three-dimensional prototypes of ideas with low-cost materials such as sticks, card stock, and modeling clay; these concrete representations invite others to engage in refining the concept. Additionally, in shaping many of the appendixes of this book, we take a similar approach, recommending that you create a visual or diagram to communicate key parts of the analysis. We also suggest questions to use when discussing the analysis with other members in the field, organization, or frontline setting. This design was purposive, applying practical insight from social science.

When you take the time to externalize a new idea, get it out of your head, and make it concrete, there is the potential that you can use it as a resource to create or shape meaning in a social system. Sketches, visual diagrams, three-dimensional prototypes, photos, and videos are artifacts that socially skilled actors use to move a concept or change idea forward.[43] Through an in-depth study of product manufacturing, Paul Carlile conceptualized these tools as "boundary objects" because if they are used well, they can bridge significant differences in professional language or foundational beliefs, or they can cross department or organizational boundaries.[44] Other people have embraced this terminology because it draws attention to the important work that artifacts can sometimes play in social interactions.

There are infinite examples of ways to create useful boundary objects in a particular context. As the proliferation of video collections on YouTube and Vimeo reveals, hardware and software developments decrease the costs and skills required to create videos. With a little practice or concerted effort to use the "smart art" feature of word processing programs or screen capture capability on computers, anyone can useful artifacts. Figure 8.2 illustrates such an example, a simple idea of trade-offs in project management, a technical analysis tool to improve coordinating activities in an implementation project. The simple diagram illustrates a fundamental point that is important to keep in mind when initiating something new: there are inherent trade-offs of quality, time, and resources. If you desire high quality, you must invest either in time or resources (money, people, knowledge) or both. When used in a nonprofit where these trade-offs are often not acknowledged, this diagram can enable a supervisor to lead her team into a realistic conversation about how to create a work plan for the project. Because it illustrates often ignored trade-offs, it can be significant in a strategic action field if used to facilitate planning conversations.

Figure 8.3 provides another heuristic that can be useful in working with groups. It represents a well-established concept in group development: convergence and divergence. Although groups might come together with a shared purpose, when people share their ideas, they begin by diverging, offering many

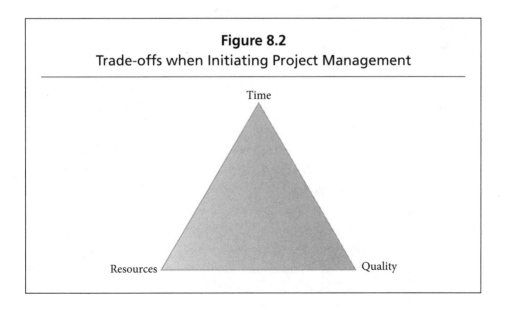

Figure 8.2
Trade-offs when Initiating Project Management

Time

Resources Quality

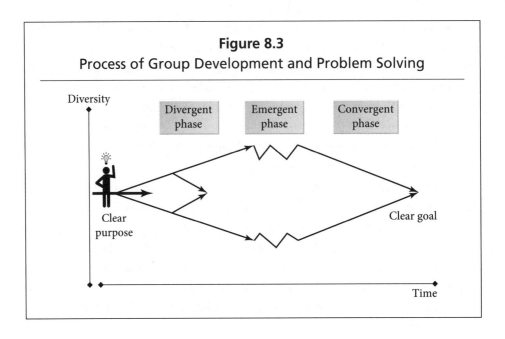

Figure 8.3

Process of Group Development and Problem Solving

Diversity

Divergent phase

Emergent phase

Convergent phase

Clear purpose

Clear goal

Time

different perspectives. Think of what happens in a brainstorming session. Some people find this process energizing because of all of the possibilities, and others find it terrifying because of all of the possibilities. After some time has passed, though, the group goes through a phase where something new is beginning to crystalize—what is called on the visual the emergent phase but often is experienced by participants as the groan zone. It is difficult when a group is on the verge of shared clarity but not yet there. When ideas converge, people come to agreement on the direction and a clear goal or result emerges. Jodi's research with colleague Kathryn Quick reveals that in citizen engagement projects, some facilitators use this heuristic as a significant boundary object to help orient participants as to where they are in the process.[45] For goal-oriented participants, it enabled them to trust the process. For those who thrive on creative idea generation, it reminded them that they ultimately needed come to some result.

Many artifacts are brought into use all the time in social systems to move implementation ideas forward. Such tools provide content, but their significance depends entirely on people who are able to engage others through their application. If used to facilitate conversation and analysis, they operate as boundary objects, allowing differently situated individuals to consider what is and what could be changed in implementation processes.

In highlighting social skill, we are explicitly directing attention to the competencies necessary to develop to engage others in grappling with the uncertainty and ambiguity that surround many decisions. Emotional intelligence, reflection on action, and use of material artifacts are specific practices that can help engage others. Yet as we have seen, there are other particular mechanisms in social systems that also deserve consideration.

Activating Authority and Using Culture

As we have stressed throughout, there are common influences—laws and regulations, market conditions, legitimizing forces, beliefs and values—that cut across strategic action fields. But the way they come together with participants and resources is unique to that place, directly influencing how the core program is enacted. It is fundamentally a social process. As Jim Spillaine and colleagues conclude from their studies of education reform, "Implementation practice is not simply a function of an individual agent's ability, skill and cognition; rather it is constituted in the interaction of administrators, teachers, students and their situation in the execution of particular tasks."[46] Thus, what happens in these interactions is significant in shaping what is considered legitimate. As a result, professional norms, as well as the shared beliefs and values developed from the work, are essential components for many change processes. In thinking about how to improve mandated standardized test implementation, administrators and teachers might be open to instituting rest times and nutritious snacks between exams, but they are unlikely to let students watch Japanese anime videos to unwind (even though the latter is what middle school students would prefer!). Culture is rarely a leading indicator of change; it emerges from the interactions of resources and technology from within the bounds of the social structure and often helps to sustain the status quo.[47]

Culture also can be what eats strategy for lunch. Strategic action field theory does suggest that creating new or unearthing existing resources is a powerful way to challenge the existing order of things and enable other feasible options for actions to crystalize.[48] For example, receiving a large new grant creates new financial resources and may destabilize the normal operation of things. In this way, it can provide a new opportunity for shifting implementation activities. Similarly, hiring talented staff or engaging external experts may create moments when new ways of working can be considered and embraced. Activating other latent sources of authority, such as politicians' self-interest or opportunities to comment on government regulations, might be similarly effective.

Although the interactions of culture and political and economic authority are complex and their consequences impossible to predict, two things are helpful in improving our awareness of how people effectively use them in improving public value creation in implementation.

First, while we earlier discussed the importance of grounding the problem and exploring the behavioral base of a policy or program, it is important to frame what comes out of this analysis in relevant terms. Framing is how people encourage others to understand things. It can be done formally through marketing, media stories, politicians' or leaders' speeches, or more informally in how topics are introduced and reinforced in social settings. Frames can also be communicated through more subtle means—stories, metaphors, or visual images or brands—which can cognitively anchor them while the details of a strategy are being worked out.[49] Many social science disciplines point to the significance of framing in shaping others' understanding and mobilizing them into action.[50]

While there are important nuances in the arguments, frame analysis in general suggests that it is more effective to base new frames on the legitimate authority or values already salient in a context.[51] Doctors may be more open to embracing a new program framed as an "empirical support intervention" than high-school-educated welfare caseworkers would. The differences in their formal education backgrounds influence what types of evidence they think is compelling. Coalitions of nonprofit advocacy organizations are more easily engaged in new "movements" than program evaluation firms are. Consider the influences of authority and culture that bound the implementation setting when exploring potential frames. If authority is primarily exerted through market logic and mechanisms, a new process or approach is more compelling framed with a terminology of competitiveness and efficiency, bottom lines, and market feasibility. If political authority is more salient, the significance of equity, due process, and transparency may be more compelling.

This idea relates to dynamics within strategic action fields. Think of the point, discussed earlier in this book, about the debates that often happen at the beginning of an implementation process. Actors discuss viable options, narrowing in on some elements that seem reasonable for accomplishing the desirable outcomes. In those debates, many options are considered, and what is selected is often driven either by what is already operating or by some leaders who can frame an alternative. Strategic action field theory is also clear that fields evolve; alternative problem frames swirl around the boundaries of the field waiting for a moment to reexert themselves.[52] If part of the change agenda involves a fundamental reorientation of the tasks or outcomes of implementation, some potent sources of framing might be gleaned from initial ideas when the policy or program was introduced. Alternatively, there may be larger social frames—the urgency of a global recession, the need for global competitiveness, the information age—that provide potent reference points.

At first blush, attending to framing as a means for influencing others and introducing new options for change strikes some people as inane and others as deceitful. But we assure you that it is neither. Strategic action requires engaging other people starting from where they are at and what they value. If an implementer frames desired change processes or results in terms that others do not understand, then the implementer failed before she even started. In doing the adaptive work necessary of helping people step away from the familiar into new territory, framing is essential.

A second way to work with authority and culture present in the strategic action field is to purposively engage others. In chapter 6, we discussed a range of implementation activities that can be used to engage different types of target groups, from participatory approaches to coercive compliance with sanctions. There exists a similar continuum for how one might engage other system actors in improving implementation. It is useful to consider the range of possible options because conventional approaches that have worked in the past in one context might not always be potent enough to support the degree of change needed.

There is a spectrum of activities that enables clearer thinking about the range of engagement activities. On one end are activities focused on informing or consulting various stakeholders through fact sheets, open meetings, or focus groups. These are appropriate approaches when the key change elements are largely decided and feedback needs to be solicited to improve or validate the approach. In the middle are formal advisory groups, polling, or conferences that seek to involve others in thinking about implementation challenges and possible solutions. These techniques were used often in both the HHF and QRS situations because of the diverse people who felt invested in the outcomes of program implementation.

There are still others who see engagement as a way to involve citizens or target group members in actual coproduction as a means to hone implementation activities. For example, in some public sector innovation projects, particularly in

Europe, governments are actively engaging citizens in public services redesign.[53] While originally argued as a means for increasing democratic participation or building legitimacy with the public, implementers are finding that engaging citizens actually enables a process that leads to better, more comprehensive solutions. As consultant Christian Bason writes, "Public sector organizations desperately need citizens' participation to better understand what they experience, how their experience could be improved, and their behavior might be changed."[54] Like the designers who experienced hospital emergency rooms to understand what needed to be changed, such engagement provides more complete information that can ground the problem.

Yet the engagement methods referenced in table 8.4 can be used for more than just providing information to implementation decision makers. They can be applied to unearth the knowledge and resources present at different levels in implementation systems and coproduce agreement about strategies for improvement. Often valuable knowledge about day-to-day implementation activities is decentralized in a system, particularly the information held by frontline staff who are delivering programs or working with clients. There is an experience gap between these professionals and people who make decisions about strategy and resource investment. Participatory processes like Future Search or the technique used in Art of Hosting can create a setting where these differences can be bridged, research into a technical solution to an implementation problem can be shared, and change strategies can be developed and refined. It has the potential to lead to more accurate and timely adjustments in implementation practice because it both draws on technical knowledge and customizes it to particular situations through engaging all elements of the system.

But this type of engagement takes time and sometimes might not seem worth the investment, particularly in resource-strapped initiatives. Certainly one must adopt an appropriate engagement approach. Yet because any change, any new activities must be considered legitimate for them to be embraced and integrated into standard operations, engagement is not an optional activity. If engaged, people will contribute their time, knowledge, curiosity, and talents. They will make connections with people outside the setting and bring in talent that can help solve technical challenges—how to create a website, automate a process, market an innovation. In environments strapped for financial resources, such engagement is essential. Without it, barriers to change will not be easily overcome and new ones will develop.

BRINGING IT ALL TOGETHER

In this concluding chapter, we have distinguished between technical and adaptive challenges to heuristically allow elaboration on important elements of each. In practice, however, these challenges emerge and evolve simultaneously. Leading effective implementation change requires the ability to draw on specific technical expertise while demonstrating social skills relevant to that context, while still communicating across the full implementation system. This is a tall order. Most of us tend to gravitate toward one skill set or the other; some are policy wonks who enjoy digging into the technical mechanisms underlying a problem, while others are relational experts who can successfully navigate even the most stressful social situations. Traditional training in public affairs that distinguishes between policy analysis and public management fuels this chasm. However, effective implementation practice must integrate both.

This integration requires deliberate practice and reflection. In appendix H, we provide an implementation improvement blueprint to help serve as a guide, or boundary object, as you lead change in your own implementation settings. We summarize some important questions to consider regarding the technical and adaptive aspects of leading change within a particular implementation setting. Like gardening, however, effective implementation is as much of an art as it is a science. Each strategic action field is its own portion of the larger implementation system garden, with its plants, landscape, and microclimate. Strategies that are useful to improve growth and change in one part of the system might not work as well in other settings. In this chapter, we have provided a language to describe some of the common challenges that emerge across implementation settings. But ultimately, effective implementation is about skillful practice.

The pursuit of effective implementation has led some leaders to focus on instrumental means to affect change most directly. Some fields invest considerable resources in training and coaching teams focused around particular program logic. Our analysis here suggests that while these efforts might be successful in integrating the program in the short term, they are not likely to create improvements that allow continuous improvement and lasting change. A more promising tactic is to work within the strategic action fields to create structures and cultures focused on improvement-oriented ongoing adjustments. There is a range of options, many of which we have suggested in this chapter. Obviously we are not prescribing options. Rather, we have tried to lay out a range that implementers might assemble given the tasks they face and the contexts within which changes will be carried out.

It is no wonder that civil servants and nonprofit professionals burn out on their jobs. Implementation is hard, and it is often a thankless task. It is much easier to blame the system, or the authorizing organization, or the service organization, or the frontline worker for a program failure than it is to wrestle with the complexity of implementation. Yet too often in the press for simple answers and high expectations of public service, many people find it easier not to engage. We hope that you see that there is no blame here. Through honing your own understanding of and your own commitment to strategic action within implementation settings, you can become a more powerful force of change in implementation systems. Implementation practice is about learning and continual improvement.

Policy Field Audit

Public policy and program implementation is complex in part because it involves so many diverse institutions. Sometimes the relationships between these institutions are formalized with government tools such as grants and contracts. Other times, they are informal, based on affiliation or history. A policy field audit can help make sense of these institutional realities.

Policy fields are bounded networks among organizations carrying out a substantive policy and program area in a particular place.[1] Therefore, a policy field analysis begins by identifying a substantive policy or program area of interest. For many professionals, their organization's mission or role helps define this substantive topic area. It might fall neatly within one policy domain, such as public education or renewable energy, or it might cross a number of policy areas; for example, economic development can involve transportation, housing, small business development, and land use policies.

Step 1

Step 1 focuses on identifying the specific federal, state, and local institutions involved in implementing this program or addressing this substantive issue. After brainstorming a list, consider the following questions:

1. *Which organizations have an interest in this policy or program?* Interests can come from staff expertise or organizational reputation, as well as their assessment of the economic, political, or ideological significance of engaging in the work.

2. *Which organizations have power to make change related to it?* Power can come from many sources, including funding, program expertise, research know-how, or communications infrastructure.

3. *Where does administrative authority lie?* In policy systems, all organizations possess some political authority, yet some organizations are given authority to mandate compulsion to change because of the power of law, public investment of funding, or both. Chapter 4 explores how the internal operations of these organizations shape implementation processes. But they also are important to identify at the policy field level.

Once identified, policy field institutions can be summarized in an annotated list, perhaps organized by sector or interest area. Significant institutions, in terms of substantial power or interest, can be called out with asterisks or bold font. This list will be helpful to inform the other parts of the policy field analysis.

Step 2

Step 2 involves cataloguing the laws, public funding streams (and their forms), and other important implementation resources in use in the field:

1. What are the important national, state, or local laws establishing the policy or authorizing public funding?

2. What policy tools are in use? Policy tools have been defined as "an identifiable method through which collective action is structured to address a policy problem."[2] These tools typically leverage the authority or resources of government, or both, and are structured as grants, contracts, vouchers, regulations, tax expenditures, and so on. Refer to table 4.3 in chapter 4 for examples of common policy tools. Consider how the policy tools in use might affect conditions or create implementation constraints within the field.

3. What other significant implementation resources are available to support implementation activities? Implementation resources have been defined as "individuals or organizations that can help implementing units learn about policy, best practices for doing policy, or professional reforms meant to change the character of services delivered to clients."[3] As noted in table 4.3, an array of nonmonetary implementation resources might be important in shaping what is happening in the field.

It is likely most helpful to arrange the policy tools and implementation resources in a table format, categorizing them by types or level of influence. Throughout, you might want to use some of the ideas discussed in chapter 4 to structure this table.

Policy Field Visual Diagram

After identifying the institutions involved in a particular policy field and describing the tools and implementation resources in use, it is often useful to create a visual diagram to illustrate key institutions and relationships. To do so, follow two steps.

Step 1

This step documents the important relationships between the institutions identified in part 1: public agencies at national, regional/state, and local levels; philanthropies; nonprofit and private service providers; purveyors or intermediaries; research or evaluation organizations; nonprofit members; and advocacy agencies. In network analysis, these are conventionally described as the ties that link organizations together. Three types of formal relationships or ties are particularly significant to understand at the beginning of policy field analysis:

1. Funding
2. Legal accountability
3. Service linkages

Because these relationships are more difficult to communicate, we advise a second step.

Step 2

Step 2 creates a visual representation of the field and relationships, particularly if you want to use the results of your analysis with others. The specific conventions of the visual representation should be customized to the audience and shaped to reflect the main analysis points you learned through investigation. Some options to consider are:

- Arrange important institutions horizontally by the level of government at which they operate: national, regional/state, local.
- Use different colors or shapes to designate public, private, and nonprofit organizations.
- Shade organizations with high levels of authority.
- Use different colors to differentiate different types of relationships.

This step-by-step approach allows a descriptive analysis of the macroconditions of the policy environment that directly shapes implementation of your policy or program of interest.

By identifying the major accountabilities and resources, you describe and share with others the forces that structure some of the perspectives those different field actors bring to the implementation process.

Program Process Flow

U sed in business operations management and design, program process flow analysis can yield valuable insight into how ideals are operationalized in an organizational context. Often a diagram is used to create a visual representation of the technology and sequencing of tasks. It illustrates how inputs are transformed into outputs. Because creating these diagrams can often provide a valuable learning experience for staff who might have little opportunity to come up from the details of day-to-day tasks, the steps emphasize engaging others in their development. Obviously they can also be created by a single individual familiar with the level of detail required for the intended use.

These process diagrams can be used in monitoring, program refinement, and building awareness among a service team. They can be aligned with management information systems tracking and used to assess potential backlogs or improper sequencing.

Step 1: Convene frontline staff or target group members, or both, who are familiar with the full range of activities carried out to deliver the program. Brainstorm the engagement and intake process with the target population.

Step 2: Arrange the activities in a sequential manner, left to right, top to bottom, bottom to top (whichever graphical representation accurately represents your context).

Step 3: Designate the steps of the process, including any branching options or feedback mechanisms structured into the process with arrows (single-headed or double wherever relevant).

Step 4: Add any final graphic designators for substantively important activities (e.g., those conducted by other organizations, those for which data are systematically gathered).

Step 5: Engage relevant stakeholders in analysis of the program process flow. Write out or discuss with others the following questions:

- What is most notable about this image? Consider its scope and complexity. Does it match the task at hand?

- Where are potential places where implementation challenges might result? What could be the cause?

- What options are available for making the program process more efficient?

- What options are available for improving effectiveness in interacting with the target group?

Organization Program Integration Audit

To understand how a particular program is situated within an existing organization, it is helpful to conduct an audit of the organization-program fit along several important dimensions.

Step 1

Set the bounds of your analysis. Often it is sufficient to compare the program of interest to the entire organization. However, sometimes it might be useful to broaden the scope of the analysis. For example, if an organization operates many disparate programs, selecting another program or two for comparison in addition to the whole organization might be useful.

Step 2

Use a table to represent the key elements of comparison. Table D.1 provides a template. First consider the organization as a whole on the particular factors. Then consider how the specific program being implemented can be described in relation to this same factor.

Step 3

Spend some time looking at the results of both the organization and program columns in the table. Consider the alignment between the program and the organization on each of the six factors. The following questions can be used to guide group discussions about the fit and potential changes.

- *Target audience*: Does the program target the same market that is targeted by other programs within the organization? Does the organization have prior

Table D.1
Organization Program Integration Audit (OPIA) Template

Key Factors	Organization	Program (s)
Target audiences	Describe the current constituencies or markets of the organization.	Describe the audience served or engaged in the program.
Program technology	Describe the current program technologies in use in the organization.	Describe the core program technology in use or proposed for this program.
Structure	Describe the current structures in use within the organization.	Describe how the program is structured to facilitate coordination.
Financial resources	Describe the funding sources and their overall characteristics.	Describe the funding sources for the program.
Culture and power	Describe how the culture and power distribution in the organization facilitate or impede integration.	Describe the extent to which culture and power support integration and the value of the program.
Key external relationships	Describe the key actors or institutions understood to be significant by senior organizational managers.	Describe the key relationships external to the organization for program delivery.

experience with the program's target market? Could serving this program's target market detract from or enhance services provided to the organization's other target market?

- *Program technology*: How similar (or dissimilar) is the technology for the focal program to the technology for other programs within the organization? Does the program expand or stretch the organization's current technology? How much? Is this feasible? Are new resources needed to accommodate the technology?

- *Structure*: Does the location of the program within the structure of the organization facilitate or impede the delivery of the program activities? What changes, if any, to the organization's structure are needed? Are these changes feasible?

- *Resources*: How does funding for this program compare with other funding to the organization? What proportion of total organizational funding does this program represent? What challenges, if any, might this present?

- *Culture*: How do the values underlying this program fit with the values of the organization? Is there potential for conflict? How important are shared beliefs and values for successful coordination of this program? Is more or less socialization of staff necessary for this program?

- *Key external relationships*: Do senior managers understand the significance of key external actors for this program? Can time be allocated to nurture and support the development of these relationships?

Frontline Interactions Audit appendix E

The diversity of public policies and programs, as well as the many settings where they are implemented, creates distraction sometimes from analytically focusing on the front lines, where the implementation system interacts with the target group of the policy or program.

To understand a particular situation and be able to describe it to others, it is often helpful to do a quick audit of the situation.

Step 1

Consider the most appropriate source of information for the audit. Do you or other professionals understand enough about frontline interactions to recount typical experiences? Does some structured observation need to occur?

Step 2

Use table E.1 as a template. Describe the key elements significant for understanding the nature of frontline interactions in your context or area of your own implementation analysis.

Step 3

Once you have described the situation, it is important to consider its implications in shaping frontline implementation. Write out or discuss with others the following questions:

- How does the nature of target group engagement shape the interactions?
- What is the significance of the label given to the target groups? What assumptions does it communicate? What are the moral issues at work in this categorization?

Table E.1
Frontline Interactions Audit Template

Key Factors	Specific Questions to Consider
Target group	
• Nature of the engagement • Descriptive labels • Diversity	• Participatory? Voluntary? Mandatory? • How is the target group referred to at the front lines? Other parts of the system? (for example, "clients," "home owners," "patients") • Is the target group homogeneous, mixed, or heterogeneous in relation to program objectives
Interaction structure	
• Communication medium • Duration • Information and communication infrastructure	• Is the interaction face-to-face, in close or distanced physical proximity? Is it facilitated by technology through a website or portable app or phone? • Are the interactions typically fleeting, one time, multiple times, or is there continuity of contact over an extended number of times? • Is there an established process for standardization or customization? Is an information technology infrastructure provided?
Social significance	
• Expectations • Value • Power of information	• Does the target group have expectations of transactional interactions, emotional connection, customization? Something else? • How significant are the program benefits in the target group's livelihood? What is the importance of the program in their lives? • Are there disparities in information between the target group and system? Are they acknowledged?

- What is significant about how the interaction is structured?

- Given that we know target-group expectations shape assessments of quality, is the interaction structured in ways that are consistent with policy or program intent?

- Are there variations in the target-group expectations across different members? Is that significant in program satisfaction?

- How much vulnerability does the target group experience in the interactions? Is this something to be capitalized on or minimized to achieve desired policy results?

Target Experiences Analysis

arget group members have experiences when interacting with public systems that are often obscured for implementers who are used to seeing and thinking from an operations- or systems-centered viewpoint. The target experiences analysis helps create a series of tools that capture information important to understanding frontline implementation from the perspective of the target groups. As such, it can provide valuable insight into current implementation conditions.

Step 1

Collect information about the groups targeted for change by the policy or program. This step can be as informal or formal as necessary and involve harvesting from published sources of information or collecting original data; often the approach is dictated by time and resource constraints. It should focus on getting background information that influences how the target group experiences the public service interaction.

A range of structured information options could be pursued during this stage:

- Literature review of qualitative studies that rely on data from interviews, observation, or focus groups with the target groups
- Observation and informal discussion with target group members at the point of interaction
- Posing as a client (or multiple types of people posing as clients) experiencing the service interaction
- Developing a sampling framework and gathering original data through interviews, focus groups, or surveys
- A combination of these options

Describe the physical, economic, or social context within which the target group members experience the policy or program. Uncover what happens before, during, and after the interaction. Focus on identifying salient moments that contribute to positive experiences or detract from them.

Step 2

Create personae to represent key experiences from the information gathered. These composite characters should bring together important demographic and social realities important in the application. In most projects, only three to five personae should be developed; these representative profiles help to humanize frontline implementation conditions and highlight important distinctions among the target group members.

Most often, personae are written out, providing fictitious names, photos, and key aspects of their lives relevant to the behavior the policy or program seeks to influence. Supplemental graphs or diagrams also can be provided. Communicate the essential elements of the personae so as to create empathy among the readers with their situations.

Step 3

This final step requires some abductive logic, applying what is represented in the personae and considering how that might affect worldview and experiences with the policy or program.[1] However, it is necessary to move from the perspective of the system into the larger context of the larger world, in which the public policy or program interacts with an array of other social, economic, and environmental factors.

Given the composite profiles, consider how implementation system operations interact with these personae. Think about the interactions step-by-step (use some of the information gathered in the frontline interactions audit). Consider various relevant questions including:

- What would be the actions, feelings, perceptions, and frame of mind brought to the interaction by the personae?

- What are the salient moments in which strong emotions or experiences might be possible?

Answering such questions can be a way to capture and map an array of significant experiences. The results can be represented in a time line, a flowchart, sequences of photos or sketches, or whatever else might most evocatively represent how these people experience the system. Sometimes it is useful to think through and write out scenarios, narrative accounts used to explore experiences from the target group members' point of view. One created for each persona might reflect, for example, how a changed economic environment might influence different experiences of the program.

This analysis lays out a multistaged approach to deepening understanding of target group experiences with implementation systems. In its application, consider when key products from this analysis need to be presented to others involved in implementation and improvements. Some questions for using these materials include:

- What does this snapshot reveal about target group members that is obscured in current conceptions of implementation?
- Which moments of interaction are most salient for different types of target group members?
- Where might our attention for making changes to improve implementation be focused?

Implementation Dynamics and Outcomes Analysis

In this book, we see implementation systems as created by the activities within interrelated yet distinct strategic action fields. To better understand how implementation activities unfold within a system, it is important to describe and analyze actual dynamics occurring at different scales in a system. Whereas previous appendixes focus on cataloguing the participants, resources, and technologies operating at various levels, this tool helps highlight how authority and culture shape what is created and how it changes.

To provide a way forward, take some time to do some analysis of the dynamics and desirable outcomes in the implementation system. (We illustrate how to apply this framework in the two cases described in chapter 7.)

Step 1

Describe the desired results of policy or program implementation. As discussed in chapter 1, there are many possible indicators of implementation effectiveness. We find it most helpful to consider changes in the system and groups targeted by the policy or program. Since so much of implementation activities focus on improving quality, it is also important to articulate both quality results and ultimate policy outcomes.

In some cases, such indicators of implementation effectiveness can be developed through a formalized process (retreats, meetings) and made visible to people throughout the implementation system. At other times, they remain implicit in the operation of the implementation system. Clear articulation of the terms used to define effectiveness can, in and of itself, bring clarity to implementation and any attempts to improve it.

Table G.1
Indicators of Implementation Effectiveness

	Process Quality Results	Ultimate Outcomes
Change in systems operations	Quality of program delivery	Integration of program processes into daily operations
Change in target groups	Target group satisfaction, engagement with the program	Desired change in the behaviors or conditions of the target group

Step 2

Analyze variation in the core program as it exists within different strategic fields. In our examples in this book, we have focused on a number of sites: policy field, authorizing organization, service organizations, and front lines. Often it is appropriate to describe variations in the core program across these levels. As we have emphasized throughout, while there might be a technological core, the activities undertaken as part of the program's change process are often modified, adapted, or even subverted in different contexts.

Depending on your work or position, it might be more desirable to describe variations in the core program not across levels in the system but among different strategic action fields at that same scale; for example, a state-level program manager working in an authorizing organization might want to compare program technologies across service organizations receiving contracts to provide the same service.

In describing the core program, consider the following questions (refer back to chapter 3 to see each item explained in detail, as they refer to the key dimensions of viable options, logic of change, and activity coordination). In this setting:

- What are we trying to accomplish? What is the range of activities considered appropriate to address the problem?

- What assumptions are being made about the target group? About the staff working at the front lines? The activities instituted to make the change?

- How are activities being coordinated to achieve the objectives? How is work structured to allow for communication?

As you gather answers to these questions from each implementation setting, approach each with a clean slate. Do not assume that the understanding from one place can be applied elsewhere. Remember that these are distinct (although related) strategic action fields.

You may want to present your discoveries in a table or adaptations to a visual program process flow (described in appendix C).

Step 3

Once the variations in the core program are established, seek to understand how things came to be the way they are in particular contexts. As described in chapter 3, this is an analysis of the mechanisms that shape social structure and dynamics within a strategic action field. Table G.2 can be used to summarize key

Table G.2
Mechanisms of Authority and Culture That Shape Social Structure and Influence Social Dynamics in Strategic Action Fields

	Establishing Viable Options	Identifying the Logic of Change	Coordinating Activities
Overarching question	What do we want to accomplish? What is the range of activities considered appropriate to address the problem?	How will we bring about change in the target population?	How will activities be coordinated to accomplish the objectives? How is work structured to allow for communication?
Political and economic authority			
Laws and regulations Market conditions			
Culture			
Legitimizing practices Beliefs and values			

mechanisms at work; while not all mechanisms are likely to be present, this table provides a systematic way to summarize them (refer back to chapter 3 to see each cell explained in detail). This type of analysis can help point to disjuncture in an implementation system.

Step 4

Summarize the key challenges that have emerged during the implementation process. Describe how these challenges have affected the resulting program and the extent to which this might affect the intended public value results and outcomes, identified in step 1. Conclude with your assessment of the critical challenges to address as you move forward.

Implementation Improvement Blueprint

mplementation problems come bundled with both technical and adaptive challenges. Technical challenges are those for which cause and effect can be described, solutions are known, and tactics for adoption can be shared and replicated from setting to setting. Adaptive challenges are those that are more ambiguous and involve values and power, beliefs and authority.

We provide some guiding questions to help facilitate learning about technical and adaptive challenges in a particular implementation setting. These lists are by no means exhaustive. Rather, they are intended to help you highlight the technical and social skills you need to lead learning in the implementation system within which you find yourself.

Technical Challenges

Setting the Problem

1. *Scientific inquiry.* What more can be learned about the needs or constraints of the target population? What have others found to be most effective at creating the types of process and outcome changes desired by the program?

2. *Public values.* Consider how the indicators of implementation that are effective relevant to your context (from appendix G) relate to the threats described in table 8.3. What are the potential threats to creating public value associated with existing or proposed changes to the program?

Behavioral Change

1. *Diagnosing the behavioral problem.* What is the behavioral change or alteration of conditions desired by this policy or program? What is the

psychological target? What are the levers being applied to make this change?

2. *Identifying biases.* Review the list of common behavioral biases in table 8.3. Which might be prevalent in your context? What alternative strategies could more closely address this behavior?

Aligning Coordination

1. *Coordination constraints.* To what extent do the existing coordinating systems match the technological tasks at hand? How could additional structure or flexibility be added to the system, where needed, to improve the coordination of the program?

2. *Diagnosing the coordination problem.* Are there inefficiencies in the coordination system? Where? How might these be addressed by a continuous improvement model?

3. *Use of performance information.* How could performance information being collected in the system be used to promote more efficiency? How could additional incentives or sanctions be used to better facilitate coordination? Is this appropriate?

Adaptive Challenges

Social Skill

1. *Emotional intelligence.* Step outside your own experience in the implementation system. How might others, in different positions or operating at different levels, feel about the operations of this implementation system? What might be their priorities and motivations for making improvements?

2. *Reflective practice.* Reflect back on a moment of surprise that you experienced in the implementation setting where you are situated. (For example: When did things not go as you expected? When did someone else have an unexpected reaction to an announcement or event? Were there any unintended consequences from a new program idea?) What might be causing these events? What might you learn from them to inform your next actions?

3. *Heuristics.* What boundary objects might be most relevant in your strategic action field? Drawings? Videos? Metaphors? How could you visually represent the important challenges you need others to engage with and address?

Activating Authority and Using Culture

1. *Framing.* How could you use conceptual frames, analogies, and metaphors to describe challenges that must be addressed? How might they pivot from common reference points but be used to facilitate learning or new thinking?

2. *Purposive engagement.* How might be it strategic to engage others in your implementation setting? To gain information? Coproduce improvements in the program? Improve outcomes? Review the engagement methods in table 8.4 to identify which of them might be most useful in this setting.

NOTES

PREFACE

1. We agree with James March and Johan Olsen, who say: "It is that governance becomes less a matter of engineering than of gardening; less a matter of hunting than of gathering." James G. March and Johan P. Olsen, "Organizing Political Life: What Administrative Reorganization Tells Us about Government," *American Political Science Review* 77, no. 2 (1983): 281–96. A similar idea is elaborated by Johan Olsen, who says, "Reformers are institutional gardeners more than architects and engineers. They reinterpret codes of behavior, impact causal and normative beliefs, . . . develop organized capabilities, and improve adaptability." Johan P. Olsen, "Understanding Institutions and Logics of Appropriateness: Introductory Essay" (ARENA working paper 13, no. 07, Centre for European Studies, 2007).

PART ONE

1. Johan P. Olsen, "Understanding Institutions and Logics of Appropriateness: Introductory Essay" (ARENA working paper 13, no. 07, Centre for European Studies, 2007), 10.

2. Sue Phillips, introduction to *The Practical Gardening Encyclopedia* (Surrey, UK: Colour Library Direct, 1997).

CHAPTER ONE

1. While details are taken from research about the Patient Protection and Affordable Care Act in Colorado, all individuals' names and roles are fictitious, created to illustrate the multilevel implementation analysis presented in this book.

2. These points were made in the governor's report: Office of the Governor of Colorado, "The State of Health: Colorado's Commitment to Become the Healthiest State" (Denver: Office of the Governor of Colorado, 2013), http://www.cohealthinfo.com/wp-content/uploads/2014/08/The-State-of-Health-Final-April-2013.pdf. For the initial state comparisons, see Commonwealth Fund. "Health System Data Center," online scorecard (2014), http://datacenter.commonwealthfund.org/scorecard/low-income/7/colorado/.

3. The Supreme Court ruling in 2012 (*National Federation of Independent Businesses* v. *Sebelius*) upheld the provisions of the Affordable Care Act but limited the federal government's abilities to impose penalties if the states did not pursue Medicaid expansion under the bill. But Colorado followed twenty-five other states and launched the program expansion in 2014 because of the financial benefits it brings.

4. Jeffrey L. Pressman and Aaron Wildavsky, *Implementation: How Great Expectations in Washington Are Dashed in Oakland or Why It's Amazing That Federal Programs Work at All*, 3rd ed. (Berkeley: University of California Press, 1984).

5. Richard E. Matland, "Synthesizing the Implementation Literature: The Ambiguity-Conflict Model of Policy Implementation," *Journal of Public Administration Research and Theory* 5, no. 2 (1995): 145–74; William T. Gormley Jr., "Regulatory Issue Networks in a Federal System," *Polity* 18, no. 4 (1986): 595–620.

6. Daniel A. Mazmanian, and Paul A. Sabatier, *Implementation and Public Policy* (Glenview, IL: Scott, Foresman, 1983), 21.

7. Paul A. Sabatier and Hank C. Jenkins-Smith, *Policy Change and Learning: An Advocacy Coalition Approach*, ed. Paul A. Sabatier and Hank C. Jenkins-Smith (Boulder, CO: Westview Press, 1993); Michael Hill and Peter Hupe, *Implementing Public Policy: An Introduction to the Study of Operational Governance*, 2nd ed. (Thousand Oaks, CA: SAGE, 2008).

8. While there is a long tradition of defining and considering public value in public administration and management, recently there has been a resurgence of attention across a number of subfields in public affairs. For illustrations, see John Bryson, Barbara Crosby, and Laura Bloomberg,

"Public Value Governance: Moving beyond Traditional Public Administration and the New Public Management," *Public Administration Review* 74, no. 4 (2014): 444–56.

9. Pressman and Wildavsky expressed this idea in the 1984 edition of their important book, *Implementation,* through an essay entitled, "Implementation as Evolution." Yet in the more recent developments in implementation sciences that we discuss in greater detail in chapter 2, the philosophical foundations of this task are often overlooked.

10. For our definition, we follow the lead of scholar Barry Bozeman, *Public Values and Public Interest: Counterbalancing Economic Individualism* (Washington, DC: Georgetown University Press, 2007). In this book, Bozeman defines public values as those values "providing normative consensus about (a) the rights, benefits, and prerogatives to which citizens should (and should not) be entitled; (b) the obligations of citizens to society, the state, and one another; and (c) the principles on which government policies should be based" (131).

11. This is a well-established tenet in organizational studies. Pamela S. Tolbert and Richard H. Hall, *Organizations: Structures, Processes, and Outcomes,* 10th ed. (Upper Saddle River, NJ: Prentice Hall, 2009); and in public administration, Hal G. Rainey, *Understanding and Managing Public Organizations,* 4th ed. (San Francisco: Jossey-Bass, 2009) with considerable empirical exploration of the multiple competing ways that organizational effectiveness is defined. As a result, a multicomponent framework such as the one suggested here is recommended.

12. Evelyn Z. Brodkin, "Implementation as Policy Politics," in *Implementation and the Policy Process: Opening Up the Black Box*, ed. Dennis J. Palumbo and Donald J. Calista (Westport, CT: Greenwood Press, 1990), 107–18.

13. Bryson, Crosby, and Bloomberg, "Public Value Governance," 444–56.

14. In her published work on this topic, author Stephanie Moulton defines these sources as "public value institutions," including formal policies and political authority. See Stephanie Moulton, "Putting Together the Publicness Puzzle: A Framework for Realized Publicness," *Public Administration Review* 69, no. 5 (2009): 889–900; Barry Bozeman and Stephanie Moulton, "Integrative Publicness: A Framework for Public Management Strategy and

Performance," *Journal of Public Administration Research and Theory* 21, no. S3 (2011): S363–80.

15. Moulton, "Putting Together the Publicness Puzzle," 889–900; Stephanie Moulton, "The Authority to Do Good: Publicly Responsible Behavior among Private Mortgage Lenders," *Public Administration Review* 72, no. 3 (2012): 430–39.

16. For example, see Lisa Blomgren Bingham, Tina Nabatchi, and Rosemary O'Leary, "The New Governance: Practices and Processes for Stakeholder and Citizen Participation in the Work of Government," *Public Administration Review* 65, no. 5 (2005): 547–58; Tina Nabatchi, "Putting the 'Public' Back in Public Values Research: Designing Participation to Identify and Respond to Values," *Public Administration Review* 72, no. 5 (2012): 699–708.

17. Robbie Waters Robichau and Laurence E. Lynn Jr., "The Implementation of Public Policy: Still the Missing Link," *Policy Studies Journal* 37, no. 1 (2009): 21–36; Laurence J. O'Toole, "Policy Recommendations for Multi-Actor Implementation: An Assessment of the Field," *Journal of Public Policy* 6, no. 2 (1986): 181–210.

18. Richard W. Scott, *Institutions and Organizations: Ideas and Interests*, 3rd ed. (Thousand Oaks, CA: SAGE, 2008); Jessica E. Sowa, Sally C. Selden, and Jodi R. Sandfort, "No Longer 'Unmeasurable'? A Multi-Dimensional Integrated Model of Nonprofit Organizational Effectiveness," *Nonprofit and Voluntary Sector Quarterly* 33, no. 4 (2004): 711–28.

19. This is a long-standing principle of business management in service firms where quality involves a comparison of expectations with performance. See A. Parasuraman, Valarie A. Zeithaml, and Leonard L. Berry, "A Conceptual Model of Service Quality and Its Implications for Future Research," *Journal of Marketing* 49, no. 4 (1985): 41–50.

20. In fact, difficulty evaluating quality has been a rationale for nonprofit or public provision of services such as nursing home or health care rather than corporate actors. According to this rationale, because nonprofit and public organizations are not driven to maximize profit and shareholder value (the "nondistribution constraint"), they can invest more resources in difficult-to-measure but potentially important quality outcomes. Along these lines, some studies have confirmed higher quality of care for nursing

home patients in nonprofit and public organizations compared with private firms—for example, lower doses of sedative use and a higher ratio of staff to patients. For an early summary, see Burton A. Weisbrod, "The Future of the Nonprofit Sector: Its Entwining with Private Enterprise and Government," *Journal of Policy Analysis and Management* 16, no. 4 (1997): 541–55.

21. Within public management, there is an extensive literature on public service motivation and public service values. For classic examples, see James L. Perry and Lois Recascino Wise, "The Motivational Bases of Public Service," *Public Administration Review* 50, no. 3 (1990): 367–73, and James L. Perry, "Antecedents of Public Service Motivation," *Journal of Public Administration Research and Theory* 7, no. 2 (1997): 181–97.

22. Carl May, "A Rational Model for Assessing and Evaluating Complex Interventions in Health Care," *BMC Health Services Research* 6, no. 11 (2006): 1–11; Gregory Aarons, Charles Glisson, Phillip D. Green, Kimberly Hoagwood, Kelly J. Kelleher, John A. Landsverk, John R. Weisz, Bruce Chorpita, Robert Gibbons, Evelyn Polk Green, Peter S. Jensen, Kelly Kelleher, John Landsverk, Stephen Mayberg, Jeanne Miranda, Lawrence Palinkas, and Sonja Schoenwald, "The Organizational Social Context of Mental Health Services and Clinician Attitudes toward Evidence-Based Practice: A United States National Study," *Implementation Science* 7 (2012): 1–15.

23. Our thinking here has been influenced by systems dynamics theory. For a good overview, see Melanie Mitchell, *Complexity: A Guided Tour* (New York: Oxford University Press, 2011).

24. We are significantly influenced in this conceptualization by Neil Fligstein and Doug McAdam, *A Theory of Fields* (New York: Oxford University Press, 2012); Neil Fligstein and Doug McAdam, "Toward a General Theory of Strategic Action Fields," *Sociological Theory* 29, no. 1 (2011): 1–26, and their students. Other political theorists describe a similar construct in trying to understand complex governance. Elinor Ostrom, for example, uses the terminology "action arenas" and "action situation." Michael D. McGinnis, "An Introduction to IAD and the Language of the Ostrom Workshop: A Simple Guide to a Complex Framework," *Policy Studies Journal* 39, no. 1 (2011): 169–83; Elinor Ostrom, "Institutional Rational Choice: An Assessment of the Institutional Analysis and Development

Framework," in *Theories of the Policy Process*, 2nd ed., ed. Paul A. Sabatier (Boulder, CO: Westview Press, 2007), 21–64. However, our professional experience leads us to more deeply embrace the strategic action field theory because it helps provide more analytical leverage on understanding systems dynamics over time at multiple, nested levels.

25. Yeheskel Hasenfeld and Robert English, "Organizational Technology," in *Human Service Organizations: A Book of Readings*, ed. Yeheskel Hasenfeld (Englewood Cliffs, NJ: Prentice Hall, 1983); Richard Daft, *Organizational Theory and Design*, 9th ed. (Boston: South-Western, 2006); Jodi Sandfort, "Human Service Organizational Technology," in *Human Services as Complex Organizations*, 2nd ed., ed. Yeheskel Hasenfeld (New York: SAGE, 2010), 269–90.

26. The notion of nested strategic action fields is a central element of Fligsten and McAdam's theory. See Fligstein and McAdam, *A Theory of Fields*.

27. Carl May, "Towards a General Theory of Implementation," *Implementation Science* 8 (2013): 8.

28. A number of implementation and governance scholars take this conceptual and empirical approach, including Hill and Hupe, *Implementing Public Policy*; Larry L. Kiser and Elinor Ostrom, "The Three Worlds of Action: A Metatheoretical Synthesis of Institutional Approaches," in *Strategies of Political Inquiry*, ed. Elinor Ostrom (Beverly Hills, CA: SAGE, 1982); Donald S. Van Meter and Carl E. Van Horn, "The Policy Implementation Process: A Conceptual Framework," *Administration and Society* 6, no. 4 (1975): 445–88; Robichau and Lynn, "The Implementation of Public Policy"; Peter J. May and Soren C. Winter, "Politicians, Managers, and Street-Level Bureaucrats: Influences on Policy Implementation," *Journal of Public Administration Research and Theory* 19, no. 3 (2007): 453–76; Eve E. Garrow and Oscar Grusky, "Institutional Logic and Street-Level Discretion: The Case of HIV Test Counseling," *Journal of Public Administration Research and Theory* 23, no. 1 (2012): 103–31. In fact, in an examination of implementation scholarship from 2003 to 2013, we find that 13 percent of the sample of 1,509 articles employed a multilevel framework in their investigation; Jodi Sandfort, Stephen Roll, and Stephanie Moulton, "Assessing Policy and Program Implementation Research," Working paper (2014).

29. This oversight largely occurred because implementation had an overt managerial orientation; it initially focused on providing explanations for why policy ideals were not easily being realized. The implementation problem was initially framed as forcing the system to correspond to policymakers' idealized notions rather than emphasizing understanding the social dynamics of a policy and strategically intervening.

30. For this terminology of key problem solvers, we are grateful to the work of David K. Cohen and Susan Moffitt, *The Ordeal of Equality: Did Federal Regulation Fix the Schools?* (Cambridge, MA: Harvard University Press, 2009).

31. Donald P. Moynihan, "Managing for Results in an Impossible Job: Solution or Symbol?" *International Journal of Public Administration* 28, no. 3 (2005): 213–31, and *The Dynamics of Performance Management: Constructing Information and Reform* (Washington, DC: Georgetown University Press, 2008); Beryl A. Radin, *Challenging the Performance Movement: Accountability, Complexity, and Democratic Values* (Washington, DC: Georgetown University Press, 2006).

32. Cohen and Moffitt, *The Ordeal of Equality*.

33. For describing the intellectual tradition shared by Simon and Bardach, we are grateful for the unpublished essay by Michael Barzeley and Fred Thompson, "Making Public Management a Design-Oriented Science" (unpublished working paper, School of Economics and Political Science and Willamette University, 2007).

34. Donald A Schön, *The Reflective Practitioner: How Professionals Think in Action* (New York: Basic Books, 1983).

35. Classic studies classify public policies by type, as distributive, constituent, regulative, and redistributive following a typology developed by scholar Theodore J. Lowi, "Four Systems of Policy, Politics, and Choice," *Public Administration Review* 32, no. 4 (1972): 298–310.

36. For more information on the current status of QRS in states, see QRIS National Learning Network, "QRIS State Contacts and Map," (QRIS National Learning Network, February 2014), http://www.qrisnetwork.org/qris-state-contacts-map (accessed March 2014).

37. O'Toole, "Policy Recommendations for Multi-Actor Implementation," 202–203.

CHAPTER TWO

1. David Easton, *A Systems Analysis of Political Life* (Chicago: University of Chicago Press, 1965).

2. Paul A. Sabatier and Hank C. Jenkins-Smith, *Policy Change and Learning: An Advocacy Coalition Approach* (Boulder, CO: Westview Press, 1993).

3. Charles O. Jones, *An Introduction to the Study of Policy* (Pacific Grove, CA: Duxbury Press, 1977); James E. Anderson, *Public Policy Making* (New York: Holt, 1977).

4. Jeffrey L. Pressman and Aaron Wildavsky, *Implementation: How Great Expectations in Washington Are Dashed in Oakland or Why It's Amazing That Federal Programs Work at All*, 3rd ed. (Berkeley: University of California Press, 1984); Malcolm L. Goggin, Ann Bowman, James P. Lester, and Laurence J. O'Toole, "Studying the Dynamics of Public Policy Implementation: A Third-Generation Approach," *Implementation and the Policy Process: Opening up the Black Box*, ed. Dennis J. Palumbo and Donald J. Calista (Westport, CT: Greenwood Press, 1990), 181–97; Michael Hill and Peter Hupe, *Implementing Public Policy: An Introduction to the Study of Operational Governance*, 2nd ed. (Thousand Oaks, CA: SAGE, 2008).

5. Paul A. Sabatier, "Top-Down and Bottom-Up Approaches to Implementation Research: A Critical Analysis and Suggested Synthesis," *Journal of Public Policy* 6, no. 1 (1986): 21–48.

6. Eugene Bardach, *The Implementation Game* (Cambridge, MA: MIT Press, 1977).

7. Donald S. Van Meter and Carl E. Van Horn, "The Policy Implementation Process: A Conceptual Framework," *Administration and Society* 6, no. 4 (1975): 445–88; Daniel A. Mazmanian and Paul A. Sabatier, *Implementation and Public Policy* (Glenview, IL: Scott, Foresman, 1983); Daniel A. Mazmanian and Paul A. Sabatier, *Implementation and Public Policy*, 3rd ed. (Lanham, MD: University Press of America, 1989); Paul A. Sabatier and Daniel A. Mazmanian, "The Implementation of Public Policy: A Framework of Analysis," *Policy Studies Journal* 8, no. 4 (1980): 538–60.

8. Mazmanian and Sabatier, *Implementation and Public Policy*.

9. Paul Berman, *The Study of Micro and Macro Implementation of Social Policy* (Santa Monica, CA: Rand, 1978); Paul Berman, "Educational Change: An Implementation Paradigm," *Improving Schools: Using What We Know*, ed. Michael B. Kane and Rolf Lehming (Beverly Hills, CA: SAGE, 1981), 253–86; Richard F. Elmore, "Backward Mapping: Implementation Research and Policy Decisions," *Political Science Quarterly* 94, no. 4 (1979): 601–16; Michael Lipsky, *Street-Level Bureaucracy: Dilemmas of the Individual in Public Services* (New York: Russell Sage Foundation, 1980).

10. Berman, *Study of Micro and Macro Implementation*; Berman, "Educational Change."

11. Benny Hjern and David O. Porter, "Implementation Structures: A New Unit of Administrative Analysis," *Organization Studies* 2, no. 3 (1981): 211–27; Benny Hjern and Chris Hull, "Implementation Research as Empirical Constitutionalism," *European Journal of Political Research* 10, no. 2 (1982): 105–15.

12. Steven Maynard-Moody and Michael Musheno, *Cops, Teachers, Counselors: Stories from the Front Lines of Public Services* (Ann Arbor: University of Michigan Press, 2003); Ann Chih Lin, *Reform in the Making: The Implementation of Social Policy in Prison* (Princeton, NJ: Princeton University Press, 2000); Jodi R. Sandfort, "Moving beyond Discretion and Outcomes: Examining Public Management from the Front-Lines of the Welfare System," *Journal of Public Administration Research and Theory* 10, no. 4 (2000): 729–56.

13. See Video Brief on Backwards Mapping at www.hubertproject.org. This was developed from an application of these seminal papers: Elmore, "Backward Mapping," 601–16; Richard F. Elmore, *Forward and Backward Mapping: Reversible Logic in the Analysis of Public Policy* (Dordrecht, NL: Springer Netherlands, 1985).

14. Malcolm L. Goggin, "The 'Too Few Cases/Too Many Variables' Problem in Implementation Research," *Political Research Quarterly* 39, no. 2 (1986): 328–47; Laurence J. O'Toole, "Policy Recommendations for Multi-Actor Implementation: An Assessment of the Field," *Journal of Public Policy* 6, no. 2 (1986): 181–210.

15. Goggin, "'Too Few Cases/Too Many Variables.'"

16. Goggin et al., "Studying the Dynamics of Public Policy Implementation," 181–97; Richard E. Matland, "Synthesizing the Implementation Literature: The Ambiguity-Conflict Model of Policy Implementation," *Journal of Public Administration Research and Theory* 5, no. 2 (1995): 145–74; Bo Rothstein, *Just Institutions Matter: The Moral and Political Logic of the Universal Welfare State* (Cambridge: Cambridge University Press, 1998); Paul A. Sabatier, "An Advocacy Coalition Framework of Policy Change and the Role of Policy-Oriented Learning Therein," *Policy Sciences* 21, nos. 2–3 (1988): 129–68; Helen Ingram and Anne Schneider, "Improving Implementation through Framing Smarter Statutes," *Journal of Public Policy* 10, no. 1 (1990): 67–88.

17. Goggin et al., "Studying the Dynamics of Public Policy Implementation," 181–97.

18. Sabatier, "Top-Down and Bottom-Up Approaches to Implementation Research," 21–48; Sabatier and Jenkins-Smith, *Policy Change and Learning*; Christopher M. Weible, Paul Sabatier, and Kelly McQueen, "Themes and Variations: Taking Stock of the Advocacy Coalition Framework," *Policy Studies Journal* 37, no. 1 (2009): 121–40.

19. Weible et al., "Themes and Variations."

20. Adrian Smith, "Policy Networks and Advocacy Coalitions: Explaining Policy Change and Stability in UK Industrial Pollution Policy?" *Environmental Planning C: Government and Policy* 18, no. 1 (2000): 95–114.

21. Patricia W. Ingraham, "Toward a More Systematic Consideration of Policy Design," *Policy Studies Journal* 15, no. 4 (1987): 611–28; Ingram and Schneider, "Improving Implementation through Framing Smarter Statutes."

22. Matland, "Synthesizing the Implementation Literature," 145–74.

23. Woodrow Wilson, "The Study of Administration," *Political Science Quarterly* 2, no. 2 (1887): 197–222.

24. For example, Dwight Waldo, *The Administrative State* (New York: Ronald, 1948).

25. Laurence E. Lynn, "The Myth of the Bureaucratic Paradigm: What Traditional Public Administration Really Stood For," *Public Administration Review* 61, no. 2 (2001): 144–60.

26. For a comprehensive review of the study of public management, see Hal Rainey, *Understanding and Managing Public Organizations*, 5th ed. (San Francisco: Jossey-Bass, 2014).

27. Laurence J. O'Toole, "Research on Policy Implementation: Assessment and Prospects," *Journal of Public Administration Research and Theory* 10, no. 2 (2000): 263–88.

28. This quote is from Harland Cleveland, *The Future Executive: A Guide for Tomorrow's Managers* (New York: Harper & Row, 1972).

29. Hill and Hupe, *Implementing Public Policy*, 131.

30. Laurence E. Lynn, Carolyn J. Heinrich, and Carolyn J. Hill, *Improving Governance: A New Logic for Empirical Research* (Washington, DC: Georgetown University Press, 2001); Christopher Pollitt and Peter Hupe, "Talking about Government," *Public Management Review* 13, no. 5 (2011): 641–58; George F. Frederickson, "Whatever Happened to Public Administration? Governance, Governance Everywhere," in *The Oxford Handbook of Public Management*, ed. Ewan Ferlie, Laurence E. Lynn, and Christopher Pollitt (Oxford: Oxford University Press, 2005); R.A.W. Rhodes, "Governance and Public Administration," in *Debating Governance: Authority, Steering, and Democracy*, ed. Jon Pierre (New York: University of Oxford Press, 2000), 54–90.

31. O'Toole, "Research on Policy Implementation," 263–88.; Hill and Hupe, *Implementing Public Policy*.

32. For an overview of this research, see Carolyn J. Heinrich, Carolyn J. Hill, and Laurence E. Lynn, *Governance as an Organizing Theme for Empirical Research* (Washington, DC: Georgetown University Press, 2004).

33. Paul J. DiMaggio and Walter W. Powell, "The Iron Cage Revisited: Institutional Isomorphism and Collective Rationality in Organizational Fields," *American Sociological Review* 48, no. 2 (1983): 147–60; Lynne G. Zucker, "Institutional Theories of Organization," *Annual Review of Sociology* 13 (1987): 443–64; Walter W. Powell, *The New Institutionalism in Organizational Analysis* (Chicago: University of Chicago Press, 1991).

34. Laurence E. Lynn, Carolyn J. Heinrich, and Carolyn J. Hill, "Studying Governance and Public Management: Challenges and Prospects," *Journal of Public Administration Research and Theory* 10, no. 2 (2000): 234.

35. This list is a slight modification of what appears in their book (Lynn et al., *Improving Governance*, 14).

36. Kenneth J. Meier, Laurence J. O'Toole, and Sean Nicholson-Crotty, "Multilevel Governance and Organizational Performance: Investigating the Political-Bureaucratic Labyrinth," *Journal of Policy Analysis and Management* 23, no. 1 (2004): 31–47.

37. Melissa Forbes, Carolyn J. Hill, and Laurence E. Lynn, "The Logic of Governance in Health Care Delivery," *Public Management Review* 9, no. 4 (2007): 453–77.

38. Lynn et al., "Multilevel Governance."

39. Elinor Ostrom, Roy Gardner, and James Walker, *Rules, Games, and Common-Pool Resources* (Ann Arbor: University of Michigan Press, 1994); Elinor Ostrom, "Background on the Institutional Analysis and Development Framework," *Policy Studies Journal* 39, no. 1 (2011): 7–27; Larry L. Kiser and Elinor Ostrom, "The Three Worlds of Action: A Metatheoretical Synthesis of Institutional Approaches," *Strategies of Political Inquiry*, ed. Elinor Ostrom (Beverly Hills, CA: SAGE, 1982).

40. Elinor Ostrom, "Institutional Rational Choice: An Assessment of the Institutional Analysis and Development Framework," in *Theories of the Policy Process,* ed. Paul Sabatier (Boulder, CO: Westview Press, 2007).

41. Ostrom, "Background on Institutional Analysis"; Kiser and Ostrom, "Three Worlds of Action."

42. Hill and Hupe, *Implementing Public Policy.*

43. H. Brinton Milward and Keith Provan, *A Manager's Guide to Choosing and Using Collaborative Networks* (Washington, DC: IBM Center for the Business of Government, 2006), 9.

44. Meier et al., "Multilevel Governance and Organizational Performance."

45. For a review of this approach, see Stanley Wasserman and Joseph Galaskiewicz, ed. *Advances in Social Network Analysis: Research in the Social and Behavioral Sciences* (Thousand Oaks, CA: SAGE, 1994); David Knoke and Song Yang, *Social Network Analysis*, vol. 154 (Thousand Oaks, CA: SAGE, 2008).

46. Walter W. Powell, "Neither Markets nor Hierarchy: Network Forms of Organization," *Research in Organizational Behavior* 12 (1990): 295–336.

47. While there is arguably an important difference between cooperation, coordination, collaborative, and integrative management, these distinctions are often not made in these studies. See Jodi R. Sandfort and H. Brinton Milward, "Collaborative Service Provision in the Public Sector," in *Handbook of Inter-Organizational Relations*, ed. Steve Cropper, Mark Ebbers, Chris Huxham, and Peter Smith Ring (Oxford: Oxford University Press, 2008), 147–74.

48. This list comes from Erik-Hans Klijn, "Networks and Inter-Organizational Management: Challenging, Steering, Evaluation and the Role of Public Actors in Public Management," ed. Ewan Ferlie, Laurence Lynn, and Christopher Pollitt, *The Oxford Handbook of Public Management* (Oxford: Oxford University Press, 2005), 257–72.

49. Robert Agranoff and Michael McGuire, *Collaborative Public Management: New Strategies for Local Governments* (Washington, DC: Georgetown University Press, 2003).

50. For a review, see R. Karl Rethemeyer and Deneen M. Hatmaker, "Network Management Reconsidered: An Inquiry into Management of Network Structures in Public Sector Service Provision," *Journal of Public Administration Research and Theory* 18, no. 4 (2008): 617–46; Kimberley R. Isett, Ines A. Mergel, Kelly LeRoux, Pamela A. Mischen, and R. Karl Rethemeyer, "Networks in Public Administration Scholarship: Understanding Where We Are and Where We Need to Go," *Journal of Public Administration Research and Theory* 21, no. S1 (2011): S157–73; Keith G. Provan and Patrick Kenis, "Modes of Network Governance: Structure, Management, and Effectiveness," *Journal of Public Administration Research and Theory* 18, no. 2 (2008): 229–52.

51. Keith Provan and H. Brinton Milward, "A Preliminary Theory of Interorganizational Network Effectiveness: A Comparison of Four Community Mental Health Systems," *Administrative Sciences Quarterly* 40, no. 1 (1995): 125–57.

52. See also H. Brinton Milward and Keith G. Provan, "Governing the Hollow State," *Journal of Public Administration, Research and Theory* 10, no. 2

(2000): 359–80; H. Brinton Milward and Keith G. Provan, "Measuring Network Structure," *Public Administration* 76, no. 2 (1998): 387–407; Keith G. Provan and H. Brinton Milward, "Do Networks Really Work? A Framework for Evaluating Public-Sector Organizational Networks," *Public Administration Review* 61, no. 4 (2001): 414–23.

53. O'Toole, "Policy Recommendations for Multi-Actor Implementation," 181–210.

54. Lester Salamon, *The Tools of Government: A Guide to the New Governance* (Oxford: Oxford University Press, 2002), 19.

55. Lester M. Salamon, "Rethinking Public Management: Third-Party Government and the Changing Forms of Government Action," *Public Policy* 29 (1981): 255–75.

56. Ingram and Schneider, "Improving Implementation," 72.

57. Milward and Provan, "Governing the Hollow State."

58. Lester Salamon, *Tools of Government.*

59. For social regulation, see Kenneth Meier and Michael Licari, "The Effect of Cigarette Taxes on Cigarette Consumption, 1955 through 1994," *American Journal of Public Health* 87, no. 7 (1997): 1126–30; Michael Licari and Kenneth Meier, "Regulation and Signaling: When a Tax Is Not Just a Tax," *Journal of Politics* 62, no. 3 (2000), 875–85. For government corporations, see James Mitchell, *The American Experiment with Government Corporations*, (Armonk, NY: M. E. Sharpe, 1999). For loan guarantees, see C. Howard, "Tax Expenditures," *The Tools of Government: A Guide to the New Governance*, ed. Lester Salamon (Oxford: Oxford University Press, 2002), 490–510.

60. Timothy Conlan, *From New Federalism to Devolution: Twenty-five Years of Intergovernmental Reform.* (Washington, DC: Brookings Institution Press, 1998); Daniel Elazar, "The Shaping of Intergovernmental Relations in the Twentieth Century," *Annals of the American Academy of Political and Social Science* 359 (1965): 10–22; Paul Posner and Mary T. Wrightson, "Block Grants: A Perennial, but Unstable, Tool of Government," *Publius* 26, no. 3 (1996): 87–108.

61. Trevor L. Brown, Matthew Potoski, and David M. Van Slyke, "Managing Public Service Contracts: Aligning Values, Institutions, and Markets," *Public Administration Review* 66, no. 3 (2006): 323–31.

62. Robert Agranoff and Michael McGuire, *Collaborative Public Management: New Strategies for Local Governments* (Washington, DC: Georgetown University Press, 2003); Robert Blair, "Policy Tools Theory and Implementation Networks: Understanding State Enterprise Zone Partnerships," *Journal of Public Administration Research and Theory* 12, no. 2 (2002): 161–90; Barbara Romzek and Jocelyn Johnston, "Reforming State Social Services through Contracting: Linking Implementation and Organization Culture," in *Advancing Public Management: New Developments in Theory Methods and Practice,* ed. Jeffrey Brudney, Laurence O'Toole, and Hal G. Rainey (Washington, DC: Georgetown University Press, 2000), 173–95; Barbara Romzek and Jocelyn Johnston, "Effective Contract Implementation and Management: A Preliminary Model," *Journal of Public Administration Research and Theory* 12, no. 3 (2002): 423–53; Kieron Walsh, *Contracting for Change* (Oxford: Oxford University Press, 1997); Brown et al., "Managing Public Service Contracts."

63. David E. Campbell, Martin R. West, and Paul E. Peterson, "Participation in a National, Means-Tested School Voucher Program," *Journal of Policy Analysis and Management* 24, no. 3 (2005): 523–41; William G. Howell, "Dynamic Selection Effects in Means-Tested, Urban School Voucher Programs," *Journal of Policy Analysis and Management* 23, no. 2 (2004): 225–50; Helen F. Ladd, "School Vouchers: A Critical View," *Journal of Economic Perspectives* 16, no. 4 (2002), 3–24; Howard M. Levin, "Educational Vouchers: Effectiveness, Choice, and Costs," *Journal of Policy Analysis and Management* 17, no. 3 (1998): 373–92; Scott Susin, "Rent Vouchers and the Price of Low-Income Housing," *Journal of Public Economics* 83, no. 1 (2002), 109–52.

64. Lawrence F. Katz, Jeffrey R. Kling, and Jeffrey B. Liebman, "Moving to Opportunity in Boston: Early Results of a Randomized Mobility Experiment," *Quarterly Journal of Economics* 116, no. 2 (2001): 607–54.

65. For an example, see Daniel P. Moynihan, *Maximum Feasible Misunderstanding: Community Action in the War on Poverty* (New York: Free Press, 1969).

66. Carol Hirschon Weiss, "Evaluating Social Programs: What Have We Learned?" *Society* 25, no. 1 (1987): 40–45.

67. In 1951, political scientist Harold Lasswell called for a "policy orientation" to help address some of the most vexing social problems of the time.

68. Pressman and Wildavsky, *Implementation*; David Easton, *A Systems Analysis of Political Life* (Chicago: University of Chicago Press, 1965); Graham Allison, *Essence of Decision: Explaining the Cuban Missile Crisis* (Boston: Little, Brown, 1972).

69. Donald E. Stokes, "Political and Organizational Analysis in the Policy Curriculum," *Journal of Policy Analysis and Management* 6, no. 1 (1986): 45–55.

70. Sabatier and Jenkins-Smith, *Policy Change and Learning*.

71. For example, see Yehezkel Dror, "Policy Analysts: A New Professional Role in Government Service," *Public Administration Review* 27, no. 3 (1967): 197–203.

72. Laurence E. Lynn, "Art, Science, or Profession?" *Public Management as Art, Science and Profession* (Chatham, NJ: Chatham House, 1996).

73. For a summary article, see Norman Beckman, "Policy Analysis for the Congress," *Public Administration Review* 37, no. 3 (1977): 237–44.

74. Alice Rivlin, *Systematic Thinking for Social Action* (Washington, DC: Brookings Institution, 1971).

75. For example, see Walter Williams, *Social Policy Research and Analysis: The Experience in the Federal Social Agencies* (New York: American Elsevier, 1971).

76. David Braybrooke and Charles Lindblom, *A Strategy of Decision: Policy Evaluation as a Social Process* (New York: Free Press, 1963).

77. Aaron Wildavsky, *Speaking Truth to Power: The Art and Craft of Policy Analysis*, 2nd ed. (New Brunswick, NJ: Transaction Publishers, 1987), 17.

78. For a good review of what economists can and cannot contribute to policy analysis, see Rebecca M. Blank, "What Do Economists Have to Contribute to Policy Decision-Making?" *Quarterly Review of Economics and Finance* 42 (2002): 817–24.

79. For a classic example, see Davis B. Bobrow and John S. Dryzek, *Policy Analysis by Design* (Pittsburgh, PA: University of Pittsburgh Press, 1987); Deborah Stone, *Policy Paradox: The Art of Political Decision Making*, 3rd ed. (New York: Norton, 2011).

80. For example, see the discussion of implementation factors in the policy analysis textbook: David L. Weimer and Aidan R. Vining, *Policy Analysis: Concepts and Practice*, 4th ed. (Upper Saddle River, NJ: Pearson Education, 2005).

81. Per Nilsen, Christian Ståhl, Kerstin Roback, and Paul Cairney, "Never the Twain Shall Meet? A Comparison of Implementation Science and Policy Implementation Research," *Implementation Science* 8, no. 63 (2013); Harald Saetren, "Facts and Myths about Research on Public Policy Implementation: Out-of-Fashion, Allegedly Dead, But Still Very Much Alive and Relevant," *Policy Studies Journal* 33, no. 4 (2005): 559–82; Jodi Sandfort, Stephen Roll, and Stephanie Moulton, "Assessing Policy and Program Implementation Research," under review, *Administration and Society* (2014).

82. Martin P. Eccles and Brian S. Mittman, "Welcome to Implementation Science," *Implementation Science*, no. 1 (2006): 1.

83. Everett M. Rogers, *Diffusion of Innovations* (New York: Free Press, 1995).

84. These key points come from a very helpful, comprehensive review done by Trisha Greenhalgh, Glenn Robert, Fraser MacFarlane, Paul Bate, and Olivia Kyriakidou, "Diffusion of Innovations in Service Organizations: Systematic Review and Recommendations," *Milbank Quarterly* 82, no. 4 (2004): 581–629.

85. Emmanuelle C. Gira, Michelle L. Kessler, and John Poertner, "Influencing Social Workers to Use Research Evidence in Practice: Lessons from Medicine and the Allied Health Professions," *Research on Social Work Practice* 14, no. 2 (2004): 68–79; Gregory Aarons et al., "The Organizational Social Context of Mental Health Services and Clinician Attitudes toward Evidence-Based Practice: A United States National Study," *Implementation Science* 7 (2012): 1–15; Richard Grol and Michel Wensing, "What Drives Change? Barriers to and Incentives for Achieving Evidence-Based Practice," *Medical Journal Australia* 180, no. S8 (2004): S57–S60.

86. Carl May and Tracy Finch, "Implementing, Embedding, and Integrating Practices: An Outline of Normalization Process Theory," *Sociology* 43, no. 3 (2009): 535–54; Carl May, "A Rational Model for Assessing and Evaluating Complex Interventions in Health Care," *BMC Health Services Research* 6 (2006): 11; Carl R. May, Frances Mair, Tracy Finch, Anne MacFarlane,

Christopher Dowrick, Shaun Treweek, Tim Rapley, Luciana Ballini, Bie Nio Ong, Anne Rogers, Elizabeth Murray, Glyn Elwyn, France Légaré, Jane Gunn, and Victor M. Montori, "Development of a Theory of Implementation and Integration: Normalization Process Theory," *Implementation Science* 4, no. 29 (2009).

87. Joseph A. Durlak and Emily P. DuPre, "Implementation Matters: A Review of Research on the Influence of Implementation on Program Outcomes and the Factors Affecting Implementation," *American Journal of Community Psychology* 41, nos. 3–4 (2008): 327–50; Dean L. Fixsen, Sandra F. Naoom, Karen A. Blase, Robert M. Friedman, Barbara Burns, and Frances Wallace, *Implementation Research: A Synthesis of the Literature* (Tampa, FL: National Implementation Research Center, 2005); Greenhalgh et al., "Diffusion of Innovations in Service Organizations"; Duncan C. Meyers, Joseph A. Durlak, and Abraham Wandersman, "The Quality Implementation Framework: A Synthesis of Critical Steps in the Implementation Process," *American Journal of Community Psychology* 50, nos. 3–4 (2012): 462–80.

88. Greenhalgh et al., "Diffusion of Innovations in Service Organizations," 595.

89. Rachel G. Tabak, Elaine C. Khoong, David A. Chambers, and Ross C. Brownson, "Bridging Research and Practice: Models for Dissemination and Implementation Research," *American Journal of Preventive Medicine* 43, no. 3 (2012): 337–50.

90. Some illustrative studies are Erum Nadeem, Alissa Gleacher, and Rinad S. Beidas, "Consultation as an Implementation Strategy for Evidence-Based Practices across Multiple Contexts: Unpacking the Black Box," *Administration and Policy in Mental Health and Mental Health Services Research* 40, no. 6 (2013): 439–50; Frank P. Deane, Retta Andresen, Trevor P. Crowe, Lindsay G. Oades, Joseph Ciarrochi, and Virginia Williams, "A Comparison of Two Coaching Approaches to Enhance Implementation of a Recovery-Oriented Service Model," *Administration and Policy in Mental Health and Mental Health Services Research* 6 (2013): 1–8; Sarah Kate Bearman, John R. Weisz, Bruce F. Chorpita, Kimberly Hoagwood, Alyssa Ward, and Ana M. Ugueto, "More Practice, Less Preach? The Role of Supervision Processes and Therapist Characteristics in EBP Implementation," *Administration and Policy in Mental Health and Mental Health Services Research* 40, no. 6 (2013): 518–29. Yet as Gira and colleagues, "Influencing Social Workers," reveal, there are

rarely such tactics that can consistently be applied to systems change across contexts.

91. Nilsen et al., "Never the Twain Shall Meet?"

92. Meyers et al., "The Quality Implementation Framework." Their Quality Implementation Framework has a tool, the Quality Implementation Self-Assessment Rating Scale, developed for application.

93. For example, in Tabak et al., "Bridging Research and Practice," only 13 percent of the 61 conceptual models in use incorporated policy. Nilsen et al., "Never the Twain Shall Meet?" also make this point.

94. Laura J. Damschroder, David C. Aron, Rosalind E. Keith, Susan R. Kirsh, Jeffery A. Alexander, and Julie C. Lowery, "Fostering Implementation of Health Services Research Findings into Practice: A Consolidated Framework for Advancing Implementation Science," *Implementation Science* 4 (January 2009): 50. Also see Abraham Wandersman, Jennifer Duffy, Paul Flaspohler, Rita Noonan, Keri Lubell, Lindsey Stillman, Morris Blachman, Richard Dunville, and Janet Saul, "Bridging the Gap between Prevention Research and Practice: The Interactive Systems Framework for Dissemination and Implementation," *American Journal of Community Psychology* 41, nos. 3–4 (2008): 171–81.

95. See Sandfort et al., "Assessing Policy and Program Implementation Research," table 6. This contrasts sharply with other topical areas, many of which do not have any implementation studies using this research approach.

96. On Amir, Dan Ariely, Alan Cooke, David Dunning, Nicholas Epley, Uri Bneezy, Botond Koszegi, Donald Lightenstein, Nina Mazar, Sedhil Mullainathan, Drazen Prelec, Eldar Shafir, and Jose Silva, "Psychology, Behavioral Economics, and Public Policy," *Marketing Letters* 16, nos. 3–4 (2005): 443–54.

97. Richard H. Thaler and Cass R. Sunstein, *Nudge: Improving Decisions about Health, Wealth, and Happiness* (New Haven, CT: Yale University Press, 2008).

98. Herbert A. Simon, *Administrative Behavior,* 3rd ed. (New York: Free Press; 1948, revised 1976); Herbert A. Simon, "A Behavioral Model of Rational Choice," *Quarterly Journal of Economics* 69, no. 1 (1955): 99–118.

99. Stanley Milgram, "Behavioral Study of Obedience," *Journal of Abnormal and Social Psychology* 67, no. 4 (1963): 371.

100. Amos Tversky and Daniel Kahneman, "Judgment under Uncertainty: Heuristics and Biases," *Science* 185, no. 4157 (1974): 1124–31, and "Prospect Theory: An Analysis of Decisions under Risk," *Econometrica* 47 (1979): 263–91; Amos Tversky and Daniel Kahneman, "The Framing of Decisions and the Psychology of Choice," *Science* 211, no. 4481 (1981): 453–58.

101. Daniel Kahneman, "Maps of Bounded Rationality: Psychology for Behavioral Economics," *American Economic Review* 93, no. 5 (2003): 1449.

102. Eric J. Johnson and Daniel Goldstein, "Do Defaults Save Lives?" *Science* 112 (2003): 1338–39.

103. Ibid.; Eric J. Johnson and Daniel G. Goldstein, "Defaults and Donation Decisions," *Transplantation* 78, no. 12 (2004): 1713–16.

104. Brigitte C. Madrian and Dennis F. Shea, "The Power of Suggestion: Inertia in 401(k) Participation and Savings Behavior," *Quarterly Journal of Economics* 116, no. 4 (2001): 1149–87; James J. Choi, David Laibson, Brigitte C. Madrian, and Andrew Metrick, "Defined Contribution Pensions: Plan Rules, Participant Choices, and the Path of Least Resistance," in *Tax Policy and the Economy,* ed. James Poterba (Cambridge, MA: MIT Press, 2002), 67–114.

105. For examples in the United States and Great Britain, see Behavioural Insights Team, https://www.gov.uk/government/organisations/behavioural-insights-team; National Institute on Aging, "Psychological Science and Behavioral Economics in the Service of Public Policy," meeting summary, National Institutes of Health, Washington, D.C., May 22, 2013, http://www.nia.nih.gov/sites/default/files/psychological_science_and_behavioral_economics.pdf .

106. Edward. L. Glaeser, "Paternalism and Psychology," *University of Chicago Law Review* 73 (2006): 144.

107. Michael S. Barr, Sendhil Mullainathan, and Eldar Shafir, "Behavorally Informed Regulation," in *The Behavioral Foundations of Public Policy,* ed. Eldar Shafir (Princeton, NJ: Princeton University Press, 2012), 457.

108. Wolfgang Pesendorfer, "Behavioral Economics Comes of Age: A Review Essay on Advances in Behavioral Economics," *Journal of Economic Literature* 44, no. 3 (2006): 712–21.

109. Amir et al., "Psychology, Behavioral Economics, and Public Policy."

110. Ann Chih Lin, *Reform in the Making: The Implementation of Social Policy in Prison* (Princeton, NJ: Princeton University Press, 2000).

CHAPTER THREE

1. For an application to policy implementation, see Michael J. R. Butler and Peter M. Allen, "Understanding Policy Implementation Processes as Self-Organizing Systems," *Public Management Review* 10, no. 3 (2008): 421–40. For more about the development of complexity theory in the natural sciences, see Melanie Mitchell, *Complexity: A Guided Tour* (New York: Oxford University Press, 2011).

2. Richard E. Matland, "Synthesizing the Implementation Literature: The Ambiguity-Conflict Model of Policy Implementation," *Journal of Public Administration Research and Theory* 5, no. 2 (1995): 145–74.

3. Malcolm L. Goggin, "The 'Too Few Cases/Too Many Variables' Problem in Implementation Research," *Political Research Quarterly* 39, no. 2 (1986): 328–47.

4. Neil Fligstein and Doug McAdam, *A Theory of Fields* (Oxford: Oxford University Press, 2012).

5. Ibid.

6. W. Richard Scott, *Organizations: Rational, Natural and Open Systems*, 5th ed. (Upper Saddle River, NJ: Prentice Hall, 1986).

7. Fligstein and McAdam, *Theory of Fields*. In our review of this theory, there are a considerable number of peer review articles (thirty-four) published since 2010. The vast majority (89 percent) focus on macrolevel systems in society, while a smaller number apply it to organizations; this undoubtedly reflects the originators' sociological background. For a selection of these articles, see Seth Abrutyn, "Toward a Theory of Institutional Ecology: The Dynamics of Macro Structural Space," *Review of European Studies* 4, no. 5 (2012): 167–81; Dustin Avent-Holt, "The Political Dynamics of

Market Organization: Cultural Framing, Neoliberalism, and the Case of Airline Deregulation," *Sociological Theory* 30, no. 4 (2013): 283–302; Stephan Bernhard, "Beyond Constructivism: The Political Sociology of an EU Policy Field," *International Political Sociology* 5, no. 4 (2011): 426–45; Edward. J. Carberry and Brayden G. King, "Defensive Practice Adoption in the Face of Organizational Stigma: Impression Management and the Diffusion of Stock Option Expensing," *Journal of Management Studies* 49, no. 7 (2012): 1137–67; Marie-Laure Djelic, "When Limited Liability Was (Still) an Issue: Mobilization and Politics of Signification in 19th-Century England," *Organization Studies* 34, nos. 5–6 (2013): 595–621; Hayriye Ozen and Sukru Ozen, "Interactions in and between Strategic Action Fields: A Comparative Analysis of Two Environmental Conflicts in Gold-Mining Fields in Turkey," *Organization and Environment* 24, no. 4 (2011): 343–63; Thomas K. Rudel and Patrick Meyfroidt, "Organizing Anarchy: The Food Security–Biodiversity–Climate Crisis and the Genesis of Rural Land Use Planning in the Developing World," *Land Use Policy* 36 (2014): 239–47; Marc Schneiberg, "Movements as Political Conditions for Diffusion: Anti-Corporate Movements and the Spread of Cooperative Forms in American Capitalism," *Organization Studies* 34, nos. 5–6 (2013): 653–82.

8. Previous scholars have described strategic action fields and implementation levels as nested "Russian dolls." While we agree with the nesting imagery, the shell around each Russian doll is hard and impermeable—creating an entirely distinct yet nested entity. In contrast, we suggest that the social structure at each level acts as a "permeable membrane."

9. Our ideas here are shaped by writings in organizational science that refer to this as *technology*: Yeheskel Hasenfeld, *Human Service Organizations* (Englewood Cliffs, NJ: Prentice Hall, 1983); Richard Daft, *Organizational Theory and Design*, 9th ed. (Boston: South-Western, 2006); and Jodi Sandfort, "Human Service Organizational Technology," in *Human Services as Complex Organizations*, 2nd ed., ed. Yeheskel Hasenfeld (New York: SAGE, 2010), 269–90.

10. Jeffrey Pressman and Aaron Wildavsky, *Implementation: How Great Expectations in Washington Are Dashed in Oakland or Why It's Amazing That Federal Programs Work at All,* 3rd ed. (Berkeley: University of California Press, 1984), 212.

11. For example, Richard Matland's typology categorizes policies based on the degree of ambiguity and conflict. Technology is captured in the dimension of ambiguity—policies can either have clear goals and clear means (technologies) for addressing the goals, or they can be ambiguous, lacking clarity around the goals or the appropriate technologies to achieve the goals. While classifying the overall ambiguity in a policy might be useful heuristically, in practice it oversimplifies some of the most important features of technology that need to be understood to improve implementation. See Matland, "Synthesizing the Implementation Literature," 145–74.

12. In this ambition, we follow the path of other scholars who have undertaken analysis to bring insight into complex processes such as leadership; see Barbara Crosby and John Bryson, *Leadership Can Be Taught* (San Francisco: Jossey-Bass, 2005).

13. The concept of domains comes from the organizational sociology and the business literature on strategic management, where organizations make decisions about their core activities in light of their skills and resources and the competitive environment. For example, see James D. Thompson, *Organizations in Action* (New York: McGraw-Hill, 1967); Michael E. Porter, *Competitive Strategy* (New York: Free Press, 1980).

14. For example, Pressman and Wildavsky, *Implementation,* refer to "causal logic" when discussing implementation.

15. For example, Pressman and Wildavsky, *Implementation,* and Daniel A. Mazmanian and Paul A. Sabatier, *Implementation and Public Policy* (Lanham, MD: University Press of America, 1989).

16. This distinction was developed by Yeheskel Hasenfeld, *Human Service Organizations* (Englewood Cliffs, NJ: Prentice Hall, 1983).

17. Mazmanian and Sabatier, *Implementation and Public Policy.*

18. The classic summary of this research comes from Louis W. Fry, "Technology—Structure Research," *Academy of Management Journal* 25, no. 3 (1982): 532–52.

19. Trevor L. Brown, Matthew Potoski, and David M Van Slyke, "Managing Public Service Contracts: Aligning Values, Institutions, and Markets," *Public Administration Review* 66, no. 3 (2006): 323–31.

20. Michael D. Cohen, James G. March, and Johan P. Olsen, "A Garbage Can Model of Organizational Choice," *Administrative Science Quarterly* 17, no. 1 (1972): 1–25; John W. Kingdon, *Agendas, Alternatives, and Public Policies*, 2nd ed. (New York: HarperCollins, 1995).

21. Peter M. Blau and W. Richard Scott, *Formal Organizations: A Comparative Approach* (San Francisco: Chandler, 1962); Mark C. Suchman, "Managing Legitimacy: Strategic and Institutional Approaches," *Academy of Management Review* 20, no. 3 (1995): 571–610.

22. For example, see Mazmanian and Sabatier, *Implementation and Public Policy*.

23. Gary L Wamsley and Mayer N. Zald, "The Political Economy of Public Organizations," *Public Administration Review* 33, no. 1 (1973): 62–73; Barry Bozeman, *All Organizations Are Public: Bridging Public and Private Organizational Theories* (San Francisco: Jossey-Bass, 1987); Stephanie Moulton, "Putting Together the Publicness Puzzle: A Framework for Realized Publicness," *Public Administration Review* 69, no. 5 (2009): 889–900.

24. Bozeman, *All Organizations Are Public*.

25. David Osborne and Ted Gaebler, *Reinventing Government: How the Entrepreneurial Spirit Is Transforming the Public Sector* (New York: Plume Books, 1992).

26. Leisha DeHart-Davis, "Green Tape: A Theory of Effective Organizational Rules," *Journal of Public Administration Research and Theory* 19, no. 2 (2009): 361–84.

27. This point is made in Fligstein and McAdams, *Theory of Fields*, but is also present in organizational studies since the 1940s. See Hal G. Rainey, *Understanding and Managing Public Organizations*, 4th ed. (San Francisco: Jossey-Bass, 2009) for an overview and for graphic illustration in terms of the significance of the form and amount of financial resources in shaping nonprofit organizational operations.

28. More about the way implementation resources can shape strategic action field activities is discussed in chapter 4, building off of the work of Heather Hill. See Heather C. Hill, "Understanding Implementation: Street-Level Bureaucrats' Resources for Reform," *Journal of Public Administration Research and Theory* 13, no. 3 (2003): 265–82.

29. Clifford Geertz, *The Interpretation of Cultures* (New York: Basic Books, 1973).

30. For a more detailed explanation of this definition, see Anne M. Khademian, *Working with Culture: The Way the Job Gets Done in Public Programs* (Washington, DC: CQ Press, 2002).

31. Karl E. Weick, *Sensemaking in Organizations* (Thousand Oaks, CA: SAGE, 1995).

32. See Fligstein and McAdam, *Theory of Fields*, chap. 2.

33. Ann Chih Lin, *Reform in the Making: The Implementation of Social Policy in Prison* (Princeton, NJ: Princeton University Press, 2000), 8.

34. Ibid., 166.

35. See the standards document: http://www.homeownershipstandards.com/Home/Home.aspx.

36. Sometimes this is referred to as institutionalization: Paul J. DiMaggio and Walter W. Powell, "The Iron Cage Revisited: Institutional Isomorphism and Collective Rationality in Organizational Fields," *American Sociological Review* 48, no. 2 (1983): 147–60.

37. The best-known framework used for management education is Edgar H. Schein, *Organizational Culture and Learning* (San Francisco: Jossey-Bass, 1992).

38. Weick, *Sensemaking*; Khademian, *Working with Culture*; Jodi Sandfort, "Moving beyond Discretion and Outcomes: Examining Public Management from the Front-Lines of the Welfare System," *Journal of Public Administration Research and Theory* 10, no. 4 (2000): 729–56.

39. Jodi Sandfort, "The Structural Impediments to Human Service Collaboration: The Case of Frontlines Welfare Reform Implementation," *Social Service Review* 73, no. 3 (1999): 314–39.

40. Linda Smircich, Peter Frost, Larry Moore, M. Louis, M. Lundberg, and Joanne Martin, "Is the Concept of Culture a Paradigm for Understanding Organizations and Ourselves?" *Organizational Culture* 23 (1985): 55–72.

41. Christopher Ansell, *Schism and Solidarity in Social Movements: The Politics of Labor in the French Third Republic* (Cambridge: Cambridge University Press, 2001).

42. In a simplified way, this is the main thrust of the advocacy coalition framework that has been used extensively to analyze policymaking in the environmental area. Paul A. Sabatier and Hank C. Jenkins-Smith, *Policy Change and Learning: An Advocacy Coalition Approach* (Boulder, CO: Westview Press, 1993); Christopher M. Weible, Paul A. Sabatier, and Kelly McQueen, "Themes and Variations: Taking Stock of the Advocacy Coalition Framework," *Policy Studies Journal* 37, no. 1 (2009): 121–40.

PART TWO

1. Peter Block, *Community: The Structure of Belonging* (San Francisco: Berrett-Koehler, 2008), 29.

2. Peter Senge, C. Otto Scharmer, Joseph Jaworski, and Betty Sue Flowers, *Presence: Human Purpose and the Field of the Future* (New York: Crown, 2008), 145.

CHAPTER FOUR

1. Edward Goetz and Mara S. Sidney, "Local Policy Subsystems and Issue Definition: An Analysis of Community Development Policy Change," *Urban Affairs Review* 32, no. 40 (1997): 490–512; H. Brinton Milward and Gary L. Wamsley, "Policy Subsystems, Networks, and the Tools of Public Management," in *Public Policy Formation*, ed. Thomas A. J. Koonen and Kenneth Hanf (Boulder, CO: Westview Press, 1984), 105. In some cases—see Walter J. M. Kickert, Eric-Hans Klijn, and Joop F. M. Koppenjan, *Managing Complex Networks: Strategies for the Public Sector* (London: SAGE, 1997)—they are also referred to as a type of "policy network." The most consistent use with that offered here were the "localized implementation structures," discussed by Benny Hjern and David O. Porter, "Implementation Structures: A New Unit of Administrative Analysis," *Organization Studies* 2, no. 3964 (1981): 211–27.

2. There is a well-developed literature on organizational fields discussed later in this chapter. This literature, along with other social theories, forms the foundation of the policy field framework we use. See Melissa Stone and Jodi R. Sandfort, "Building a Policy Fields Framework to Inform Research in Nonprofit Organizations," *Nonprofit and Voluntary Sector Quarterly* 38, no. 6 (2009): 1054–75; Jodi R. Sandfort, "Nonprofits within Policy Fields," *Journal of Policy Analysis and Management* 29, no. 3 (2010): 637–44.

3. Hjern and Porter, "Implementation Structures." A similar idea can be found in the literature on policy subsystems: Milward and Wamsley, "Policy Subsystems"; Paul A. Sabatier, "An Advocacy Coalition Framework of Policy Change and the Role of Policy-Oriented Learning Therein," *Policy Sciences* 21, nos. 2–3 (1988): 129–68; Paul A. Sabatier and Hank C. Jenkins-Smith, *Policy Change and Learning: An Advocacy Coalition Approach* (Boulder, CO: Westview Press, 1993).

4. If policy fields are equivalent to markets, policy domains are equivalent to industries; see Paul Burstein, "Policy Domains: Organization, Culture and Policy Outcomes," *Annual Review of Sociology* 17, no. 1 (1991): 327–50.

5. Research about state diffusion of policy ideas tends to focus on broad policy parameters rather than implementation specifics. Joe Soss, Richard C. Fording, and Sanford F. Schram, *Disciplining the Poor: Neoliberal Paternalism and the Persistent Power of Race* (Chicago: University of Chicago Press, 2011); Frances Stokes Berry and William D. Berry, "Innovation and Diffusion Models in Policy Research," in *Theories of the Policy Process*, ed. Paul A. Sabatier (Boulder, CO: Westview Press, 1999), 169–200; Brenda K. Bushouse, *University Preschool: Policy Change, Stability, and the Pew Charitable Trusts* (Albany, NY: SUNY Press, 2009). Also see Christopher M. Weible, Paul A. Sabatier, and Kelly McQueen, "Themes and Variations: Taking Stock of the Advocacy Coalition Framework," *Policy Studies Journal* 37, no. 1 (2009): 121–40, who reflect that although considerable studies have examined their related advocacy coalition framework, few have done so in such a systematic or comparative way.

6. Stone and Sandfort, "Building a Policy Fields Framework." Sandfort, "Nonprofits within Policy Fields," 637–44.

7. Laurence O'Toole Jr., *American Intergovernmental Relations: Foundations, Perspectives, and Issues*, vol. 4 (Washington, DC: Congressional Quarterly Press, 2007); Chung-Lae Cho and Deil S. Wright, "The Devolution Revolution in Intergovernmental Relations in the 1990s: Changes in Cooperative and Coercive State-National Relations as Perceived by State Administrators," *Journal of Public Administration Research and Theory* 14, no. 4 (2004): 447–68.

8. O'Toole, *American Intergovernmental Relations*.

9. Cho and Wright, "The Devolution Revolution in Intergovernmental Relations in the 1990s," 447–68; John E. Chubb, "The Political Economy of Federalism," *American Political Science Review* 79, no. 4 (1985): 994–1015; Daniel J. Elazar, "The Shaping of Intergovernmental Relations in the Twentieth Century," *Annals of the American Academy of Political and Social Science* 359, no. 1 (1965): 10–22; Paul Peterson, *The Price of Federalism* (Washington, DC: Brookings Institution, 1995); O'Toole, *American Intergovernmental Relations*.

10. Some scholars even argue that implementation challenges are really indicators of the larger success in a federalist system based on the separation of powers at the core of a Madisonian government. See Barbara Ferman, "When Failure Is Success: Implementation and Madisonian Government," in *Implementation and the Policy Process: Opening up the Black Box*, ed. Dennis J. Palumbo and Donald J. Calista (New York: Greenwood Press, 1990), 39–50.

11. These and other astute points are made in Martha Derthinck, *Keeping the Compound Republic* (Washington, DC: Brookings Institution Press, 2001).

12. Chris Skelcher, "Public-Private Partnerships and Hybridity," in *The Oxford Handbook of Public Management*, ed. Ewan Ferlie, Laurence E. Lynn Jr., and Christopher Pollitt (Oxford: Oxford University Press, 2005), 347–70; Jodi R. Sandfort and H. Brinton Milward, "Collaborative Service Provision in the Public Sector," in *Handbook of Inter-Organizational Relations*, ed. Steve Cropper, Mark Ebbers, Chris Huxham, and Peter Smith Ring (Oxford: Oxford University Press, 2008), 147–74; Steven Rathgeb Smith and Michael Lipsky, *Non-Profits for Hire: The Welfare State in the Age of Contracting* (Cambridge, MA: Harvard University Press, 1993); Lester Salamon, *Partners in Public Service: Government-Nonprofit Relations in the Modern Welfare State* (Baltimore, MD: Johns Hopkins University Press, 1995).

13. Lester Salamon, *The Tools of Government: A Guide to the New Governance* (Oxford: Oxford University Press, 2002).

14. Laurence J. O'Toole, "Treating Networks Seriously," *Public Administration Review* 57, no. 1 (1997): 45.

15. As Keith G. Provan, Amy Fish, and Joerg Sydow note in "Interorganizational Networks at the Network Level: A Review of the Empirical Literature on

Whole Networks," *Journal of Management* 33, no. 3 (2007): 479–516, the research on whole networks has been slower to develop, largely because of the costs and complexity of studying whole networks over time.

16. Paul DiMaggio, "State Expansion and Organizational Fields," in *Organizational Theory and Public Policy*, ed. Richard Hall and Robert Quinn (Beverly Hills, CA: SAGE, 1983), 147–61. For a more general articulation of institutional theory, see Paul J. DiMaggio and Walter W. Powell, "The Iron Cage Revisited: Institutional Isomorphism and Collective Rationality in Organizational Fields," in *The New Institutionalism in Organizational Analysis*, ed. Walter W. Powell and Paul J. DiMaggio (Chicago: University of Chicago Press, 1991).

17. This differs from the assumption of other scholars, such as political scientists embracing the advocacy coalition approach: Paul A. Sabatier and Hank C. Jenkins-Smith, *Policy Change and Learning: An Advocacy Coalition Approach* (Boulder, CO: Westview Press, 1993); Weible et al., "Themes and Variations: Taking Stock of the Advocacy Coalition Framework," 121–40, who stress the competition for scarce resources among subgroups. The strategic action field theory underpinning our analysis integrates both perspectives.

18. For an overview of this approach in the public sector, see Trevor L. Brown, Matthew Potoski, and David M. Van Slyke, "Trust and Contract Completeness in the Public Sector," *Local Government Studies* 33, no. 4 (2007): 607–23; Anthony M. Bertelli and Craig R. Smith, "Relational Contracting and Network Management," *Journal of Public Administration Research and Theory* 20, no. 1 (2010): i21-i40.

19. Erik-Hans Klijn and Jurian Edelenbos, "Metagovernance as Network Management," in *Theories of Democratic Network Governance*, ed. Eva Sorenson and Jacob Torfing (New York: Palgrave Macmillan, 2008).

20. Others have noted this as well. See Robert McGuire and Michael McGuire, "Inside the Matrix: Integrating the Paradigms of Intergovernmental and Network Management," *International Journal of Public Administration* 26, no. 12 (2003): 1401–22; Laurence O'Toole, "The Theory-Practice Issue in Policy Implementation Research," *Public Administration* 82, no. 2 (2004): 309–29.

21. This idea was first documented by Benny Hjern and David O. Porter, "Implementation Structures: A New Unit of Administrative Analysis," *Organization Studies* 2, no. 3964 (1981): 211–27, in their helpful article describing the function of local implementation structures.

22. Here we are articulating a more general definition of ways organizations participate within policy fields. An earlier publication of Sandfort's, "Nonprofits within Policy Fields," describes the roles played by nonprofit organizations within two different policy fields. In these two contexts, nonprofits provided professional membership services, policy advocacy, systems change, program administration, capacity building, and service delivery.

23. Stephen Goldsmith and William Eggers showcase this in their book *Governing by Network* (Washington, DC: Brookings Institutions Press, 2004).

24. In theories of the state, nonprofit organizations are sometimes conceptualized as intermediary institutions interfacing between citizens and government. In various literatures, the term also is used to represent organizations carrying out dramatically different roles; for example, see David Brown and Archana Kalegaonkar, "Support Organizations and the Evolution of the NGO Sector," *Nonprofit and Voluntary Sector Quarterly* 31, no. 2 (2002): 231–58, or Meredith Honig, "The New Middle Management: Intermediary Organizations in Education Policy Implementation," *Educational Evaluation and Policy Analysis* 26, no. 1 (2004): 65–87. For conceptual clarity, we modify a framework developed by Glickman and Servon describing the roles of community economic development intermediaries focused on building capacity in programs, organizations, networks, finances, and policy. See Norman Glickman and Lisa J. Servon, "More Than Bricks and Sticks: What Is Community Development Capacity?" *Housing Policy Debate* 9, no. 3 (1998): 497 or Norman Glickman, "By the Numbers: Measuring Community Development Corporations' Capacity," *Journal of Planning Education and Research* 22, no. 3 (2003): 240–56.

25. Parents as Teachers National Center (2014), http://www.parentsasteachers.org/.

26. Keith Provan, and H. Brinton Milward, "A Preliminary Theory of Interorganizational Network Effectiveness: A Comparative Study of Four Community Mental Health Systems," *Administrative Science Quarterly* 40 (1995): 1–33.

27. Interestingly, many more of these are the focus of scholarly inquiry, likely because they are created from a visible, public initiative.

28. James Mahoney, "Path Dependence in Historical Sociology," *Theory and Society* 29, no. 4 (2000): 507–48; Paul Pierson, "Increasing Returns, Path Dependence, and the Study of Politics," *American Political Science Review* 94, no. 2 (2000): 251–67; Paul A. David, "Why Are Institutions the 'Carriers of History'? Path Dependence and the Evolution of Conventions, Organizations and Institutions," *Structural Change and Economic Dynamics* 5, no. 2 (1994): 205–20.

29. Heather C. Hill, "Understanding Implementation: Street-Level Bureaucrats' Resources for Reform," *Journal of Public Administration Research and Theory* 13, no. 1(2003): 265–82.

30. We explore this literature in detail in chapter 6. See Michael Lipsky, *Street-Level Bureaucracy: Dilemmas of the Individual in Public Services* (New York: Russell Sage Foundation, 1980).

31. Erik-Hans Klijn, Jurian Edelenbos, and Bram Steijn, "Trust in Governance Networks: Its Impacts on Outcomes," *Administration and Society* 42, no. 2 (2010): 193–221.

32. Eric-Hans Klijn and Geert R. Teisman, "Strategies and Games in Networks," in *Managing Complex Networks: Strategies for the Public Sector*, ed. Walter J. M. Kickert, Eric-Hans Klijn, and Joop F. M. Koppenjan (London: SAGE, 1997), 98–118; Jodi R. Sandfort, "The Structural Impediments to Human Service Collaboration: The Case of Frontline Welfare Reform Implementation," *Social Service Review* 73, no. 3 (1999): 314–39.

33. Salamon, *The Tools of Government*, 19.

34. Ibid.

35. A short video about policy field analysis is available at http://www.hubert project.org.

36. In addition to players, Bryson also talks about context setters, subjects, and the crowd as stakeholders in change process. See John M. Bryson, "What to Do When Stakeholders Matter," *Public Management Review* 6, no. 1 (2004): 21–53.

37. There are other techniques for teaching this type of analysis in the classroom; see Jodi Sandfort and Melissa Stone, "Analyzing Policy Fields: Helping Students Understand Complex State and Local Contexts," *Journal of Public Affairs Education* 14, no. 2 (2008): 129–48.

38. John M. Bryson, Fran Ackermann, Colin Eden, and Charles B. Finn, *Visible Thinking: Unlocking Causal Mapping for Practical Business Results* (Hoboken, NJ: Wiley, 2004); Sandfort and Stone, "Analyzing Policy Fields," 129–48.

39. Minnesota's historically civically engaged business, United Way, and private philanthropic funders also are active players, providing about $24 million to the field in 2007. Private business leaders created the nonprofit Minnesota Early Learning Foundation to fund research and development in the field.

40. DiMaggio and Powell, "The Iron Cage Revisited"; Susan M. Miller and Stephanie Moulton, "Publicness in Policy Environments: A Multilevel Analysis of Substance Abuse Treatment Services," *Journal of Public Administration Research and Theory* 24, no. 3 (2014): 553–89.

41. William D. Berry and Brady Baybeck, "Using Geographic Information Systems to Study Interstate Competition," *American Political Science Review* 99, no. 4 (2005): 505–19; Charles R. Shipan and Craig Volden, "The Mechanisms of Policy Diffusion," *American Journal of Political Science* 52, no. 4 (2008): 840–57.

CHAPTER FIVE

1. For example, see Hal G. Rainey, *Understanding and Managing Public Organizations* (San Francisco: Jossey-Bass, 2014).

2. Robert D. Behn, "The Big Questions of Public Management," *Public Administration Review* 55, no. 4 (1995): 313–24.

3. Robbie Waters Robichau and Laurence E. Lynn Jr., "The Implementation of Public Policy: Still the Missing Link," *Policy Studies Journal* 37, no. 1 (2009): 21–36.

4. W. Richard Scott, *Organizations as Rational, Natural and Open Systems,* 5th ed. (New York: Prentice Hall, 2003), 11.

5. James G. March and Herbert Alexander Simon, *Organizations* (New York: Wiley, 1958).

6. James G. March and Johan P. Olsen, "Organizing Political Life: What Administrative Reorganization Tells Us about Government," *American Political Science Review* 77, no. 2 (1983): 281–96.

7. Paul Berman, *The Study of Micro and Macro Implementation of Social Policy* (Santa Monica, CA: Rand, 1978).

8. Ibid.

9. Laurence E. Lynn, Carolyn J. Heinrich, and Carolyn J. Hill, *Improving Governance: A New Logic for Empirical Research* (Washington, DC: Georgetown University Press, 2001).

10. For example, see Joe Soss, Sanford F. Schram, Thomas P. Vartanian, and Erin O'Brien, "Setting the Terms of Relief: Explaining State Policy Choices in the Devolution Revolution," *American Journal of Political Science* 45, no. 2 (2001): 378–95.

11. For example, see Carolyn J. Heinrich and Elizabeth Fournier, "Dimensions of Publicness and Performance in Substance Abuse Treatment Organizations," *Journal of Policy Analysis and Management* 23, no. 1 (2004): 49–70; Susan Meyer Goldstein and Michael Naor, "Linking Publicness to Operations Management Practices: A Study of Quality Management Practices in Hospitals," *Journal of Operations Management* 23, no. 2 (2005): 209–28; Jaap Dronkers and Péter Robert, "Differences in Scholastic Achievement of Public, Private Government-Dependent, and Private Independent Schools: A Cross-National Analysis," *Educational Policy* 22, no. 4 (2008): 541–77.

12. For example, see differences between substance abuse providers operating in different states: Susan M. Miller and Stephanie Moulton. "Publicness in Policy Environments: A Multilevel Analysis of Substance Abuse Treatment Services," *Journal of Public Administration Research and Theory* 24, no. 3 (2014): 553–89.

13. For example, see David M. Van Slyke, "Agents or Stewards: Using Theory to Understand the Government-Nonprofit Social Service Contracting Relationship," *Journal of Public Administration Research and Theory* 17, no. 2 (2007): 157–87.

14. Kenneth D. Boulding, "General Systems Theory: The Skeleton of Science," *Management Science* 2, no. 3 (1956): 127–39; Daniel Katz and Robert L. Kahn, *The Social Psychology of Organizations* (New York: Wiley, 1978).

15. Jeffrey Pfeffer and Gerald R. Salancik, *The External Control of Organizations: A Resource Dependence Perspective* (New York: Harper, 1978).

16. Paul J. DiMaggio and Walter W. Powell, "The Iron Cage Revisited: Institutional Isomorphism and Collective Rationality in Organizational Fields," *American Sociological Review* 48, no. 2 (1983): 284–301.

17. Peter Senge, *The Fifth Discipline: The Art and Practice of the Learning Organization*, rev. ed. (New York: Doubleday, 2006).

18. Pamela Herd, Thomas DeLeire, Hope Harvey, and Donald P. Moynihan, "Shifting Administrative Burden to the State: The Case of Medicaid Take-Up," *Public Administration Review* 73, no. s1 (2013): S69-S81.

19. Ibid.

20. Raymond E. Miles, Charles C. Snow, Alan D. Meyer, and Henry J. Coleman, "Organizational Strategy, Structure, and Process," *Academy of Management Review* 3, no. 3 (1978): 546–62.

21. Sanjay K. Pandey and Patrick G. Scott, "Red Tape: A Review and Assessment of Concepts and Measures," *Journal of Public Administration Research and Theory* 12, no. 4 (2002): 553–80.

22. David Osborne and Ted Gaebler, *Reinventing Government: How the Entrepreneurial Spirit Is Transforming Government* (Reading, MA: Addison-Wesley, 1992).

23. Theodore H. Poister, *Measuring Performance in Public and Nonprofit Organizations* (San Francisco: Jossey-Bass, 2003).

24. William G. Ouchi, "Markets, Bureaucracies, and Clans," *Administrative Science Quarterly* 25, no. 1 (1980): 129–41.

25. Donald P. Moynihan, "The Normative Model in Decline? Public Service Motivation in the Age of Governance," in *Motivation in Public Management: The Call of Public Service,* ed. James L. Perry and Annie Hondeghem (Oxford and New York: Oxford University Press, 2008), 247–67.

26. Jay R. Galbraith, "Organization Design: An Information Processing View," *Interfaces* 4, no. 3 (1974): 28–36.

27. Herbert A. Simon, *Administrative Behavior,* vol. 3. (New York: Free Press, 1948, revised 1976).

28. Barbara S. Romzek, "Enhancing Accountability," *Handbook of Public Administration,* 2nd ed., ed. James L. Perry (San Francisco: Jossey-Bass, 1996), 102; Barbara S. Romzek and Patricia Wallace Ingraham, "Cross Pressures of Accountability: Initiative, Command, and Failure in the Ron Brown Plane Crash," *Public Administration Review* 60, no. 3 (2000): 240–53; Barbara S. Romzek and Melvin J. Dubnick, "Accountability in the Public Sector: Lessons from the *Challenger* Tragedy," *Public Administration Review* 47, no. 3 (1987): 227–38.

29. See Mike Bresnen, Anna Goussevskaia, and Jacky Swan, "Embedding New Management Knowledge in Project-Based Organizations," *Organization Studies* 25, no. 9 (2004): 1535–55; Dianne Waddell, "Program Management: The Next Step in the Evolution of Project Management?," *Problems and Perspectives in Management,* no. 3 (2005): 160–68; Joann Hackos and Janice Redish, *User and Task Analysis for Interface Design* (New York: Wiley, 1998).

30. Kathryn Tout and Jennifer Cleveland, *Evaluation of Parent Aware: Minnesota's Quality Rating and Improvement System* (Washington, DC: Child Trends, 2014).

31. Initial evaluation of the first year of statewide expansion of the program stressed that generally coaches were successful in customizing their support for providers, establishing positive relationships, customizing coaching, and engaging more providers in all steps.

32. Raymond E. Miles, Charles C. Snow, Alan D. Meyer, and Henry J. Coleman, "Organizational Strategy, Structure, and Process," *Academy of Management Review* 3, no. 3 (1978): 546–62.

33. Kirsten Gronbjerg's early research long ago suggested that the characteristics of revenue sources themselves exert a distinct influence on nonprofit organizational operation. Kirsten Gronbjerg, *Understanding Nonprofit Funding: Managing Revenues in Social Services and Community Development Organizations* (San Francisco: Jossey-Bass, 1993).

CHAPTER SIX

1. Mary Jo Bitner, Bernard H. Booms, and Lois A. Mohr, "Critical Service Encounters: The Employee's Viewpoint," *Journal of Marketing* 58, no. 4

(1994): 95–106; Linda L. Price, Eric J. Arnould, and Patrick Tierney, "Going to Extremes: Managing Service Encounters and Assessing Provider Performance," *Journal of Marketing* 59, no. 2 (1995): 83–97.

2. A. Parasuraman, Valarie A. Zeithaml, and Leonard L. Berry, "A Conceptual Model of Service Quality and Its Implications for Future Research," *Journal of Marketing* 49, no. 4 (1985): 41–50.

3. David Osborne and Ted Gaebler, *Reinventing Government: How the Entrepreneurial Spirit Is Transforming the Public Sector* (New York: Plume Books, 1992).

4. A number of political theorists explore this in detail. For an alternative conception and embrace of the multiple manifestations of "public work," see Harry C. Boyte, *Common Wealth: A Return to Citizen Politics* (London: Collier Macmillan, 1989) or Harry Boyte, *The Citizen Solution* (Minneapolis: University of Minnesota Press, 2008).

5. Henry Mintzberg, "Managing Government, Governing Management," *Harvard Business Review* (May–June 1996): 77.

6. Michael Lipsky, *Street-Level Bureaucracy: Dilemmas of the Individual in Public Services* (New York: Russell Sage Foundation, 1980).

7. Ibid., xiii.

8. Richard E. Matland, "Synthesizing the Implementation Literature: The Ambiguity-Conflict Model of Policy Implementation," *Journal of Public Administration Research and Theory* 5, no. 2 (1995): 145–74.

9. Joel F. Handler, *The Conditions of Discretion: Autonomy, Community, Bureaucracy* (New York: Russell Sage Foundation, 1986); Matland, "Synthesizing"; and many others.

10. Barry Bozeman, *Bureaucracy and Red Tape* (Upper Saddle River, NJ: Prentice Hall, 2000).

11. Steven Maynard-Moody and Michael Musheno, "State Agent or Citizen Agent: Two Narratives of Discretion," *Journal of Public Administration Research and Theory* 10, no. 2 (2000): 329–58; Jodi R. Sandfort, "Moving Beyond Discretion and Outcomes: Examining Public Management from the Front-Lines of the Welfare System," *Journal of Public Administration Research and Theory* 10, no. 4 (2000): 729–56; Pamela Herd, Thomas

DeLeire, Hope Harvey, and Donald P. Moynihan, "Shifting the Administrative Burden to the State: A Case Study of Medicaid Take-Up," *Public Administration Review* 73, no. s1 (2013): S69–S81.

12. Lipsky, *Street-Level Bureaucracy*, xii.

13. Janet Coble Vinzant and Lane Crothers, *Street-Level Leadership: Discretion and Legitimacy in Front-Line Public Service* (Washington, DC: Georgetown University Press, 1998).

14. This focus was initiated in Lipsky's initial work and continued through many studies. See, for example, Evelyn Z. Brodkin, "Bureaucracy Redux: Management Reformism and the Welfare State," *Journal of Public Administration Research and Theory* 17, no. 1 (2006): 1–17; Steven Maynard-Moody and Michael Musheno, *Cops, Teachers, Counselors: Stories from the Front Lines of Public Services* (Ann Arbor: University of Michigan Press, 2003); Steven Maynard-Moody and Shannon Portillo, "Street-Level Bureaucracy Theory," in *The Oxford Handbook of American Bureaucracy*, ed. Robert F. Durant (Oxford: Oxford University Press, 2000); Carolyn J. Hill, "Casework Job Design and Client Outcomes in Welfare-to-Work Offices," *Journal of Public Administration Research and Theory* 16, no. 2 (2005): 263–88; Heather C. Hill, "Understanding Implementation: Street-Level Bureaucrats' Resources for Reform," *Journal of Public Administration Research and Theory* 13, no. 3 (2003): 265–82.

15. For a great example of each when dealing with similar populations, see Maynard-Moody and Musheno, *Cops, Teachers, Counselors*, for the former; and Joe Soss, Richard Fording, and Sanford F. Schram, "The Organization of Discipline: From Performance Management to Perversity and Punishment," *Journal of Public Administration Research and Theory* 21, no. s2 (2011): S203–32, and John Brehm and Scott Gates, *Working, Shirking, and Sabotage: Bureaucratic Response to a Democratic Public* (Ann Arbor: University of Michigan Press, 1997) for the latter.

16. Eve E. Garrow and Oscar Grusky, "Institutional Logic and Street-Level Discretion: The Case of HIV Test Counseling," *Journal of Public Administration Research and Theory* 23, no. 1 (2012): 103–31; Maynard-Moody and Portillo, "Street-Level Bureaucracy Theory."

17. Many scholars discuss the significance of the social construction of the target groups in policy design and implementation. A comprehensive statement of the core ideas can be found in Anne Larason Schneider and Helen Ingram, *Policy Design for Democracy* (Lawrence: University of Kansas, 1997).

18. Jeffrey Prottas's *People Processing: The Street-Level Bureaucrats in Public Service Bureaucracies* (Lanham, MD: Lexington Books, 1979) discussed the moral nature of this process almost forty years ago. The idea was elaborated by Yeheskel Hasenfeld, *Human Service Organizations* (Englewood Cliffs, NJ: Prentice Hall, 1983); Celeste Watkins-Hayes, *The New Welfare Bureaucrats* (Chicago: University of Chicago, 2009); Joe Soss, Richard C. Fording, and Sanford F. Schram, *Disciplining the Poor: Neoliberal Paternalism and the Persistent Power of Race* (Chicago: University of Chicago Press, 2011); Maynard-Moody and Musheno, *Cops, Teachers, Counselors*; Lael R. Keiser, "State Bureaucratic Discretion and the Administration of Social Welfare Programs: The Case of Social Security Disability," *Journal of Public Administration Research and Theory* 9, no. 1 (1999): 87–106.

19. This useful distinction was first made by Albert C. Hyde, "Feedback from Customers, Clients, and Captives," *Bureaucrat* 20, no. 4 (1991): 49–53. It was reinforced in a more recent article by Trevor Brown, "Coercion versus Choice: Citizen Evaluations of Public Service Quality across Methods of Consumption," *Public Administration Review* 67, no. 3 (2007): 559–72.

20. Joe Soss, "Talking Our Way to Meaningful Explanations: A Practice-Centered View of Interviewing for Interpretative Research," in *Interpretation and Method: Empirical Research Methods and the Interpretive Turn*, ed. Dvora Yanow and Peregrine Schwartz-Shea (London: M. E. Sharp, 2007), 127–49.

21. Richard H. Thaler and Shlomo Benartzi, "Save More Tomorrow: Using Behavioral Economics to Increase Employee Saving," *Journal of Political Economy* 112, no. s1 (2004): S164–87.

22. As R. Kent Weaver notes in "Compliance Regimes and Barriers to Behavioral Change," *Governance: An International Journal of Policy, Administration, and Institutions* 27, no. 2 (2013): 243–65, there is a considerable literature spanning political science, economics, psychology, and law

about why individuals and businesses do not comply with public policies. His review provides a comprehensive consideration of these issues.

23. Richard E. Matland, "Synthesizing the Implementation Literature: The Ambiguity-Conflict Model of Policy Implementation," *Journal of Public Administration Research and Theory* 5, no. 2 (1995): 145–74.

24. Steven Maynard-Moody and Michael Musheno, "State Agent or Citizen Agent: Two Narratives of Discretion," *Journal of Public Administration Research and Theory* 10, no. 2 (2000): 334.

25. Watkins-Hayes, *The New Welfare Bureaucrats*, 11.

26. For example, see David K. Cohen, "Revolution in One Classroom," *Educational Evaluation and Policy Analysis* 12, no. 3 (1990): 311–29; David K. Cohen, Milbrey W. McLaughlin, and Joan Talbert, *Teaching for Understanding: Challenges for Policy and Practice* (San Francisco: Jossey-Bass, 1993); James P. Spillane and John S. Zeuli, "Reform and Mathematics Teaching: Exploring Patterns of Practice in the Context of National State Reforms," *Educational Evaluation and Policy Analysis* 21, no. 1 (1999): 1–27; David K. Cohen and Heather C. Hill, *Learning Policy: When State Education Reform Works* (New Haven, CT: Yale University Press, 2001); Meredith I. Honig, ed., *New Directions in Education Policy Implementation: Confronting Complexity* (Albany: State University of New York Press, 2006).

27. These specific findings come from Maynard-Moody and Musheno, *Cops, Teachers, Counselors*; and Watkins-Hayes, *The New Welfare Bureaucrats*.

28. Aaron R. Lyon, Kristy Ludwig, Evalynn Romano, Skyler Leonard, Ann Vander Stoep, and Elizabeth McCauley, "'If It's Worth My Time, I Will Make the Time': School-Based Providers' Decision-Making about Participating in an Evidence-Based Psychotherapy Consultation Program," *Administration and Policy in Mental Health and Mental Health Services Research* 40, no. 6 (2013): 467–81.

29. In addition, the "evidence-based practices" ideal is based on a number of assumptions about staff that do not necessarily hold. First, it assumes that staff are professionally trained and embrace the legitimacy of empirical research, particularly experimental control studies with randomized assignments of participants to various treatment conditions. Yet, there are many other forms of knowledge that staff find more legitimate, such as

experience. Second, members of minority groups reasonably question the applicability of such studies to their groups. Third, it is assumed that the existence of this research base should guarantee its adoption. The fallacy of that assumption echoes the findings of the first generation of policy researchers that we discuss in chapter 2.

30. Maynard-Moody and Musheno, *Cops, Teachers, Counselors,* 22.

31. Ibid., 88.

32. Ibid., 44.

33. Marcia K. Meyers and Susan Vorsanger, "Street-Level Bureaucrats and the Implementation of Public Policy," in *Handbook of Public Administration,* ed. B. Guy Peters and John Pierre (Thousand Oaks, CA: SAGE, 2003), 245–55.

34. Garrow and Grusky, "Institutional Logic and Street-Level Discretion." In addition, see Charles Glisson, Anthony Hemmelgarn, Philip Green, and Nathaniel J. Williams, "Randomized Trial of the Availability, Responsiveness and Continuity (ARC) Organizational Intervention for Improving Youth Outcomes in Community Mental Health Programs," *Journal of the American Academy of Child and Adolescent Psychiatry* 52, no. 5 (2013): 493–500; Gregory A. Aarons et al., "The Organizational Social Context of Mental Health Services and Clinician Attitudes toward Evidence-Based Practice: A United States National Study," *Implementation Science* 7 (2012): 1–15.

35. Garrow and Grusky, "Institutional Logic and Street-Level Discretion," 122.

36. There is a growing literature about coproduction in public services. See Elinor Ostrom, "Crossing the Great Divide: Coproduction, Synergy, and Development," *World Development* 24, no. 6 (1996): 1073–87; John Alford, "Why Do Public-Sector Clients Coproduce?: Toward a Contingency Theory," *Administration and Society* 34, no. 1 (2002): 32–56; Tony Bovaird, "Beyond Engagement and Participation: User and Community Coproduction of Public Services," *Public Administration Review* 67, no. 5 (2007): 846–60; Kathryn S. Quick and Martha S. Feldman, "Distinguishing Participation and Inclusion," *Journal of Planning Education and Research* 31, no. 3 (2011): 272–90.

37. T. Elder and E. Powers, "The Incredible Shrinking Program," *Research on Aging* 28 (2006): 341–58; L. D. Shore-Sheppard, "Stemming the Tide? The

Effect of Expanding Medicaid Eligibility on Health Insurance Coverage," *BE Journal of Economic Analysis & Policy* 8, no. 6 (2008): 287–303.

38. See James L. Perry, Trent A. Engbers, and So Yun Jun, "Back to the Future? Performance-Related Pay, Empirical Research, and the Perils of Persistence," *Public Administration Review* 69, no. 1 (2008): 39–51, for a systematic review of the literature published between 1977 and 2008, as well as the history of pay-for-performance initiatives in national and state governments.

39. Donald P. Moynihan, *The Dynamics of Performance Management: Constructing Information and Reform* (Washington, DC: Georgetown University Press, 2008); Gwyn Bevan and Christopher Hood, "What's Measured Is What Matters: Targets and Gaming in the English Public Health System," *Public Administration* 84, no. 3 (2006): 517–38; Beryl A. Radin, *Challenging the Performance Movement: Accountability, Complexity, and Democratic Values* (Washington, DC: Georgetown University Press, 2006).

40. Bevan and Hood, "What's Measured Is What Matters," 517–38.

41. This discussion of the HHF assistance process is described in detail in the dissertation of scholar Blair Russell, a research assistant working with OHFA on the evaluation of the HHF program. Blair D. Russell, "Examining the Barriers to Public Assistance Take-Up: Evidence from a Foreclosure Mitigation Program in Ohio" (PhD dissertation, Ohio State University, 2013), https://etd.ohiolink.edu.

42. Nigel Cross, "Designerly Ways of Knowing," *Design Studies* 3, no. 4 (1982): 221–27; Nigel Cross, "From a Design Science to a Design Discipline: Understanding Designerly Ways of Knowing and Thinking," in *Design Research Now*, ed. R. Michel (Basel: Birkhauser, 2007), 41–54; Nigel Cross, *Design Thinking* (London: Bloomsbury Academic, 2011). In addition, a number of scholars have explored the distinct design reasoning, showing how it differs from the logic of analysis and evaluation, which uses deductive and inductive reasoning to determine what should be or what is. Drawing on the work of philosopher Charles Peirce, they explore the concept of abductive reasoning, which imagines what might be based on data and experience. For a

discussion of this tradition see Cross's work, as well as that by Maria Gonzalez and Willem Haselager, "Creativity: Surprise and Abductive Reasoning, *Semiotica* 153, no. 1 (2005): 325–41 and other articles in a special issue of *Semiotica* 153 (2005).

43. Lipsky, *Street-Level Bureaucracy*.

PART THREE

1. Donald A Schön, *Educating the Reflective Practitioner: Toward a New Design for Teaching and Learning in the Professions* (San Francisco: Jossey-Bass, 1987), 4.

2. Henry Mintzberg, "Rethinking Strategic Planning Part I: Pitfalls and Fallacies," *Long Range Planning* 27, no. 3 (1994): 13.

3. Peter M. Senge, *The Fifth Discipline: The Art and Practice of the Learning Organization* (New York: Doubleday, 1990); Parker Palmer, *Let Your Life Speak: Listening for the Voice of Vocation* (San Francisco: Jossey-Bass, 1999).

4. Scholars note that most often change occurs in such ways, in terms consistent with the existing norms of the strategic action field (SAF) and in ways that do not challenge the existing order. These are incremental changes that are stressed in the organizational decision-making literature. For example, see Charles E. Lindblom, "The Science of Muddling Through," *Public Administration Review* 19, no. 2 (1959): 79–88.

5. Scholars consider this to be rare and discuss it in terms of punctured equilibrium. For an example, see ibid.

CHAPTER SEVEN

1. Annie Lowrey, "Treasury Faulted in Effort to Relieve Homeowners," *New York Times*, April 12, 2012, http://www.nytimes.com/2012/04/12/business/economy/treasury-department-faulted-in-effort-to-relieve-homeowners.html?_r=0.

2. Christy L. Romero, Office of the Special Inspector General for the Troubled Asset Relief Program, "Factors Affecting Implementation of the Hardest Hit Fund," 2013, http://www.sigtarp.gov/audit%20reports/sigtarp_hhf_audit.pdf.

3. Jeffrey Pressman and Aaron Wildavsky, *Implementation: How Great Expectations in Washington Are Dashed in Oakland or Why It's Amazing That Federal Programs Work at All,* 3rd ed. (Berkeley: University of California Press, 1984).

4. Much of the background information about the program is from the information on the program website: http://www.treasury.gov/initiatives/finan cial-stability/TARP-Programs/housing/hhf/Pages/default.aspx.

5. From Section 2 of EESA, as cited in the Treasury RFP for the HHF program. Department of the Treasury, "Housing Finance Agency Innovation Fund for the Hardest Hit Housing Markets ("HFA Hardest-Hit Fund"): Guidelines for HFA Proposal Submission," http://www.treasury.gov/initiatives/ financial-stability/TARPPrograms/housing/Documents/HFA_Proposal_ Guidelines_-_1st_Rd.pdf.

6. SIGTARP, "Factors Affecting Implementation of the Hardest Hit Fund."

7. For example, see Daniel Immergluck, "Neighborhoods in the Wake of the Debacle: Intrametropolitan Patterns of Foreclosed Properties," *Urban Affairs Review* 46, no. 1 (2010): 3–36.

8. Politically, Treasury also faced pressures to expend TARP funds quickly. By distributing the funds to the states as block grants and giving them discretion for allocation, Treasury was able to meet the deadline for expending TARP funds.

9. From Ohio's proposal to Treasury: "Ohio's inter-agency team used current unemployment claims matched against 2008 tax returns to estimate that 287,600 households that had a member receiving unemployment compensation as of April 12, 2010 also had an outstanding mortgage. Approximately 30 percent of those 287,600 unemployed homeowners may be in need of mortgage assistance, assuming that 11 percent of households are delinquent on their mortgage, and 19 percent of homeowners seeking foreclosure prevention assistance are current on their mortgage. Therefore, the inter-agency team estimated that 86,280 unemployed households in Ohio could be eligible for Restoring Stability if they meet the other eligibility criteria." Ohio Housing Financing Agency, "Restoring Stability: A Save the Dream Initiative," http://www.treasury.gov/initiatives/financial-

stability/programs/housing-programs/hhf/Documents/HHFfinalproposal%
204–11–2011.pdf (April 11, 2011).

10. Ohio Housing Financing Agency, "Restoring Stability: A Save the Dream Initiative."

11. US Department of the Treasury, "Hardest Hit Fund: Third Quarter 2013 Performance Summary," http://www.treasury.gov/initiatives/financial-sta bility/reports/Documents/Q3%202013%20Hardest%20Hit%20 Fund%20 Program%20Performance%20Summary%20FINAL%2012.17.13.pdf (Sept. 30, 2013).

12. While the general structures of the interventions were similar, there was much more variation between states on programmatic details such as eligibility requirements and the structure and duration of assistance.

13. See, for example, Senator Sherrod Brown (Democrat, Ohio) urging Treasury to reconsider the limit on use of HHF funds to pay for legal aid and counseling. Sherrod Brown to Timothy Geithner, June 1, 2010, in "Sen. Brown Urges Sec. Geithner to Expand Access to Legal Aid and Counseling Assistance Programs," http://www.brown.senate.gov/newsroom/press/re lease/sen-brown-urges-sec-geithner-to-expand-access-to-legal-aid-and-counseling-assistance-programs (June 1, 2010).

14. US Department of the Treasury, "Hardest Hit Fund: Third Quarter 2013 Performance Summary."

15. A description of this process is provided in a research article evaluating take-up assistance through the HHF program. See Blair Russell, Stephanie Moulton, and Rob Greenbaum, "Accessibility, Transaction Costs and the Take-up of Mortgage Assistance for Distressed Homeowners," *Journal of Housing Economics* 24, no. C (2014): 57–74.

16. Ibid.

17. OHFA worked with "LeanOhio," an initiative of the Ohio Department of Administrative Services, to streamline the intake and application process for HHF homeowners. Highlights from this initiative are published online at LeanOhio, "Simplified Process Aims to Make "Saving the Dream" 9 Times Faster for Struggling Homeowners" (August 1, 2012), http://lean.ohio.gov/Results/OHFAEligibilityDeterminationJuly2012.aspx.

18. Warren Staley and Duane Benson, "Tax Dollars Well-Spent? It's Possible," *Star Tribune*, January 17, 2013.

19. National Research Council, *Who Cares for America's Children? Child Care Policy for the 1990s*, ed. Cheryl D. Hayes, John L. Palmer, and Martha J. Zaslow (Washington, DC: National Academy Press: 1990); Janet C. Gornick and Marcia K. Meyers, *Families That Work: Policies for Reconciling Parenthood and Employment* (New York: Russell Sage Foundation, 2003); Brenda K. Bushouse, *Universal Preschool: Policy Change, Stability, and the Pew Charitable Trusts* (Albany, NY: SUNY Press, 2009).

20. This implementation detail—in which some types of programs (school-run, Head Start, and nationally accredited child care centers) are automatically awarded the highest Parent Aware rating—was also highly controversial. Fundamentally, it reflected conflicting cultural norms in the policy field—some actors asserting that schools or Head Start programs are more "professional" and thus not necessarily affected by a voluntary program like QRS.

21. Aisha Ray, *Parents Priorities in Selecting Early Care and Education Programs: Implications for Minnesota's Quality Rating and Improvement Systems*, Minnesota Early Learning Foundation, 2008, http://www.pasrmn.org/MELF/Parent_Aware_Pilot_Research.

22. Dave Hage, *Into the Fray: How a Funders Coalition Restored Momentum for Early Learning in Minnesota*, 2011, http://fcd-us.org/resources/fray-how-funders-coalition-restored-momentum-early-learning-minnesota.

23. Kathryn Tout, Rebecca Starr, Jennifer Cleveland, Sharah Friese, Margaret Soli, and Ladia Albertson-Junkans, *Statewide Expansion of Parent Aware: Year 1 Implementation Report*, Parent Aware for School Readiness, 2011, http://www.pasrmn.org/work/research.

24. Richard Chase and Jennifer Valorose, *Child Care Use in Minnesota: Report of the 2009 Statewide Household Child Care Survey* (St. Paul, MN: Wilder Research Center, 2010). http://www.wilder.org/WilderResearch/Publications/Studies/Child%20Care%20Use%20in%20Minnesota%202009/Child%20Care%20Use%20in%20Minnesota,%20Full%20Report.pdf (accessed October 2, 2013).

CHAPTER EIGHT

1. Ronald A. Heifetz and Marty Linsky, *Leadership on the Line: Staying Alive through the Dangers of Leading* (Boston: Harvard Business School Press, 2002); Ronald A. Heifetz, *Leadership without Easy Answers* (Cambridge, MA: Belknap Press of Harvard University, 1994). In the first book, Heifetz actually discusses technical challenges as "type I" and adaptive challenges as "type II" and "type III." Type II is when the problem is definable but there are no clear-cut solutions available. In type III, the problem definition is not clear-cut and technical fixes are not available. While certainly all are present in implementation reform, we focus on the more simplistic differentiation for now.

2. Heifetz and Linsky, *Leadership on the Line*, 58.

3. John Dewey, *The Public and Its Problems* (New York: Holt, 1927).

4. Jean Lave and Etienne Wenger, *Situated Learning: Legitimate Peripheral Participation* (Cambridge: Cambridge University Press, 1991); John Forester, *The Deliberative Practitioner: Encouraging Participatory Planning Processes* (Cambridge, MA: MIT Press, 1999).

5. Eugene Bardach, *A Practical Guide for Policy Analysis: The Eightfold Path to More Effective Problem Solving*, 3rd ed. (Washington, DC: CQ Press: 2009); David Weimer and Aidan Vining, *Policy Analysis: Concepts and Practice*, 2nd ed. (Englewood Cliffs, NJ: Prentice Hall, 1992).

6. Mark H. Moore, *Creating Public Value: Strategic Management in Government* (Cambridge, MA: Harvard University Press, 1995).

7. Adam Dahl and Joe Soss, "Neoliberalism for the Common Good? Public Value-Governance and the Downsizing of Democracy," *Public Administration Review* 74, no. 4 (2014): 496–504.

8. Barry Bozeman, *Public Values and Public Interest: Counterbalancing Economic Individualism* (Washington, DC: Georgetown University Press, 2007), 132.

9. For a discussion of the original eight criteria, see ibid.

10. This is in line with Bozeman's criteria to "ensure subsistence and human dignity" (see note 8).

11. This harsh example actually occurred in the 1932 Tuskegee Syphilis Study, where nearly four hundred African American men were denied treatment for a curable disease so that the study would have a true control group. Bozeman, *Public Values and Public Interest*.

12. This is similar to network scholars' definition of capacity-building networks. For example, see Brinton H. Milward and Keith G. Provan, *A Manager's Guide to Choosing and Using Collaborative Networks* (Washington, DC: IBM Center for the Business of Government, 2006).

13. This is similar to Bozeman's criteria for "provider availability." Bozeman, *Public Values and Public Interest*.

14. This criterion is similar to Bozeman's criteria for "mechanisms for values articulation and aggregation." Bozeman, *Public Values and Public Interest*.

15. Some scholars of democracy make this point even more strongly than we do here. For example, see Adam Dahl and Joe Soss, "Neoliberalism for the Common Good? Public Value-Governance and the Downsizing of Democracy," *Public Administration Review* 74, no. 4 (2014): 496–504.

16. For example, see Pierre Koning and Carolyn J. Heinrich, "Cream-Skimming, Parking and Other Intended and Unintended Effects of High-Powered, Performance-Based Contracts," *Journal of Policy Analysis and Management* 32, no. 3 (2013): 461–83.

17. Our understanding of complex and complicated systems is influenced by the field of knowledge management and the work of David Snowden. For a relevant video, see Cognitive Edge, http://cognitive-edge.com/library/more/video/introduction-to-the-cynefin-framework/. Also see David J. Snowden and Mary E. Boone, "A Leader's Framework for Decision Making," *Harvard Business Review* (November 2007): 1–12.

18. Thirty-five years ago, Richard Elmore described these two fundamentally different approaches to redesign in "Backward Mapping: Implementation Research and Policy Decisions," *Political Science Quarterly* 94, no. 4 (1980): 601–16.

19. Ibid., 602.

20. On Amir, Dan Ariely, Alan Cooke, David Dunning, Nicholas Epley, Uri Gneezy, and Botond Koszegi, "Psychology, Behavioral Economics, and Public Policy," *Marketing Letters* 16, nos. 3–4 (2005): 443–54.

21. R. Kent Weaver, "Target Compliance: The Final Frontier of Policy Implementation," *Brookings Issues in Governance Studies* 27 (2009).

22. Richard H. Thaler and Shlomo Benartzi, "Save More Tomorrow: Using Behavioral Economics to Increase Employee Saving," supplement to *Journal of Political Economy* 112, no. s1 (2004): S164–87.

23. Brigitte C. Madrian and Dennis F. Shea, "The Power of Suggestion: Inertia in 401(k) Participation and Savings Behavior," *Quarterly Journal of Economics* 116, no. 4 (2001): 1149–87.

24. D. Kahneman and A. Tversky, "Prospect Theory: An Analysis of Decisions under Risk," *Econometrica* 47 (1979): 263–91.

25. Thaler and Benartzi, "Save More Tomorrow."

26. Story recounted in Tim Brown, *Change by Design* (New York: Harper Business, 2009), 50.

27. This fundamental idea is from contingency theory. For the classic study, see Paul Lawrence and Jay W. Lorche, *Organizations and Environment* (Cambridge, MA: Harvard Business School, Division of Research, 1967); James D. Thompson. *Organizations in Action* (New York: McGraw-Hill, 1967).

28. Karen J. Fryer, Jiju Antony, and Alex Douglas, "Critical Success Factors of Continuous Improvement in the Public Sector: A Literature Review and Some Key Findings," *TQM Magazine* 19, no. 5 (2007): 497–517.

29. Ibid., 497–517.

30. Like other state governments, Ohio embraced an approach called LEAN. According to its website: "The mission of Lean Ohio is to make government services in Ohio simpler, faster, better, and less costly. Using continuous improvement methods such as Lean and Six Sigma, Ohio's state agencies are cutting red tape, removing inefficiencies, improving customer service, and achieving measurable results." See Ohio Department of Administrative Services, "About Lean Ohio," http://lean.ohio.gov/.

31. Ohio Department of Administrative Services, Lean Ohio, "Simplified Process Aims to Make 'Saving the Dream' 9 Times Faster for Struggling Homeowners," August 2012, http://lean.ohio.gov/Results/OHFAEligibility DeterminationJuly2012.aspx.

32. This important point about the different uses of performance information is not new. See Robert D. Behn, "Why Measure Performance? Different Purposes Require Different Measures," *Public Administration Review* 63, no. 5 (2003): 586–606.

33. For a discussion of the appropriateness of rewards and sanctions applied to contracting in the public sector, see Trevor L. Brown, Matthew Potoski, and David M. Van Slyke, "Managing Public Service Contracts: Aligning Values, Institutions, and Markets," *Public Administration Review* 66, no. 3 (2006): 323–31.

34. For additional discussion of normative control and appealing to intrinsic motivation, see Donald P. Moynihan, "The Normative Model in Decline? Public Service Motivation in the Age of Governance," *Public Service Motivation: State of the Science and Art* 4 (2008): 247–67. For a discussion of trust-based contracting, see David M. Van Slyke, "Agents or Stewards: Using Theory to Understand the Government-Nonprofit Social Service Contracting Relationship," *Journal of Public Administration Research and Theory* 17, no. 2 (2007): 157–87.

35. Our thinking about this is influenced by the work of Carl May and his colleagues' normalization process theory, developed to explain how to effectively integrate evidence-based practice into clinical practice. However, we remain less convinced than May that significant adaptations might not occur during enactment. Carl R. May, Frances Mari, Tracy Finch, Anne MacFarlane et al., "Development of a Theory of Implementation and Integration: Normalization Process Theory," *Implementation Science* 4, no. 29 (2009): 1–9; Carl May, "Towards a General Theory of Implementation," *Implementation Science* 8, no. 1 (2013): 18.

36. David Snowden and Mary Boone, "A Leader's Framework for Decision Making," *Harvard Business Review* (November 2007): 1–12.

37. Daniel Goleman, "What Makes a Leader?" *Harvard Business Review* (November–December 1998): 93–102. Goleman, a psychologist, was a science reporter at the *New York Times* but built off the research of John Mayer and Peter Salovey.

38. In this work, Schön followed in the important shoes of Herbert Simon, Edgar Schein, and Nathan Glazer, who had identified a gap between professional knowledge and the demands of real-world practice. See

Donald A. Schön, *The Reflective Practitioner: How Professionals Think in Action* (New York: Basic Books, 1983) and *Educating the Reflective Practitioner: Toward a New Design for Teaching and Learning in the Professions* (San Francisco: Jossey-Bass, 1987).

39. Ibid.

40. Martha S. Feldman and Wanda J. Orlikowski, "Theorizing Practice and Practicing Theory," *Organization Science* 22, no. 5 (2011): 1240–53; John Forester, "Learning to Improve Practice: Lessons from Practice Stories and Practitioners' Own Discourse Analyses (or Why Only the Loons Show Up)," *Planning Theory and Practice* 13, no. 1 (2012): 11–26; Chris Huxham and Siv Vangen, *Managing to Collaborate: The Theory and Practice of Collaborative Advantage* (New York: Routledge, 2005).

41. Schön, *The Reflective Practitioner*, 268.

42. Ronald A. Heifetz and Marty Linsky, *Leadership on the Line: Staying Alive through the Dangers of Leading* (Boston: Harvard Business School Press, 2002).

43. It is well recognized that material objects become significant artifacts when they are used to alter relationships and results. For example, see Bruno Latour, *Reassembling the Social: An Introduction to Actor-Network Theory* (Oxford: Oxford University Press, 2005); Martha S. Feldman, Anne Khademian, Helen Ingram, and Anne Scheider, "Ways of Knowing and Inclusive Management Practices," *Public Administration Review* 66, no. S1 (2006): S89–S99; Martha S. Feldman and Anne M. Khademian, "The Role of the Public Manager in Inclusion: Creating Communities of Participation," *Governance* 20, no. 2 (2007): 305–24; Jodi Sandfort and Kathryn Quick, "Deliberative Technology in Use: Learning from the Art of Hosting," forthcoming in *Public Administration Review*.

44. Paul Carlile, "A Pragmatic View of Knowledge and Boundaries: Boundary Objects in New Product Development," *Organizational Science* 13, no. 4 (2002): 442–55.

45. Sandfort and Quick, "Deliberative Technology in Use."

46. Jim Spillane, Brian Reiser, and Todd Reimer, "Policy Implementation and Cognition: Reframing and Refocusing Implementation Research," *Review of Educational Research* 72, no. 3 (2002): 412.

47. Anne M. Khademian, *Working with Culture: The Way the Job Gets Done in Public Programs* (Washington DC: CQ Press, 2002); Edgar Schein, *Organizational Culture and Learning* (Cambridge, MA: Harvard University Press, 1992).

48. Neil Fligstein and Doug McAdam, *A Theory of Fields* (New York: Oxford University Press, 2012); "Social Skill and the Theory of Fields," *Sociological Theory* 19, no. 2 (2001): 105–25.

49. George Lakoff and Mark Johnson, *Philosophy in the Flesh: The Embodied Mind and Challenge to Western Philosophy* (New York: Basic Books, 1999). Schön, *The Reflective Practitioner*, also talks about generative metaphors—creating new perceptions, explanations, and inventions.

50. Erving Goffman, *Frame Analysis: An Essay on the Organization of Experience* (London: Harper & Row, 1974); Donald A. Schön and Martin Rein, *Frame Reflection: Toward the Resolution of Intractable Policy Controversies* (New York: Basic Books, 1995); George Lakoff, *The Political Mind: A Cognitive Scientist's Guide to Your Brain and Its Politics* (New York: Penguin Books, 2009).

51. Ibid.

52. Fligstein and McAdams, *Theory of Fields*.

53. Christian Bason, *Leading Public Sector Innovation: Co-Creating for a Better Society* (Bristol, UK: Policy Press, 2010); Tony Bovaird, "Beyond Engagement and Participation: User and Community Coproduction in Public Services," *Public Administration Review* (September–October 2007): 846–60.

54. Bason, *Leading Public Sector Innovation*, 154.

APPENDIX A

1. For an overview, see the policy field analysis video at www.hubertproject.org. The scholarly grounding is found in Jodi R. Sandfort and Melissa Middleton Stone, "Analyzing Policy Fields: Helping Students Understand Complex Policy Environments," *Journal of Public Affairs Education* 14, no. 2 (2008): 128–45; Melissa Stone and Jodi R. Sandfort, "Building a Policy Fields Framework to Inform Research in Nonprofit Organizations," *Nonprofit and Voluntary Sector Quarterly* 38, no. 6 (2009): 1054–75.

2. Lester Salamon, *The Tools of Government: A Guide to the New Governance* (Oxford: Oxford University Press, 2002).

3. Heather C. Hill, "Understanding Implementation: Street-Level Bureaucrats' Resources for Reform," *Journal of Public Administration Research and Theory* 13, no. 3 (July 2003): 269.

APPENDIX F

1. For more on abductive logic and its long tradition in philosophy and social science, see Peirce Edition Project, eds., *The Essential Peirce: Selected Philosophical Writings* (Bloomington: University of Indiana Press, 1998); Nigel Cross, *Design Thinking* (London: Bloomsbury Academic, 2011).

BIBLIOGRAPHY

PREFACE

March, James G., and Johan P. Olsen. "Organizing Political Life: What Administrative Reorganization Tells Us about Government." *American Political Science Review* 77, no. 2 (1983): 281–96.

Olsen, Johan P. "Understanding Institutions and Logics of Appropriateness: Introductory Essay." Centre for European Studies. ARENA working paper 13, no. 7 (2007).

PART ONE INTRODUCTION

Olsen, Johan P. "Understanding Institutions and Logics of Appropriateness: Introductory Essay." Centre for European Studies. ARENA working paper 13, no. 7 (2007).

Phillips, Sue. *The Practical Gardening Encyclopedia*. Surrey, UK: Colour Library Direct, 1997.

CHAPTER ONE

Aarons, Gregory, Charles Glisson, Phillip D. Green, Kimberly Hoagwood, Kelly J. Kelleher, John A. Landsverk, John R. Weisz, Bruce Chorpita, Robert Gibbons, Evelyn Polk Green, Peter S. Jensen, Stephen Mayberg, Jeanne Miranda, Lawrence Palinkas, and Sonja Schoenwald. "The Organizational Social Context of Mental Health Services and Clinician Attitudes toward Evidence-Based

Practice: A United States National Study." *Implementation Science*, no. 7 (2012): 1–15.

Barzeley, Michael, and Fred Thompson. "Making Public Management a Design-Oriented Science." Working paper, School of Economics and Political Science, Willamette University, OR, 2007.

Bingham, Lisa B., Tina Nabatchi, and Rosemary O'Leary. "The New Governance: Practices and Processes for Stakeholder and Citizen Participation in the Work of Government." *Public Administration Review* 65, no. 5 (2005): 547–58.

Bozeman, Barry. *Public Values and Public Interest: Counterbalancing Economic Individualism.* Washington, DC: Georgetown University Press, 2007.

Bozeman, Barry, and Stephanie Moulton. "Integrative Publicness: A Framework for Public Management Strategy and Performance." *Journal of Public Administration Research and Theory* 21, no. S3 (2011): S363–80.

Brodkin, Evelyn Z. "Implementation as Policy Politics." In *Implementation and the Policy Process: Opening up the Black Box*, edited by Dennis J. Palumbo and Donald J. Calista, 107–18. Westport, CT: Greenwood Press, 1990.

Bryson, John, Barbara Crosby, and Laura Bloomberg. "Public Value Governance: Moving beyond Traditional Public Administration and the New Public Management." *Public Administration Review* 74, no. 4 (2014): 444–56.

Cohen, David K., and Susan Moffitt. *The Ordeal of Equality: Did Federal Regulation Fix the Schools?* Cambridge, MA: Harvard University Press, 2009.

Commonwealth Fund. "Health System Data Center." http://datacenter.common wealthfund.org/scorecard/low-income/7/colorado/.

Daft, Richard. *Organizational Theory and Design*, 9th ed. Boston: South-Western, 2006.

Fligstein, Neil, and Doug McAdam. "Toward a General Theory of Strategic Action Fields." *Sociological Theory* 29, no. 1 (2011): 1–26.

———. *A Theory of Fields.* New York: Oxford University Press, 2012.

Garrow, Eve E., and Oscar Grusky. "Institutional Logic and Street-Level Discretion: The Case of HIV Test Counseling." *Journal of Public Administration Research and Theory* 23, no. 1 (2012): 103–31.

Gormley, Jr., William T. "Regulatory Issue Networks in a Federal System." *Polity* 18, no. 4 (1986): 595–620.

Hasenfeld, Yeheskel, and Robert English. "Organizational Technology." In *Human Service Organizations: A Book of Reading*. Englewood Cliffs, NJ: Prentice Hall, 1983.

Hill, Michael, and Peter Hupe. *Implementing Public Policy: An Introduction to the Study of Operational Governance*, 2nd ed. Thousand Oaks, CA: SAGE, 2008.

Kiser, Larry L., and Elinor Ostrom. "The Three Worlds of Action: A Metatheoretical Synthesis of Institutional Approaches." In *Strategies of Political Inquiry*, edited by Elinor Ostrom. Beverly Hills, CA: SAGE, 1982.

Lowi, Theodore J. "Four Systems of Policy, Politics, and Choice." *Public Administration Review* 32, no. 4 (1972): 298–310.

Matland, Richard E. "Synthesizing the Implementation Literature: The Ambiguity-Conflict Model of Policy Implementation." *Journal of Public Administration Research and Theory* 5, no. 2 (1995): 145–74.

May, Carl. "A Rational Model for Assessing and Evaluating Complex Interventions in Health Care." *BMC Health Services Research* 6, no. 11 (2006): 1–11.

————. "Towards a General Theory of Implementation." *Implementation Science* 8 (2013): 1–14.

May, Peter J., and Soren C. Winter. "Politicians, Managers, and Street-Level Bureaucrats: Influences on Policy Implementation." *Journal of Public Administration Research and Theory* 19, no. 3 (2007): 453–76.

Mazmanian, Daniel A., and Paul A. Sabatier. *Implementation and Public Policy*. Glenview, IL: Scott, Foresman, 1983.

McGinnis, Michael D. "An Introduction to IAD and the Language of the Ostrom Workshop: A Simple Guide to a Complex Framework." *Policy Studies Journal* 39, no. 1 (2011): 169–83.

Mitchell, Melanie. *Complexity: A Guided Tour*. New York: Oxford University Press, 2011.

Moulton, Stephanie. "Putting Together the Publicness Puzzle: A Framework for Realized Publicness." *Public Administration Review* 69, no. 5 (2009): 889–900.

_____. "The Authority to Do Good: Publicly Responsible Behavior among Private Mortgage Lenders." *Public Administration Review* 72, no. 3 (2012): 430–39.

Moynihan, Donald P. "Managing for Results in an Impossible Job: Solution or Symbol?" *International Journal of Public Administration* 28, no. 3 (2005): 213–31.

_____. *The Dynamics of Performance Management: Constructing Information and Reform*. Washington, DC: Georgetown University Press, 2008.

Nabatchi, Tina. "Putting the 'Public' Back in Public Values Research: Designing Participation to Identify and Respond to Value." *Public Administration Review* 72, no. 5 (2012): 699–708.

O'Toole, Laurence J. "Policy Recommendations for Multi-Actor Implementation: An Assessment of the Field." *Journal of Public Policy* 6, no. 2 (1986): 181–210.

Office of the Governor of Colorado. "The State of Health: Colorado's Commitment to Become the Healthiest State." Denver: Office of the Governor of Colorado, 2013. http://www.cohealthinfo.com/wp-content/uploads/2014/08/The-State-of-Health-Final-April-2013.pdf.

Ostrom, Elinor. "Institutional Rational Choice: An Assessment of the Institutional Analysis and Development Framework." In *Theories of the Policy Process*, 2nd ed., edited by Paul A. Sabatier, 21–64. Boulder, CO: Westview Press, 2007.

Parasuraman, A., Valarie A. Zeithaml, and Leonard L. Berry. "A Conceptual Model of Service Quality and Its Implications for Future Research." *Journal of Marketing* 49, no. 4 (1985): 41–50.

Perry, James L. "Antecedents of Public Service Motivation." *Journal of Public Administration Research and Theory* 7, no. 2 (1997): 181–97.

Perry, James L., and Lois Recascino Wise. "The Motivational Bases of Public Service." *Public Administration Review* 50, no. 3 (1990): 367–73.

Pressman, Jeffrey L., and Aaron Wildavsky. *Implementation: How Great Expectations in Washington Are Dashed in Oakland or Why It's Amazing That Federal Programs Work at All*, 3rd ed. Berkeley: University of California Press, 1984.

QRIS National Learning Network. "QRIS State Contacts and Map." QRIS National Learning Network, February 2014. http://www.qrisnetwork.org/qris-state-contacts-map.

Radin, Beryl A. *Challenging the Performance Movement: Accountability, Complexity, and Democratic Values*. Washington, DC: Georgetown University Press, 2006.

Rainey, Hal G. *Understanding and Managing Public Organizations*, 4th ed. San Francisco: Jossey-Bass, 2009.

Robichau, Robbie W., and Laurence E. Lynn, Jr. "The Implementation of Public Policy: Still the Missing Link." *Policy Studies Journal* 37, no. 1 (2009): 21–36.

Sabatier, Paul A., and Hank C. Jenkins-Smith, eds. *Policy Change and Learning: An Advocacy Coalition Approach*. Boulder, CO: Westview Press, 1993.

Sandfort, Jodi. "Human Service Organizational Technology." In *Human Services as Complex Organizations*, 2nd ed., edited by Yeheskel Hasenfeld, 269–90. New York: SAGE, 2010.

Schön, Donald A. *The Reflective Practitioner: How Professionals Think in Action*. New York: Basic Books, 1983.

Scott, Richard W. *Institutions and Organizations: Ideas and Interests*, 3rd ed. Thousand Oaks, CA: SAGE, 2008.

Sowa, Jessica E., Sally C. Selden, and Jodi R. Sandfort. "No Longer 'Unmeasurable'? A Multi-Dimensional Integrated Model of Nonprofit Organizational Effectiveness." *Nonprofit and Voluntary Sector Quarterly* 33, no. 4 (2004): 711–28.

Tolbert, Pamela S., and Richard H. Hall. *Organizations: Structures, Processes, and Outcomes*, 10th ed. Upper Saddle River, NJ: Prentice Hall, 2009.

Van Meter, Donald S., and Carl E. Van Horn. "The Policy Implementation Process: A Conceptual Framework." *Administration and Society* 6, no. 4 (1975): 445–88.

Weisbrod, Burton A. "The Future of the Nonprofit Sector: Its Entwining with Private Enterprise and Government." *Journal of Policy Analysis and Management* 16, no. 4 (1997): 541–55.

CHAPTER TWO

Aarons, Gregory, et al. "The Organizational Social Context of Mental Health Services and Clinician Attitudes toward Evidence-Based Practice: A United States National Study." *Implementation Science* 7 (2012): 1–15.

Agranoff, Robert, and Michael McGuire. *Collaborative Public Management: New Strategies for Local Governments*. Washington, DC: Georgetown University Press, 2003.

Allison, Graham. *Essence of Decision: Explaining the Cuban Missile Crisis*. Boston: Little, Brown, 1972.

Amir, On, Dan Ariely, Alan Cooke, David Dunning, Nicholas Epley, Uri Bneezy, Botond Koszegi, Donald Lightenstein, Nina Mazar, Sedhil Mullainathan, Drazen Prelec, Eldar Shafir, and Jose Silva. "Psychology, Behavioral Economics, and Public Policy." *Marketing Letters* 16, nos. 3–4 (2005): 443–54.

Anderson, James E. *Public Policy Making*. New York: Holt, 1977.

Bardach, Eugene. *The Implementation Game*. Cambridge, MA: MIT Press, 1977.

Barr, Michael S., Sendhil Mullainathan, and Eldar Shafir. "Behavorally Informed Regulation." In *The Behavioral Foundations of Public Policy*, edited by Eldar Shafir. Princeton, NJ: Princeton University Press, 2012.

Bearman, Sarah Kate, John R. Weisz, Bruce F. Chorpita, Kimberly Hoagwood, Alyssa Ward, and Ana M. Ugueto. "More Practice, Less Preach? The Role of Supervision Processes and Therapist Characteristics in EBP Implementation." *Administration and Policy in Mental Health and Mental Health Services Research* 40, no. 6 (2013): 518–29.

Beckman, Norman. "Policy Analysis for the Congress." *Public Administration Review* 37, no. 3 (1977): 237–44.

Behavioural Insights Team. https://www.gov.uk/government/organisations/behavioural-insights-team.

Berman, Paul. *The Study of Micro and Macro Implementation of Social Policy*. Santa Monica, CA: Rand, 1978.

———. "Educational Change: An Implementation Paradigm." *Improving Schools: Using What We Know*, edited by Michael B. Kane and Rolf Lehming, 253–86. Beverly Hills, CA: SAGE, 1981.

Blair, Robert. "Policy Tools Theory and Implementation Networks: Understanding State Enterprise Zone Partnerships." *Journal of Public Administration Research and Theory* 12, no. 2 (2002): 161–90.

Blank, Rebecca M. "What Do Economists Have to Contribute to Policy Decision?" *Quarterly Review of Economics and Finance* 42 (2002): 817–24.

Bobrow, Davis B., and John S. Dryzek. *Policy Analysis by Design*. Pittsburgh, PA: University of Pittsburgh Press, 1987.

Braybrooke, David, and Charles Lindblom. *A Strategy of Decision: Policy Evaluation as a Social Process*. New York: Free Press, 1963.

Brown, Trevor L., Matthew Potoski, and David M. Van Slyke. "Managing Public Service Contracts: Aligning Values, Institutions, and Markets." *Public Administration Review* 66, no. 3 (2006): 323–31.

Campbell, David E., Martin R. West, and Paul E. Peterson. "Participation in a National, Means-Tested School Voucher Program." *Journal of Policy Analysis and Management* 24, no. 3 (2005): 523–41.

Choi, James J., David Laibson, Brigitte C. Madrian, and Andrew Metrick. "Defined Contribution Pensions: Plan Rules, Participant Choices, and the Path of Least Resistance." In *Tax Policy and the Economy*, edited by James Poterba, 67–114. Cambridge, MA: MIT Press, 2002.

Cleveland, Harland. *The Future Executive: A Guide for Tomorrow's Managers*. New York: Harper & Row, 1972.

Conlan, Timothy. *From New Federalism to Devolution: Twenty-Five Years of Intergovernmental Reform*. Washington, DC: Brookings Institution Press, 1998.

Damschroder, Laura J., David C. Aron, Rosalind E. Keith, Susan R. Kirsh, Jeffery A. Alexander, and Julie C. Lowery. "Fostering Implementation of Health Services Research Findings into Practice: A Consolidated Framework for Advancing Implementation Science." *Implementation Science* 4 (January 2009): 50.

Deane, Frank P., Retta Andresen, Trevor P. Crowe, Lindsay G. Oades, Joseph Ciarrochi, and Virginia Williams. "A Comparison of Two Coaching Approaches to Enhance Implementation of a Recovery-Oriented Service Model." *Administration and Policy in Mental Health and Mental Health Services Research* 6 (2013): 1–8.

DiMaggio, Paul J., and Walter W. Powell. "The Iron Cage Revisited: Institutional Isomorphism and Collective Rationality in Organizational Fields." *American Sociological Review* 48, no. 2 (1983): 147–60.

Dror, Yehezkel. "Policy Analysts: A New Professional Role in Government Service." *Public Administration Review* 27, no. 3 (1967): 197–203.

Durlak, Joseph A., and Emily P. DuPre. "Implementation Matters: A Review of Research on the Influence of Implementation on Program Outcomes and the

Factors Affecting Implementation." *American Journal of Community Psychology* 41, nos. 3–4 (2008): 327–50.

Easton, David. *A Systems Analysis of Political Life*. Chicago: University of Chicago Press, 1965.

Eccles, Martin P., and Brian S. Mittman. "Welcome to Implementation Science." *Implementation Science*, no. 1 (2006): 1.

Elazar, Daniel. "The Shaping of Intergovernmental Relations in the Twentieth Century." *Annals of the American Academy of Political and Social Science* 359 (1965): 10–22.

Elmore, Richard F. "Backward Mapping: Implementation Research and Policy Decisions." *Political Science Quarterly* 94, no. 4 (1979): 601–16.

_____. *Forward and Backward Mapping: Reversible Logic in the Analysis of Public Policy*. Dordrecht, NL: Springer Netherlands, 1985.

Fixsen, Dean L., Sandra F. Naoom, Karen A. Blase, Robert M. Friedman, Barbara Burns, and Frances Wallace. *Implementation Research: A Synthesis of the Literature*. Tampa, FL: National Implementation Research Center, 2005.

Forbes, Melissa, Carolyn J. Hill, and Laurence E. Lynn. "The Logic of Governance in Health Care Delivery." *Public Management Review* 9, no. 4 (2007): 453–77.

Frederickson, George F. "Whatever Happened to Public Administration? Governance, Governance Everywhere." In *The Oxford Handbook of Public Management*, edited by Ewan Ferlie, Laurence E. Lynn, and Christopher Pollitt. Oxford: Oxford University Press, 2005.

Gira, Emmanuelle C., Michelle L. Kessler, and John Poertner. "Influencing Social Workers to Use Research Evidence in Practice: Lessons from Medicine and the Allied Health Professions." *Research on Social Work Practice* 14, no. 2 (2004): 68–79.

Glaeser, Edward. L. "Paternalism and Psychology." *University of Chicago Law Review* 73 (2006): 144.

Goggin, Malcolm L. "The 'Too Few Cases/Too Many Variables' Problem in Implementation Research." *Political Research Quarterly* 39, no. 2 (1986): 328–47.

Goggin, Malcolm L., Ann Bowman, James P. Lester, and Laurence J. O'Toole. "Studying the Dynamics of Public Policy Implementation: A Third-Generation

Approach." *Ion Implementation and the Policy Process: Opening up the Black Box*, edited by Dennis J. Palumbo and Donald J. Calista, 181–97. Westport, CT: Greenwood Press, 1990.

Greenhalgh, Trisha, Glenn Robert, Fraser MacFarlane, Paul Bate, Olivia Kyriakidou. "Diffusion of Innovations in Service Organizations: Systematic Review and Recommendation." *Milbank Quarterly* 82, no. 4 (2004): 581–629.

Grol, Richard, and Michel Wensing. "What Drives Change? Barriers to and Incentives for Achieving Evidence-Based Practice." *Medical Journal Australia* 180, no. S8 (2004): S57–S60.

Heinrich, Carolyn J., Carolyn J. Hill, and Laurence E. Lynn. *Governance as an Organizing Theme for Empirical Research*. Washington, DC: Georgetown University Press, 2004.

Hill, Michael, and Peter Hupe. *Implementing Public Policy: An Introduction to the Study of Operational Governance*, 2nd ed. Thousand Oaks, CA: SAGE, 2008.

Hjern, Benny, and Chris Hull. "Implementation Research as Empirical Constitutionalism." *European Journal of Political Research* 10, no. 2 (1982): 105–15.

Hjern, Benny, and David O. Porter. "Implementation Structures: A New Unit of Administrative Analysis." *Organization Studies* 2, no. 3 (1981): 211–27.

Howard, C. "Tax Expenditures." In *The Tools of Government: A Guide to the New Governance*, edited by Lester Salamon, 490–510. Oxford: Oxford University Press, 2002.

Howell, William G. "Dynamic Selection Effects in Means-Tested, Urban School Voucher Programs." *Journal of Policy Analysis and Management* 23, no. 2 (2004), 225–50.

Ingraham, Patricia W. "Toward a More Systematic Consideration of Policy Design." *Policy Studies Journal* 15, no. 4 (1987): 611–28.

Ingram, Helen, and Anne Schneider. "Improving Implementation through Framing Smarter Statutes." *Journal of Public Policy* 10, no. 1 (1990): 67–88.

Isett, Kimberley R., Ines A. Mergel, Kelly LeRoux, Pamela A. Mischen, and R. Karl Rethemeyer. "Networks in Public Administration Scholarship: Understanding Where We Are and Where We Need to Go." *Journal of Public Administration Research and Theory* 21, no. S1 (2011): S157–73.

Johnson, Eric J., and Daniel G. Goldstein. "Defaults and Donation Decisions." *Transplantation* 78, no. 12 (2004): 1713–16.

———. "Do Defaults Save Lives?" *Science* 112 (2003): 1338–39.

Jones, Charles O. *An Introduction to the Study of Policy*. Pacific Grove, CA: Duxbury Press, 1977.

Kahneman, Daniel. "Maps of Bounded Rationality: Psychology for Behavioral Economics." *American Economic Review* 93, no. 5 (2003): 1449.

Kahneman, Daniel, and Amos Tversky. "Prospect Theory: An Analysis of Decisions under Risk." *Econometrica* 47 (1979): 263–91.

Katz, Lawrence F., Jeffrey R. Kling, and Jeffrey B. Liebman. "Moving to Opportunity in Boston: Early Results of a Randomized Mobility Experiment." *Quarterly Journal of Economics* 116, no. 2 (2001): 607–54.

Kiser, Larry L., and Elinor Ostrom. "The Three Worlds of Action: A Metatheoretical Synthesis of Institutional Approaches." *Strategies of Political Inquiry*, edited by Elinor Ostrom. Beverly Hills, CA: SAGE, 1982.

Klijn, Erik-Hans. "Networks and Inter-Organizational Management: Challenging, Steering, Evaluation and the Role of Public Actors in Public Management." In *The Oxford Handbook of Public Management*, edited by Ewan Ferlie, Laurence Lynn, and Christopher Pollitt, 257–72. Oxford: Oxford University Press, 2005.

Knoke, David, and Song Yang. *Social Network Analysis*. Thousand Oaks, CA: SAGE, 2008.

Ladd, Helen F. "School Vouchers: A Critical View." *Journal of Economic Perspectives* 16, no. 4 (2002), 3–24.

Levin, Howard M. "Educational Vouchers: Effectiveness, Choice, and Costs." *Journal of Policy Analysis and Management* 17, no. 3 (1998): 373–92.

Licari, Michael, and Kenneth Meier. "Regulation and Signaling: When a Tax Is Not Just a Tax." *Journal of Politics* 62, no. 3 (2000), 875–85.

Lin, Ann Chih. *Reform in the Making: The Implementation of Social Policy in Prison*. Princeton, NJ: Princeton University Press, 2000.

Lipsky, Michael. *Street-Level Bureaucracy: Dilemmas of the Individual in Public Services*. New York: Russell Sage Foundation, 1980.

Lynn, Laurence E. "Art, Science, or Profession?" In *Public Management as Art, Science and Profession*. Chatham, NJ: Chatham House, 1996.

_____. "The Myth of the Bureaucratic Paradigm: What Traditional Public Administration Really Stood For." *Public Administration Review* 61, no. 2 (2001): 144–60.

Lynn, Laurence E., Carolyn J. Heinrich, and Carolyn J. Hill. "Studying Governance and Public Management: Challenges and Prospects." *Journal of Public Administration Research and Theory* 10, no. 2 (2000): 234.

_____. Improving Governance: *A New Logic for Empirical Research*. Washington, DC: Georgetown University Press, 2001.

Madrian, Brigitte C., and Dennis F. Shea. "The Power of Suggestion: Inertia in 401(k) Participation and Savings Behavior." *Quarterly Journal of Economics* 116, no. 4 (2001): 1149–87.

Matland, Richard E. "Synthesizing the Implementation Literature: The Ambiguity-Conflict Model of Policy Implementation." *Journal of Public Administration Research and Theory* 5, no. 2 (1995): 145–74.

May, Carl. "A Rational Model for Assessing and Evaluating Complex Interventions in Health Care." *BMC Health Services Research* 6 (2006): 11.

May, Carl, and Tracy Finch. "Implementing, Embedding, and Integrating Practices: An Outline of Normalization Process Theory." *Sociology* 43, no. 3 (2009): 535–54.

May, Carl R., Frances Mair, Tracy Finch, Anne MacFarlane, Christopher Dowrick, Shaun Treweek, Tim Rapley, Luciana Ballini, Bie Nio Ong, Anne Rogers, Elizabeth Murray, Glyn Elwyn, France Légaré, Jane Gunn, and Victor M. Montori. "Development of a Theory of Implementation and Integration: Normalization Process Theory." *Implementation Science* 4, no. 29 (2009).

Maynard-Moody, Steven, and Michael Musheno. *Cops, Teachers, Counselors: Stories from the Front Lines of Public Services*. Ann Arbor: University of Michigan Press, 2003.

Mazmanian, Daniel A., and Paul A. Sabatier. *Implementation and Public Policy*. Glenview, IL: Scott, Foresman, 1983.

Meier, Kenneth, and Michael Licari. "The Effect of Cigarette Taxes on Cigarette Consumption, 1955 through 1994."*American Journal of Public Health* 87, no. 7 (1997): 1126–30.

Meier, Kenneth J., Laurence J. O'Toole, and Sean Nicholson-Crotty. "Multilevel Governance and Organizational Performance: Investigating the Political-Bureaucratic Labyrinth." *Journal of Policy Analysis and Management* 23, no. 1 (2004): 31–47.

Meyers, Duncan C., Joseph A. Durlak, and Abraham Wandersman. "The Quality Implementation Framework: A Synthesis of Critical Steps in the Implementation Process." *American Journal of Community Psychology* 50, nos. 3–4 (2012): 462–80.

Milgram, Stanley. "Behavioral Study of Obedience." *Journal of Abnormal and Social Psychology* 67, no. 4 (1963): 371.

Milward, Brinton, and Keith G. Provan. "Measuring Network Structure." *Public Administration* 76, no. 2 (1998): 387–407.

———. "Governing the Hollow State." *Journal of Public Administration, Research and Theory* 10, no. 2 (2000): 359–80.

———. *A Manager's Guide to Choosing and Using Collaborative Networks*. Washington, DC: IBM Center for the Business of Government, 2006.

Mitchell, James. *The American Experiment with Government Corporations.* Armonk, NY: M. E. Sharpe, 1999.

Moynihan, Daniel P. *Maximum Feasible Misunderstanding: Community Action in the War on Poverty*. New York: Free Press, 1969.

Nadeem, Erum, Alissa Gleacher, and Rinad S. Beidas. "Consultation as an Implementation Strategy for Evidence-Based Practices across Multiple Contexts: Unpacking the Black Box." *Administration and Policy in Mental Health and Mental Health Services Research* 40, no. 6 (2013): 439–50.

National Institute on Aging. "Psychological Science and Behavioral Economics in the Service of Public Policy," meeting summary, National Institutes of Health, Washington, D.C., May 22, 2013. http://www.nia.nih.gov/sites/default/files/psychological_science_and_behavioral_economics.pdf.

Nilsen, Per, Christian Ståhl, Kerstin Roback, and Paul Cairney. "Never the Twain Shall Meet? A Comparison of Implementation Science and Policy Implementation Research." *Implementation Science* 8, no. 63 (2013).

O'Toole, Laurence J. "Policy Recommendations for Multi-Actor Implementation: An Assessment of the Field." *Journal of Public Policy* 6, no. 2 (1986): 181–210.

———. "Research on Policy Implementation: Assessment and Prospects." *Journal of Public Administration Research and Theory* 10, no. 2 (2000): 263–88.

Ostrom, Elinor. "Institutional Rational Choice: An Assessment of the Institutional Analysis and Development Framework." In *Theories of the Policy Process*, edited by Paul Sabatier. Boulder, CO: Westview Press, 2007.

———. "Background on the Institutional Analysis and Development Framework." *Policy Studies Journal* 39, no. 1 (2011): 7–27.

Ostrom, Elinor, Roy Gardner, and James Walker. *Rules, Games, and Common-Pool Resources*. Ann Arbor: University of Michigan Press, 1994.

Pesendorfer, Wolfgang. "Behavioral Economics Comes of Age: A Review Essay on Advances in Behavioral Economics." *Journal of Economic Literature* 44, no. 3 (2006): 712–21.

Pollitt, Christopher, and Peter Hupe. "Talking about Government." *Public Management Review* 13, no. 5 (2011): 641–58.

Posner, Paul, and Mary T. Wrightson. "Block Grants: A Perennial, but Unstable, Tool of Government." *Publius* 26, no. 3, (1996): 87–108.

Powell, Walter W. "Neither Markets nor Hierarchy: Network Forms of Organization." *Research in Organizational Behavior* 12 (1990): 295–336.

———. *The New Institutionalism in Organizational Analysis*. Chicago: University of Chicago Press, 1991.

Pressman, Jeffrey L., and Aaron Wildavsky. *Implementation: How Great Expectations in Washington Are Dashed in Oakland or Why It's Amazing That Federal Programs Work at All*, 3rd ed. Berkeley: University of California Press, 1984.

Provan, Keith G., and Patrick Kenis. "Modes of Network Governance: Structure, Management, and Effectiveness." *Journal of Public Administration Research and Theory* 18, no. 2 (2008): 229–52.

Provan, Keith, and H. Brinton Milward. "A Preliminary Theory of Interorganizational Network Effectiveness: A Comparison of Four Community Mental Health Systems." *Administrative Sciences Quarterly* 40, no. 1 (1995): 125–57.

———. "Do Networks Really Work? A Framework for Evaluating Public-Sector Organizational Networks." *Public Administration Review* 61, no. 4 (2001): 414–23.

Rainey, Hal. *Understanding and Managing Public Organizations*, 5th ed. San Francisco: Jossey-Bass, 2014.

Rethemeyer, R. Karl, and Deneen M. Hatmaker. "Network Management Reconsidered: An Inquiry into Management of Network Structures in Public Sector Service Provision." *Journal of Public Administration Research and Theory* 18, no. 4 (2008): 617–46.

Rhodes, R.A.W. "Governance and Public Administration." In *Debating Governance: Authority, Steering, and Democracy*, edited by Jon Pierre, 54–90. New York: University of Oxford Press, 2000.

Rivlin, Alice. *Systematic Thinking for Social Action*. Washington, DC: Brookings Institution, 1971.

Rogers, Everett M. *Diffusion of Innovations*. New York: Free Press, 1995.

Romzek, Barbara, and Jocelyn Johnston. "Reforming State Social Services through Contracting: Linking Implementation and Organization Culture." In *Advancing Public Management: New Developments in Theory Methods and Practice*, edited by Jeffrey Brudney, Laurence O'Toole, and Hal G. Rainey, 173–95. Washington, DC: Georgetown University Press, 2000.

———. "Effective Contract Implementation and Management: A Preliminary Model." *Journal of Public Administration Research and Theory* 12, no. 3 (2002): 423–53.

Rothstein, Bo. *Just Institutions Matter: The Moral and Political Logic of the Universal Welfare State*. Cambridge: Cambridge University Press, 1998.

Sabatier, Paul A. "Top-Down and Bottom-Up Approaches to Implementation Research: A Critical Analysis and Suggested Synthesis." *Journal of Public Policy* 6, no. 1 (1986): 21–48.

———. "An Advocacy Coalition Framework of Policy Change and the Role of Policy-Oriented Learning Therein." *Policy Sciences* 21, nos. 2–3 (1988): 129–68.

Sabatier, Paul A., and Hank C. Jenkins-Smith. *Policy Change and Learning: An Advocacy Coalition Approach*. Boulder, CO: Westview Press, 1993.

Sabatier, Paul A., and Daniel A. Mazmanian. "The Implementation of Public Policy: A Framework of Analysis." *Policy Studies Journal* 8, no. 4 (1980): 538–60.

Saetren, Harald. "Facts and Myths about Research on Public Policy Implementation: Out-of-Fashion, Allegedly Dead, But Still Very Much Alive and Relevant." *Policy Studies Journal* 33, no. 4 (2005): 559–82.

Salamon, Lester M. "Rethinking Public Management: Third-Party Government and the Changing Forms of Government Action." *Public Policy* 29, no. 3 (1981): 255–75.

———. *The Tools of Government: A Guide to the New Governance*. Oxford: Oxford University Press, 2002.

Sandfort, Jodi R. "Moving Beyond Discretion and Outcomes: Examining Public Management from the Front-Lines of the Welfare System." *Journal of Public Administration Research and Theory* 10, no. 4 (2000): 729–56.

Sandfort, Jodi R., and H. Brinton Milward. "Collaborative Service Provision in the Public Sector." In *Handbook of Inter-Organizational Relations*, edited by Steve Cropper, Mark Ebbers, Chris Huxham, and Peter Smith Ring, 147–74. Oxford: Oxford University Press, 2008.

Sandfort, Jodi, Stephen Roll, and Stephanie Moulton, "Assessing Policy and Program Implementation Research." Working paper, 2014.

Simon, Herbert A. *Administrative Behavior*. New York: Free Press, 1948, revised 1976.

———. "A Behavioral Model of Rational Choice." *Quarterly Journal of Economics* 69, no. 1 (1955): 99–118.

Smith, Adrian. "Policy Networks and Advocacy Coalitions: Explaining Policy Change and Stability in UK Industrial Pollution Policy?" *Environmental Planning C: Government and Policy* 18, no. 1 (2000): 95–114.

Stokes, Donald E. "Political and Organizational Analysis in the Policy Curriculum." *Journal of Policy Analysis and Management* 6, no. 1 (1986): 45–55.

Stone, Deborah. *Policy Paradox: The Art of Political Decision Making*, 3rd ed. New York: Norton, 2011.

Susin, Scott. "Rent Vouchers and the Price of Low-Income Housing." *Journal of Public Economics* 83, no. 1 (2002), 109–52.

Tabak, Rachel G., Elaine C. Khoong, David A. Chambers, and Ross C. Brownson. "Bridging Research and Practice: Models for Dissemination and Implementation Research." *American Journal of Preventive Medicine* 43, no. 3 (2012): 337–50.

Thaler, Richard H., and Cass R. Sunstein. *Nudge: Improving Decisions about Health, Wealth, and Happiness.* New Haven, CT: Yale University Press, 2008.

Tversky, Amos, and Daniel Kahneman. "Judgment under Uncertainty: Heuristics and Biases." *Science* 185, no. 4157 (1974): 1124–31.

————. "The Framing of Decisions and the Psychology of Choice." *Science* 211, no. 4481 (1981): 453–58.

Van Meter, Donald S., and Carl E. Van Horn. "The Policy Implementation Process: A Conceptual Framework." *Administration and Society* 6, no. 4 (1975): 445–88.

Waldo, Dwight. *The Administrative State.* New York: Ronald, 1948.

Walsh, Kieron. *Contracting for Change.* Oxford: Oxford University Press, 1997.

Wandersman, Abraham, Jennifer Duffy, Paul Flaspohler, Rita Noonan, Keri Lubell, Lindsey Stillman, Morris Blachman, Richard Dunville, and Janet Saul. "Bridging the Gap between Prevention Research and Practice: The Interactive Systems Framework for Dissemination and Implementation." *American Journal of Community Psychology* 41, nos. 3–4 (2008): 171–81.

Wasserman, Stanley, and Joseph Galaskiewicz, eds. *Advances in Social Network Analysis: Research in the Social and Behavioral Sciences.* Thousand Oaks, CA: SAGE, 1994.

Weible, Christopher M., Paul Sabatier, and Kelly McQueen. "Themes and Variations: Taking Stock of the Advocacy Coalition Framework." *Policy Studies Journal* 37, no. 1 (2009): 121–40.

Weimer, David L., and Aidan R. Vining. *Policy Analysis: Concepts and Practice,* 4th ed. Upper Saddle River, NJ: Pearson Education, 2005.

Weiss, Carol H. "Evaluating Social Programs: What Have We Learned?" *Society* 25, no. 1 (1987): 40–45.

Wildavsky, Aaron. *Speaking Truth to Power: The Art and Craft of Policy Analysis*, 2nd ed. New Brunswick, NJ: Transaction Publishers, 1987.

Williams, Walter. *Social Policy Research and Analysis: The Experience in the Federal Social Agencies*. New York: American Elsevier, 1971.

Wilson, Woodrow. "The Study of Administration." *Political Science Quarterly* 2, no. 2 (1887): 197–222.

Zucker, Lynne G. "Institutional Theories of Organization." *Annual Review of Sociology* 13 (1987): 443–64.

CHAPTER THREE

Abrutyn, Seth. "Toward a Theory of Institutional Ecology: The Dynamics of Macro Structural Space." *Review of European Studies* 4, no. 5 (2012): 167–81.

Ansell, Christopher. *Schism and Solidarity in Social Movements: The Politics of Labor in the French Third Republic*. Cambridge: Cambridge University Press, 2001.

Avent-Holt, Dustin. "The Political Dynamics of Market Organization: Cultural Framing, Neoliberalism, and the Case of Airline Deregulation." *Sociological Theory* 30, no. 4 (2013): 283–302.

Bernhard, Stephan. "Beyond Constructivism: The Political Sociology of an EU Policy Field." *International Political Sociology* 5, no. 4 (2011): 426–45.

Blau, Peter M., and W. Richard Scott. *Formal Organizations: A Comparative Approach*. San Francisco: Chandler, 1962.

Bozeman, Barry. *All Organizations Are Public: Bridging Public and Private Organizational Theories*. San Francisco: Jossey-Bass, 1987.

Brown, Trevor L., Matthew Potoski, and David M. Van Slyke. "Managing Public Service Contracts: Aligning Values, Institutions, and Markets." *Public Administration Review* 66, no. 3 (2006): 323–31.

Butler, Michael J. R., and Peter M. Allen. "Understanding Policy Implementation Processes as Self-Organizing Systems." *Public Management Review* 10, no. 3 (2008): 421–40.

Carberry, Edward J., and Brayden G. King. "Defensive Practice Adoption in the Face of Organizational Stigma: Impression Management and the Diffusion of Stock Option Expensing." *Journal of Management Studies* 49, no. 7 (2012): 1137–67.

Cohen, Michael D., James G. March, and Johan P. Olsen. "A Garbage Can Model of Organizational Choice." *Administrative Science Quarterly* 17, no. 1 (1972): 1–25.

Crosby, Barbara, and John Bryson. *Leadership Can Be Taught*. San Francisco: Jossey-Bass, 2005.

Daft, Richard. *Organizational Theory and Design*, 9th ed. Boston: South-Western, 2006.

DeHart-Davis, Leisha. "Green Tape: A Theory of Effective Organizational Rules." *Journal of Public Administration Research and Theory* 19, no. 2 (2009): 361–84.

DiMaggio, Paul J., and Walter W. Powell. "The Iron Cage Revisited: Institutional Isomorphism and Collective Rationality in Organizational Fields." *American Sociological Review* 48, no. 2 (1983): 147–60.

Djelic, Marie-Laure. "When Limited Liability Was (Still) an Issue: Mobilization and Politics of Signification in 19th-Century England." *Organization Studies* 34, nos. 5–6 (2013): 595–621.

Fligstein, Neil, and Doug McAdam. *A Theory of Fields*. Oxford: Oxford University Press, 2012.

Fry, Louis W. "Technology-Structure Research." *Academy of Management Journal* 25, no. 3 (1982): 532–52.

Geertz, Clifford. *The Interpretation of Cultures*. New York: Basic Books, 1973.

Goggin, Malcolm L. "The 'Too Few Cases/Too Many Variables' Problem in Implementation Research." *Political Research Quarterly* 39, no. 2 (1986): 328–47.

Hasenfeld, Yeheskel. *Human Service Organizations*. Englewood Cliffs, NJ: Prentice Hall, 1983.

Hill, Heather C. "Understanding Implementation: Street-Level Bureaucrats' Resources for Reform." *Journal of Public Administration Research and Theory* 13, no. 3 (2003): 265–82.

Khademian, Anne M. *Working with Culture: The Way the Job Gets Done in Public Programs*. Washington, DC: CQ Press, 2002.

Kingdon, John W. *Agendas, Alternatives, and Public Policies*, 2nd ed. New York: HarperCollins, 1995.

Lin, Ann Chih. *Reform in the Making: The Implementation of Social Policy in Prison*. Princeton, NJ: Princeton University Press, 2000.

Matland, Richard E. "Synthesizing the Implementation Literature: The Ambiguity-Conflict Model of Policy Implementation." *Journal of Public Administration Research and Theory* 5, no. 2 (1995): 145–74.

Mazmanian, Daniel A., and Paul A. Sabatier. *Implementation and Public Policy*. Lanham, MD: University Press of America, 1989.

Mitchell, Melanie. *Complexity: A Guided Tour*. New York: Oxford University Press, 2011.

Moulton, Stephanie. "Putting Together the Publicness Puzzle: A Framework for Realized Publicness." *Public Administration Review* 69, no. 5 (2009): 889–900.

Osborne, David, and Ted Gaebler. *Reinventing Government: How the Entrepreneurial Spirit Is Transforming the Public Sector*. New York: Plume Books, 1992.

Ozen, Hayriye, and Sukru Ozen. "Interactions in and between Strategic Action Fields: A Comparative Analysis of Two Environmental Conflicts in Gold-Mining Fields in Turkey." *Organization and Environment* 24, no. 4 (2011): 343–63.

Porter, Michael E. *Competitive Strategy*. New York: Free Press, 1980.

Pressman, Jeffrey, and Aaron Wildavsky. *Implementation: How Great Expectations in Washington Are Dashed in Oakland or Why It's Amazing That Federal Programs Work at All*, 3rd ed. Berkeley: University of California Press, 1984.

Rainey, Hal G. *Understanding and Managing Public Organizations*, 4th ed. San Francisco: Jossey-Bass, 2009.

Rudel, Thomas K., and Patrick Meyfroidt. "Organizing Anarchy: The Food Security–Biodiversity–Climate Crisis and the Genesis of Rural Land Use Planning in the Developing World." *Land Use Policy* 36 (2014): 239–47.

Sabatier, Paul A., and Hank C. Jenkins-Smith. *Policy Change and Learning: An Advocacy Coalition Approach*. Boulder, CO: Westview Press, 1993.

Sandfort, Jodi. "The Structural Impediments to Human Service Collaboration: The Case of Frontlines Welfare Reform Implementation." *Social Service Review* 73, no. 3 (1999): 314–39.

———. "Moving Beyond Discretion and Outcomes: Examining Public Management from the Front-Lines of the Welfare System." *Journal of Public Administration Research and Theory* 10, no. 4 (2000): 729–56.

———. "Human Service Organizational Technology." In *Human Services as Complex Organizations*, 2nd ed., edited by Yeheskel Hasenfeld, 269–90. New York: SAGE, 2010.

Schein, Edgar H. *Organizational Culture and Learning*. San Francisco: Jossey-Bass, 1992.

Schneiberg, Marc. "Movements as Political Conditions for Diffusion: Anti-Corporate Movements and the Spread of Cooperative Forms in American Capitalism." *Organization Studies* 34, nos. 5–6 (2013): 653–82.

Scott, W. Richard. *Organizations: Rational, Natural and Open Systems*, 5th ed. Upper Saddle River, NJ: Prentice Hall, 1986.

Smircich, Linda, Peter Frost, Larry Moore, M. Louis, M. Lundberg, and Joanne Martin. "Is the Concept of Culture a Paradigm for Understanding Organizations and Ourselves?" *Organizational Culture* 23 (1985): 55–72.

Suchman, Mark C. "Managing Legitimacy: Strategic and Institutional Approaches." *Academy of Management Review* 20, no. 3 (1995): 571–610.

Thompson, James D. *Organizations in Action*. New York: McGraw-Hill, 1967.

Wamsley, Gary L., and Mayer N. Zald. "The Political Economy of Public Organizations." *Public Administration Review* 33, no. 1 (1973): 62–73.

Weible, Christopher M., Paul A. Sabatier, and Kelly McQueen. "Themes and Variations: Taking Stock of the Advocacy Coalition Framework." *Policy Studies Journal* 37, no. 1 (2009): 121–40.

Weick, Karl E. *Sensemaking in Organizations*. Thousand Oaks, CA: SAGE, 1995.

CHAPTER FOUR

Berry, Frances Stokes, and William D. Berry. "Innovation and Diffusion Models in Policy Research." In *Theories of the Policy Process*, edited by Paul A. Sabatier, 169–200. Boulder, CO: Westview Press, 1999.

Berry, William D., and Brady Baybeck. "Using Geographic Information Systems to Study Interstate Competition." *American Political Science Review* 99, no. 4 (2005): 505–19.

Bertelli, Anthony M., and Craig R. Smith. "Relational Contracting and Network Management." *Journal of Public Administration Research and Theory* 20, no. 1 (2010): i21–i40.

Brown, David, and Archana Kalegaonkar. "Support Organizations and the Evolution of the NGO Sector." *Nonprofit and Voluntary Sector Quarterly* 31, no. 2 (2002): 231–58.

Brown, Trevor L., Matthew Potoski, and David M. Van Slyke. "Trust and Contract Completeness in the Public Sector." *Local Government Studies* 33, no. 4 (2007): 607–23.

Bryson, John M. "What to Do When Stakeholders Matter." *Public Management Review* 6, no. 1 (2004): 21–53.

Bryson, John M., Fran Ackermann, Colin Eden, and Charles B. Finn. *Visible Thinking: Unlocking Causal Mapping for Practical Business Results*. Hoboken, NJ: Wiley, 2004.

Burstein, Paul. "Policy Domains: Organization, Culture and Policy Outcomes." *Annual Review of Sociology* 17, no. 1 (1991): 327–50.

Bushouse, Brenda K. *University Preschool: Policy Change, Stability, and the Pew Charitable Trusts*. Albany, NY: SUNY Press, 2009.

Cho, Chung-Lae, and Deil S. Wright. "The Devolution Revolution in Intergovernmental Relations in the 1990s: Changes in Cooperative and Coercive State-National Relations as Perceived by State Administrators." *Journal of Public Administration Research and Theory* 14, no. 4 (2004): 447–68.

Chubb, John E. "The Political Economy of Federalism." *American Political Science Review* 79, no. 4 (1985): 994–1015.

David, Paul A. "Why Are Institutions the 'Carriers of History'? Path Dependence and the Evolution of Conventions, Organizations and Institutions." *Structural Change and Economic Dynamics* 5, no. 2 (1994): 205–20.

Derthinck, Martha. *Keeping the Compound Republic*. Washington, DC: Brookings Institution Press, 2001.

DiMaggio, Paul. "State Expansion and Organizational Fields." *Organizational Theory and Public Policy*, edited by Richard Hall and Robert Quinn, 147–61. Beverly Hills, CA: SAGE, 1983.

DiMaggio, Paul J., and Walter W. Powell. "The Iron Cage Revisited: Institutional Isomorphism and Collective Rationality in Organizational Fields." In *The New Institutionalism in Organizational Analysis*, edited by Walter W. Powell and Paul J. DiMaggio. Chicago: University of Chicago Press, 1991.

Elazar, Daniel J. "The Shaping of Intergovernmental Relations in the Twentieth Century." *Annals of the American Academy of Political and Social Science* 359, no. 1 (1965): 10–22.

Ferman, Barbara. "When Failure Is Success: Implementation and Madisonian Government." In *Implementation and the Policy Process: Opening Up the Black Box*, edited by Dennis J. Palumbo and Donald J. Calista, 39–50. Westport, CT: Greenwood Press, 1990.

Glickman, Norman. "By the Numbers: Measuring Community Development Corporations' Capacity." *Journal of Planning Education and Research* 22, no. 3 (2003): 240–56.

Glickman, Norman, and Lisa J. Servon. "More Than Bricks and Sticks: What Is Community Development Capacity?" *Housing Policy Debate* 9, no. 3 (1998): 497.

Goetz, Edward, and Mara S. Sidney. "Local Policy Subsystems and Issue Definition: An Analysis of Community Development Policy Change." *Urban Affairs Review* 32, no. 40 (1997): 490–512.

Goldsmith, Stephen, and William Eggers. *Governing by Network* (Washington, DC: Brookings Institution Press, 2004).

Hill, Heather C. "Understanding Implementation: Street-Level Bureaucrats' Resources for Reform." *Journal of Public Administration Research and Theory* 13, no. 1 (2003): 265–82.

Hjern, Benny, and David O. Porter. "Implementation Structures: A New Unit of Administrative Analysis." *Organization Studies* 2, no. 3964 (1981): 211–27.

Honig, Meredith. "The New Middle Management: Intermediary Organizations in Education Policy Implementation." *Educational Evaluation and Policy Analysis* 26, no. 1 (2004): 65–87.

Kickert, Walter J. M., Eric-Hans Klijn, and Joop F. M. Koppenjan. *Managing Complex Networks: Strategies for the Public Sector*. London: SAGE, 1997.

Klijn, Eric-Hans, and Geert R. Teisman. "Strategies and Games in Networks." In *Managing Complex Networks: Strategies for the Public Sector*, edited by Walter J. M. Kickert, Eric-Hans Klijn, and Joop F. M. Koppenjan, 98–118. London: SAGE, 1997.

Klijn, Erik-Hans, and Jurian Edelenbos. "Metagovernance as Network Management." In *Theories of Democratic Network Governance*, edited by Eva Sorenson and Jacob Torfing. New York: Palgrave Macmillan, 2008.

Klijn, Erik-Hans, Jurian Edelenbos, and Bram Steijn. "Trust in Governance Networks: Its Impacts on Outcomes." *Administration and Society* 42, no. 2 (2010): 193–221.

Lipsky, Michael. *Street-Level Bureaucracy: Dilemmas of the Individual in Public Services*. New York: Russell Sage Foundation, 1980.

Mahoney, James. "Path Dependence in Historical Sociology." *Theory and Society* 29, no. 4 (2000): 507–48.

McGuire, Robert, and Michael McGuire. "Inside the Matrix: Integrating the Paradigms of Intergovernmental and Network Management." *International Journal of Public Administration* 26, no. 12 (2003): 1401–22.

Miller, Susan M., and Stephanie Moulton. "Publicness in Policy Environments: A Multilevel Analysis of Substance Abuse Treatment Services." *Journal of Public Administration Research and Theory* 24, no. 3 (2014): 553–89.

Milward, Brinton H., and Gary L. Wamsley. "Policy Subsystems, Networks, and the Tools of Public Management." In *Public Policy Formation*, edited by Thomas A. J. Koonen and Kenneth Hanf. Boulder, CO: Westview Press, 1984.

O'Toole, Laurence J. "Treating Networks Seriously." *Public Administration Review* 57, no. 1, (1997): 45.

————. "The Theory–Practice Issue in Policy Implementation Research." *Public Administration* 82, no. 2 (2004): 309–29.

————. *American Intergovernmental Relations: Foundations, Perspectives, and Issues*, vol. 4. Washington, DC: Congressional Quarterly Press, 2007.

Parents as Teachers National Center. (2014). http://www.parentsasteachers.org/.

Peterson, Paul. *The Price of Federalism*. Washington, DC: Brookings Institution Press, 1995.

Pierson, Paul. "Increasing Returns, Path Dependence, and the Study of Politics." *American Political Science Review* 94, no. 2 (2000): 251–67.

Provan, Keith G., Amy Fish, and Joerg Sydow. "Interorganizational Networks at the Network Level: A Review of the Empirical Literature on Whole Networks." *Journal of Management* 33, no. 3 (2007): 479–516.

Provan, Keith, and H. Brinton Milward. "A Preliminary Theory of Interorganizational Network Effectiveness: A Comparative Study of Four Community Mental Health Systems." *Administrative Science Quarterly* 40 (1995): 1–33.

Sabatier, Paul A. "An Advocacy Coalition Framework of Policy Change and the Role of Policy-Oriented Learning Therein." *Policy Sciences* 21, nos. 2–3 (1988): 129–68.

Sabatier, Paul A., and Hank C. Jenkins-Smith. *Policy Change and Learning: An Advocacy Coalition Approach*. Boulder, CO: Westview Press, 1993.

Salamon, Lester. *Partners in Public Service: Government-Nonprofit Relations in the Modern Welfare State*. Baltimore, MD: Johns Hopkins University Press, 1995.

———. *The Tools of Government: A Guide to the New Governance*. Oxford: Oxford University Press, 2002.

Sandfort, Jodi R. "The Structural Impediments to Human Service Collaboration: The Case of Frontline Welfare Reform Implementation." *Social Service Review* 73, no. 3 (1999): 314–39.

———. "Nonprofits within Policy Fields." *Journal of Policy Analysis and Management* 29, no. 3 (2010): 637–44.

Sandfort, Jodi R., and H. Brinton Milward. "Collaborative Service Provision in the Public Sector." In *Handbook of Inter-Organizational Relations*, edited by Steve Cropper, Mark Ebbers, Chris Huxham, and Peter Smith Ring, 147–74. Oxford: Oxford University Press, 2008.

Sandfort, Jodi, and Melissa Stone. "Analyzing Policy Fields: Helping Students Understand Complex State and Local Contexts." *Journal of Public Affairs Education* 14, no. 2 (2008): 129–48.

Shipan, Charles R., and Craig Volden. "The Mechanisms of Policy Diffusion." *American Journal of Political Science* 52, no. 4 (2008): 840–57.

Skelcher, Chris. "Public-Private Partnerships and Hybridity." In *The Oxford Handbook of Public Management*, edited by Ewan Ferlie, Laurence E. J. Lynn, and Christopher Pollitt, 347–70. Oxford: Oxford University Press, 2005.

Smith, Steven Rathgeb, and Michael Lipsky. *Non-Profits for Hire: The Welfare State in the Age of Contracting*. Cambridge, MA: Harvard University Press, 1993.

Soss, Joe, Richard C. Fording, and Sanford F. Schram. *Disciplining the Poor: Neoliberal Paternalism and the Persistent Power of Race*. Chicago: University of Chicago Press, 2011.

Stone, Melissa, and Jodi R. Sandfort. "Building a Policy Fields Framework to Inform Research in Nonprofit Organizations." *Nonprofit and Voluntary Sector Quarterly* 38, no. 6 (2009): 1054–75.

Weible, Christopher M., Paul A. Sabatier, and Kelly McQueen. "Themes and Variations: Taking Stock of the Advocacy Coalition Framework." *Policy Studies Journal* 37, no. 1 (2009): 121–40.

CHAPTER FIVE

Behn, Robert D. "The Big Questions of Public Management." *Public Administration Review* 55, no. 4 (1995): 313–24.

Berman, Paul. *The Study of Micro and Macro Implementation of Social Policy*. Santa Monica, CA: RAND, 1978.

Boulding, Kenneth D. "General Systems Theory: The Skeleton of Science." *Management Science* 2, no. 3 (1956): 127–39.

Bresnen, Mike, Anna Goussevskaia, and Jacky Swan. "Embedding New Management Knowledge in Project-Based Organizations." *Organization Studies* 25, no. 9 (2004): 1535–55.

DiMaggio, Paul J., and Walter W. Powell. "The Iron Cage Revisited: Institutional Isomorphism and Collective Rationality in Organizational Fields." *American Sociological Review* 48, no. 2 (1983): 284–301.

Dronkers, Jaap, and Péter Robert. "Differences in Scholastic Achievement of Public, Private Government-Dependent, and Private Independent Schools: A Cross-National Analysis." *Educational Policy* 22, no. 4 (2008): 541–77.

Galbraith, Jay R. "Organization Design: An Information Processing View." *Interfaces* 4, no. 3 (1974): 28–36.

Goldstein, Susan Meyer, and Michael Naor. "Linking Publicness to Operations Management Practices: A Study of Quality Management Practices in Hospitals." *Journal of Operations Management* 23, no. 2 (2005): 209–28.

Gronbjerg, Kirsten. *Understanding Nonprofit Funding: Managing Revenues in Social Services and Community Development Organizations.* San Francisco: Jossey-Bass, 1993.

Hackos, Joann, and Janice Redish. *User and Task Analysis for Interface Design.* New York: Wiley, 1998.

Heinrich, Carolyn J., and Elizabeth Fournier. "Dimensions of Publicness and Performance in Substance Abuse Treatment Organizations." *Journal of Policy Analysis and Management* 23, no. 1 (2004): 49–70.

Herd, Pamela, Thomas DeLeire, Hope Harvey, and Donald P. Moynihan. "Shifting Administrative Burden to the State: The Case of Medicaid Take-Up." *Public Administration Review* 73, no. s1 (2013): S69–S81.

Katz, Daniel, and Robert L. Kahn. *The Social Psychology of Organizations.* New York: Wiley, 1978.

Lynn, Laurence E., Carolyn J. Heinrich, and Carolyn J. Hill. *Improving Governance: A New Logic for Empirical Research.* Washington, DC: Georgetown University Press, 2001.

March, James G., and Johan P. Olsen. "Organizing Political Life: What Administrative Reorganization Tells Us about Government." *American Political Science Review* 77, no. 2 (1983): 281–96.

March, James G., and Herbert Alexander Simon. *Organizations.* Oxford: Wiley-Blackwell, 1958.

Miles, Raymond E., Charles C. Snow, Alan D. Meyer, and Henry J. Coleman. "Organizational Strategy, Structure, and Process." *Academy of Management Review* 3, no. 3 (1978): 546–62.

Miller, Susan M., and Stephanie Moulton. "Publicness in Policy Environments: A Multilevel Analysis of Substance Abuse Treatment Services." *Journal of Public Administration Research and Theory* 24, no. 3 (2014): 553–89.

Moynihan, Donald P. "The Normative Model in Decline? Public Service Motivation in the Age of Governance." In *Motivation in Public Management: The Call of Public Service*, ed. James L. Perry and Annie Hondeghem, 247–67. Oxford: Oxford University Press, 2008.

Osborne, David, and Ted Gaebler. *Reinventing Government: How the Entrepreneurial Spirit Is Transforming Government*. Reading, MA: Addison-Wesley, 1992.

Ouchi, William G. "Markets, Bureaucracies, and Clans." *Administrative Science Quarterly* 25, no. 1 (1980): 129–41.

Pandey, Sanjay K., and Patrick G. Scott. "Red Tape: A Review and Assessment of Concepts and Measures." *Journal of Public Administration Research and Theory* 12, no. 4 (2002): 553–80.

Pfeffer, Jeffrey, and Gerald R. Salancik. *The External Control of Organizations: A Resource Dependence Perspective*. New York: Harper & Row, 1978.

Poister, Theodore H. *Measuring Performance in Public and Nonprofit Organizations*. San Francisco: Jossey-Bass, 2003.

Rainey, Hal G. *Understanding and Managing Public Organizations*. San Francisco: Jossey-Bass, 2014.

Robichau, Robbie Waters, and Laurence E. Lynn Jr. "The Implementation of Public Policy: Still the Missing Link." *Policy Studies Journal* 37, no. 1 (2009): 21–36.

Romzek, Barbara, S. "Enhancing Accountability." In *Handbook of Public Administration*, 2nd ed., edited by James L. Perry. San Francisco: Jossey-Bass, 1996.

Romzek, Barbara S., and Melvin J. Dubnick. "Accountability in the Public Sector: Lessons from the *Challenger* Tragedy." *Public Administration Review* 47, no. 3 (1987): 227–38.

Romzek, Barbara S., and Patricia Wallace Ingraham. "Cross Pressures of Accountability: Initiative, Command, and Failure in the Ron Brown Plane Crash." *Public Administration Review* 60, no. 3 (2000): 240–53.

Scott, W. Richard. *Organizations as Rational, Natural and Open Systems*, 5th ed. New York: Prentice Hall, 2003.

Senge, Peter. *The Fifth Discipline: The Art and Practice of the Learning Organization*. New York: Doubleday, 2006.

Simon, Herbert A. *Administrative Behavior*, vol. 3. New York: Free Press, 1948, revised 1976.

Soss, Joe, Sanford F. Schram, Thomas P. Vartanian, and Erin O'Brien. "Setting the Terms of Relief: Explaining State Policy Choices in the Devolution Revolution." *American Journal of Political Science* 45, no. 2 (2001): 378–95.

Tout, Kathryn, and Jennifer Cleveland. *Evaluation of Parent Aware: Minnesota's Quality Rating and Improvement System, Year 2 Evaluation Report*. Washington, DC: Child Trends, 2014.

Van Slyke, David M. "Agents or Stewards: Using Theory to Understand the Government-Nonprofit Social Service Contracting Relationship." *Journal of Public Administration Research and Theory* 17, no. 2 (2007): 157–87.

Waddell, Dianne. "Program Management: The Next Step in the Evolution of Project Management?" *Problems and Perspectives in Management*, no. 3 (2005): 160–68.

CHAPTER SIX

Aarons, Gregory, et al. "The Organizational Social Context of Mental Health Services and Clinician Attitudes toward Evidence-Based Practice: A United States National Study." *Implementation Science* 7 (2012): 15.

Alford, John. "Why Do Public-Sector Clients Coproduce? Toward a Contingency Theory." *Administration and Society* 34, no. 1 (2002): 32–56.

Bevan, Gwyn, and Christopher Hood. "What's Measured Is What Matters: Targets and Gaming in the English Public Health System." *Public Administration* 84, no. 3 (2006): 517–38.

Bitner, Mary Jo, Bernard H. Booms, and Lois A. Mohr. "Critical Service Encounters: The Employee's Viewpoint." *Journal of Marketing* 58, no. 4 (1994): 95–106.

Bovaird, Tony. "Beyond Engagement and Participation: User and Community Coproduction of Public Services." *Public Administration Review* 67, no. 5 (2007): 846–60.

Boyte, Harry C. *CommonWealth: A Return to Citizen Politics*. London: Collier Macmillan, 1989.

Boyte, Harry. *The Citizen Solution*. Minneapolis: University of Minnesota Press, 2008.

Bozeman, Barry. *Bureaucracy and Red Tape.* Upper Saddle River, NJ: Prentice Hall, 2000.

Brehm, John, and Scott Gates. *Working, Shirking, and Sabotage: Bureaucratic Response to a Democratic Public.* Ann Arbor: University of Michigan Press, 1997.

Brodkin, Evelyn Z. "Bureaucracy Redux: Management Reformism and the Welfare State." *Journal of Public Administration Research and Theory* 17, no. 1 (2006): 1–17.

Brown, Trevor. "Coercion versus Choice: Citizen Evaluations of Public Service Quality across Methods of Consumption." *Public Administration Review* 67, no. 3 (2007): 559–72.

Coble, Janet Vinzan, and Lane Crothers. *Street-Level Leadership: Discretion and Legitimacy in Front-Line Public Service.* Washington, DC: Georgetown University Press, 1998.

Cohen, David K. "Revolution in One Classroom." *Educational Evaluation and Policy Analysis* 12, no. 3 (1990): 311–29.

Cohen, David K., and Heather C. Hill. *Learning Policy: When State Education Reform Works.* New Haven, CT: Yale University Press, 2001.

Cohen, David K., Milbrey W. McLaughlin, and Joan Talbert. *Teaching for Understanding: Challenges for Policy and Practice.* San Francisco: Jossey-Bass, 1993.

Cross, Nigel. "Designerly Ways of Knowing." *Design Studies* 3, no. 4 (1982): 221–27.

Cross, Nigel. "From a Design Science to a Design Discipline: Understanding Designerly Ways of Knowing and Thinking." *Design Research Now*, edited by R. Michel, 41–54. Basel: Birkhauser, 2007.

Cross, Nigel. *Design Thinking.* London: Bloomsbury Academic, 2011.

Elder, T., and E. Powers. "The Incredible Shrinking Program." *Research on Aging* 28 (2006): 341–58.

Garrow, Eve, and Oscar Grusky. "Institutional Logic and Street-Level Discretion: The Case of HIV Test Counseling." *Journal of Public Administration Research and Theory* 23, no. 1 (2013): 122.

Glisson, Charles, Anthony Hemmelgarn, Philip Green, and Nathaniel J. Williams. "Randomized Trial of the Availability, Responsiveness and Continuity (ARC) Organizational Intervention for Improving Youth Outcomes in Community Mental Health Programs." *Journal of the American Academy of Child and Adolescent Psychiatry* 52, no. 5 (2013): 493–500.

Gonzalez, Maria, and Willem Haselager. "Creativity: Surprise and Abductive Reasoning." *Semiotica* 153, no. 1 (2005): 325–41.

Handler, Joel F. *The Conditions of Discretion: Autonomy, Community, Bureaucracy.* New York: Russell Sage Foundation, 1986.

Hasenfeld, Yeheskel. *Human Service Organizations.* Englewood Cliffs, NJ: Prentice Hall, 1983.

Herd, Pamela, Thomas DeLeire, Hope Harvey, and Donald P. Moynihan. "Shifting the Administrative Burden to the State: A Case Study of Medicaid Take-Up." *Public Administration Review* 73, no. s1 (2013): S69–S81.

Hill, Carolyn J. "Casework Job Design and Client Outcomes in Welfare-to-Work Offices." *Journal of Public Administration Research and Theory* 16, no. 2 (2005): 263–88.

Hill, Heather C. "Understanding Implementation: Street-Level Bureaucrats' Resources for Reform." *Journal of Public Administration Research and Theory* 13, no. 3 (2003): 265–82.

Honig, Meredith I., ed. *New Directions in Education Policy Implementation: Confronting Complexity.* Albany: State University of New York Press, 2006.

Hyde, Albert C. "Feedback from Customers, Clients, and Captives." *Bureaucrat* 20, no. 4 (1991): 49–53.

Keiser, Lael R. "State Bureaucratic Discretion and the Administration of Social Welfare Programs: The Case of Social Security Disability." *Journal of Public Administration Research and Theory* 9, no. 1 (1999): 87–106.

Lipsky, Michael. *Street-Level Bureaucracy: Dilemmas of the Individual in Public Services.* New York: Russell Sage Foundation, 1980.

Lyon, Aaron R., Kristy Ludwig, Evalynn Romano, Skyler Leonard, Ann Vander Stoep, and Elizabeth McCauley. "'If It's Worth My Time, I Will Make the Time': School-Based Providers' Decision-Making About Participating in an Evidence-Based Psychotherapy Consultation Program." *Administration and*

Policy in Mental Health and Mental Health Services Research 40, no. 6 (2013): 467–81.

Matland, Richard E. "Synthesizing the Implementation Literature: The Ambiguity-Conflict Model of Policy Implementation." *Journal of Public Administration Research and Theory* 5, no. 2 (1995): 145–74.

Maynard-Moody, Steven, and Michael Musheno. "State Agent or Citizen Agent: Two Narratives of Discretion." *Journal of Public Administration Research and Theory* 10, no. 2 (2000): 329–58.

———. *Cops, Teachers, Counselors: Stories from the Front Lines of Public Service.* Ann Arbor: University of Michigan Press, 2003.

Maynard-Moody, Steven, and Shannon Portillo. "Street-Level Bureaucracy Theory." In *The Oxford Handbook of American Bureaucracy*, edited by Robert F. Durant. New York: Oxford University Press, 2000.

Meyers, Marcia K., and Susan Vorsanger. "Street-Level Bureaucrats and the Implementation of Public Policy." In *Handbook of Public Administration*, edited by B. Guy Peters and John Pierre, 245–55. Thousand Oaks, CA: SAGE, 2003.

Mintzberg, Henry. "Managing Government, Governing Management." *Harvard Business Review* (May–June 1996): 77.

Moynihan, Donald P. *The Dynamics of Performance Management: Constructing Information and Reform.* Washington, DC: Georgetown University Press, 2008.

Osborne, David, and Ted Gaebler. *Reinventing Government: How the Entrepreneurial Spirit Is Transforming the Public Sector.* New York: Plume Books, 1992.

Ostrom, Elinor. "Crossing the Great Divide: Coproduction, Synergy, and Development." *World Development* 24, no. 6 (1996): 1073–87.

Parasuraman, A., Valarie A. Zeithaml, and Leonard L. Berry. "A Conceptual Model of Service Quality and Its Implications for Future Research." *Journal of Marketing* 49, no. 4 (1985): 41–50.

Perry, James, Trent A. Engbers, and So Yun Jun. "Back to the Future? Performance-Related Pay, Empirical Research, and the Perils of Persistence." *Public Administration Review* 69, no. 1 (2008): 39–51.

Price, Linda L., Eric J. Arnould, and Patrick Tierney. "Going to Extremes: Managing Service Encounters and Assessing Provider Performance." *Journal of Marketing* 59, no. 2 (1995): 83–97.

Prottas, Jeffrey. *People Processing: The Street-Level Bureaucrats in Public Service Bureaucracies.* Lanham, MD: Lexington Books, 1979.

Quick, Kathryn S., and Martha S. Feldman. "Distinguishing Participation and Inclusion." *Journal of Planning Education and Research* 31, no. 3 (2011): 272–90.

Radin, Beryl. *Challenging the Performance Movement: Accountability, Complexity, and Democratic Values.* Washington, DC: Georgetown University Press, 2006.

Russell, Blair D. "Examining the Barriers to Public Assistance Take-Up: Evidence from a Foreclosure Mitigation Program in Ohio." Doctoral dissertation, Ohio State University, 2013. https://etd.ohiolink.edu.

Sandfort, Jodi R. "Moving Beyond Discretion and Outcomes: Examining Public Management from the Front-Lines of the Welfare System." *Journal of Public Administration Research and Theory* 10, no. 4 (2000): 729–56.

Schneider, Anne L., and Helen Ingram. *Policy Design for Democracy.* Lawrence: University of Kansas, 1997.

Shore-Sheppard, L. D. "Stemming the Tide? The Effect of Expanding Medicaid Eligibility on Health Insurance Coverage." *BE Journal of Economic Analysis and Policy* 8, no. 6 (2008): 287–303.

Soss, Joe. "Talking Our Way to Meaningful Explanations: A Practice-Centered View of Interviewing for Interpretative Research." In *Interpretation and Method: Empirical Research Methods and the Interpretive Turn*, edited by Dvora Yanow and Peregrine Schwartz-Shea, 127–49. London: M. E. Sharp, 2007.

Soss, Joe, Richard C. Fording, and Sanford F. Schram. *Disciplining the Poor: Neoliberal Paternalism and the Persistent Power of Race.* Chicago: University of Chicago Press, 2011.

———. "The Organization of Discipline: From Performance Management to Perversity and Punishment." *Journal of Public Administration Research and Theory* 21, no. s2 (2011): S203–32.

Spillane, James P., and John S. Zeuli. "Reform and Mathematics Teaching: Exploring Patterns of Practice in the Context of National State Reforms." *Educational Evaluation and Policy Analysis* 21, no. 1 (1999): 1–27.

Thaler, Richard H., and Shlomo Benartzi. "Save More Tomorrow: Using Behavioral Economics to Increase Employee Saving." *Journal of Political Economy* 112, no. s1 (2004): S164–87.

Watkins-Hayes, Celeste. *The New Welfare Bureaucrats*. Chicago: University of Chicago Press, 2009.

Weaver, Kent. "Compliance Regimes and Barriers to Behavioral Change." *Governance: An International Journal of Policy, Administration, and Institutions* 27, no. 2 (2013): 243–65.

CHAPTER SEVEN

Brown, Sherrod. "Sen. Brown Urges Sec. Geithner to Expand Access to Legal Aid and Counseling Assistance Programs." June 1, 2010. http://www.brown.senate.gov/newsroom/press/release/sen-brown-urges-sec-geithner-to-expand-access-to-legal-aid-and-counseling-assistance-programs.

Bushouse, Brenda K. *Universal Preschool: Policy Change, Stability, and the Pew Charitable Trusts*. Albany, NY: SUNY Press, 2009.

Chase, Richard, and Jennifer Valorose. "Child Care Use in Minnesota: Report of the 2009 Statewide Household Child Care Survey." St. Paul, MN: Wilder Research Center, 2010. http://www.wilder.org/WilderResearch/Publications/Studies/Child%20Care%20Use%20in%20Minnesota%202009/Child%20Care%20Use%20in%20Minnesota,%20Full%20Report.pdf.

Gornick, Janet C., and Marcia K. Meyers. *Families That Work: Policies for Reconciling Parenthood and Employment*. New York: Russell Sage Foundation, 2003.

Hage, David. "Into the Fray: How a Funders Coalition Restored Momentum for Early Learning in Minnesota." 2011. http://fcd-us.org/resources/fray-how-funders-coalition-restored-momentum-early-learning-minnesota.

Immergluck, Daniel. "Neighborhoods in the Wake of the Debacle: Intrametropolitan Patterns of Foreclosed Properties." *Urban Affairs Review* 46, no. 1 (2010): 3–36.

Lean Ohio. "Simplified Process Aims to Make 'Saving the Dream' 9 Times Faster for Struggling Homeowners." August 1, 2012. http://lean.ohio.gov/Results/ OHFAEligibilityDeterminationJuly2012.aspx.

Lowrey, Annie. "Treasury Faulted in Effort to Relieve Homeowners." *New York Times,* April 12, 2012. http://www.nytimes.com/2012/04/12/business/economy/ treasury-department-faulted-in-effort-to-relieve-homeowners.html?_r=0.

National Research Council. *Who Cares for America's Children? Child Care Policy for the 1990s,* edited by Cheryl D. Hayes, John L. Palmer, and Martha J. Zaslow. Washington, DC: National Academy Press, 1990.

Office of the Special Inspector General for the Troubled Asset Relief Program. "Factors Affecting Implementation of the Hardest Hit Fund" by Christy L. Romero. 2013. http://www.sigtarp.gov/audit%20reports/sigtarp_hhf_audit.pdf.

Ohio Housing Financing Agency. "Restoring Stability: A Save the Dream Initiative." April 11, 2011. http://www.treasury.gov/initiatives/financial-stability/pro grams/housing-programs/hhf/Documents/HHFfinalproposal%204–11–2011 .pdf.

Pressman, Jeffrey, and Aaron Wildavsky. *Implementation: How Great Expectations in Washington Are Dashed in Oakland or Why It's Amazing That Federal Programs Work at All,* 3rd ed. Berkeley: University of California Press, 1984.

Ray, Aisha. *Parents' Priorities in Selecting Early Care and Education Programs: Implications for Minnesota's Quality Rating and Improvement Systems.* Minnesota Early Learning Foundation. 2008. http://www.pasrmn.org/MELF/ Parent_Aware_Pilot_Research.

Russell, Blair, Stephanie Moulton, and Rob Greenbaum. "Accessibility, Transaction Costs and the Take-up of Mortgage Assistance for Distressed Homeowners." Forthcoming in *Journal of Housing Economics* 24, no. C (2014): 57–74.

Staley, Warren, and Duane Benson, "Tax Dollars Well-Spent? It's Possible." *Star Tribune,* January 17, 2013.

Tout, Kathryn, Rebecca Starr, Jennifer Cleveland, Sharah Friese, Margaret Soli, and Ladia Albertson-Junkans. *Statewide Expansion of Parent Aware: Year 1 Implementation Report.* Parent Aware for School Readiness. 2011. http://www .pasrmn.org/work/research.

US Department of the Treasury. "Hardest Hit Fund: Third Quarter 2013 Performance Summary." September 30, 2013. http://www.treasury.gov/initiatives/financial-stability/reports/Documents/Q3%202013%20Hardest%20Hit%20Fund%20Program%20Performance%20Summary%20FINAL%2012.17.13.pdf.

————. "Housing Finance Agency Innovation Fund for the Hardest Hit Housing Markets ("HFA Hardest-Hit Fund"): Guidelines for HFA Proposal Submission." http://www.treasury.gov/initiatives/financial-stability/TARPPrograms/housing/ Documents/ HFA_Proposal_Guidelines_-_1st_Rd.pdf.

CHAPTER EIGHT

Amir, On, Dan Ariely, Alan Cooke, David Dunning, Nicholas Epley, Uri Gneezy, and Botond Koszegi. "Psychology, Behavioral Economics, and Public Policy." *Marketing Letters* 16, nos. 3–4 (2005): 443–54.

Bardach, Eugene. *A Practical Guide for Policy Analysis: The Eightfold Path to More Effective Problem Solving*, 3rd ed. Washington, DC: CQ Press, 2009.

Bason, Christian. *Leading Public Sector Innovation: Co-Creating for a Better Society*. Bristol, UK: Policy Press, 2010.

Behn, Robert D. "Why Measure Performance? Different Purposes Require Different Measures." *Public Administration Review* 63, no. 5 (2003): 586–606.

Bovaird, Tony. "Beyond Engagement and Participation: User and Community Coproduction in Public Services," *Public Administration Review* (September–October 2007): 846–60.

Bozeman, Barry. *Public Values and Public Interest: Counterbalancing Economic Individualism*. Washington, DC: Georgetown University Press, 2007.

Brown, Tim. *Change by Design*. New York: Harper Business, 2009.

Brown, Trevor L., Matthew Potoski, and David M. Van Slyke. "Managing Public Service Contracts: Aligning Values, Institutions, and Markets." *Public Administration Review* 66, no. 3 (2006): 323–31.

Bryson, John. *Strategic Planning for Public and Nonprofit Organizations: A Guide to Strengthening and Sustaining Organizational Achievement*. San Francisco: Jossey-Bass, 2011.

Carlile, Paul. "A Pragmatic View of Knowledge and Boundaries: Boundary Objects in New Product Development." *Organizational Science* 13, no. 4 (2002): 442–55.

Dahl, Adam, and Joe Soss. "Neoliberalism for the Common Good? Public Value-Governance and the Downsizing of Democracy." *Public Administration Review* 74, no. 4 (2014): 496–504.

Dewey, John. *The Public and Its Problems*. New York: Holt, 1927.

Elmore, Richard F. "Backward Mapping: Implementation Research and Policy Decisions." *Political Science Quarterly* 94, no. 4 (1980): 601–16.

Feldman, Martha S., and Anne M. Khademian. "The Role of the Public Manager in Inclusion: Creating Communities of Participation." *Governance* 20, no. 2 (2007): 305–24.

Feldman, Martha S., Anne Khademian, Helen Ingram, and Anne Scheider. "Ways of Knowing and Inclusive Management Practices." *Public Administration Review* 66, no. S1 (2006): S89–S99.

Feldman, Martha S., and Wanda J. Orlikowski. "Theorizing Practice and Practicing Theory." *Organization Science* 22, no. 5 (2011): 1240–53.

Fisher, Roger, William L. Ury, and Bruce Patton. *Getting to Yes: Negotiating Agreement without Giving In*. New York: Penguin Books, 1991.

Fligstein, Neil. "Social Skill and the Theory of Fields." *Sociological Theory* 19, no. 2 (2001): 105–25.

Flockhart, Andrew. "Raising the Profile of Social Enterprises: The Use of Social Return on Investment (SROI) and Investment Ready Tools (IRT) to Bridge the Financial Credibility Gap." *Social Enterprise Journal* 1, no. 1 (2005): 29–42.

Forester, John. *The Deliberative Practitioner: Encouraging Participatory Planning Processes*. Cambridge, MA: MIT Press, 1999.

————. "Learning to Improve Practice: Lessons from Practice Stories and Practitioners' Own Discourse Analyses (or Why Only the Loons Show Up)." *Planning Theory and Practice* 13, no. 1 (2012): 11–26.

Fryer, Karen J., Jiju Antony, and Alex Douglas. "Critical Success Factors of Continuous Improvement in the Public Sector: A Literature Review and Some Key Findings." *TQM Magazine* 19, no. 5 (2007): 497–517.

Goffman, Irving. *Frame Analysis: An Essay on the Organization of Experience*. London: Harper & Row, 1974.

Goleman, Daniel. "What Makes a Leader?" *Harvard Business Review* (November–December 1998): 93–102.

Harry, Mikel, and Richard Schroeder. *Six Sigma: The Breakthrough Management Strategy Revolutionizing the World's Top Corporations*. New York: Random House, 2005.

HBR Guide to Project Management. Cambridge, MA: Harvard Business Review Press, 2013.

Heifetz, Ronald A. *Leadership without Easy Answers*. Cambridge, MA: Belknap Press of Harvard University, 1994.

Heifetz, Ronald A., and Marty Linsky. *Leadership on the Line: Staying Alive through the Dangers of Leading*. Boston: Harvard Business School Press. 2002.

Huxham, Chris, and Siv Vangen. *Managing to Collaborate: The Theory and Practice of Collaborative Advantage*. New York: Routledge, 2005.

Kahneman, D., and A. Tversky. "Prospect Theory: An Analysis of Decisions under Risk." *Econometrica* 47 (1979): 263–91.

Khademian, Anne M. *Working with Culture: The Way the Job Gets Done in Public Programs*. Washington, DC: CQ Press, 2002.

Koning, Pierre, and Carolyn J. Heinrich. "Cream-Skimming, Parking and Other Intended and Unintended Effects of High-Powered, Performance-Based Contracts." *Journal of Policy Analysis and Management* 32, no. 3 (2013): 461–83.

Krueger, Richard, and Mary Anne Casey. *Focus Groups: A Practical Guide for Applied Research*, 4th ed. Thousand Oaks, CA: SAGE, 2008.

Lakoff, George. *The Political Mind: A Cognitive Scientist's Guide to Your Brain and Its Politics*. New York: Penguin Books, 2009.

Lakoff, George, and Mark Johnson. *Philosophy in the Flesh: The Embodied Mind and Challenge to Western Philosophy*. New York: Basic Books, 1999.

Langbein, Laura I. *Public Program Evaluation: A Statistical Guide*. London: M. E. Sharpe, 2012.

Latour, Bruno. *Reassembling the Social: An Introduction to Actor-Network Theory*. Oxford: Oxford University Press, 2005.

Lave, Jean, and Etienne Wenger. *Situated Learning: Legitimate Peripheral Participation*. Cambridge: Cambridge University Press, 1991.

Lawrence, Paul, and Jay W. Lorche. *Organizations and Environment*. Cambridge, MA: Harvard Business School, Division of Research, 1967.

Lundquist, Leah, Jodi Sandfort, Cris Lopez et al. *Cultivating Change in the Academy: Practicing the Art of Hosting Conversations That Matter within the University of Minnesota*. Minneapolis: University of Minnesota, 2013.

Madrian, Brigitte C., and Dennis F. Shea. "The Power of Suggestion: Inertia in 401(k) Participation and Savings Behavior," *Quarterly Journal of Economics* 116, no. 4 (2001): 1149–87.

May, Carl M. "Towards a General Theory of Implementation." *Implementation Science* 8, no. 1 (2013): 18.

May, Carl M., Frances Mari, Tracy Finch, Anne MacFarlane et al. "Development of a Theory of Implementation and Integration: Normalization Process Theory." *Implementation Science* 4, no. 29 (2009): 1–9.

Milward, Brinton H., and Keith G. Provan. *A Manager's Guide to Choosing and Using Collaborative Networks*. Washington, DC: IBM Center for the Business of Government, 2006.

Mishan, Edward J., and Euston Quah. *Cost-Benefit Analysis*. London: Routledge, 2007.

Moore, Mark H. *Creating Public Value: Strategic Management in Government*. Cambridge, MA: Harvard University Press, 1995.

Moynihan, Donald P. "The Normative Model in Decline? Public Service Motivation in the Age of Governance." *Public Service Motivation: State of the Science and Art* 4 (2008).

Ohio Department of Administrative Services. "Simplified Process Aims to Make 'Saving the Dream' 9 Times Faster for Struggling Homeowners." Lean Ohio, August 2012.

_____. "About Lean Ohio." August 1, 2012. http://lean.ohio.gov/.

The Power of Suggestion: Inertia in 401(k) Participation and Savings Behavior. Washington, DC: National Bureau of Economic Research, 2000.

Quinn, Robert E., and Sue R. Faerman. *Becoming a Master Manager: A Competing Values Approach*, 5th ed. San Francisco: Jossey-Bass, 2010.

Ringquist, Evan. *Meta-Analysis for Public Management and Policy*. San Francisco: Jossey-Bass, 2013.

Rubin, Herbert J., and Irene S. Rubin. *Qualitative Interviewing: The Art of Hearing Data*, 3rd ed. Thousand Oaks, CA: SAGE, 2011.

Sandfort, Jodi, and Kathryn Quick. "Deliberative Technology in Use: Learning from the Art of Hosting." Forthcoming in *Public Administration Review*.

Schein, Edgar. *Organizational Culture and Learning*. Cambridge, MA: Harvard University Press, 1992.

Schön, Donald A. *The Reflective Practitioner: How Professionals Think in Action*. New York: Basic Books, 1983.

_____. *Educating the Reflective Practitioner: Toward a New Design for Teaching and Learning in the Professions*. San Francisco: Jossey-Bass, 1987.

Schön, Donald A., and Martin Rein. *Frame Reflection: Toward the Resolution of Intractable Policy Controversies*. New York: Basic Books, 1995.

Schwartz, Peter. *The Art of the Long View: Planning for the Future in an Uncertain World*. New York: Currency/Doubleday, 1996.

Schwarz, Roger. *The Skilled Facilitator: A Comprehensive Resource for Consultants, Facilitators, Managers, Trainers and Coaches*, 2nd ed. San Francisco: Jossey-Bass, 2002.

Simmons, Annette, and Doug Lipman, *The Story Factor*, 2nd ed. New York: Basic Books, 2006.

Snowden, David, and Mary Boone. "A Leaders' Framework for Decision Making." *Harvard Business Review* (November 2007): 1–12.

Spillane, Jim, Brian Reiser, and Todd Reimer. "Policy Implementation and Cognition: Reframing and Refocusing Implementation Research." *Review of Educational Research* 72, no. 3 (2002): 412.

Thaler, Richard H., and Shlomo Benartzi. "Save More Tomorrow: Using Behavioral Economics to Increase Employee Saving." *Journal of Political Economy* 112, no. s1 (2004): S164–87.

Thompson, James D. *Organizations in Action*. New York: McGraw-Hill, 1967.

Van Slyke, David M. "Agents or Stewards: Using Theory to Understand the Government-Nonprofit Social Service Contracting Relationship." *Journal of Public Administration Research and Theory* 17, no. 2 (2007): 323–31.

Weaver, R. Kent. "Target Compliance: The Final Frontier of Policy Implementation." *Brookings Issues in Governance Studies* 27 (2009): 243–65.

Weimer, David, and Aidan Vining. *Policy Analysis Concepts and Practice*, 2nd ed. Englewood Cliffs, NJ: Prentice Hall, 1992.

Weisbord, Marvin, and Sandra Janoff. *Future Search: Getting the Whole System in the Room for Vision, Commitment, and Action*, 3rd ed. San Francisco: Berrett-Koehler, 2010.

INDEX

Actors: competition between field, 90; establishing viable program options, 120–121; HHF policy field, 114–117; identifying logic of change, 121–125; public agencies as, 115; QRS, 118–119. *See also* Multiactor networks

Adaptive challenges: activating authority and using culture, 255–258, 285; confronting, 25, 27; engaging others in change, 246–249, 285; implementation improvement blueprint for, 284–285; iterative approach of, 246; practices for improving effectiveness, 227; tactics and tools for, 246–248; technical versus, 226–227

Advocacy coalition framework (ACF), 41–42

Affordable Care Act (ACA): implementation in Colorado, 5–9, 26, 112; measuring effectiveness of, 13; policy fields in implementation of, 103–104; Supreme Court ruling on, 6, 87

Agranoff, R., 48

American Journal of Preventative Medicine, 58

Ansell, C., 96

Antony, J., 232

Applying Science in Early Childhood Programs and Systems (Halle, Metz, and Martinez-Beck), 130

Art of the Long View, The (Schwartz), 248

Asset specificity, 80

Auditing: frontline interactions, 182–186, 271–273; organization-program integration, 158–162, 267–270; policy fields, 131–133, 261–262

Authority: activating change within existing, 255–258, 285; bottom-up, 39–43, 64; distribution of resources and, 18; legitimate, 84; political and economic, 85–86; summarizing mechanisms of, 281; top-down, 37–39, 41–43, 64. *See also* Political processes and authority

Authorizing roles of organizations, 143–146

Backward mapping, 40–41, 238

Bardach, E., 27

Bason, C., 258

Becoming a Master Manager (Quinn and Faerman), 232

Behavioral change: choice architecture and, 238–239, 242–243; complexities of programs focusing on, 77–78; diagnosing problems for, 283–284; exploring assumptions about, 237–238. *See also* Behavioral economics

Behavioral economics: applying to target groups, 63; biases affecting, 62–63, 240–242, 284; diagnosing behaviors underlying problems, 239–240; influencing decision making with, 61–62

Benartzi, S., 230, 239, 240

Berman, P., 39, 143

Best practices, 93–94, 98

Boiled frog syndrome, 148
Bottom-up authority: backward mapping delineating, 40–41; frameworks toward integrating, 41–43; summary of, 64; theories on, 39–41
Boundary objects, 252–253
Bounded rationality, 60
Bozeman, B., 86, 235
Braybrooke, D., 55
British National Health Service, 181
Brown, M., 7
Brown, T., 176
Bryson, J., 248
BUILD initiative, 118, 135
Buysse, V., 130

Carlile, P., 252
Casey, M. A., 248
Challenges. *See* Technical challenges; Adaptive challenges
Change: achieving effective system, 236; choice architects' role in, 60; core program processes for, 229–230; core program's causal logic for, 76–79, 81, 85, 95; dependence on technology to effect, 74; disruption and opportunities for, 193; engaging others in, 246–249, 257–258, 285; failing to implement public values with, 235–237; as goal of effective implementation, 225; indicating program effectiveness, 213; individuals who can lead, 226; institutional sanctioning of, 83; knowing contexts for, 25; making sense of with ACF, 41–42; policy implementation and process of, 12; process leading to, 192; quality of user experience and, 15–16; technology's role in, 17–18; types of outcomes from, 14–15. *See also* Adaptive challenges; Leading change; Technical challenges
Chih Lin, A., 92
Child Care Aware of Minnesota, 119, 135, 157
Child Care Resources, 218, 219–220
Child Trends, 118, 119
Children Care Policy Research Consortium, 118
Children's Health Insurance Program, 7
Choice architects, 60, 239
Choice architecture, 238–239, 242–243
Clan organizing, 153–154

Cleveland, H., 44
Collective action, 19–20
Colorado Department of Health Care Policy and Financing, 7, 16
Colorado Health Foundation, 7, 8
Community policing, 124–125
Competition between field actors, 90
Connect with Health Colorado exchange, 5, 6, 7, 8, 26, 104
Consolidated Framework for Implementation Research (CFIR), 59
Contexts, 19, 25
Coordinating activities: aligning coordination systems, 243–245, 284; for core programs, 79–81, 85; frontline workers' role in, 179–181; organizational continuum for, 152–154; role of policy fields in, 125–128
Core programs: carrying out with strategic action fields, 74–82; causal logic of change for, 76–79, 81, 85, 95; change process enacted by front lines, 178–179; combining processes of, 81–82; coordinating activities for, 79–81, 85; creating change with three processes of, 229–230; enacted by frontline staff, 166, 174–181; establishing viable options for, 75–76, 81, 85, 95; focusing analysis on, 68–69, 96–97; front line coordination of activities, 179–181; grounding approach of, 230, 233–235, 237; HHF objectives, 200–201; how policy fields coordinate activities for, 125–128; identifying logic of change for policy field, 121–125; identifying public values of, 234–235; influences shaping QRS, 214–220; institutions integrating change in, 150–152; integrating of by organizations, 148–154; making changes to, 227; organizational coordination of, 152–154; organizations' role to create viable options, 149–150; policy fields and development of, 120–131; recognizing failure to implement public values, 235–237; shaped by frontline implementation, 189; shaping of HHF by social structure and dynamics, 201–209; strategic action fields within, 71–73; unpacking and implementing, 25, 26–27. *See also* Coordinating activities; Logic of change; Policy implementation; Viable program options
Cost-Benefit Analysis, 232

Creating Public Value (Moore), 234

Cross, N., 196

Cultivating Change in the Academy (Lundquist and others), 248

Culture: activating authority using, 255–258; analyzing for organization-program integration audit, 268–269; critical influence on effective implementation, 91–92; evaluating organization-program integration with, 160–161; as influence in social action, 18; legitimizing practices, 93–94; shared beliefs and values in, 94–96; in strategic action fields, 85

Customer-centric service, 169–170, 188

Decision making: bounded rationality and, 60; creating choice architecture for, 238–239, 242–243; explaining with IAD framework, 46; influencing with behavioral economics, 61–62; institutional boundaries for, 141; policy analysis as aid to, 55

Dewey, J., 227

Diagnostic and Statistical Manual of Mental Disorders, 179

Dimensional publicness, 86

Douglas, A., 232

Dynamics of implementation: about, 195–196; Hardest Hit Fund, 196–211; legal and regulatory environment in social structures, 86–89; Quality Rating and Improvement System, 211–222; shaping of core programs by, 201–209. *See also* Implementation dynamics and outcomes analysis

Early childhood education. *See* Quality Rating and Improvement System

Early Childhood Funders Collaborative, 118

Early Learning Council, 119

Easton, D., 37

Economic authority, 85–86

Economic Development Administration, 38

Ecosystem metaphor, 70–73

Effective implementation: aligning coordination systems, 243–245, 284; behavioral theory's measure of, 41; change as goal of, 225; complexity of measuring, 79–80; cultural influences critical to, 91–92; defining, 11–12; diagnosing behaviors underlying problems, 239–240; exploring behavioral base, 237–243; grounding approach to core programs, 230, 233–235, 237; identifying public values of program, 234–235; indicators of, 14, 201, 202, 212–213, 280; leading change for, 259–260; measuring, 12–16; overview, 191–194; performance targets for frontline workers, 180–181; principles of, 24–28; public value created by, 198; recognizing behavioral biases, 62–63, 240–242, 284; recognizing failure to implement public values, 235–237; skills required for, 228. *See also* Behavioral change

Eggers, W., 112

Elmore, R., 40–41, 238

Emergency Economic Stabilization Act (EESA), 115, 198–199

Emotional intelligence, 249–250, 284

Empirically supported interventions (ESIs), 57

Empirically supported treatments (ESTs), 57

Evidence-based practice (EBP), 57

Evidence-informed practice (EIP), 57

External Control of Organizations, The (Pfeffer and Salancik), 147

External relationships of organizations, 161–162

Faerman, S. R., 232

Failures in implementation: investigating Great Society programs, 37–39; recognizing, 235–237

Fannie Mae, 115

Financial resources, 160–161

Fisher, R., 248

Fligstein, N., 85

Flockhart, A., 232

Focus Groups (Krueger and Casey), 248

For profit organizations, 111

Framing, 256–257, 285

Freddie Mac, 115

Front lines: about, 163–166, 188–189; activities for target groups by, 176–178; adopting viable options, 175–178; analyzing HHF interactions on, 184, 185–186; bending policy to salient values of, 92; change process enacted by, 178–179; coordinating program activities, 179–181; discovering behavioral biases from, 242; effectiveness of, 181–188; enacting core programs,

Front lines *(continued)*
166, 174–181; enacting policies for target members, 22–23, 24; frontline interactions audit, 182–186, 271–273; HHF implementation by, 208–209; impact on behavioral change, 239; implementing policies from, 16–17; involving in program process flow analysis, 265–266; occupations in, 166–168; performance targets for, 180–181; as strategic action fields, 171–174; street-level bureaucrats in, 40, 165, 168, 172–173, 175; target groups of, 169–171; viewing as strategic action field, 69; work and discretion required by, 168–169. *See also* Frontline analysis

Frontline analysis: about, 181–182; frontline interactions audit, 182–186, 271–273; target experiences analysis, 186–188, 275–277

Frontline workers. *See* Front lines

Fryer, K. J., 232

Future Search (Weisbord and Janoff), 248

Gaebler, T., 153, 164

Gaming, 180–181

Geertz, C, 91

Getting to Yes (Fisher, Ury, and Patton), 248

Goggin, M., 41

Goldsmith, S., 112

Goleman, D., 249–250

Goodnow, F., 43

Governance, 176

Governance and management: attributes of perspective, 36; defining governance, 44; historical studies in, 43–44; multiactor networks in, 36, 44, 47–50, 64; multilevel nature of, 44–47; research on policy tools, 50–52. *See also* Multilevel governance research; States

Governance tools research, 50–52

Governing by Network (Goldsmith and Eggers), 112

Government-sponsored entities (GSEs), 115

Great Society programs, 43, 52–54

Greater Twin Cities United Way and Head Start Early Funders collaborative, 135

Green tape, 88

Greenhalgh, T., 58

Grusky, O., 176

Hall, T., 50

Halle, T., 130

Hardest Hit Fund (HHF): about, 28–30, 114; applying governance tools research to, 52; authorizing and service delivery roles within, 145; comparing with QRS, 32; dynamics of implementation for, 196–211; front line adjustments in, 179; frontline analysis for, 184, 185–186; how core programs came together in Ohio, 129, 131; implementation resources for, 122–124; indicators of effective implementation, 201, 202; involving national stakeholders in, 115–116; logic of change in, 210–211; measuring complex outcomes of, 204–205; objectives for, 200–201; organizations mobilized to support, 149; policy field actors for, 114–117; poor application follow-through for, 244; potential benefits of, 197–198; program intent and public value of, 198–201; shaped by social structure and dynamics, 201–209; threats to perceived value of, 209–211

Harry, M., 232

HBR Guide to Project Management, 232

Head Start programs, 53, 135, 170

Health care policies: Colorado's ACA implementation, 5–9, 26, 112; multiple strategic action fields for, 18–19; predicting implementation success of, 58; reforms of national, 5–6

HealthCare.gov online enrollment, 18

Heifetz, R., 226

Heinrich, C., 45

Heuristics and diagrams, 252–254, 284

Hill, C., 45

Hill, H., 124

Hill, M., 44, 46–47

Hjern, B., 39–40, 47, 50, 105

Homeowner Emergency Mortgage Assistance Program, 203

Hood, C., 181

HOPE NOW, 116

Hupe, P., 44, 46–47

Implementation. *See* Policy implementation; Perspectives on Implementation

Implementation dynamics and outcomes analysis: about, 196, 223; comparing HHF and

QRS cases, 32; describing key mechanisms influencing, 281; HHF, 28–30; indicators of implementation effectiveness, 280; learning to do, 28; QRS programs for, 29, 30–31; steps in, 279–282

Implementation improvement blueprint, 283–285

Implementation (Pressman and Wildavsky), 37–39

Implementation science, 56–59

Implementation Science, 56

Implementation structures, 39–40, 47–50

Indicators of effective implementation, 14, 201, 202, 212–213, 280

Ingraham, P., 42

Ingram, H., 42, 50

Inputs, 17, 265–266

Institutional analysis and development (IAD) framework, 46

Intermediary institutions. *See* Organizations

International Association for Public Participation, 248

Interventions: addressing technical and adaptive aspects of, 226–227; analyzing policies and programs via, 36; behavioral economics and Save More Tomorrow, 239–240; effect of culture on, 92; ensuring compliance of target groups to, 170; grounding theories in, 64; improving HHF application follow-through, 244; leading learning by grounding problem for, 237; testing in controlled settings, 63

Janoff, S., 248

Johnson, L. B., 52

Kahneman, D., 61, 240

Krueger, R., 248

Langbein, L. I., 232

Lasswell, H., 54

Leading change: activating authority and using culture, 255–258, 285; aligning coordination systems, 243–245, 284; considering target group needs and interests, 236–237; diagnosing behaviors underlying problems, 239–240; distinguishing between technical and adaptive challenges, 226–227; engaging others in change, 246–249, 257–258, 285; exploring assumptions about behavioral change, 237–238; grounding approach of core programs, 230, 233–235, 237; influencing others with framing, 256–257, 285; overview, 259–260; recognizing common behavioral biases, 62–63, 240–242, 284; social skills for, 249–255, 284

Legal and regulatory environment, 86–89

Legitimate authority, 84

Lindbom, C., 55

Linsky, M., 226

Lipman, D., 248

Lipsky, M., 40, 165, 172, 175, 188

Local entities: implementing QRS in Minnesota, 119

Logic of change: based on beliefs of implementers, 95–96; change process enacted by front lines, 178–179; core programs and, 76–79, 81, 85; identifying for policy field, 121–125; integrating through institutions, 150–152; public value of HHF and, 210–211

Logic of governance framework, 45

Lundquist, L., 248

Lynn, L., 45

Manning, N., 8, 16, 17

Mapping: multiactor networks, 47–48; policy fields, 133–136; relationships in policy field analysis, 263–264; using backward mapping, 40–41

Martinez-Beck, I., 130

Martinez, S., 5, 6, 17

Matland, R., 42–43

Maxwell, K., 130

May, C., 19, 57

Maynard-Moody, S., 171, 173–174

Mazmanian, D., 11, 39, 41, 58

McAdams, D., 85

McGuire, M., 48

Medicaid, 6, 7, 148–149, 179

Medicare, 7, 8

Meier, K., 45

Meta-Analysis for Public Management and Policy (Ringquist), 232

Metz, A., 130

Meyers, D., 58

Milgram, S., 60

Milward, B., 48, 49, 114

Minnesota Association for the Education of Young Children, 119
Minnesota Center for Professional Development, 119
Minnesota Early Learning Foundation, 119
Minnesota Office of Early Learning, 119
Mintzberg, H., 165
Mishan, E., 232
Moore, M., 234
Mortgage Bankers Association, 115, 116
Motivation, 154
Moving to Opportunity (MTO) demonstration, 53
Multiactor networks: about, 64; analyzing policies and programs via, 36; defining, 47; mapping, 47–48; research on, 48–50; studies in mental health, 49
Multilevel governance research: about, 64; benefits of, 47; defining governance levels in, 45–46; history of, 44–45; IAD framework of, 46; logic of governance framework in, 45; multiple governance framework in, 46–47
Multilevel implementation systems: ecosystem metaphors applied to, 70–73; governance framework of, 46–47; understanding, 100–101. See also Hardest Hit Fund; Quality Rating and Improvement System
Musheno, M., 171, 173–174

National Association for the Education of Young Children, 118
National Center for Community Policing, 124
National Center on Child Care Quality, 118
National Council of State Housing Agencies, 115, 116
National Economic Council, 116
National Foreclosure Mitigating Counseling (NFMC), 116–117
National Partnership for Reinventing Government, 164
Networks: policy fields as bounded, 103–104, 107; policy fields viewed as, 108–109
New public management, 26
New York Times, 196, 249
Nonprofit organizations: involvement in policy fields, 111; as QRS policy field actors, 118, 119; support for HHF, 116, 117
Nudge (Thaler and Sunstein), 60

Occupational identities, 172
Occupations in front lines, 166–168
Office of Affordable Housing Research (OAHR), 117
Ohio Capital Corporation for Housing (OCCH), 116
Ohio Department of Commerce, 116
Ohio Governor's Office, 116
Ohio Homeowner Assistance LLC (OHA), 116
Ohio Housing Finance Agency (OHFA), 116, 185, 186, 200, 205, 207
Organization-program integration audit (OPIA): advantages of, 158–162; conducting, 267–269; template for, 268
Organizational analysis: organization-program integration audit, 158–162, 267–270; program process flow analysis for, 155–158; uses for, 155
Organizational fields, 108–109
Organizations: aligning and reinforcing program activities within, 230; analyzing policies and programs via, 36; authorizing and service delivery by, 143–146; dimensional publicness of, 86; existing within policy fields, 22, 24; Fannie Mae and Freddie Mac as intermediary, 115; filtering problems and solutions through, 131–132; identifying policy field, 261–262; implementing policies as, 16; institutional sanctioning of change, 83; institutions within policy fields, 110–119; integrating change in core programs, 150–152; integration of core programs by, 148–154; as integrators, 141, 161; interpreting legal authorization of, 87–89; involved in policy fields, 110–119; mapping relationships between, 263–264; organization-program integration audit, 158–162, 267–270; in policy fields, 111, 112–113; program process flow analysis for, 155–158; as QRS policy field actors, 118; role in policy implementation, 139–142; social structures of, 141; as strategic action fields, 145–148; viewing as strategic action field, 69. See also Multiactor networks
Osborne, D., 153, 164
Ostrom, E., 46
Ostrom, V., 46
O'Toole, L., 32, 45, 50

Outputs: about, 17; analyzing with program process flow, 265–266; describing with logic of governance framework, 45; indicating public values failure, 235–237. *See also* Implementation dynamics and outcomes analysis

Palmer, P., 192
Parent Aware for School Readiness, 119, 130, 212, 215, 217, 218, 219, 220
Parents as Teachers model, 113
Patton, B., 248
Paulsell, D., 130
People processing, 77–78, 208
Performance targets for front lines, 180–181
Perspectives on implementation: errors in historic, 67–69; governance and management, 43–52; overview, 35–36; policy and program evaluations, 36, 52–64; political processes and authority, 36, 37–43
Pfeffer, J., 147
Philanthropies: involvement in policy fields, 111; as QRS policy field actors, 118, 119; role in implementing changes, 112
Policy analysis: as aid to decision making, 55; objectives of, 65; as social process, 54–56. *See also* Policy field analysis
Policy and program evaluation: attributes of perspective, 36; behavioral economics, 59–64; implementation science, 56–59; origins of, 52–54; policy analysis as social process, 54–56
Policy cases. *See* Hardest Hit Fund; Quality Rating and Improvement System
Policy field actors. *See* Actors
Policy field analysis: about, 136; auditing policy fields, 131–133, 261–262; beginning, 261; diagramming relationships for, 263–264; policy field maps, 133–136
Policy field visual diagram, 263–264
Policy fields: about, 21–22, 103–104, 136–137; actors for HHF, 114–117; aligning coordination activities inherited from, 243–245, 284; assembling core programs in, 120; auditing, 131–133, 261–262; as bounded networks, 103–104, 107; changes in QRS, 217; competition between actors in, 90; complexity of, 106–107; coordinating core program activities, 125–128; defined, 21,

24, 261; establishing viable options for, 120–121; filtering problems and solutions through institutions, 131–132; formation of, 105; how core programs come together, 129–131; identifying logic of change for, 121–125; institutions within, 110–119; intergovernmental negotiations within, 107–108; mapping, 133–136; organizations embedded within, 146–147; as strategic action fields, 108–109; types of tools used by, 126–128; viewing as strategic action field, 69. *See also* Policy field analysis
Policy implementation: ADA policies in Colorado, 5–9, 26, 112; change occurring during, 12; collective action's role in, 19–20; complexity of implementing ADA, 8; contracting out versus in-house production of activities, 80; cultivating effective, 24–28; defining, 11–12; distribution of resources and authority in, 18; embedded practices complicating, 82–83; failures of top-down authority in, 37–39; influencing with behavioral economics, 61–62; levels within system of, 16–17; measuring effectiveness of, 12–16; organizations' role in, 139–142; policy design and, 42–43; as policy practice, 23–24; quality of user experience and, 15–16; role of culture in, 18; scale in, 20–23; similarity of implementation science studies with, 58; strategic action fields and, 17; suffering from errors in scale, 25; technology used for, 17–18; tools supporting technical challenges, 230, 231–232; ultimate outcomes of, 14–15; unintended effects of, 26. *See also* Policy analysis; Policy fields; Policy tools
Policy tools: evaluating those used, 262; program process flow analysis, 155–158; research on, 50–52; supporting technical challenges, 230, 231–232; tactics for adaptive challenges, 246–248; types of, 126–128
Policymakers, 37–39, 62–63
Political processes and authority: attributes of perspective, 36; concepts of political authority, 85–86; Easton's influence on theories of, 37; implementation frameworks for, 41–43; scholarship on bottom-up

Political processes and authority *(continued)*
  authority, 39–43, 64; using top-down
  authority, 37–39, 41–43, 64
Politics and Administration (Goodnow), 43
Porter, D., 105
Pressman, J., 37–39, 74, 197
Private financial institutions, 115
Problem solving practices, 27–28
Professional membership associations, 113
Program process flow analysis, 155–158,
  265–266
Provan, K., 48, 49, 114
Public Administration Review, 176
Public agencies: implementing HHF, 116;
  involvement in policy fields, 110, 111; as
  national actor in policy field, 115; as QRS
  policy field actors, 118, 119
Public Program Foundation (Langbein), 232
Public service: customer-centric, 169–170,
  188; quality of implementation tied to,
  15–16; street-level bureaucrats and, 40,
  165, 168, 172–173, 175; work and discretion required in, 168–169
Public service providers: involvement in policy
  fields, 111; occupational and social identities of, 172–174. *See also* Front lines; Social
  skills
Public value: considering potential threats to,
  283; created by effective implementation,
  198; failure to implement, 235–237; HHF
  and threats to perceived, 209–211; HHF
  program intent and, 198–201; identifying,
  234–235; QRS and threats to, 220–222
Purveyors, 111, 113

QRS National Learning Network, 118
Quah, E., 232
Quality Rating and Improvement System
  (QRS): comparing with HHF, 32; how core
  programs came together in Minnesota,
  129, 130, 131; implementation dynamics
  for, 211–222; implementation resources
  for, 122–124; indicators of effectiveness for,
  212–213; influences shaping core program,
  214–220; mapping policy fields for Minnesota, 134; organizational support of, 149;
  policy field actors for, 117–119; program
  process flow analysis, 155–158; programs
  of, 29, 30–31, 114; public value threats in,

236, 237; role of philanthropies in, 112;
  threats to perceived value of, 220–222
Quest for Quality, The (Wesley and Buysse),
  130
Quick, K., 254
Quinn, R. E., 232

Race to the Top-Early Learning Challenge,
  130, 212, 216, 217
RAND, 118
Random innovation, 55
Reflection, 250–252, 284
*Reflective Practitioner and Education of a
  Reflective Practitioner, The* (Schön), 250
Reinventing Government (Osborne and Gae-
  bler), 153, 164
Research organizations: involvement in policy
  fields, 112; as QRS policy field actors, 118;
  support for HHF, 117
Resonant collective identity, 96
Resource dependence theory, 147
Restoring Stability System (RSS), 185
Ringquist, E., 232
Rivlin, A., 55
Rogers, E., 57

Sabatier, P., 11, 39, 41, 58
Salamon, L., 50, 126, 127, 128
Salanicik, G., 147
Save the Dream Ohio, 116–117, 185, 205, 206,
  207, 210
Scale: suffering from errors in, 25; understand-
  ing implementation, 20–23
Schneider, A., 42, 50
Schön, D., 250–251
Schroeder, R., 232
Schwartz, P., 248
Schwarz, R., 248
Schön, D., 27–28
Science, 61
Science of the Artificial (Simon), 27
Senge, P., 192
Service delivery by organizations, 143–146
Simmons, A., 248
Simon, H., 60
Simon, H. A., 27
Six Sigma (Harry and Schroeder), 232
Six Sigma process, 244
Skilled Facilitator, The (Schwarz), 248

Social skills: blueprint for improving, 284; displaying, 249–255; emotional intelligence, 249–250, 284; purposive use of heuristics and diagrams, 252–254, 284; reflection, 250–252, 284; required for change, 246

Social structures: analyzing for organization-program integration audit, 268; complicating policy implementation, 82–83; dimensional publicness and, 86; dynamics of legal and regulatory environment in, 86–89; engaging others in change of, 246–249, 285; evaluating cultural norms and values of, 91–96; of institutions, 141; legitimizing practices in, 93–94; logic of change and beliefs of implementers, 95–96; market conditions and, 89–91; occupational and social identities of frontline workers, 171–172; policy fields and, 105; political and economic authority in, 84–86; shaping QRS program, 214–220; understanding shared beliefs and values of culture, 94–96

Soss, J., 170

Speaking Truth to Power (Wildavsky), 55

Spillaine, J., 255

Start Early Funders Coalition, 119

"State of Public Administration, The" (Wilson), 43

States: examples of authorizing organizations among, 143–144; implementation of HHF, 114–115, 116–117; implementing HHF program technologies, 202–209; mapping policy fields for Minnesota early childhood education, 134; QRS implementation in Minnesota, 118–119. *See also* Hardest Hit Fund; Quality Rating and Improvement System

Story Factor, The (Simmons and Lipman), 248

Strategic action fields: about, 17–18, 96–98; aligning coordination activities inherited from, 243–245, 284; analyzing implementation using, 69–74; assessing social structures and dynamics of, 82–95; carrying out core programs, 74–82; challenging existing orders with new resources, 255–256; contexts effecting, 19; coordinating activities in, 79–81, 85; ecosystem metaphor applied to, 70–73; engaging others in change, 246–249, 285; establishing

viable options, 75–76, 81, 85, 95; existence of multiple, 18–19; framing and, 256–257, 284; front lines as, 171–174; identifying logic of change, 76–79, 81, 85; market conditions and, 89–91; organizations as, 145–148; policy fields as, 108–109; power and culture in, 85

Strategic Planning for Public and Nonprofit Organizations (Bryson), 248

Street Level Bureaucracy (Lipsky), 40

Street-level bureaucrats, 40, 165, 168, 172–173, 175. *See also* Front lines

Sunstein, C., 60

Systems: aligning coordination, 243–245, 284; changes in operations of, 14–15; disconnect between target group behavior and operations of, 10; levels within policy implementation, 16–17; understanding multilevel implementation, 100–101

Target experiences analysis, 186–188, 275–277

Target groups: about, 169–171; analyzing experiences of, 186–188, 275–277; analyzing for organization-program integration audit, 267–269; applying behavioral economics to, 63; changes in, 14–15; choice architecture for, 238–239, 242–243; customer-centric service for, 169–170, 188; disconnect between system operation and behavior of, 10; engagement continuum of activities for, 176–178; failing to consider needs or interests of, 236–237; finding consensus of views on implementation effectiveness, 13–14; frontline workers allegiance to, 172; homeowners as HHF, 207; policy analyses focus on, 56; uncovering assumptions about behavior of, 239; understanding perspectives and behaviors of, 23

Technical challenges: adaptive versus, 226–227; confronting, 25, 27; coordinating performance information, 245; creating choice architectures, 238–239, 242–243; evaluating public value failure, 235–237; exposing assumptions about behavioral change, 237–238; implementation improvement blueprint for, 283–284; practices for improving effectiveness,

Technical challenges *(continued)*
227; recognizing and applying behavioral biases, 62–63, 240–242, 284; tactics and tools to address, 230, 231–232

Technology: analyzing for organization-program integration audit, 268; asset specificity and program, 80; change dependent on, 74; confronting challenges in implementing, 25, 27; defined, 17; influence of IT staff on organizations, 146; required for behavioral change and people processing, 77–78; suggested by implementation resources, 124–125. *See also* Technical challenges

Templates: frontline interactions audit, 272; organization-program integration audit, 268

Temporary Assistance for Needy Families (TANF), 144

Thaler, R., 60, 239, 240

Tools of Government, The (Salamon), 126, 127

Top-down authority: frameworks toward integrating, 41–43; studies on, 37–39; summary of, 43, 64

Total Quality Management movement, 244

Tout, K., 130

"Toward a General Theory of Strategic Action Fields" (Fligstein and McAdams), 85

TQM Magazine, 232

Troubled Asset Relief Program (TARP), 28, 29, 115, 197, 199, 204

Trust in policy fields and networks, 125–126

Tversky, A., 61, 240

United Way, 216

University of Minnesota Center for Early Education and Development, 135, 157

Ury, W. L., 248

US Department of Health and Human Services, 7, 118

US Department of Housing and Urban Development, 116, 117

US Department of Treasury, 29, 114, 115, 129, 149, 197, 199, 201, 202–203, 207

US Supreme Court, 6, 87

Viable program options: adopted on front lines, 175–178; analyzing how policy field actors establish, 120–121; establishing for core programs, 75–76, 81, 85, 95; organizations role in creating, 149–150

Violent Crime Control and Law Enforcement Act, 124

Walkins-Hayes, C, 172

Wang, C., 8, 16, 17

War on Poverty, 52, 104

Weaver, K., 176, 239

Weisbord, M., 248

Weiss, C., 53

Wesley, P. M., 130

Wildavsky, A., 37–39, 55, 74, 197

Wilson, W., 43